W9-BEM-956

RESEARCH
IN
EDUCATION

RESEARCH IN EDUCATION

fourth edition

JOHN W. BEST

PRENTICE-HALL, INC., Englewood Cliffs, New Jersey 07632

Library of Congress Cataloging in Publication Data

Best, John W
    Research in education.

    Includes bibliographies and indexes.
    1.   Educational research.   I.   Title.
LB1028.B4   1981   370'.7'8   80-26245
ISBN 0-13-774026-3

editorial/production supervision and interior design: CATHIE MICK MAHAR
cover design: 20/20 Services Inc.
manufacturer buyer: EDMOND W. LEONE

© 1981, 1977, 1970, 1959 by PRENTICE-HALL, INC., *Englewood Cliffs, N.J. 07632*

All rights reserved. No part of this book
may be reproduced in any form or
by any means without permission in writing
from the publisher.

Printed in the United States of America

10   9   8   7   6   5   4   3   2   1

Prentice-Hall International, Inc., *London*
Prentice-Hall of Australia Pty. Limited, *Sydney*
Prentice-Hall of Canada, Ltd., *Toronto*
Prentice-Hall of India Private Limited, *New Delhi*
Prentice-Hall of Japan, Inc., *Tokyo*
Prentice-Hall of Southeast Asia Pte. Ltd., *Singapore*
Whitehall Books Limited, *Wellington, New Zealand*

Contents

THREE

FOUR

FIVE

SIX

TEN

Preface

This book has been written for use as a research reference or as a text in an introductory course in research methods, for graduate students enrolled in a research seminar, for those writing a thesis, or for those who carry on research as a professional activity. All professional workers should be familiar with the methods of research and, if only as consumers, should understand some of the techniques of problem identification, hypothesis formulation, the construction and use of data-gathering instruments, and the analysis of data. They should also be able to interpret research reports that appear in professional publications.

No introductory course can be expected to confer research competence, nor can any book present all relevant information. Research skill and understanding cannot be achieved without the necessary intellectual qualities and extensive training and experience. Some graduate students have found it profitable to carry on a modest study as a way of learning about research.

This fourth edition of *Research in Education* expands and attempts to clarify a number of ideas presented in previous editions. Additional concepts, procedures and examples have been added, a few deleted.

The topics included in Chapter Seven and Chapter Eight, detailing the use of descriptive and inferential statistical analysis, Chapter Nine, listing an extensive range of references in education and in allied behavioral fields, and Chapter Ten, indicating ways of presenting a written research report, may be peripheral to some course objectives. It is not suggested that all these topics be included in a course. It is recommended that instructors use them selectively and in the sequence that is most appropriate.

The author is indebted to many students and colleagues, more than can be acknowledged by name. To the unknown manuscript reviewers, he expresses his appreciation for their helpful suggestions. To his wife, Solveig Ager Best, he is grateful for her constant encouragement.

John W. Best

RESEARCH
IN
EDUCATION

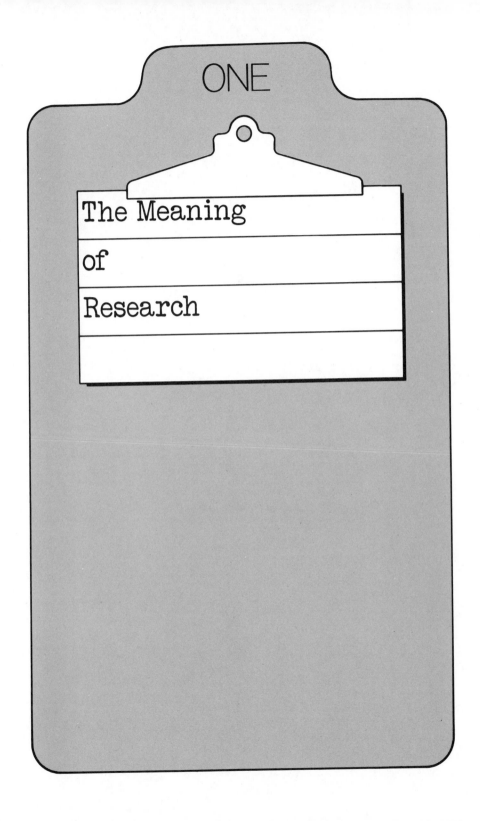

ONE

The Meaning

of

Research

THE SEARCH FOR KNOWLEDGE

Human beings are the unique product of their creation and evolution. In contrast to other forms of animal life, their more highly developed nervous system has enabled them to develop sounds and symbols (letters and numbers) that make possible the communication and recording of their questions, observations, experiences, and ideas.

It is understandable that their greater curiosity, implemented by their control of symbols, would lead them to speculate about the operation of the universe, the great forces beyond their own control. Over many centuries, people began to develop what seemed to be plausible explanations. Attributing the forces of nature to the working of supernatural powers, they believed that the gods, at their whims, manipulated the sun, the stars, the wind, the rain, and the lightning.

The appearance of the medicine man or the priest, who claimed special channels of communication with the gods, led to the establishment of a system of religious authority passed on from one generation to another. A rigid tradition developed and a dogma of Nature's processes, explained in terms of mysticism and the authority of the priesthood, became firmly rooted, retarding for centuries further search for truth.

But gradually people began to see that the operations of the forces of Nature were not as capricious as they had been led to believe. They began to observe an orderliness in the universe, certain cause-and-effect relationships, and discovered that, under certain conditions, events could be predicted with reasonable accuracy. However, these explanations were often rejected if they seemed to conflict with the dogma of religious authority. Curious persons who raised questions were often punished and even put to death when they persisted in expressing doubts suggested by such unorthodox explanations of natural phenomena.

This reliance on empirical evidence or personal experience challenged the sanction of vested authority and represented an important step in the direction of scientific inquiry. Such pragmatic observation, however, was largely unsystematic and further limited by the lack of an objective method. Observers were likely to overgeneralize on the basis of incomplete experience or evidence, to ignore complex factors operating simultaneously, or to let their feelings and prejudices influence both their observations and their conclusions.

It was only when people began to think systematically about thinking itself that the era of logic began. The first systematic approach to reasoning, attributed to Aristotle and the Greeks, was the deductive method. The categorical syllogism was one model of thinking that prevailed among early philosophers. Syllogistic reasoning established a logical relationship between a *major premise, a minor premise,* and a *conclusion.* A major premise is a self-evident assumption, previously established by metaphysical truth or dogma, concerning a relationship; a minor premise is a particular case related to the major premise. Given the logical relationship of these premises, it leads to an inescapable conclusion.

A typical Aristotelian categorical syllogism follows:

Major premise . . . . All men are mortal.
Minor premise . . . . Socrates is a man.
        Conclusion . . . . Socrates is mortal.

This deductive method, moving from the general assumption to the specific application, made an important contribution to the development of modern problem solving. But it was not fruitful in arriving at new truths. The acceptance of incomplete or false major premises based on old dogmas or unreliable authority could only lead to error. Semantic difficulties often resulted from shifting definitions of the terms involved.

Centuries later, Francis Bacon advocated the application of direct observation of phenomena, arriving at conclusions or generalizations through the evidence of many individual observations. This inductive process of moving from specific observations to the generalization freed logic from some of the hazards and limitations of deductive thinking. Bacon recognized the obstacle that the deductive process placed in the way of discovering new truths: it started with old dogmas that religious or intellectual authorities had already accepted and could be expected to arrive at few new truths. These impediments to the discovery of truth, which he termed "idols," were exposed in his *Novum Organum,* written in 1620.

The following story, attributed to Bacon, expresses his revolt against the authority of the written word, an authority that dominated the search for truth during the Middle Ages:

In the year of our Lord, 1432, there arose a grievous quarrel among the brethren over the number of teeth in the mouth of a horse. For thirteen days the disputation raged without ceasing. All the ancient books and chronicles were fetched out, and wonderful and ponderous erudition was made manifest. At the beginning of the fourteenth day a youthful friar of goodly bearing asked his learned superiors for permission to add a word, and straightway, to the wonder of the disputants, whose deep wisdom he sorely vexed, he beseeched them in a manner coarse and unheard of, to look in the mouth of a horse and find answers to their questionings. At this, their dignity being grievously hurt, they waxed exceedingly wroth; and joining in a mighty uproar they flew upon him and smote him hip and thigh and cast him out forthwith. For, said they, "Surely Satan hath tempted this bold neophyte to declare unholy and unheard-of ways of finding truth, contrary to all the teachings of the fathers." After many days of grievous strife the dove of peace sat on the assembly, and they, as one man, declaring the problem to be an everlasting mystery because of a dearth of historical and theological evidence thereof, so ordered the same writ down.[1]

The method of inductive reasoning proposed by Bacon, a method new to the field of logic, but widely used by the scientists of his time, was not hampered by false premises, by the inadequacies and ambiguities of verbal symbolism, or by the absence of supporting evidence.

But the inductive method alone did not provide a completely satisfactory system for the solution of problems. Random collection of individual observations without a unifying concept or focus often obscured investigations, and therefore rarely led to a generalization or theory.

The deductive method of Aristotle and the inductive method of Bacon were fully integrated in the work of Charles Darwin in the nineteenth century. During his early career his observations of animal life failed to lead to a satisfactory theory of man's development. The concept of the struggle for existence in Thomas Malthus' *Essay on Population* intrigued Darwin and suggested the assumption that natural selection explains the origin of different species of animals. This hypothesis provided a needed focus for his investigations. He proceeded to deduce specific consequences suggested by the hypothesis. The evidence gathered confirmed the hypothesis that biological change in the process of natural selection, in which favorable variations were preserved and unfavorable variations destroyed, resulted in the formation of new species.

The major premise of the older deductive method was gradually replaced by an assumption or hypothesis which was subsequently tested by the collection and logical analysis of data. This deductive-inductive method is now recognized as an example of a scientific approach.

John Dewey suggested a pattern that is helpful in identifying the elements of a deductive-inductive process:

A METHOD OF SCIENCE

1. Identification and definition of the problem

---

[1] Francis Bacon as cited by C. E. K. Mees, "Scientific Thought and Social Reconstruction," *American Scientist* 22 (1934):13–14.

2. Formulation of a hypothesis—a hunch, an assumption, or an intelligent guess

3. Collection, organization, and analysis of data

4. Formulation of conclusions

5. Verification, rejection, or modification of the hypothesis by the test of its consequences in a specific situation.

While this pattern is a useful reconstruction of some methods of scientific inquiry, it is not to be considered the *only* scientific method. There are many ways of applying logic and observation to problem solving. An overly rigid definition of the research process would omit many ways in which researchers go about their tasks. The planning of a study may include a great deal of exploratory activity, which is frequently intuitive or speculative and, at times, a bit disorderly. Although researchers must eventually identify a precise and significant problem, their object may initially be vague and poorly defined. They may observe situations that seem to suggest certain possible cause-and-effect relationships and even gather some preliminary data to examine for possible relevancy to their vaguely conceived problem. At this stage, imagination and much speculation are essential to the formulation of a clearly defined problem that is susceptible to the research process. Many students of research rightly feel that problem identification is one of the most difficult and most crucial steps of the research process.

THE HYPOTHESIS

After a problem has been identified, certain answers or solutions in the form of hypotheses may be formulated. These hunches, educated guesses, or speculations may be based upon past experience, informal observation, or information gained from others. In everyday situations those who confront problems often propose informal hypotheses that can be tested directly. For example, when a lamp fails to light when the switch is turned on, several informal hypotheses come to mind:

1. The plug is not properly connected to the wall outlet.

2. The bulb is burned out.

3. The fuse is burned out or the circuit breaker tripped.

4. There has been a power failure in the neighborhood.

Each of these speculations can be tested directly by checking the plug connection, substituting a bulb known to be in working condition, inspecting the fuse or circuit breaker, or by noting whether or not other lights in the house or in neighbors' houses are on.

The Research Hypothesis

The research or scientific hypothesis is a formal affirmative statement predicting a single research outcome, a tentative explanation of the relationship between two or more variables. It limits the focus of the investigation to a definite target and determines what observations are to be made.

A number of years ago the hypothesis was formulated that there is a positive causal relationship between cigarette smoking and the incidence of coronary heart disease. This hypothesis proposed a tentative explanation that led to many studies comparing the incidence of heart disease among cigarette smokers and nonsmokers. As a result of these extensive studies, the medical profession now generally accepts the conclusion that this relationship has been established.

In the behavioral sciences, the variables may be abstractions that cannot be observed. These variables must be defined operationally, by describing some incidents or samples of actual behavior that are concrete enough to be observed directly. The relationship between these observable incidents may be deduced as consistent or inconsistent with the consequences of the hypothesis. Thus, the hypothesis may be judged to be probably true or probably false.

For example, one might propose the hypothesis that third grade children taught the Chisanbop hand calculating process would learn to perform the basic arithmetic processes more effectively than those using the conventional method. Children would be randomly assigned to two groups, one taught the Chisanbop system (experimental group) and the other using the conventional method (control group). The experiment would be carried on for a period of nine months. If the hypothesis were true, the mean scores of the experimental group on a standardized arithmetic achievement test would be significantly higher than those of the control group.

The Null Hypothesis (H_o)

In the early stage of their study, researchers state an affirmative scientific or research hypothesis as a prediction of the outcome that they propose to test. Later, at the stage of the statistical analysis of the observed data, they restate the hypothesis in negative or null form.

For example, the previous research hypothesis would be restated: There is *no significant difference* in the arithmetic achievement of students taught the Chisanbop system of hand calculation and those using the conventional method.

The null hypothesis relates to a statistical method of interpreting conclusions about population characteristics inferred from the variable relationships observed in samples. The null hypothesis asserts that observed differences or relationships merely result from chance errors inherent in the sampling process. If the researcher rejects the null hypothesis, he or she accepts the research hypothesis, concluding that the magnitude of the observed variable relationship is probably too great to attribute to sampling error.

The logic of the use of the null hypothesis, which may be confusing to students, is explained in greater detail in the discussions of sampling error and the central limit theorem in Chapter Eight.

SAMPLING

The primary purpose of research is to discover principles that have universal application, but to study a whole population in order to arrive at generalizations would be impracticable, if not impossible. Some populations are so large that their characteristics could not be measured; before the measurement had been completed the population would have changed.

Imagine the difficulty of conducting a reading experiment with all American fifth grade children as subjects. The study of a population of this size would require the services of thousands of researchers, the expenditure of millions of dollars, and hundreds of thousands of class hours.

Fortunately, the process of sampling makes it possible to draw valid inferences or generalizations on the basis of careful observation of variables within a relatively small proportion of the population. A measured value based upon sample data is a *statistic*. A population value inferred from a statistic is a *parameter*.

A population is any group of individuals that have one or more characteristics in common that are of interest to the researcher. The population may be all the individuals of a particular type or a more restricted part of that group. All public school teachers, all male secondary school teachers, all elementary school teachers, or all Chicago kindergarten teachers may be populations.

A sample is a small proportion of a population selected for observation and analysis. By observing the characteristics of the sample, one can make certain inferences about the characteristics of the population from which it is drawn. Contrary to some popular opinion, samples are not selected haphazardly; they are chosen randomly in a systematic way, so that chance or the operation of probability can be utilized.

Randomness

The concept of randomness has been basic to scientific observation and research. It is based upon the assumption that, while individual events cannot be predicted with accuracy, aggregate events can. Sir Francis Galton (1822–1911) wrote, "I know of scarcely anything so apt to impress the imagination as the wonderful form of cosmic order expressed by the 'law of frequency or error.' This law would have been personified by the Greeks and deified, if they had known it. It reigns with serenity and in complete self-effacement amidst the wildest confusion. The huger the mob, the greater the apparent anarchy, the more perfect its sway. It is the supreme law of unreason. Whenever a large sample of chaotic elements are taken in hand and marshalled in the order of their magnitude, an unsuspected and most beautiful form of regularity proves to have been latent all along."

Randomization has two important applications in research:

1. Selecting groups of individuals for observation that are representative of the population about which the researcher wishes to generalize.

2. Equating experimental and control groups in an experiment. Assigning individuals by random assignment is the best method of providing for their equivalence.

It is important to note that a random sample is not necessarily an identical representation of the population. Characteristics of successive random samples drawn from the same population may differ to some degree, but it is possible to estimate their variation from the population characteristics and from each other. The variation, known as sampling error, does not suggest that a mistake has been made in the process, but that with randomization, certain predictable chance variations are observed.

The topic of sampling error is considered in greater detail in Chapter Eight, in the discussion of the central limit theorem, the standard error of the mean, and the level of significance.

The Simple Random Sample

The individual observations or individuals are chosen in such a way that each has an equal chance of being selected, and that each choice is independent of any other choice. If we wished to draw a sample of 50 individuals from a population of 600 students enrolled in a school, we could place the 600 names in a container and, blindfolded, draw one name at a time until the sample of 50 was selected. This procedure is cumbersome and is rarely used.

Random Numbers

A more convenient way of selecting a random sample, or assigning individuals to experimental and control groups so that they are equated, is by the use of a table of random numbers. Many such tables have been generated by computers producing a random sequence of digits. *The Million Random Digits with 100,000 Normal Deviates* of the RAND Corporation[2] and the *Table of 105,000 Random Decimal Digits* of the Interstate Commerce Commission[3] are frequently used.

When using a table, it is necessary to assign consecutive numbers to each member of the population from which the sample is to be selected. Then, entering the table at any page, row, or column, the sample can be selected from 100 to 999, three digits; and from 1000 to 9999, four digits. When a duplicated number or a number larger than the population size is encountered, it is skipped and the process continues until the desired sample size is selected.

As an illustration, let us assume that a sample of 30 is to be selected from a serially numbered population of 835. Using a portion of a table of random numbers reproduced here, 30 three-digit numbers are selected by reading from left to right. When using the table of random numbers to select a sample, one must number the population members serially. Then, enter the table at any page, row or column at random, and the sample can be selected by reading to the left, right, up, down, or diagonally. For populations up to 99 in number, two digits are selected; from 100–999, three digits; and from 1000 to 9999, four digits.

These 30 numbered members of the population comprise the sample. If this group were to be divided into two equated groups of 15 each, the first 15 could compose one group and the second 15 the other. There are many varieties of random assignment, such as assigning the odd numbers to one group (1, 3, 5, 7, . . .) and the even numbers (2, 4, 6, 8, . . .) to the other. It is apparent that in order to select a random sample, conscious selection of any particular individual or obser-

---

[2] RAND Corporation, *A Million Random Digits with 100,000 Normal Deviates* (New York: Free Press, 1965).

[3] *Table of 105,000 Random Decimal Digits* (Washington, D.C.: Bureau of Transport Economics and Statistics, Interstate Commerce Commission, Statement No. 4914, File No. 261-A-1). Prepared for the Commission by H. Burke Horton and R. Tynes Smith III.

TABLE 1 An Abbreviated Table of Random Numbers

50393	13330	92982	17442	63378	02050		
09038	31974	22381	24289	72341	61530		
82066	06997	44590	23445	72731	61407		
91340	84979	39117	89344	46694	95596		

The sample

503	426	197	161	590	~~913~~	444
~~931~~	337	422	530	~~234~~	408	669
333	802	381	820	457	497	
092	050	242	660	273	~~939~~	
~~982~~	090	~~897~~	699	~~161~~	117	
074	383	234	744	407	~~893~~	

In selecting this sample, eight numbers were deleted. Numbers 931, 982, 897, 913, 939, and 893 were deleted because they were larger than the population of 835 described. Numbers 234 and 161 were deleted because they duplicated previous selections.

vation must not enter the process. The size of the sample may or may not be significantly related to its adequacy. A large sample, carelessly selected, may be biased and inaccurate, whereas a smaller one, carefully selected, may be relatively unbiased and accurate enough to make satisfactory inference possible.

In addition to care in the sampling process, defining the population about which inferences are to be made is extremely important. When the now defunct *Literary Digest* drew its sample for the purpose of predicting the results of the 1936 presidential election, subjects were chosen from the pages of telephone directories and from automobile registration lists. The prediction of Alfred Landon's victory over Franklin D. Roosevelt proved to be wrong and a postelection analysis revealed that the population for which the prediction was made was not the same population sampled. Large numbers of eligible voters did not own automobiles and were not telephone subscribers, and consequently were not included in the sample.

The Systematic Sample

If a population can be accurately listed, or is finite, a type of systematic selection will provide what approximates a random sample. A systematic sample consists of the selection of each *n*th term from a list. For example, if a sample of 200 were to be selected from a telephone directory, with 200,000 listings, one would select the first name by selecting a randomly selected name from a randomly selected page. Then every thousandth name would be selected until the sample of 200 names was complete. If the last page were reached before the desired number had been selected, the count would continue from the first page of the directory. Systematic samples of automobile owners could be selected in similar fashion from a state licensing bureau list or file, or a sample of eighth grade students from a school attendance roll.

The Stratified Random Sample

At times it is advisable to subdivide the population into smaller homogeneous groups in order to get more accurate representation. For example, in making an income study of wage earners in a community, a true sample would approximate the same relative number from each socioeconomic level of the whole community. If the proportion were 15 percent professional workers, 10 percent managers, 20 percent skilled workers, and 55 percent unskilled workers, the sample should include approximately the same proportions in order to be considered representative. Within each subgroup a random selection should be used. This process gives the researcher a more representative sample than one selected from the entire community, which might be unduly weighted by a preponderance of unskilled workers.

In addition to, or instead of, socioeconomic status, such characteristics as age, sex, extent of formal education, racial origin, religious or political affiliation, or rural-urban residence might provide a basis for choosing a stratified sample. The characteristics of the entire population must be carefully considered together with the purposes of the study before a stratified sample is decided upon.

The Area or Cluster Sample

The area or cluster sample is a variation of the simple random sample, particularly appropriate when the population of interest is infinite, where a list of the members of the population does not exist, or when the geographic distribution of the individuals is widely scattered. Suppose for the purpose of a survey we wanted to select a sample of all public school elementary teachers in the United States. A simple random sample would be impracticable.

From the 50 states a random sample of 20 could be selected. From the 20 states, all counties could be listed and a random sample of 80 counties selected. From the 80 counties, all of the school districts could be listed and a random sample of 30 school districts selected. It would not be difficult to compile a list of all elementary teachers from the 30 school districts and a random sample of 500 teachers selected. This successive random sampling of states, counties, school districts, and finally of individuals would involve a relatively efficient and inexpensive method of selecting a sample of individuals.

This method of sampling is likely to introduce an element of sample bias because of the unequal size of some of the subsets selected. Only when a simple random sample would be impracticable is this method recommended.

Nonprobability Samples

Some nonprobability sampling procedures may produce samples that do not accurately reflect the characteristics of a population of interest. Such samples may lead to unwarranted generalizations and should not be used if random selection is practicable.

Educational researchers, because of administrative limitations in randomly selecting and assigning individuals to experimental and control groups, often use available classes as samples. The status of groups may be equated by such statistical means as the analysis of covariance. In certain types of descriptive studies, the use of available samples may restrict generalizations to similar populations. For example, when a psychology professor uses Introduction to Psychology classes as subjects, he or she may safely generalize only to other similar groups of psychology students.

A sample made up of those who volunteer to participate in a study may represent a biased sample. Volunteers are not representative of a total population, for volunteering results in a selection of individuals who are different and who really represent a population of volunteers. In a sense, those who respond to a mailed questionnaire are volunteers and may not reflect the characteristics of all who were on the mailing list. It may be desirable to send another copy of the instrument to nonrespondents with an appeal for their participation.

Sample Size

There is usually a trade-off between the desirability of a large sample and the feasibility of a small one. The ideal sample is large enough to serve as an adequate representation of the population about which the researcher wishes to generalize, and small enough to be selected economically, in terms of subject availability, expense in both time and money, and complexity of data analysis. There is no fixed number or percentage of subjects that determines the size of an adequate sample. It may depend upon the nature of the population of interest or the data to be gathered and analyzed. A national opinion poll randomly selects a sample of about 1500 subjects as a reflection of the opinions of a population of more than 150 million United States citizens of voting age, with an error factor of from two to three percent.

Prior to the second decade of the twentieth century, statisticians believed that samples should be relatively large so that the normal probability table could be used to estimate sampling error,[4] explained by the central limit theorem. The work of William Sealy Gosset in 1915, in which he developed data on the probability distribution of small sample means (Students' *t* distribution), led to the effective use of small samples. Gosset's contribution made feasible research studies that necessarily had to be limited to a small number of subjects. Small-sample research has made a significant contribution to statistical analysis of research data, particularly in experimental studies.

It is often stated that samples of 30 or more are to be considered large samples and those with fewer than 30, small samples. It is approximately at this sample size of 30 that the magnitude of Student's *t* critical values for small samples approach the *z* critical values of the normal probability table for large samples. (See Chapter Eight for a discussion of *z* and *t* critical values.)

More important than size is the care with which the sample is selected. The ideal method is random selection, letting chance or the laws of probability determine which members of the population are to be selected. When random sampling is employed, whether the sample is large or small, the errors of sampling may be estimated, giving researchers an idea of the confidence that they may place in their findings.

In summary, several practical observations about sample size are listed:

1. The larger the sample, the smaller the magnitude of sampling error.

2. Survey-type studies probably should have larger samples than needed in experimental studies.

3. When sample groups are to be subdivided into smaller groups to be compared, the researcher initially should select large enough samples so that the subgroups are of adequate size for his or her purpose.

4. In mailed questionnaire studies, since the percentage of responses may be as low as 20 to 30 percent, a larger initial sample mailing is indicated.

5. Subject availability and cost factors are legitimate considerations in determining appropriate sample size.

---

[4] See Chapter Eight for a discussion of sampling error and students' distribution.

THE ROLE OF THEORY

At this stage in the discussion, a statement about theory would be appropriate. To many people the term *theory* suggests an ivory tower, something unreal, something of little practical value. To the contrary, a theory establishes a cause-and-effect relationship between variables with the purpose of explaining and predicting phenomena. Those who engage in pure research devote their energies to the formulation of theories and may not be concerned with their practical application. When a theory has been established it may suggest many applications of practical value. John Dewey once said that there was nothing more practical than a good theory.

Theories about the relationship between the position of the earth and other moving celestial bodies were essential to the successful launching and return of manned space vehicles. Theories of the behavior of gases were essential to the development of refrigeration and air-conditioning. Controlled atomic energy could not have been achieved without the establishment of theories about the nature of mass and energy and the structure of the atom. The real purpose of scientific method is prediction, the discovery of certain theories or generalizations that anticipate future occurrences with maximum probability.

THE SOCIAL SCIENCES

The term *science* may be thought of as an approach or attitude rather than a field of subject matter. By attempting to apply the rigorous controls of systematic observation and analysis used in the physical and biological sciences to areas of social behavior, the social sciences have grown and have advanced humanity's knowledge of itself. The fields of anthropology, economics, education, political science, psychology, and social psychology have become recognized as sciences by many authorities. To the extent that these studies are founded on scientific methodology, they are sciences. There are some who reject this concept, still defining science in terms of areas of subject matter rather than as methodology. Historically their position can be readily explained. Since scientific methods were first used in the investigation of physical phenomena, tradition has identified science with the physical world. Only within the last century has the methodology of science been applied to the study of various areas of human behavior. Since these are newer areas of investigation their results have not achieved the acceptance and status that come with the greater maturity and longer tradition of the physical sciences. There exist today bodies of opinion in politics, religion, and some academic disciplines that man is not the proper study of mankind.

The uniformity of nature is a reasonable assumption in the world of physical objects and their characteristics, but in the area of social behavior, such assumptions are not warranted. Human nature is much more complex than the sum of its many discrete elements, even if they could be isolated and identified. Because human nature is so complex, it is much more difficult to develop sound theories of human behavior than it is to predict occurrences in the physical world.

1. No two persons are alike in feelings, drives, or emotions. What may be a reasonable prediction for one may be useless for another.

2. No one person is completely consistent from one moment to another. Human behavior is influenced by the interaction of the individual with every changing element in his environment, often in a way that is difficult to predict.

3. Human beings are influenced by the research process itself. They are influenced by the attention that is focused on them when under investigation and influenced by the knowledge that their own behavior is being observed.

4. The behavioral sciences have been limited by a lack of adequate definitions. Accurate operational definitions are essential to the development of a sophisticated science. Such traits as intelligence, learning, hostility, anxiety, or motivation are not directly observable. As constructs they can only be postulated, and since they cannot be seen, heard, or felt, they can only be inferred by test scores, or by observed hostile or aggressive acts, skin responses, pulse rates, or persistence at a task.

But even constructs for which useful descriptive instruments *are* available account for only limited sources of variation; they yield only partial definitions. For example, intelligence, as defined operationally by a score on an intelligence test, is not a satisfactory measure of the type of intelligence that individuals are called upon to demonstrate in a variety of situations outside a formal academic environment.

In the physical sciences, many complex constructs have been more effectively defined in operational terms. Time is one such construct; time is a function of the motion of the earth in relation to the sun, measured by the rotation of a hand on the face of a circular scale in precise units. Weight is a construct involving the laws of gravitation, measured by springs, torsion devices, levers, or electronic adaptations of these instruments.

The instruments which measure such constructs are devised so that they are consistent, to a maximum degree, with known physical laws and forces, and yield valid descriptions in a variety of situations. An international bureau prescribes standards for these devices so that they may provide precise operational definitions of the constructs.

Although the problems of discovering theories of human behavior are difficult, they may not be insoluble. Behavioral scientists will need to carry on their investigations as carefully and rigorously as have physical scientists. However, one must not overestimate the exactness of the physical sciences, for theoretical speculations and probability estimates are also inherent characteristics.

Today we live in a world that attests to the progress of physical science. Many diseases have been conquered. The Salk and Sabin vaccines promise to rid the world of poliomyelitis. Human life span has been increased markedly in some countries, actually by almost two-thirds in the past century. People have traveled at several times the speed of sound; they enjoy a more adequate diet, perform less physical labor, and suffer less from the discomforts of excessive heat and cold. They have entertainment available, at home or in their car, at the turn of a switch, and enjoy more leisure than they could have dreamed of a century ago. The splitting of the atom, space travel, and such developments in the field of electronics as the laser and the silicon chip, promise improvements and adventures that are beyond the scope of human imagination. All these improvements have resulted from the investigation of physical science.

However, there is less confidence about the improvement of the nonphysical aspects of our world. Despite all their marvelous gadgets, there is some question about whether people are happier or more satisfied, or whether their basic needs are being fulfilled more effectively today than they were a century ago. The fear of nuclear plant failures and the uncertainty about the safe disposal of nuclear waste is uppermost in the minds of people throughout the world. Dependence upon an ever-increasingly expensive supply of petroleum threatens systems of transportation, the heating of buildings, and society's basic economic structure. The consequences of hot and cold wars and intergroup tensions and conflicts have become more frightening with the development of paralyzing methods of social protest and more sophisticated means of destruction.

Scientific methods must be applied with greater vigor and imagination to the behavioral aspects of our culture. The development of the behavioral sciences and their application to education and other human affairs presents one of the twentieth century's greatest challenges.

WHAT IS RESEARCH?

How is research related to scientific method? The terms *research* and *scientific method* are sometimes used synonymously in educational discussions. Although it is true that the terms have some common elements of meaning, a distinction would be helpful.

For the purposes of this discussion, *research* is considered to be the more formal, systematic, and intensive process of carrying on a scientific method of analysis. Scientific method in problem solving may be an informal application of problem identification, hypothesis formulation, observation, analysis, and conclusion. You could reach a conclusion about the reason your car wouldn't start or why a fire occurred in an unoccupied house by employing a scientific method, but the processes involved would not likely be as structured as those of research. Research is a more systematic activity directed toward discovery and the development of an organized body of knowledge. *Research may be defined as the systematic and objective analysis and recording of controlled observations that may lead to the development of generalizations, principles, or theories, resulting in prediction and possibly ultimate control of events.*

Since definitions of this sort are rather abstract, a summary of some of the characteristics of research may help to clarify its spirit and its meaning.

1. Research is directed toward the solution of a problem. The ultimate goal is to discover cause-and-effect relationships between variables, though researchers often have to settle for the useful discovery of a systematic relationship, for lack of enough evidence to establish one of cause-and-effect.

2. Research emphasizes the development of generalizations, principles, or theories that will be helpful in predicting future occurrences. Research usually goes beyond the specific objects, groups, or situations investigated and infers characteristics of a target population from the sample observed. Research is more than information retrieval, the simple gathering of information. Although many school research departments gather and tabulate statistical information that may be useful in decision making, these activities are not properly termed research.

3. Research is based upon observable experience or empirical evidence. Certain interesting questions do not lend themselves to research procedures because they cannot be observed. Research rejects revelation and dogma as methods of establishing knowledge and accepts only what can be verified by observation.

4. Research demands accurate observation and description. Researchers use quantitative measuring devices, the most precise form of description. When this is not possible or appropriate, they use qualitative or nonquantitative descriptions of their observations. They select or devise valid data-gathering procedures and, when feasible, employ mechanical, electronic, or psychometric devices to refine observation, description, and analysis of data.

5. Research involves gathering new data from primary or first-hand sources or using existing data for a new purpose. Teachers frequently assign a so-called research project that involves writing a paper dealing with the life of a prominent person. The students are expected to read a number of encyclopedias, books, or periodical references, and synthesize the information in a written report. This is not research, for the data are not new. Merely reorganizing or restating what is already known and has already been written, valuable as it may be as a learning experience, is not research. It adds nothing to what is known.

6. Although research activity may at times be somewhat random and unsystematic, it is more often characterized by carefully designed procedures, always applying rigorous analysis. Although trial and error are often involved, research is rarely blind, shotgun investigation—trying something to see what happens.

7. Research requires expertise. The researcher knows what is already known about the problem and how others have investigated it. He or she has searched the related literature carefully, and is also thoroughly grounded in the terminology, the concepts, and the technical skill necessary to understand and analyze the data gathered.

8. Research strives to be objective and logical, applying every possible test to validate the procedures employed, the data collected, and the conclusions reached. The researcher attempts to eliminate personal bias. There is no attempt to persuade or to prove an emotionally held conviction. The emphasis is on testing rather than on proving the hypothesis. Although absolute objectivity is as elusive as pure righteousness, the researcher tries to suppress bias and emotion in his or her analysis.

9. Research involves the quest for answers to unsolved problems. Pushing back the frontiers of ignorance is its goal and originality is frequently the quality of a good research project. However, previous important studies are deliberately repeated, using identical or similar procedures, with different subjects, different settings, and at a different time. This process is *replication*, a fusion of the words *repetition* and *duplication*. Replication is always desirable to confirm or to raise questions about the conclusions of a previous study. Rarely is an important finding made public unless the original study has been replicated.

10. Research is characterized by patient and unhurried activity. It is rarely spectacular and researchers must expect disappointment and discouragement as they pursue the answers to difficult questions.

11. Research is carefully recorded and reported. Each important term is defined, limiting factors are recognized, procedures are described in detail, references are carefully documented, results are objectively recorded, and conclusions are presented with scholarly caution and restraint. The written report and accompanying data are made available to the scrutiny of associates or other scholars. Any competent scholar will have the information necessary to analyze, evaluate, and even replicate the study.

12. Research sometimes requires courage. The history of science reveals that many important discoveries were made in spite of the opposition of political and religious authorities. The Polish scientist Copernicus (1473–1543) was condemned by church authorities when he announced his conclusion concerning the nature of the solar system. His theory that the sun, not the earth, was the center of the solar system, in direct conflict with the older Ptolemaic theory, angered supporters of prevailing religious dogma, who viewed his theory as a denial of the story of creation as described in the book of Genesis. Modern researchers in such fields as genetics, sexual behavior, and even business practices have aroused violent criticism from those whose personal convictions, experiences, or observations were in conflict with some of the research conclusions.

The rigorous standards of scientific research are apparent from an examination of these characteristics. The research worker should be a scholarly, imaginative person of the highest integrity, willing to spend long hours painstakingly seeking truth. However, it must be recognized that researchers are human beings. The ideals that have been listed are probably never completely realized. Like righteousness, they serve as goals to strive for, and are not all achieved by every researcher.

Many people have a superficial concept of research, picturing research workers as strange introverted individuals who, shunning the company of their fellows, find refuge in their laboratory. There, surrounded by test tubes, retorts, beakers, and other gadgets they carry on their mysterious activities. In reality the picture is quite different. Research is not at all mysterious, and is carried on by thousands of quite normal individuals, more often in teams than alone, very often in the factory, the school, or the community, as well as in the laboratory. Its importance is attested to by the tremendous amounts of time, manpower, and money spent on research by industry, universities, government agencies, and the professions. The key to the cultural development of the Western world has been research, reducing areas of ignorance by discovering new truths, which in turn lead to better predictions, better ways of doing things, and new and better products. We recognize the fruits of research: better consumer products, better ways of preventing and treating diseases, better ways of understanding the behavior of individuals and groups, and a better understanding of the world in which we live. In the field of education, we identify research with a better understanding of the individual, and a better understanding of the teaching-learning process and the conditions under which it is most successfully carried on.

PURPOSES OF RESEARCH

Fundamental or Pure Research

The discussion to this point has described research in its more formal aspects. Research has drawn its pattern and spirit from the physical sciences and has represented a rigorous, structured type of analysis. The goal of research has been seen as the development of theories by discovering broad generalizations or principles. It has employed careful sampling procedures in order to extend the findings beyond the group or situation studied. It has had little concern for the application of the findings to actual problems in areas considered to be the concern of people other than the investigator. This methodology is the approach of pure or fundamental research.

Fundamental research is usually carried on in a laboratory situation, often with animals as subjects. This type of research has been primarily the activity of psychologists rather than educators.

Applied Research

Applied research has most of the characteristics of fundamental research, including the use of sampling techniques and the subsequent inferences about the target population. However, its purpose is improving a product or a process—testing theoretical concepts in actual problem situations. Most educational research is applied research, for it attempts to develop generalizations about teaching-learning processes and instructional materials.

Fundamental research in the behavioral sciences may be concerned with the development and testing of theories of behavior. Educational research is concerned with the development and testing of theories of how students behave in an educational setting.

Action Research

Since the late 1930s there has been great interest in social psychology and education in what has been called *action research*. In education this movement has had as its goal the involvement of both research specialist and classroom teacher in the study and application of research to educational problems in a particular classroom setting.

Action research is focused on the immediate application, not on the development of theory, nor upon general application. It has placed its emphasis on a problem, here and now, in a local setting. Its findings are to be evaluated in terms of local applicability, not in terms of universal validity. Its purpose is to improve school practices and, at the same time, to improve those who try to improve the practices: to combine the research function with teacher growth in such qualities as objectivity, skill in research processes, habits of thinking, ability to work harmoniously with others, and professional spirit.

If most classroom teachers are to be involved in research activity it will probably be in the area of action research. Modest studies may be made for the purpose of trying to improve local classroom practices. It is not likely that many teachers will have the time, resources, or technical background to engage in the more formal aspects of research activity. Fundamental research must continue to make its essential contribution to behavioral theory and applied research to the improvement of educational practices. These activities, however, will be primarily the function of research specialists, many of them subsidized by universities, private and government agencies, professional associations, and philanthropic foundations.

Many observers have deprecated action research as nothing more than the application of common sense or good management. But whether or not it is worthy of the term *research,* it does apply scientific thinking and methods to real life problems and represents a great improvement over teachers' subjective judgments and decisions based upon folklore and their limited personal experiences.

In concluding this discussion it is important to realize that research may be carried on at various levels of complexity. Respectable research studies may be of the simple descriptive fact-finding variety that lead to useful generalizations. Actually, many of the early studies in the behavioral sciences were useful in providing needed generalizations about the behavior or characteristics of individuals and of groups. Subsequent experimental studies of a more complex nature needed this groundwork information to suggest hypotheses for more precise analysis. The descriptive studies of the intellectually gifted, carried on since the early 1920s by the late Lewis M. Terman and his associates, have provided useful generalizations about the characteristics of this segment of the school population. Although these studies did not explain the factors underlying giftedness, they did provide many hypotheses to be investigated by more sophisticated experimental methods.

ASSESSMENT, EVALUATION, AND DESCRIPTIVE RESEARCH

The term *descriptive research* has often been incorrectly used to describe three types of investigation that are basically different. Perhaps their superficial similarities have obscured their differences. Each of them employs the process of disciplined inquiry through the gathering and analysis of empirical data and each attempts to develop knowledge. To be done competently, each requires the expertise of the careful and systematic investigator. A brief explanation may serve to put each one in proper perspective.

Assessment is a fact-finding activity, describing conditions that exist at a particular time. No hypotheses are proposed or tested, no variable relationships are examined, and no recommendations for action are suggested.

The national census is a massive assessment type of investigation conducted by the Bureau of the Census, a division of the United States Department of Commerce. Every ten years, an enumeration of the population is conducted, with data classified by nationality, citizenship, age, sex, race, marital status, educational level, regional and community residence, employment, economic status, births, deaths, and other characteristics. These data provide a valuable basis for social analysis and government action.

In education, assessment may be concerned with the determination of progress that students have made toward educational goals. The *National Assessment of Educational Progress* (NAEP), originally known as the Committee on Assessment of the Progress of Education, has been financed by the National Center for Educational Statistics. Since 1969, a nationwide testing program has been conducted in such fields as science, mathematics, literature, reading, and social studies, in four age groupings, in various geographical areas of the country, in communities of various sizes, and in particular states, and has reported interesting evidence of the degree to which learning goals have or have not been realized.

Evaluation is concerned with the application of its findings and implies some judgment of the effectiveness, social utility, or desirability of a product, process, or program in terms of carefully defined and agreed-upon objectives or values. It may involve recommendations for action. It is not concerned with generalizations that may be extended to other settings. In education, it may seek answers to such questions as: How well is the science program developing the competencies that have been agreed upon by the faculty curriculum committee? Should the program in vocational agriculture education be dropped? Are the library facilities adequate? Should the reading textbook series currently in use be retained?

Descriptive research, unlike assessment and evaluation, is concerned with hypothesis formulation and testing, the analysis of the relationships between nonmanipulated variables, and the development of generalizations. Unlike the experimental method, in which variables are deliberately arranged and manipulated through the intervention of the researcher, in descriptive research variables that exist or have already occurred are selected and observed. This process is described as *ex post facto,* explanatory observational, or causal-comparative research in Chapter Four. Both descriptive and experimental methods employ careful sampling procedures so that generalizations may be extended to other individuals, groups, times, or settings.

TYPES OF EDUCATIONAL RESEARCH

Any attempt to classify types of educational research poses a difficult problem. The fact that practically every textbook suggests a different system of classification provides convincing evidence that there is no generally accepted scheme.

To systematize a method of presentation, however, some pattern is desirable. At the risk of seeming arbitrary, and with a recognition of the danger of oversimplification, a framework is suggested that might clarify understanding of basic principles of research methodology. It should be noted that the system of classification is not important in itself, but only has value in making the analysis of research processes more comprehensible.

Actually, *all* research involves the elements of observation, description, and the analysis of what happens under certain circumstances. A rather simple three-point analysis may be used to classify educational research. Practically all studies fall under one, or a combination, of these types.

1. *Historical research* describes *what was.* The process involves investigating, recording, analyzing, and interpreting the events of the past for the purpose of discovering generalizations that are helpful in understanding the past, understanding the present, and to a limited extent, in anticipating the future.

2. *Descriptive research* describes *what is.* It involves the description, recording, analysis, and interpretation of conditions that exist. It involves some type of comparison or contrast and attempts to discover relationships between existing nonmanipulated variables.

3. *Experimental research* describes *what will be* when certain variables are carefully controlled or manipulated. The focus is on variable relationships. As defined here, deliberate manipulation is always a part of the experimental method.

A complete chapter is devoted to each of these three types of research; to techniques of data-gathering, to areas of application, and to methods of analysis.

SUMMARY

Human beings' desire to know about their world has led them from primitive superstition to modern scientific knowledge. From mysticism, dogma, and the limitations of unsystematic observation based upon personal experience, they have examined the process of thinking itself to develop the method of deductive-inductive thinking, which has become the foundation of scientific method. Although first applied as a method of the physical sciences, the process of scientific inquiry has also become the prevailing method of the behavioral sciences.

There is no single scientific method, for scientists carry on their investigations in a number of ways. However, accuracy of observation and the qualities of imagination, creativity, objectivity, and patience are some of the common ingredients of all scientific methods.

The hypothesis is an essential research device that gives a focus to the investigation and permits researchers to reach probability conclusions. After researchers formulate an affirmative research hypothesis at the outset of their project, for the purposes of statistical analysis of their observations, they restate the hypothesis in negative or null form. This procedure facilitates inferring population characteristics from observed variable relationships as they relate to the error inherent in the sampling process.

Sampling, a deliberate rather than haphazard method of selecting subjects for observation, enables the scientist to infer conclusions about a population of interest from the observed characteristics of a relatively small number of cases. Simple random, systematic, stratified random, area or cluster, and available (nonprobability) samples have been described. Methods of determining the size of an appropriate sample are suggested and the sources of sample bias are considered.

Research has been defined as *the systematic and objective analysis and recording of controlled observations that may lead to the development of generalizations, principles or theories, resulting in prediction and possibly ultimate control of events.* The characteristics of research that may help to clarify its spirit and meaning have been presented.

Fundamental, or *pure,* research is the formal and systematic process of deductive-inductive analysis, leading to the development of theories. *Applied* research adapts the theories, developed through fundamental research, to the solution of problems. *Action* research, which may fail to attain the rigorous qualities of fundamental and applied research, attempts to apply the spirit of scientific method to the solution of problems in a particular setting, without any assumptions about the general application of findings beyond the situation studied.

The distinctions between assessment, evaluation, and descriptive research have been discussed. A scheme that classifies research as historical, descriptive, and experimental has been presented.

Readers are reminded that research is essentially an intellectual and creative activity. The mastery of techniques and processes does not confer research competence, though these skills may help the creative problem-solver to reach his or her objectives more efficiently.

EXERCISES

1. Construct two syllogisms:
    a. one that is sound
    b. one that is faulty; indicate the nature of the fallacy.

2. Illustrate the application of Dewey's steps in problem solving. Choose one of the problems listed, or one of your own:
    a. brown patches on your lawn
    b. your car won't start when you leave for home
    c. getting an economical buy on canned peaches
    d. most of the members of your class failed an examination.
3. Give an example of:
    a. a pure research problem
    b. an applied research problem
    c. an action research problem.
4. To what extent have religious institutions resisted the claims of science?
5. Is there necessarily a conflict between the disciplines of the sciences and the humanities?
6. Explain why you agree or disagree with the following statements:
    a. Excessive effort is spent on the development of theories, because they don't usually work in real situations.
    b. Science is more properly thought of as a method of problem solving, rather than as a field of knowledge.
    c. Applied research is more important than pure research in contributing to human welfare.
7. How would you select a sample of 40 college students for a morale study from a freshman class of 320?
8. From a metropolitan school district staff directory, you wish to select a sample of 300 teachers from a listing of 3800. Discuss several ways that the sample could be selected, considering the issues that may be involved.
9. What are the distinctive characteristics of descriptive research as contrasted with:
    a. assessment
    b. evaluation
    c. experimental research.
10. How is the term *research* sometimes misused in classroom assignments and television interviews?

BIBLIOGRAPHY

Barzun, Jacques. *Science: The Glorious Entertainment.* New York: Harper & Row, 1964.

Conant, James B. *Science and Common Sense.* New Haven: Yale University Press, 1951.

——. *Two Modes of Thought.* New York: Simon & Schuster, 1964.

Dewey, John. *How We Think.* Boston: Raytheon Education Co., 1933.

———. *Logic: The Theory of Inquiry.* New York: Holt, Rinehart & Winston, 1938.

EBEL, ROBERT L. "Some Limitations of Basic Research in Education." *Phi Delta Kappan* 49 (Oct. 1967): 81–84.

FEIGL, HERBERT and MAY BROADBECK. *Readings in the Philosophy of Science.* New York: Appleton-Century-Crofts, 1953.

FRANK, PHILLIP G. *The Validation of Scientific Theories.* New York: Collier Books, 1961.

HAYS, W. L. *Quantification in Psychology.* Monterey, CA: Brooks/Cole Publishing Co., 1967.

HELMSTADTER, GERALD C. *Research Concepts in Human Behavior.* New York: Appleton-Century-Crofts, 1970.

JONES, W. T. *The Sciences and the Humanities: Conflict and Reconciliation.* Berkeley: University of California Press, 1965.

KAPLAN, ABRAHAM. *The Conduct of Inquiry.* San Francisco: Chandler Publishing Co., 1964.

REAGAN, MICHAEL D. "Basic and Applied Research: A Meaningful Distinction?" *Science* 155 (Jan. 6, 1967): 1383–1386.

SKINNER, B. F. *Walden Two.* New York: Macmillan Co., 1948.

SLAVIN, ROBERT E. "Basic vs. Applied Research: A Response." *Educational Researcher* 7:2 (Feb. 1978): 15–17.

SNOW, C. P. *Two Cultures and the Scientific Revolution.* New York: Cambridge University Press, 1959.

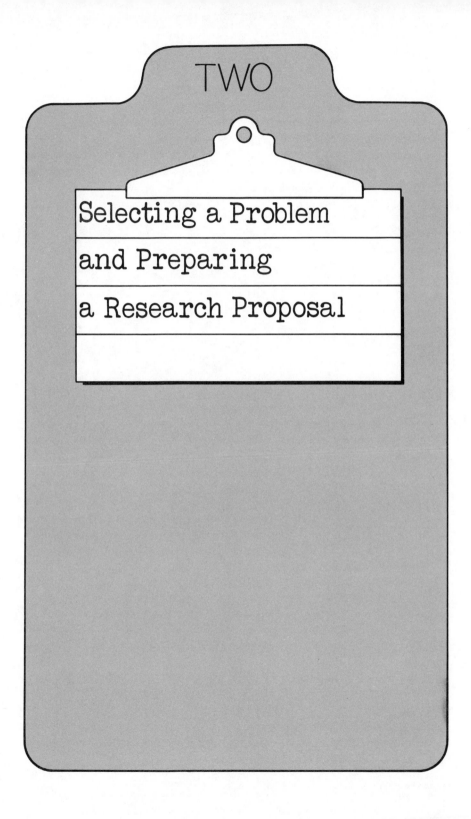

TWO

Selecting a Problem
and Preparing
a Research Proposal

One of the most difficult phases of the graduate research project is the choice of a suitable problem. Beginners are likely to select a problem that is much too broad in scope. This may be due to their lack of understanding of the nature of research and systematic problem-solving activity. It may also be due to their enthusiastic, but naïve, desire to solve an important problem quickly and immediately.

Those who are more experienced know that research is often tedious, painfully slow, and rarely spectacular. They realize that the search for truth and the solution of important problems take a great deal of time and energy and the intensive application of logical thinking. Research makes its contribution to human welfare by countless small additions to knowledge. The researcher has some of the characteristics of the ant, who brings its single grain of sand to the anthill.

Before considering the ways in which problems may be identified, a discussion of a few of the characteristics of research and the activities of the researcher would seem appropriate. Research is more often a team endeavor than an individual activity. Researchers working in groups attack problems in different ways, pooling their knowledge and ideas and sharing the results of their efforts. Highly publicized discoveries usually result from the cumulative efforts of many, working as teams over long periods of time. They are rarely the product of a single individual working in isolation.

Great discoveries rarely happen by accident. When they do, the researcher is usually well-grounded and possesses the ability, known as *serendipity,* to recognize the significance of these fortunate occurrences. He or she is imaginative enough to seize the opportunity presented and to carry it through to a fruitful conclusion. Pasteur has observed that chance favors the prepared mind.

Researchers are specialists, rather than generalists. They employ the principle of the rifle rather than the shotgun, analyzing limited aspects of broad problems. Critics have complained that much social research consists of learning more and more about less and less until the researcher knows everything about nothing. This is a clever statement, but an exaggeration. The opposite statement, equally clever and exaggerated, characterizes much ineffective problem solving: learning less and less about more and more until one knows nothing about everything.

There is a danger, however, that research activity may focus upon such fragmentary aspects of a problem that it has little relevance to the formulation of a general theory. An analysis of the relationship between a few isolated factors in a complex situation may seem attractive as a research project, but it will make little or no contribution to a body of knowledge. Research is more than compiling, counting, and tabulating data. It involves deducing the consequences of hypotheses through careful observation and the application of rigorous logic.

It is sometimes important to discover that a generalization is probably *not* true. Beginning researchers frequently associate this type of conclusion with a sense of personal failure, for they become emotionally committed to their hypotheses. Research, however, is a process of *testing*, rather than *proving*, and implies an objectivity that lets the data lead where they will.

THE ACADEMIC RESEARCH PROBLEM

Academic research projects have been subjected to much criticism, both by the academic community and by the general public. The academic research project is usually a requirement in partial fulfillment of the requirements of a graduate course or for an advanced degree. The initial motivation may not be the desire to engage in research, but the practical need of meeting a requirement. Unfortunately, few such studies make a significant contribution to the development or refinement of knowledge or to the improvement of practice. The lack of time, financial resources, experience, and expertise of the researcher, and the academic hazard of departing from a relatively safe, short-range project are, understandably, hindrances to significant contributions. But these projects are often justified on the grounds that, once students develop some research competency, they will use their "know-how" to seek solutions to basic problems and will make a contribution to the body of knowledge upon which sound practices are based. Too often this expectation is not realized, for too few students carry on further studies.

Perhaps more significant master's-degree or doctoral studies could be carried on under the direction of an advisor or major professor who is devoting his or her own energies to research on a significant problem. The efforts of degree candidates thus could be directed toward certain restricted phases of the major problem, making possible long-term longitudinal studies. Such studies as those by the late Lewis M. Terman at Stanford University of gifted children, followed over 50 years, represent the cumulative attack that is likely to yield more significant results than the uncoordinated investigations of candidates whose efforts lack this unifying direction and continuity.

Since the early 1960s, the massive participation of the federal government in the support of educational research has had great impact on graduate schools. Funds have been made available for significant long-range studies, conducted by individuals and by teams of faculty researchers, and have provided financial support and valuable apprenticeship opportunities for graduate students.

Levels of Research Projects

In the light of the varied types and purposes of students' projects, the choice of a problem will depend upon the level at which the research is done. A problem appropriate for a beginner in a first course in research would be different from that selected for the more rigorous requirements of the master's thesis or the doctoral dissertation. The first topic will necessarily be a modest one which can be carried on by an inexperienced researcher in a limited period of time. The emphasis will be placed upon the learning process of the beginning researcher, rather than on his or her actual contribution to education. This statement does not imply that the product is necessarily unimportant. It merely recognizes that the limitations of the first research project place the emphasis on learning how, with the hope that subsequent investigations will progressively yield more significant contributions to the advancement of knowledge.

Some students choose a first problem that can be expanded later into a more comprehensive treatment at the level of the master's thesis or the doctoral dissertation. The first study thus serves as an exploratory process.

Sources of Problems

The choice of a suitable problem is always difficult. Few beginners possess real problem awareness, and even the more experienced researcher hesitates at this step. It is a serious responsibility to commit oneself to a problem that will inevitably require much time and energy and which is so academically significant.

What are the most likely sources to which one may go for a suitable research problem, or from which one may develop a sense of problem awareness?

1. Many of the problems confronted in the classroom, the school, or the community lend themselves to investigation, and they are perhaps more appropriate for the beginning researcher than are problems more

remote from his own teaching experience. What organizational or management procedures are employed? How is learning material presented? To what extent does one method yield more effective results than another? How do teachers feel about these procedures? How do pupils and parents feel about them? What out-of-school activities and influences seem to affect students and the teaching-learning process?

Teachers will discover "acres of diamonds" in their own back yards, and an inquisitive and imaginative mind may discover in one of these problem areas an interesting and worthwhile research project.

2. Technological changes and curricular developments are constantly bringing forth new problems and new opportunities for research. Perhaps more than ever before, educational innovations are being advocated in classroom organization, in teaching materials and procedures, and in the application of technical devices and equipment. Such innovations as teaching by television, programmed instruction, modified alphabets, new subject matter concepts and approaches, flexible scheduling, and team teaching need to be carefully evaluated through the research process.

3. The graduate academic experience should stimulate the questioning attitude toward prevailing practices and effectively promote problem awareness. Classroom lectures, class discussions, seminar reports, and out-of-class exchanges of ideas with fellow students and professors will suggest many stimulating problems to be solved. Students who are fortunate enough to have graduate assistantships have an especially advantageous opportunity to profit from the stimulation of close professional relationships with faculty members and fellow assistants.

Reading assignments in textbooks, special assignments, research reports, and term papers will suggest additional areas of needed research. Research articles often suggest techniques and procedures for the attack on other problems. A critical evaluation may reveal faults or defects that made published findings inconclusive or misleading. Many research articles suggest problems for further investigation that may prove fruitful.

Such specialized sources as the *Education Index, Current Index to Journals in Education, Resources in Education, Dissertation Abstracts International,* and similar publications are rich sources for problem seekers. Readers are urged to consult Chapter Nine on the use of reference materials, for a detailed explanation of valuable sources.

4. Consultation with the course instructor, advisor, or major professor is helpful. Although the student should not expect research problems to be assigned, consultation with the more experienced faculty member is a desirable practice. Most students feel insecure as they approach the choice of a research problem. They wonder if the problem they

may have in mind is significant enough, feasible, and reasonably free of unknown hazards. To expect the beginner to arrive at the advisor's office with a completely acceptable problem is quite unrealistic. One of the most important functions of the research advisor is to help students clarify their thinking, achieve a sense of focus, and develop a manageable problem from one that may be vague and too complex.

The following list may suggest some problem areas from which research problems may be defined.

1. Programmed instruction—scrambled texts—teaching machines— computer-assisted instruction
2. Television instruction—closed circuit
3. Modified alphabets—Unifon—Initial Teaching Alphabet
4. Flexible scheduling
5. Team teaching
6. Evaluation of learning—reporting to parents
7. Student regulation/control
8. Evaluation of learning—practices—philosophies
9. Homework policies and practices
10. Field trips
11. School buildings and facilities—lighting—space—safety
12. Extracurricular programs
13. Student out-of-school activities—employment—recreation—cultural activity—reading—television viewing
14. Teacher out-of-school activities—employment—political activity— recreation
15. The open classroom
16. Linguistics
17. New approaches to biology/chemistry/physics
18. Language laboratories—foreign languages—reading
19. Multiple textbooks
20. Independent study programs
21. Advanced placement program
22. Audiovisual programs
23. Sociometry
24. Health services
25. Guidance-counseling programs
26. Teacher morale—annoyances and satisfactions
27. Teacher welfare—salaries—merit rating—retirement—tenure
28. Educational organizations—local, state, and national—NEA—AFT
29. Inner-city schools—the culturally deprived—Head Start—Upward Bound—tutoring
30. Preservice education of teachers—student teaching

31. In-service programs
32. Racial integration—student—teacher
33. Parochial/private school problems—tax credits
34. Follow-up of graduates—early school leavers
35. Religion and education—released time programs—dismissed time—shared time
36. Non-school sponsored social organizations or clubs
37. School district reorganization
38. Community pressures on the school—academic freedom—controversial issues
39. Legal liability of teachers
40. Cadet teaching—teacher recruitment
41. Teaching internship
42. Sex education
43. Ability grouping—acceleration—retardation/promotion
44. Special education—speech therapy—clinical services—social services
45. Problems in higher education—selection—prediction of success—graduate programs
46. Work-study programs
47. Comparison of the effectiveness of two teaching methods/procedures
48. Self-image analysis
49. Vocational objectives of students
50. History of an institution, program, or organization
51. Factors associated with the selection of teaching/nursing/social work as a career
52. Case studies
53. Socioeconomic status and academic achievement
54. Perceptions of administrative leadership
55. The effect of stress on academic achievement

For those members of the class who are not teachers, some of the problem areas listed may be appropriate in social agency, hospital, or industrial situations.

Evaluating the Problem

Before the proposed research problem can be considered appropriate, several searching questions should be raised. Only when those questions are answered in the affirmative can the problem be considered a good one.

1. Is this the type of problem that can be effectively solved through the process of research? Can relevant data be gathered to test the theory or find the answer to the problem under consideration?

2. Is the problem significant? Is an important principle involved? Would the solution make any difference as far as educational theory or practice is concerned? If not, there are undoubtedly more significant problems waiting to be investigated.

3. Is the problem a new one? Is the answer already available? Ignorance of prior studies may lead a student to spend time needlessly on a problem already investigated by some other worker.

   Although novelty or originality is an important consideration, the fact that a problem has been investigated in the past does not mean that it is no longer worthy of study. There are times when it is appropriate to replicate (repeat) a study to verify its conclusions or to extend the validity of its findings to a different situation.

4. Is research on the problem feasible? After a research project has been evaluated, there remains the problem of suitability for a particular researcher. Although the problem may be a good one, is it a good problem for me? Will I be able to carry it through to a successful conclusion? Some of the questions that should be raised are the following:

   a. Am I competent to plan and carry out a study of this type? Do I know enough about this field to understand its significant aspects and to interpret my findings? Am I skillful enough to develop, administer, and interpret the necessary data-gathering devices and procedures? Am I well grounded in the necessary knowledge of research design and statistical procedures?

   b. Are pertinent data accessible? Are valid and reliable data-gathering devices and procedures available? Will school authorities permit me to contact the students, conduct necessary experiments or administer necessary tests, interview teachers, or have access to important cumulative records? Will I be able to get the sponsorship necessary to open doors that otherwise would be closed to me?

   c. Will I have the necessary financial resources to carry on this study? What will be the expense involved in data-gathering equipment, printing, test materials, travel, and clerical help? If the project is an expensive one, what is the possibility of getting a grant from a philanthropic foundation or from such organizations as the National Institute of Education.

   d. Will I have enough time to complete the project? Will there be time to devise the procedures, select the data-gathering devices, gather and analyze the data, and complete the research report? Since most academic programs impose time limitations, certain worthwhile projects of a longitudinal type are precluded.

e. Will I have the courage and determination to pursue the study in spite of the difficulties and social hazards that may be involved? Will I be willing to work aggressively when data are difficult to gather and when others are reluctant to cooperate? Sex education, racial integration, teaching about communism, and other controversial problem areas, however, may not be appropriate for a beginning research project.

THE RESEARCH PROPOSAL[1]

The preparation of a research proposal is an important step in the research process. Many institutions require that a proposal be submitted before any project is approved. This provides a basis for the evaluation of the project and gives the advisor a basis for assistance during the period of his or her direction. It also provides a systematic plan of procedure for the researcher to follow.

The proposal is comparable to the blueprint which the architect prepares before the bids are let and building commences. The initial draft proposal is subject to modification in the light of the analysis by the student and his or her project advisor. Since good research must be carefully planned and systematically carried out, procedures that are improvised from step to step will not suffice. A worthwhile research project is likely to result only from a well-designed proposal.

The proposal format presented here should not be considered the only satisfactory sequence. Many institutions suggest other formats for the proposal.

1. The statement of the problem, either in question form or as a declarative statement. This attempt to focus on a stated goal gives direction to the research process. It must be limited enough in scope to make a definite conclusion possible. The major statement or question may be followed by minor statements or questions. The problem areas that previously have been listed in this chapter are not statements of problems. They are merely broad areas of concern from which problems may be selected.

A problem suggests a specific answer or conclusion. Usually a controversy or a difference of opinion exists. A cause-and-effect relationship may be suggested upon the basis of personal observation and experience.

[1] Compare the research proposal described here with the format or outline of a research report described in Chapter Ten.

Do children who have had kindergarten experience demonstrate greater academic achievement in the first grade than those who have not had this experience? Is participation in high school competitive athletics detrimental to academic achievement? Does racial segregation have a damaging effect upon the self-image of minority group children? Does knowledge of participation in an experiment have a stimulating effect upon the reading achievement of participants? These four questions are problem statements. They involve more than information gathering. They suggest answers or conclusions and provide a focus for research activity.

2. *The hypothesis.* It is appropriate here to formulate a major hypothesis and possibly several minor hypotheses. This approach clearly establishes the nature of the problem and the logic underlying the investigation, and gives direction to the data-gathering process. A good hypothesis has several basic characteristics:

a. It should be reasonable.

b. It should be consistent with known facts or theories.

c. It should be stated in such a way that it can be tested and found to be probably true or probably false.

d. It should be stated in the simplest possible terms.

The research hypothesis is a tentative answer to a question. It is a hunch, or an educated guess, to be subjected to the process of verification or disconfirmation. The gathering of data and the logical analysis of data relationships provide a method of confirming or disconfirming the hypothesis by deducing its consequences.

It is important that the hypothesis be formulated before data are gathered. Suppose that the researcher gathers some data and, on the basis of these, notes something that looks like the basis for an alternative hypothesis. Since any particular set of observations may display an extreme distribution, using such observations to test the hypothesis would possibly lead to an unwarranted conclusion.

The formulation of the hypothesis in advance of the data-gathering process is necessary for an unbiased investigation. It is not inappropriate to formulate additional hypotheses after data are collected, but they should be tested on the basis of new data, not on the old data that suggested them.

3. *The significance of the problem.* It is important that the researcher point out how the answer to the question or the solution to the problem can influence educational theory or practice. Careful formulation and

presentation of the implications or possible applications of knowledge helps to give the project an urgency, justifying its worth.

Failure to include this step in the proposal may well leave the researcher with a problem without significance—a search for data of little ultimate value. Many of the tabulating or "social bookkeeping" research problems should be abandoned if they do not pass the critical test of significance. Perhaps university library shelves would not groan with the weight of so many unread and forgotten dissertations if this criterion of significance had been rigorously applied. With so many gaps in educational theory, and so many areas of educational practice in need of analysis, there is little justification for the expenditure of research effort on trivial or superficial investigations.

4. Definitions, assumptions, limitations, and delimitations. It is important to define all unusual terms that could be misinterpreted. These definitions help to establish the frame of reference with which the researcher approaches the problem. The variables to be considered should be defined in operational terms. Such expressions as academic achievement and intelligence are useful concepts, but they cannot be used as criteria unless they are defined as observable samples of behavior. Academic grades assigned by teachers or scores on standardized achievement tests are operational definitions of achievement. A score on a standardized intelligence test is an operational definition of intelligence.

Assumptions are statements of what the researcher believes to be facts, but cannot verify. A researcher may state the assumption that the participant observers in the classroom, after a period of three days, will establish rapport with the students and will not have a reactive effect on the behavior to be observed.

Limitations are those conditions beyond the control of the researcher that may place restrictions on the conclusions of the study and their application to other situations. Administrative policies that preclude using more than one class in an experiment, a data-gathering instrument that has not been validated, or the inability to randomly select and assign subjects to experimental and control groups are examples of limitations.

Delimitations are the boundaries beyond which the study is not concerned. A study of the attitudes toward racial minorities may be concerned only with middle-class, fifth grade pupils, and conclusions are not to be extended beyond this population sampled.

5. Review of related literature. A summary of the writings of recognized authorities and of previous research provides evidence that the researcher is familiar with what is already known and what is still unknown and untested. Since effective research is based upon past knowledge, this step helps to eliminate the duplication of what has been done, and provides useful hypotheses and helpful suggestions for significant investigation. Citing studies that show substantial agreement and those that seem to present conflicting conclusions helps to sharpen and define understanding of existing knowledge in the problem area, provides a background for the research project, and makes the reader aware of the status of the issue. Parading a long list of annotated studies relating to the problem is ineffective and inappropriate. Only those studies that are plainly relevant, competently executed, and clearly reported should be included.

In searching related literature, the researcher should note certain important elements:

a. Reports of closely related studies that have been investigated

b. Design of the study, including procedures employed and data-gathering instruments used

c. Populations that were sampled: sampling methods employed

d. Variables that were defined

e. Extraneous variables that could have affected the findings

f. Faults that could have been avoided

g. Recommendations for further research.

Capitalizing on the reviews of expert researchers can be fruitful in providing helpful ideas and suggestions. While review articles that summarize related studies are useful, they do not provide a satisfactory substitute for an independent search. Even though the review of related literature is listed as step number 5 in the research proposal, the search for related literature is one of the first steps in the research process. It is a valuable guide to defining the problem, recognizing its significance, suggesting promising data-gathering devices, appropriate study design, and sources of data.

6. *A careful and detailed analysis of proposed research procedures.* This part of the proposal outlines the entire research plan. It describes what will be done, how it will be done, what data will be needed, what data-gathering devices will be used, how samples will be selected, and the method of analyzing the data.

7. *Time schedule.* While this step may not be required by the study advisor, a time schedule should be prepared so that the researcher may budget his or her time and energy effectively. Dividing the project into manageable parts and assigning dates for their completion helps to systematize the study and minimize the natural tendency to procrastinate. Some phases of the project cannot be started until other phases

have been completed. Such parts of the final research report as the review of related literature can be completed and typed while waiting for the data-gathering process. Since academic research projects usually involve critical time limitations and definite deadlines for filing the complete report, the planning of procedures with definite date goals is most important. From time to time the major professor or advisor may request a progress report. This device also serves as a stimulus, helping the researcher to move systematically toward the goal of a completed project.

FINDING RELATED LITERATURE

Students often waste time searching for references in an unsystematic way. The search for references is an ever-expanding process, for each reference may lead to a new list of sources. Although the order suggested does not exhaust the process of compiling a bibliography, it does provide a systematic plan for getting under way.

Researchers may consider these sources as basic:

1. *The Education Index*

2. *Resources in Education*

3. *Current Index to Journals in Education*

4. *Index to Doctoral Dissertations* and *Dissertation Abstracts International*

5. Other specialized indexes or abstracts indicated by the area of investigation

COMPUTER-GENERATED REFERENCE SOURCES

There are a number of computer-generated reference sources that may save a great deal of time and effort and provide a more complete search of the literature.

Educational Resources Information Centers (ERIC) Data Base Search

A computer data base search of ERIC documents is available at no cost from the appropriate ERIC Clearing House, or from any one of more than 500 organizations listed in the ERIC publication, *Survey of ERIC Data Base Search Services.* The subject requested will be translated by a search analyst into appropriate terms from the *Thesaurus of ERIC*

Descriptors, a controlled vocabulary of educational terms used to enter and index documents into the ERIC system.

The reproduction of any ERIC documents in 8½ × 11 inch hard copy, microfilm, or microfiche is available from *ERIC Document Reproduction Service.*[2] See Chapter Nine for a list of specialized ERIC Clearing Houses and the address of the document reproduction service.

School Research Information Service (SRIS)

This information retrieval service is operated by Phi Delta Kappa fraternity, Bloomington, Indiana. The Educational Resources Information Center, *Current Index to Journals in Education* and *Resources in Education* tapes serve as a base. A computer printout of abstracts will be furnished for a moderate fee.

Direct Access to Reference Information (DATRIX)

A development of the University Microfilms (Ann Arbor, Michigan), a division of the Xerox Corporation, this system provides computerized retrieval for *Dissertation Abstracts,* from 1928 to date. The researcher selects key words from a DATRIX Key Word List and dissertations will be cited by title, author, page and volume of *Dissertation Abstracts,* and name of university. Information on microfiche or Xerographic copy of the complete dissertation is provided and may be ordered from University Microfilms.

Psychological Abstracts Search and Retrieval Service (PASAR)

This search and retrieval service provides printouts of abstracts of psychological journal articles, monographs, reports, and parts of books. Each monthly issue of *Psychological Abstracts* provides a request form and search request guidelines. Consult the *Cumulative Subject Index to Psychological Abstracts* for appropriate key words or terms to use in making a request. A moderate fee is charged for the search.

NOTE TAKING

One of the most important research activities of the graduate student is note taking—putting materials in a form that can easily be recalled

---

[2] *How to Use ERIC Reference Tools* (Washington, D.C.: National Institute of Education, Superintendent of Documents, 1979).

and used in the future. Notes will result from speeches and lectures, class discussions, conversation, from solitary meditation, and from reading reference materials. In preparing term papers and research reports the notes that result from reading will be most significant. Without a careful, systematic system of note taking, much of what is read is quickly forgotten.

Reading-reference notes have been classified under four principal categories:

1. *Quotation.* The exact words of an author are reproduced, enclosed in quotation marks. It is essential to copy each statement accurately, and to indicate the exact page reference so that the quotations may be properly footnoted in the written report.

2. *Paraphrase.* The reader restates the author's thoughts in his or her own words.

3. *Summary.* The reader states in condensed form the contents of the article.

4. *Evaluation.* The reader records his or her own reaction, indicating agreement or disagreement, or interpreting the point of view of the writer.

A single note card may include several of these types when it seems appropriate.

A Suggested Method for Taking Notes

1. Skim the reference source before copying any notes. A bird's-eye view is essential before one can decide what material to record and use. Selecting the most significant material is an art to be cultivated.
2. Use 4" × 6" index cards. They are easily sorted by subject headings, and are large enough to include a reasonable amount of material. Some students prefer 5" × 8" cards, which are less convenient to carry but provide more space for notes.
3. File each note card under a definite topic or heading. Place the subject heading at the top of the card for convenient filing. A complete bibliographic citation should be placed at the bottom of the note card. If a book has been used, the call number should be indicated to facilitate library location in the future.
4. Include only one topic on a card. This makes organization of notes flexible. If the notes are lengthy, use consecutively numbered cards, and slip a rubber band around them before filing.

5. Be sure that notes are complete and clearly understandable, for they are not likely to be used for some time after they have been copied.

6. Distinguish clearly between a summary, a direct quotation of the author, a reference to the author's source, and an evaluative statement.

7. Don't plan to recopy or type your notes. It wastes time and increases possibility of error and confusion. Copy your notes carefully the first time.

8. Keep a supply of note cards with you at all times, so that you can jot down ideas that come to you while waiting, riding the bus, or listening to a lecture or discussion.

9. Be careful not to lose your notes. As soon as they are copied, file them in a card index box. If you must carry them with you, use the 4″ × 6″ or 5″ × 8″ accordion file folder, and be sure that your name and address is clearly printed on it.

10. Keep a permanent file of your notes. You may find the same notes useful in a number of courses or in writing a number of reports.

Lateral dominance - reading achievement

Purpose: to study relationships between dominance and reading achievement specified by Dearborn (1931), Monroe (1932), + Harris (1957).

Hypothesis: there is no significant relationship between reading achievement and: 1. hand - eye dominance 2. strength or direction of hand dominance 3. strength or direction of eye dominance 4. early, late, or no establishment of consistent hand dominance

Sample: 250 second grade pupils in 13 randomly-selected classrooms in a middle-class St. Paul, Minnesota suburb

Tests: Lorge Thorndike Intelligence Test, Level I; Harris Test of Lateral Dominence; Gates Advanced Primary Reading Tests

Analysis: Analysis of Covariance: IQ scores the covariate

Results: all three hypotheses confirmed; no significant differences at the .05 level. "Lateral dominance does not seem to be a fruitful area for seeking out determiners of individual differences in reading achievement." p.143.

Irving H. Balow and Bruce Balow, "Lateral Dominance and Reading Achievement in the Second Grade." *American Educational Research Journal,* 1: 139-43, May, 1964.

Fig. 2-1. Note Card (4″ × 6″)

PHOTOSTATIC REPRODUCTION OF REFERENCE MATERIALS

When taking notes, consider the advisability of making photostatic copies of book and journal pages so that they can be examined more efficiently at home.

Recent volumes of professional journals are available only in microfilm form in most libraries. An entire year's publication can be included on one spool of film. Many book and journal materials are reproduced on microfiche cards that may include as many as 1,000 pages on one 4 × 6 inch card. The rapid trend toward microfilming and microfiching professional literature will continue as the constantly increasing volume of published materials burdens limited shelf space.

Coin-operated microfilm and microfiche printers are found in most university libraries. Reproduction is not expensive and the quality of the copy is excellent. It is actually much more convenient to take notes from an 8½ × 11 inch print copy than from film projected on a screen.

THE BIBLIOGRAPHY

In preparing a formal report or paper, it is customary to include a bibliography, indicating the references that have been used in preparing the report. Writing a brief descriptive comment or annotation adds to the usefulness of the entries.

The most convenient way to assemble and organize the bibliography

Fig. 2-2. Bibliography Card

is by the use of bibliography cards. The card includes the call number (if the reference is a book), the name of the author, the facts of publication, and the annotation. Placing the information on cards makes it easy to assemble the author's names in the alphabetical order in which they are listed in the bibliography of the report.

THE FIRST RESEARCH PROJECT

Experience has indicated that one way to understand the methodology and processes of research is actually to engage in research. Such a project may be very modest in nature and necessarily limited by time, the experience of the student, and many other factors associated with the graduate student's home and teaching obligations. However, the methodology may be learned by this doing and thinking under the careful supervision of the instructor of the beginning course in research. Respectable research projects have been undertaken and reported on within a semester's time, even within an eight-week summer session. Although most of these studies have been of the descriptive-survey type, some simple historical and experimental studies have also been completed. The emphasis must necessarily be placed on the process rather than on the product or its contribution to the improvement of educational practice. A study chosen for this first project, however, may not be of great enough significance to serve as an appropriate thesis problem.

The full-scale project may be either an individual or a group enterprise. Groups of three to five graduate students can profitably work together on the planning of the study. Data-gathering devices may be chosen or constructed through joint enterprise. Data may be gathered within the university graduate class, or in the classrooms, schools, or communities in which the group's members teach. However, it is recommended that the next steps—organization and analysis of data and the writing of the final report—be an individual project. There is always the danger in a group project of "letting George do it," and incidentally letting George get all of the values of the experience.

This recommended combination of group effort in the initial stages and individual effort in the later stages represents a compromise that seems effective and enables students to carry through a study in a limited amount of time with reasonable opportunity for personal growth. For some of those who plan to write a thesis in partial fulfillment of degree requirements, this first project may serve as preparation. For others, it may initiate a study capable of subsequent expansion into a thesis or dissertation.

Many research course instructors believe that a more practicable requirement would be the preparation of a carefully designed research proposal, rather than a limited-scope study. There is much to be said for this point of view, for the beginning research student is inexperienced, the time is short, and there is a real danger of conveying a superficial concept of sound research. The author has assigned the study as part of the course requirement, but other instructors may find the research proposal a more effective exercise.

The following topics were selected by inexperienced student researchers who were carrying on a project in partial fulfillment of the requirements of a beginning course in educational research. Most of the topics were short, action-type descriptive studies, not based upon random selection and random assignment of subjects or observations. Notice that the wording of the titles did not imply generalization of the conclusions to a wider population. The primary purpose was a learning exercise, not a contribution to a field,of knowledge.

Topics Used by Students in a Beginning Graduate Course in Educational Research

1. The Attitudes of a Group of University Seniors toward Coeducational Dormitories.
2. The Reading Skill Development of a Deaf First Grade Child.
3. The Status of Latin in Indiana High Schools.
4. Discipline Problems at Washington High School as Viewed by a Group of Seniors.
5. A Study of the Effectiveness of Chisanbop Calculation with a Group of Third Grade Pupils.
6. The Status of Music in the Western Yearly Meeting of the Society of Friends.
7. The Rehabilitation of a Group of Heroin Addicts in a Federally-Funded Drug Treatment Center.
8. The Social Development of a Six-Year-Old Autistic Child.
9. The Effect of Trial Promotion on the Academic Achievement of a Group of Underachievers.
10. The Effects of Parent Visitation upon the Reading Performance of a Group of Fourth Grade Students.
11. The Predictive Value of Entrance Examinations at the Methodist School of Nursing.
12. The Interests of a Three-Year-Old Boy.
13. Student Participation in the Activity Program at Lawrence Central High School.

14. The Influence of Kindergarten Experience on the Subsequent Reading Achievement of a Group of Third Grade Pupils.
15. The Views of Selected Baptist Laymen, Ministers, and National Church Leaders Concerning Issues Relating to the Tradition of Separation of Church and State.
16. The Attitudes and Behavior of Freshmen and Seniors Regarding Classroom Dishonesty at Sheridan High School.
17. The Attitudes of a Group of Florida School Superintendents toward Mandated Minimum Competency Testing.
18. Authority Images of a Selected Group of Inner-City Children.
19. The Achievement of Twins, Both Identical and Fraternal, in the Lebanon, Indiana Metropolitan School District.
20. A Follow-Up Study of Non-Promoted Students at School #86.
21. A History of the Indiana Boy's School, Plainfield, Indiana.
22. A Comparative Analysis of the Self-Concepts of a Group of Gifted and Slow-Learning Children.
23. The Attitudes of a Group of High School Seniors toward Nuclear Protest Movements.
24. The Educational Backgrounds of 129 American Celebrities Listed in the 1966 Current Biography Yearbook.
25. The Attitudes of a Group of Graduate Students toward Mandated Smoking Restrictions in Public Facilities.
26. The Influence of Entering Age upon the Subsequent Achievement at First, Second, and Third Grade Levels in Washington Township.
27. The Attitudes of a Selected Group of Black and White Parents toward Busing to Achieve Racial Integration.
28. A Study of Socioeconomic Status in the Butler-Tarkington Area, a Racially Integrated Community.
29. A Follow-Up Study of the 1970 Graduates of Grace Lutheran School.
30. The Effect of Title IX, Prohibiting Sex Discrimination in Public Schools, upon the Athletic Budgets of Illinois Public Colleges and Universities.

For experienced researchers, projects would necessarily be more theory-oriented with conclusions generalized beyond the specific group observed. At this more advanced level a careful process of randomization would be desirable, if not necessary, and the research design would be much more rigorous. The details of some of the more sophisticated procedures are partially explained in subsequent chapters of this text and in other relevant sources, particularly discussion of experimental and descriptive research processes, the selection or construction of data-gathering devices, and the statistical analysis of data.

SUBMITTING A RESEARCH PROPOSAL TO A FUNDING AGENCY

Seasoned researchers may plan to submit research proposals to foundations or government agencies for financial support. The beginning researcher may not feel the need for suggestions, but it may be helpful to understand the detailed type of information that a foundation or agency would expect to receive before committing support funds.

The following is a list of suggestions for those who seek financial support:

1. Write the proposal very carefully. A carelessly written proposal suggests to the evaluators that the research project would be carelessly done.
2. State your problem in such a way that the proposal evaluators, who are capable and experienced in judging research proposals, but know nothing about your project, will be able to judge its worth and the likelihood of its contributing to a significant area of knowledge.
3. Indicate how your study will add to or refine present knowledge.
4. State your hypothesis or hypotheses in both conceptual and operational terms and in both substantive and null form.
5. Indicate that you are completely familiar with the field of investigation and are aware of all recent studies in the problem area.
6. Indicate how you propose to test your hypotheses, describing your research design and the data-gathering instruments or procedures that you will use, indicating their known validity and reliability.
7. Describe your sampling procedures, indicating how you will randomly select and randomly assign your subjects or observations.
8. Indicate the extraneous variables that must be recognized and explain how you propose to minimize their influence.
9. Explain the statistical procedures that you will employ, indicating any computer application that you will use.
10. Prepare a budget proposal estimating the funds required for:
    a. wages, including any fringe benefits
    b. purchase or rental of special equipment or supplies
    c. travel expense
    d. clerical expense
    e. additional overhead expense that may be involved
    f. publication costs
11. Provide some tangible evidence of your competence by listing:
    a. research projects that you have carried on or actively participated in
    b. a list of your scholarly journal articles, including abstracts of your studies

    c. personal letters of recommendation from researchers who are recognized authorities in your area of investigation

SUMMARY

Academic research projects are usually required in partial fulfillment of the requirements of a course or a degree program. The motivation is not always a genuine desire to engage in research and, in addition, limitations of time, money, and experience usually preclude the consideration of problems that could make significant contributions to educational theory and practice.

The choice of a suitable problem is one of the most difficult tasks facing the beginning researcher. Students tend to define problems that are too broad in scope or that deal with too fragmentary aspects of the problem. Consultation with the course instructor or advisor is particularly helpful in identifying a problem that is manageable and significant enough to justify the time and effort that will be required.

Problems are found in the teachers' daily classroom, school, and community experiences. Technological and social changes call for research evidence to chart new courses in educational practice. Graduate academic experience helps to promote problem awareness through classroom activities, the reading of research studies, and interaction with instructors, advisors, and fellow students.

A good research problem has the qualities of significance, originality, and feasibility. The researcher should evaluate a proposed problem in the light of his or her competence, the availability of data, the financial demands of the project, the limitations of time, and the possible difficulties and social hazards involved.

A research proposal is required by many institutions, and serves as a useful basis for the evaluation of a project as well as a guide for the researcher. The proposal contains a clear and concise statement of the problem, the hypothesis or hypotheses involved, a recognition of the significance of the problem, definitions of important terms, assumptions, delimitations, and limitations, a résumé of related literature, an analysis of proposed research procedures, a bibliography, and a time schedule. Some advisors request a progress report from time to time in order to evaluate the progress of the investigation.

One way to learn about research is to conduct a study in connection with the beginning research course. Another way is to write a research proposal which may involve all of the steps in the research process except the gathering and analysis of data and the formulation of conclusions. Either of these exercises gives a focus to the dicussions about research and may help in developing some competence and the research point of view. It may even encourage some teachers to conduct modest studies in their own schools during or after the completion of their graduate programs.

EXERCISES

1. The following research topics are faulty or are completely inappropriate. Revise each one, if possible, so that it describes a feasible project or proposal for this course.
   a. The Attitudes of Teachers toward Merit Rating
   b. How to Teach Poetry Most Effectively
   c. The Best Way to Teach Spelling
   d. The Evils of Alcohol
   e. Does Ability Grouping Meet the Needs of Students?
   f. The Adequacy of Law Enforcement
   g. The Hazards of Smoking
   h. Why the Discussion Method Is Better than the Lecture Method
   i. The Fallacy of Evolution
2. State a hypothesis, first in scientific or research form and then in null or statistical form.
3. Define the following terms in operational form:
   a. intelligence
   b. creativity
   c. coordination
   d. authoritarian
   e. memory.
4. In a research study, is a hypothesis to be tested always preferable to a question to be answered? Why or why not?
5. What are some of the more effective ways to find a suitable research problem?

BIBLIOGRAPHY

AGIN, AVIS P. "Overview of Recent Research in Reading." *Elementary English* 52 (March 1975): 370–375.

ANDERSON, RICHARD C. ET AL., eds. *Current Research on Instruction.* Englewood Cliffs, N.J.: Prentice-Hall, 1969.

EARLY, MARGARET. "Important Research on Reading and Writing." *Phi Delta Kappan* 57 (Jan. 1976): 298–301.

ENNIS, ROBERT H. "Operational Definitions." *American Educational Research Journal* 1 (May 1964): 183–201.

GAGE, N. L. *Handbook of Research on Teaching.* Chicago: Rand McNally & Co., 1963.

GUBA, E. G. and D. L. CLARK. "Levels of Research and Development Productivity in Schools of Education." *Educational Researcher* 7 (May 1978): 3–9.

HEARN, D. D. JOEL BURDIN, and LILLIAN KATZ, eds. *Current Research and Perspectives in Open Education.* Washington, D.C.: American Association of Elementary–Kindergarten–Nursery School Education, 1973.

HERBER, HAROLD R. ET AL., eds. *Research in Reading in the Content Areas.* Syracuse: Reading and Language Arts Center, Syracuse University, 1977.

ISAAKSON, B. L. and R. ELLSWORTH. "Teacher Attitudes toward Educational Research." *Teacher Education* 14 (Autumn 1978): 9–13.

LEHMANN, IRVIN J. and WILLIAM A. MEHERENS, eds. *Educational Research: Readings in Focus.* New York: Holt, Rinehart & Winston, 1971.

MARTIN, LYN S. and BARBARA N. PAVAN. "Current Research on Open Space, Non-Grading, Vertical Grouping, and Team Teaching." *Phi Delta Kappan* 57 (Jan. 1976): 310–315.

PEATHING, J. H. "Research and Religion." *Religious Education* 78 (Sept./Oct. 1978): 101–125.

Research in Physical Education, Recreation, and Psychomotor Function for Mentally Retarded Persons. Washington, D.C.: Information and Research Utilization Center for the Handicapped, 1976.

Review of Head Start Research Since 1969 and an Annotated Bibliography. Washington, D.C.: National Institute of Education, Superintendent of Documents, 1978.

Review of Research in Education. Itaska, IL.: F. E. Peacock, Publishers, 1973–date (Annual).

ROSENAU, M. J. "Serendipity." *Journal of Bacteriology* 29 (Feb. 1935): 91–98.

TRAVERS, R. M. W., ed. *Handbook of Research on Teaching.* 2d ed. Chicago: Rand McNally & Co., 1973.

WARD, A. W. ET AL., "Evaluation of Published Research in Education." *American Educational Research Journal* 12 (Spring 1975): 109–128.

WESTBURY, IAN and ARNOLD A. BELLACK, eds. *Research into Classroom Procedures.* New York: Teachers College Press, 1971.

ZIGLER, E. "Twenty Years of Mental Retardation Research." *Mental Retardation* 15 (June 1977): 51–53.

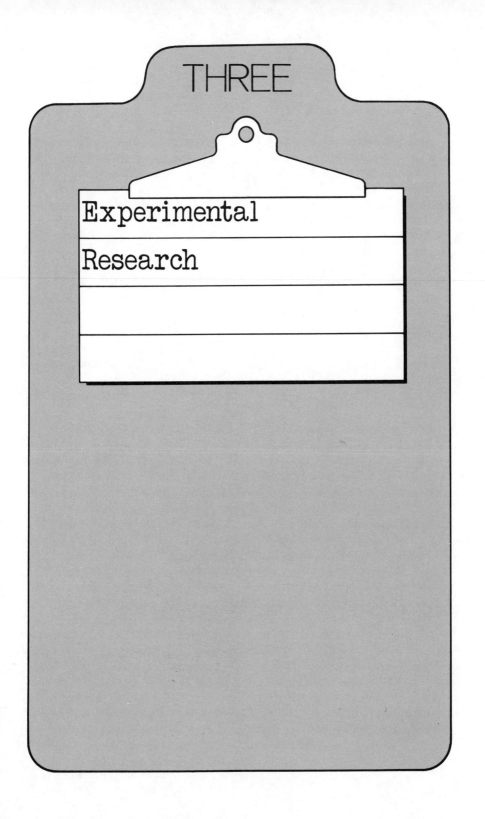

THREE

Experimental

Research

Experimental research provides a systematic and logical method for answering the question, "If this is done under carefully controlled conditions, what will happen?" Experimenters manipulate certain stimuli, treatments, or environmental conditions and observe how the condition or behavior of the subject is affected or changed. Their manipulation is deliberate and systematic. They must be aware of other factors that could influence the outcome and remove or control them in such a way that they can establish a logical association between manipulated factors and observed effects.

Experimentation provides a method of hypothesis testing. After experimenters define a problem they propose a tentative answer, or hypothesis. They test the hypothesis and confirm or disconfirm it in the light of the controlled variable relationship that they have observed. It is important to note that the confirmation or rejection of the hypothesis is stated in terms of probability rather than certainty.

Experimentation is the classic method of the science laboratory, where elements manipulated and effects observed can be controlled. It is the most sophisticated, exacting, and powerful method for discovering and developing an organized body of knowledge.

Although the experimental method finds its greatest utility in the laboratory, it has been effectively applied within nonlaboratory settings such as the classroom, where significant factors or variables can be controlled to some degree. The immediate purpose of experimentation is to predict events in the experimental setting. The ultimate purpose is to generalize the variable relationships so that they may be applied outside the laboratory to a wider population of interest.

EARLY EXPERIMENTATION

The earliest assumptions of experimental research were based upon what was known as the *law of the single variable*. John Stuart Mill defined this principle in 1872 in his work "Methods of Experimental Inquiry." He stated five rules or canons that he believed would include all types of logical procedure required to establish order among controlled events.

One of his canons, known as the *method of difference*, states:

If an instance in which the phenomenon under investigation occurs, and an instance in which it does not occur have every circumstance in common save one, that one occurring only in the former, the circumstance in which alone the two instances differ is the effect, or the cause, or an indispensable part of the cause of the phenomenon.[1]

In simpler language, if two situations are alike in every respect and one element is added to one but not the other, any difference that develops is the effect of the added element; or, if two situations are alike in every respect and one element is removed from one, but not from the other, any difference that develops may be attributed to the subtracted element.

The law of the single variable provided the basis for much early laboratory experimentation. In 1662, Robert Boyle, an Irish physicist, used this method in arriving at a principle upon which he formulated his law of gases: When temperature is held constant the volume of an ideal gas is inversely proportional to the pressure exerted upon it. In other words, when pressure is raised, volume decreases; when pressure is lowered, volume increases.

$$\frac{V_1}{V_2} = \frac{P_2}{P_1} \text{ (In Boyle's Law, } \textit{pressure} \text{ is the single variable.)}$$

A little more than a century later, Jacques A. C. Charles, a French physicist, discovered a companion principle, now known as Charles' Law. He observed that when the pressure was held constant, the volume of an ideal gas was directly proportional to the temperature. When temperature is raised, volume increases; when temperature is lowered, volume decreases.

$$\frac{V_1}{V_2} = \frac{T_1}{T_2} \text{ (In Charles' Law, } \textit{temperature} \text{ is the single variable.)}$$

FACTORIAL DESIGNS

Although the concept of the single variable proved useful in some areas of the physical sciences, it failed to provide a sound approach to experimentation in the behavioral sciences. Despite its appealing simplicity and apparent logic, it did not provide an adequate method for studying complex problems. It assumed a highly artificial and restricted relationship between single variables. Rarely, if ever, are human events the

---

[1] John Stuart Mill, *A System of Logic* (New York: Harper & Row, 1873), 222.

result of single causes. They are usually the result of the interaction of many variables, and an attempt to limit variables so that one can be isolated and observed proves impossible.

The contributions of R. A. Fisher, first applied in agricultural experimentation, have provided a much more effective way of conducting realistic experimentation in the behavioral sciences. His concept of achieving pre-experimental equation of conditions through random selection of subjects and random assignment of treatments, and his concepts of analysis of variance and analysis of covariance, made possible the study of complex interactions through factorial designs, in which the influence of more than one independent variable upon more than one dependent variable could be observed.

EXPERIMENTAL AND CONTROL GROUPS

An experiment involves the comparison of the effects of a particular treatment with that of a different treatment or of no treatment. In a simple conventional experiment reference is usually made to an *experimental group* and to a *control group.*

These groups are equated as nearly as possible. The experimental group is exposed to the influence of the factor under consideration; the control group is not. Observations are then made to determine what difference appears or what change or modification occurs in the experimental as contrasted with the control group.

However, experiments are not always characterized by a treatment-nontreatment comparison. Varying types, amounts, or degrees of the experimental factor may be applied to a number of groups. For example, an experiment to test the effectiveness of a particular medication in reducing body temperature might involve administering a massive dosage to one group, a normal dosage to a second, and a minimal dosage to a third. Since all the groups receive medication, there is no control group in the limited sense of the term, but control of the experimental factors and observation of their effects are essential elements.

VARIABLES

Independent and Dependent Variables

Variables are the conditions or characteristics that the experimenter manipulates, controls, or observes. The *independent* variables are the conditions or characteristics that the experimenter manipulates in his or her attempt to ascertain their relationship to observed phenomena. The *dependent* variables are the conditions or characteristics that appear, disappear, or change as the experimenter introduces, removes, or changes independent variables.

In educational research an independent variable may be a particular teaching method, a type of teaching material, a reward, or a period of exposure to a particular condition. The dependent variable may be a test score, the number of errors, or measured speed in performing a task. Thus, the dependent variables are the measured changes in pupil performance attributable to the influence of the independent variables.

Operational Definitions of Experimental Variables

Such variables as giftedness, academic achievement, and creativity are conceptual definitions that are defined as dictionary terms. But because they cannot be observed directly, they are vague and ambiguous and provide a poor basis for identifying variables. Much more precise and unambiguous definitions of variables would be stated in operational form, which stipulates the operation by which they could be observed and measured. Giftedness could be operationally defined as a score two or more standard deviations above the mean on the *Wechsler Adult Intelligence Scale,* academic achievement as a score on the 1973 edition of the *Stanford Achievement Test,* or creativity as a score on the *Torrance Tests of Creative Thinking.* When an operational definition is used there is no doubt about what the researcher means.

To be useful, however, operational definitions must be based upon a theory that is generally recognized as valid. Operational terms do not necessarily prove to be useful in describing variables, for they could conceivably be based upon irrelevant behavior. Defining degree of self-esteem in terms of the number of times an individual smiles per minute would not be a useful or realistic definition, even though such behavior could easily be observed and recorded.

Organismic or Attribute Variables

Organismic variables are those characteristics that cannot be altered by the experimenter. Such independent variables as age, sex, or race have already been determined, but they can be introduced or removed as variables. The question of whether eight-year-old girls show greater reading achievement than eight-year-old boys provides an example of sex as an organismic variable. The teaching procedure is the same for each group. Since sex is the variable it is not manipulated; it has already been determined.

Intervening Variables

In many types of behavioral research the relationship between the independent and dependent variables is not a simple one of stimulus to response. Certain variables which cannot be controlled or measured directly may have an important effect upon the outcome. These modifying variables intervene between the cause and the effect.

In a classroom language experiment a researcher is interested in determining the effect of immediate reinforcement upon learning the parts of speech. He or she suspects that certain factors or variables may influence the relationship, even though they cannot be observed directly. Anxiety, fatigue, and motivation, for example, may be intervening variables and are difficult to define in operational terms. These intervening variables cannot be ignored, however, and must be accounted for.

Extraneous Variables

Extraneous variables are those uncontrolled variables (i.e., variables not manipulated by the experimenter) that may have a significant influence upon the dependent variable. Many research conclusions are invalidated by the influence of these extraneous variables.

In a widely publicized study, the effectiveness of three methods of social studies teaching was compared. Intact classes were used and the researchers were unable to randomize or control such variables as teacher competence or enthusiasm, or the age, socioeconomic level, or academic ability of the student subjects. The criterion of effectiveness was achievement, measured by scores on standardized tests. It would seem clear that the many extraneous variables precluded valid conclusions about the relative effectiveness of the independent variables, which were teaching methods.

Although it is impossible to eliminate all extraneous variables, particularly in classroom research, sound experimental design enables the researcher to largely neutralize their influence.

Controlling Extraneous Variables

Variables that are not of direct interest to the researcher may be removed or their influence minimized by several methods:

Removing the variable. Variables may be controlled by eliminating them completely. Observer distraction may be removed by separating the observer from both experimental and control groups by a one-way glass partition. Some variables between subjects may be eliminated by selecting cases with uniform characteristics. Using only female subjects removes sex as a variable. (Of course, it must be remembered that not all females have uniform physical or psychological characteristics.)

Matching cases. Selecting pairs or sets of individuals with identical or nearly identical characteristics and assigning one of them to the experimental group and the other to the control group provides another method of control. This method is limited by the difficulty of matching on more than one variable. It is also likely that some individuals will be excluded from the experiment if a matching subject is not available. Matching is not considered satisfactory unless the members of the pairs or sets are randomly assigned to the treatment groups, a method known as *blocking.*

Balancing cases. Balancing cases consists of assigning subjects to experimental and control groups in such a way that the means and the variances of the groups are as nearly equal as possible. Since identical balancing of groups is impossible, the researcher must decide how much departure from equality can be tolerated without loss of satisfactory control. This method also presents a similar difficulty noted in the matching method; namely, the difficulty of equating groups on the basis of more than one characteristic or variable.

Analysis of covariance. This method permits the experimenter to eliminate initial differences on several variables between the experimental and control groups by statistical methods. Using pretest mean scores as covariates, this method is considered preferable to the conventional matching of groups. Analysis of covariance is a rather complicated statistical procedure, beyond the scope of this elementary treatment. For a complete discussion, readers may wish to consult the references by Edwards, Kerlinger, or Lindquist, listed in the chapter bibliography.

Randomization. Randomization involves pure chance selection and assignment of subjects to experimental and control groups from a limited supply of available subjects.

If two groups are involved, randomization could be achieved by tossing a coin, assigning a subject to one group if heads appeared, to the other if the toss were tails. When more than two groups are involved, dice or a table of random numbers could be used.

Randomization provides the most effective method of eliminating systematic bias and of minimizing the effect of extraneous variables. The principle is based upon the assumption that through random assignment, differences between groups result only from the operation of probability or chance. These differences are known as *sampling error* or *error variance*, and their magnitude can be estimated by the researcher.

In an experiment, differences in the dependent variables that may be attributed to the effect of the independent variables are known as *experimental variance*. The significance of an experiment may be tested by comparing experimental variance with error variance. If, at the conclusion of the experiment, the differences between experimental and control groups are too great to attribute to error variance it may be assumed that these differences are probably attributable to experimental variance.

EXPERIMENTAL VALIDITY

In order to make a significant contribution to the development of knowledge, an experiment must have two types of validity, internal validity and external validity.

Internal validity. An experiment has internal validity to the extent that the factors that have been manipulated (independent variables) actually have a genuine effect on the observed consequences (dependent variables) in the experimental setting.

External validity. The researcher would achieve little of practical value if these observed variable relationships were valid only in the experimental setting and only for those participating. External validity is the extent to which the variable relationships can be generalized to nonexperimental situations—other settings, other treatment variables, other measurement variables, and other populations.

Experimental validity is an ideal to aspire to, for it is unlikely that it can ever be completely achieved. Internal validity is very difficult to achieve in the nonlaboratory setting of the behavioral experiment where there are so many extraneous variables to attempt to control. When experimental controls are tightened to achieve internal validity, the more artificial, less realistic situation may prevail, reducing the external validity or generalizability of the experiment. Some compromise is inevitable so that a reasonable balance may be established between control and generalizability—between internal and external validity.

Threats to Experimental Validity

In educational experiments, or in any behavioral experiments conducted outside the laboratory, a number of extraneous variables are present in the situation or are generated by the experimental design and procedures. These variables influence the results of the experiment in ways that are difficult to evaluate. In a sense, they introduce rival hypotheses that could account for experimental change not attributable to the experimental variables under consideration. Although these extraneous variables cannot be completely eliminated, many of them can be identified. It is important that behavioral researchers anticipate them and take all possible precautions to minimize their influence through sound experiment design and execution.

A number of factors jeopardize the power of the experimenter to evaluate the effects of independent variables unambiguously. Donald T. Campbell and Julian C. Stanley[2] have discussed these factors in their excellent definitive treatment. They include the following:

Maturation. Subjects change in many ways over a period of time, and these changes may be confused with the effect of the independent variables under consideration. Between initial and subsequent observations subjects may become tired, bored, wiser, or influenced by the incidental learnings or experiences that they encounter through normal maturation.

History. Specific external events beyond the control of the researcher may have a stimulating or disturbing effect upon the performance of subjects. The effect of a fire drill, the emotional tirade of a teacher, a pep session, the anxiety produced by a pending examination, or a catastrophic event in the community may significantly affect the test performance of a group of students.

In some classroom experiments these external events might have a similar effect upon both experimental and control subjects, but since they are specific events, they may affect one group but not the other. The effect of these uncontrolled external events is one of the hazards inherent in experiments carried on outside the laboratory. In laboratory experiments these extraneous variables can be controlled more effectively.

Testing. The process of pretesting at the beginning of an experiment may produce a change in subjects. Tests may sensitize individuals by making them more aware of concealed purposes of the researcher and may serve as a stimulus to change. Pretesting may produce a practice effect that may make subjects more proficient in subsequent test performance. Testing presents a threat to internal validity that is common to pretest-posttest experiments.

[2] Donald T. Campbell and Julian C. Stanley, *Experimental and Quasi-experimental Designs for Research* (Chicago: Rand McNally & Company, 1963), pp. 171–246.

Interference of prior treatment.   In some types of experiments the effect of one treatment may carry over to subsequent treatments. In an educational experiment, learning produced by the first treatment is not completely erased and its influence may accrue to the advantage of the second treatment. This is one of the major limitations of the single-group, equated-materials experimental design in which the same subjects serve as members of both control and experimental groups.

Unstable instrumentation.   Unreliable instruments or techniques used to describe and measure aspects of behavior are threats to the validity of an experiment. If tests used as instruments of observation are not accurate or consistent, a serious element of error is introduced. If human observers are used to describe behavior changes in subjects, changes in their standards due to fatigue, increased insight or skill, or changes in criteria of judgment over a period of time are likely to introduce error.

Statistical regression.   Statistical regression is a phenomenon that sometimes operates in pretest-posttest situations. Subjects who score highest on a pretest are likely to score relatively lower on a retest, whereas subjects who score lowest on the pretest are likely to score higher on a retest. In pretest-retest situations there is a normal regression toward the mean. The initially highest and lowest scoring subjects are not necessarily the highest and lowest achievers. They were the highest and the lowest only on that particular pretest occasion. Failure to recognize this regression effect may lead the researcher erroneously to attribute unwarranted gain to the lowest group and loss or small gain to the highest group.

Differential selection.   Selection bias is represented by the nonequivalence of experimental and control groups, and its most effective deterrent is the random assignment of treatments to subjects. Selection bias is likely when, upon invitation, volunteers are used as members of an experimental group. Although they may appear to be equated to the nonvolunteers, their characteristics of higher motivation may introduce a bias that would invalidate reasonable comparison. Selection bias may be introduced when intact classes are used as experimental and control groups: because of scheduling arrangements an English class meeting during the fourth period may consist of particularly able students who are scheduled at that period because they are also enrolled in an advanced mathematics class.

Researchers are rarely, if ever, able to randomly select samples from the wide population of interest; consequently, generalization from samples to populations is hazardous. Samples used in most classroom experiments are usually composed of intact groups, not randomly selected individuals. They are based upon an accepted invitation to participate. Some school officials agree to participate; others refuse. One cannot assume that samples taken from cooperating schools are necessarily representative of the target population. Such schools are usually characterized by faculties that have high morale, less insecurity, greater willingness to try a new approach, and a greater desire to improve their performance. Even if all schools were willing to participate in an experiment, few administrators will permit marked departures from the normal scheduling of classes and the random selection and assignment of students to experimental and control groups.

Experimental mortality. Mortality, or loss of subjects, particularly likely in a long-term experiment, introduces a confounding element. Even though experimental and control groups are randomly selected, the survivors might represent a sample that is quite different from the unbiased sample that began the experiment. Those who survive a period of experimentation are likely to be healthier, more able, or more highly motivated than those who are absent frequently or who drop out of school and do not remain for the duration of the experiment.

The artificiality of the experimental setting. In an effort to control extraneous variables the researcher imposes careful controls which may introduce a sterile or artificial atmosphere that is not at all like the real-life situation about which generalizations are desired. The reactive effect of the experimental process is a constant threat.

Placebo-Hawthorne effect. Knowledge of participation in an experiment may introduce the extraneous variable of bias in favor of the experimental group. The medical professional has long recognized that patients who receive any medication, regardless of its real efficacy, tend to feel better or perform more effectively. In medical experiments it is important to administer harmless or inert substitutes to the control group to offset the psychological effect of medication. These substitutes, or *placebos,* are indistinguishable from the real medication under investigation and neither experimental nor control subjects know whether they are receiving medication or the placebo. The effectiveness of the true medication is the difference between the effect of the medication and that of the placebo.

What seems to be a similar psychological effect was recognized in a series of experiments at the Hawthorne Plant of the Western Electric Company in Chicago a number of years ago. The studies concerned the relationships between certain working conditions and worker output efficiency. Illumination was one of these manipulated experimental variables. It was discovered that as light intensity was increased, worker output increased. After a certain peak was apparently reached it was decided to see what effect the reduction of intensity of illumination would have. To the surprise of the researchers, as intensity was decreased by stages, output continued to increase. The researchers concluded that the attention given the workers and their awareness of participation in an experiment apparently were important motivating factors. From these studies the term *Hawthorne Effect* was introduced into psychological literature.

It has been commonly believed that this reactive effect of knowledge of participation in an experiment, the Hawthorne Effect, is similar to the placebo effect. Researchers have devised nonmedical placebos to counteract it. One such device was used in connection with an experiment involving the comparison of traditional teaching materials with a new experimental program. The control, or traditional, materials were reprinted and labeled "Experimental Method" to minimize the reactive effect.

Studies by Desmond Cook[3] have attempted to evaluate reactive effects of this type with what the author has reported as inconclusive results. Although it is believed that the Hawthorne Effect is a threat to experimental validity, it would seem that further study of the nature of this phenomenon is needed.

Contamination. Contamination is a type of bias introduced when the researcher has some previous knowledge about the subjects involved in an experiment. This knowledge of subject status may cause the researcher to convey some clue that affects the subject's reaction or may affect the objectivity of his or her judgment.

In medical research it is common practice to conceal from the subject the knowledge of who is receiving the placebo and who the experimental medication. This is known as a *blind.* Having someone other than the experimenter administer the treatments and record which subjects are receiving the medication and which the placebo provides an additional safeguard. This practice, known as a *double blind,* helps to minimize contamination.

Beginners in educational research have been known to contaminate a study by classifying student performance when they know the nature of the variable to be correlated with that performance. In a simple *ex*

---

[3] Desmond L. Cook, *The Impact of the Hawthorne Effect in Experimental Designs in Educational Research.* Final Report, Project No. 1757, Contract No. OE 3–10–041 (Washington, D.C.: U.S. Office of Education, 1967).

post facto study a member of the author's class proposed to determine the relationship between academic achievement and citizenship grades in her class. Since she proposed to assign the citizenship grades herself, it would seem apparent that an element of contamination would result. Her knowledge of the student's previous academic achievement would tend to precondition her judgment in assigning citizenship grades.

In educational studies of this type, researchers would minimize contamination if outside observers rated the subjects without any knowledge of their academic status.

After reading about these threats to experimental validity, the beginner is probably ready to conclude that behavioral research is too hazardous to attempt. Particularly outside of the laboratory, ideal experimental conditions and controls are never likely to prevail. However, an understanding of these threats is important so that the researcher can make every effort to remove or minimize their influence. If one were to wait for a research setting free from all threats no research would ever be carried on. Knowing the limitations and doing the best that he or she can under the circumstances, the researcher may conduct experiments, reach valid conclusions, provide answers to important questions, and solve significant problems.

EXPERIMENTAL DESIGN

Experimental design is the blueprint of the procedures that enable the researcher to test hypotheses by reaching valid conclusions about relationships between independent and dependent variables. Selection of a particular design is based upon the purposes of the experiment, the type of variables to be manipulated, and the conditions or limiting factors under which it is conducted. The design deals with such practical problems as how subjects are to be selected for experimental and control groups, the way variables are to be manipulated and controlled, the way extraneous variables are to be controlled, how observations are to be made, and the type of statistical analysis to be employed in interpreting data relationships.

The adequacy of experimental designs is judged by the degree to which they eliminate or minimize threats to experimental validity. Three categories are presented here:

1. *True experimental design*—employs randomization to provide for control of the equivalence of groups and exposure to treatment.

2. *Quasi-experimental design*—provides a less satisfactory degree of control, used only when randomization is not feasible.

3. *Pre-experimental design*—the least effective, for it either provides no control group, or no way of equating groups that are used.

A complete discussion of experimental design would be too complex for this introductory treatment, therefore only a few designs will be described. Readers may wish to refer to Campbell and Stanley's[4] excellent treatment, in which sixteen designs are described.

In discussing experimental designs a few symbols are used.

> *R* random selection of subjects or assignment of treatments to experimental groups
>
> *X* experimental variable manipulated
>
> *C* control variable
>
> *O* observation or test
>
> —— a line between levels indicates equated groups

True Experimental Designs

In a true experiment the equivalence of the experimental and control groups is provided by random assignment of subjects to experimental and control treatments. While it is difficult to arrange a true experimental design, particularly in school classroom research, it is the strongest type of design and should be used whenever possible. Three experimental designs have been selected for discussion:

The posttest-only, equivalent-groups design

$$\frac{R \quad X \quad O_1}{R \quad C \quad O_2}$$

This design is one of the most effective in minimizing the threats to experimental validity. Experimental and control groups are equated by random assignment. At the conclusion of the experimental period the difference between the mean test scores of the experimental and control groups are subjected to a test of statistical significance, a *t* test, or an analysis of variance. The assumption is that the means of randomly assigned experimental and control groups from the same population will differ only to the extent that random sample means from the same population will differ as a result of sampling error. If the difference between the means is too great to attribute to sampling error, the difference may be attributed to the treatment variable effect.

[4] Campbell and Stanley, *op. cit.*

Using a table of random numbers, the researcher selects 80 students from a school population of 450 sophomores. The 80 students are randomly assigned to experimental and control treatments, using the first 40 as the experimental group and the other 40 as the control group. The experimental group is taught the concepts of congruence of triangles by method X, while the control group is taught the same set of concepts by method C. All factors of time of day, treatment length in time, and other factors are equated. At the end of a three-week period the experimental and control groups are administered a test and the difference between mean scores is subjected to a test of statistical significance. The difference between mean scores is found to favor the experimental group, but not by an amount that is statistically significant. The researcher rightly concludes that the superiority of the X group could well have been the result of sampling error, and that there was no evidence of the superiority of the X method.

The pretest-posttest equivalent-groups design

$$R \quad O_1 \quad X \quad O_2 \qquad X \text{ gain} = O_2 - O_1 \qquad O_1 \quad O_3 = \text{pretests}$$
$$R \quad O_3 \quad C \quad O_4 \qquad C \text{ gain} = O_4 - O_3 \qquad O_2 \quad O_4 = \text{posttests}$$

This design is similar to the previously described design, except that pretests are administered before the application of the experimental and control treatments and posttests at the end of the treatment period. Gain scores may be compared and subjected to a test of the significance of the difference between means. This is a strong design, but there may be a possibility of the influence of the effect of testing and the interaction with the experimental variable.

Time on Task

Time available is the number of months, weeks, days, hours, or periods assigned to a part of the curriculum and is a significant factor in the learning process. However, not all learners use the time available to the same extent. These differences have an effect upon the actual amount that is learned. *Time-on-task* is the amount of time that the individual actually spends in overt learning activity. *Time-off-task* may be spent in such extraneous or distractive activity as daydreaming, looking around, moving about, scuffling, or talking to others. Time-on-task may be quantified by carefully-timed, randomly-selected observations and expressed as point scores or as a proportion of the learning period. The following classroom experiment illustrates a pretest-posttest equated groups design, using time-on-task and time-on-reading as independent variables.

TABLE I Correlates of Time-on-Task and Time-on-Reading

		Initial Attitude	Initial Comprehension	Gain in Comprehension
Time-on-task	comics	.35	.61*	.19
	books	.42*	.19	.15
Time-on-reading	comics	.09	.67*	.50*
	books	.12	−.07	.25

* significant at .05 level

Arlin and Roth[5] have reported a pretest-posttest equivalent groups study of the use of time in reading comic books and regular books during daily, 20 minute free-reading periods. Forty-two third grade pupils were randomly assigned to reading groups, one group reading comics, the other, regular books appropriate to their interests and reading levels. Random samples of as many as five, 5-second observations of each student per class period, each week for nine weeks, were made at identical times by two independent observers. A distinction was made between time-on-task and time-on-reading. Time-on-task consisted of behavior other than such distractive behavior as looking around, talking, or bothering others, regarded as time-off-task. *Time-on-reading* was identified by noting such evidence as moving the lips or tracing words on the page, using the fingers. Time-off-reading consisted of flipping the pages or turning the pages too rapidly to indicate reading.

Approximately two-thirds of the observation was for time-on-task, one third for time-on-reading. Inter-observer rating agreement was 96.7 per cent.

The *Gates-MacGinitie Reading Test* was used to measure reading comprehension, the *Arlin-Hills Attitude Survey* to measure attitude toward reading. One point was scored for each five-second time-on-task or time-on-reading observation. Time-off-task and time-off-reading observations were scored as 0 points. Total time-on-task and time-on-reading scores for each subject were tabulated and compared with attitude toward reading, initial comprehension score and reading comprehension gain score.

Some of the findings are summarized:

1. Time-on-reading spent on books was greater than that spent on comics.

2. Time-on-task spent on books was approximately equal to that spent on comics.

[5] Marshall Arlin and Gary Roth, "Pupils' Use of Time while Reading Comics and Books," *American Educational Research Journal* 15 (Sept. 1978): 201–206.

3. Time-on-reading was significantly related to gain in comprehension.

4. Good readers spent as much time on reading books as on comics and achieved similar degrees of gain in comprehension.

5. Poor readers spent less time on reading comics than books and gained less in comprehension from comics than from books.

6. Attitude toward reading was more highly correlated with time-on-task than with time-on-reading.

The authors suggest that there is some indication that comic book programs designed for poor readers may be targeted to those who are least able to profit from them.

The Solomon four-group design

$$R \quad O_1 \quad X \quad O_2$$
$$R \quad O_3 \quad C \quad O_4$$
$$R \quad \quad\quad X \quad O_5$$
$$R \quad \quad\quad C \quad O_6$$

1. Subjects are randomly assigned to four groups.

2. Two groups receive experimental treatment (X).

3. One experimental group receives a pretest (O_1).

4. Two groups (control) do not receive treatment.

5. One control group receives a pretest (O_3).

6. All four groups receive posttests $(O_2\ O_4\ O_5\ O_6)$.

The design is really a combination of the two group designs previously described, the posttest only and the pretest-posttest. It is possible to evaluate the main effects of testing, history, and maturation. A two-way analysis of variance is used to compare the four posttest scores, analysis of covariance to compare gains in O_2 and O_4.

Since this design provides for two simultaneous experiments, the advantages of a replication are incorporated. A major difficulty is finding enough subjects to randomly assign to four equivalent groups.

Quasi-Experimental Designs

These designs provide control of when and to whom the measurement is applied but, *because random assignment to experimental and control treatments has not been applied,* the equivalence of the groups is unlikely.

Of the many quasi-experimental designs, only two are described.

The pretest-posttest nonequivalent-groups design

$$O_1 \quad X \quad O_2 \qquad O_1 \quad O_3 = \text{pretests}$$
$$O_3 \quad C \quad O_4 \qquad O_2 \quad O_4 = \text{posttests}$$

This design is often used in classroom experiments when experimental and control groups are such naturally assembled groups as intact classes which may be similar. The difference between the mean of the O_1 and O_2 scores and the difference between the mean of the O_3 and O_4 scores (mean gain scores) are tested for statistical significance. Since this design may be the only feasible one, the comparison is justifiable, but the results should be interpreted cautiously.

Two first grade classes in a school were selected for an experiment. One group was exposed to the initial teaching alphabet approach to reading while the other was taught by the traditional alphabet approach. At the end of the school year both groups were administered a standardized reading test and the mean scores of the two groups were compared. The i/t/a group showed a significant superiority in test scores over the conventional alphabet group. However, without some evidence of the equivalence of the groups in intelligence, maturity, readiness, and other factors at the beginning of the experimental period, conclusions should be cautiously accepted.

The Follow Through Planned Variation Study

An interesting example of the pretest-posttest non-equivalent groups design was the *Follow Through Planned Variation Study*,[6] conceived in the late 1960s, initiated and funded by the United States Office of Education. The purpose of the program was to implement and evaluate a variety of compensatory programs, extending the services of Project Head Start for disadvantaged children into the primary grades. It was a large scale enterprise, including many innovative instructional models, involving the expenditure of more than a half billion dollars. The program extended over a period of more than nine years with more than 79,000 first, second, and third grade children participating. Of the twenty different instructional models and 170 projects, 17 models and 70 projects were selected for evaluation. Approximately 2 percent of the total number of children were included in the evaluation.

[6] *Education as Experimentation: A Planned Variation Model* (Cambridge, MA: Abt Associates, Inc., 1977). Also issued as *The Follow Through Planned Variation Experiment Series* (U.S. Office of Education, 1978).

Participation by school districts was voluntary with each district selecting the particular model that it wished to implement and helping
to choose the groups that were to be used as controls. Treatments were
not randomly assigned nor control groups randomly selected.

The unit of analysis was pupil mean gain for groups K-3 and 1–3
growth scores, statistically compared by instructional model and by project, using variants of linear regression and analysis of covariance. Outcome measures were derived from gain scores on the following measuring instruments:

1. *The Metropolitan Achievement Test Battery* covering such basic skills as
   reading comprehension, spelling, word usage and analysis, and mathematical computation, concepts and problem solving.

2. *The Raven's Coloured Matrices Test,* a non-verbal test of problem-solving
   ability, requiring the manipulation of geometric patterns, essentially
   a measure of intelligence rather than a measure of learning outcomes.

3. *The Coopersmith Self-Image Inventory,* a measure of self-esteem, but ques-
   tioned on the grounds that it required a maturity of judgment beyond
   the competence of primary age children.

4. *The Intellectual Achievement Responsibility Scale* which attempts to assess
   the child's experience of success or failure, indicating the degree to
   which the child attributes success to internal or external causes. This
   instrument was also judged to require insights beyond the maturity
   level of small children.

There have been many analyses and evaluations of the program
by official and independent agencies funded by the US Office of Education and by private philanthropic foundations. Among the evaluating
agencies were:

The United States Office of Education, Washington, D.C.

Abt Associates, Inc., Cambridge, Massachusetts

The Stanford Research Institute, Stanford, California

The Huron Institute, Cambridge, Massachusetts

The Center for Research and Curriculum Evaluation of the University
   of Illinois, Urbana, Illinois

It is unlikely that any large scale study has been scrutinized so extensively, both as to research design, procedures employed, and interpreta-

tion of the data. There have been critiques of the evaluations and critiques of the critiques with sharp disagreement on most aspects of the study.[7,8,9]

However, there is some consensus that the findings were disappointing, because most of the experimental effects were negligible. Only a few of the treatment effects produced as much as a one quarter standard deviation change. Of those that met this criterion, two instructional models with at least one positive effect were structured approaches. Three models with at least one negative effect were unstructured approaches. Few of either cognitive, structured approaches or child-centered, nonstructured approaches yielded significant effects.

Much of the disagreement centered around the reasons why the study was ineffective. Several plausible explanations have been suggested.

1. The research was deficient in design, implementation, statistical analysis and interpretation. Since experimental treatments were not randomly-selected, nor control groups randomly-assigned, mismatching resulted and comparisons were really made between different populations.

2. There was great intersite difference in effectiveness within a given instructional model. Most of the within model differences were greater than the between models difference. There may have been serious deficiencies in the competence of those who implemented the innovative procedures, even though the teachers and their teacher aides were specially trained and their activities monitored by the project sponsors.

3. The measuring instruments used may have been incompatible with the goals of the project because of inadequate identification and definition of appropriate outcome variables. The more effective instruments seemed to focus on basic skills or traditional educational goals, rather than on goals ordinarily associated with non-structured approaches to education. Some measured intellectual status, rather

[7] Ernest L. House, Gene V Glass, Leslie D. McLean and Decker F. Walker, "No Simple Answer: Critique of the Follow Through Evaluation," *Harvard Educational Review* 48 (May 1978): 128–160.

[8] Richard B. Anderson, Robert G. St Pierre, Elizabeth C. Proper and Linda B. Stebbins. "Pardon Us, But What Was the Question Again?: A Response to the Critique of the Follow Through Evaluation," *Harvard Educational Review* 48 (May 1978): 161–170.

[9] Carl E. Wisler, Gerald P. Burns, and David Iwamoto," Follow Through Redux: A Response to the Critique by House, Glass, McLean and Walker," *Harvard Educational Review* 48 (May 1978): 177–185.

than achievable learning goals. Others appeared to require a maturity of response, too complex for primary age children.

Not all reactions to the study were negative. Hodges, a member of the Follow Through Task Force, lists a number of reasons for viewing the program as significant and worth while. He states that "Just because Follow Through has not proved to be an easy, workable, inexpensive solution for all the educational problems of poor children does not mean it should be dismissed as just another failure in compensatory education."[10]

In behavioral research, the random selection and assignment of subjects to experimental and control groups may be impracticable. Because of administrative difficulties in arranging school experiments it may be necessary to use the same group as both experimental and control groups. These designs have two apparently attractive features. They can be carried on with one intact group without a noticeable reorganization of the classroom schedule. The changes in procedures and testing can be concealed within ordinary classroom routines. Artificiality can be minimized, for the procedures can be introduced without the subjects' awareness of participation in an experiment.

The Time-Series Design   At periodic intervals an observation (measurement) is applied to a unit, which may be an individual (N of 1 study) or a group of individuals. An experimental variable (X) is introduced and its effect may be judged by the change or gain in the measurement immediately following its introduction.

In the time-series experimental design, a measured change or gain after the introduction of the experimental variable in observation 3 would serve as an indication of the influence of the treatment.

This design is particularly sensitive to the failure to control the extraneous variable, history, for it is possible that some distracting, simultaneous event at the time of testing would provide a rival hypothesis for the change.

The Equivalent Time-Samples Design   Lengthening the duration of the experiment by increasing the number of time samples and adding additional randomly repeated applications of the experimental treatment would reduce the influence of history.

[10] Walter L. Hodges, "The Worth of the Follow Through Experience," *Harvard Educational Review* 48 (May 1978): p. 191.

$$
\begin{array}{c}
X \qquad\qquad X \quad X \qquad X \\
| \qquad\qquad | \quad\ | \qquad | \\
O_1\!-\!O_2\!-\!O_3\!-\!O_4\!-\!O_5\!-\!O_6\!-\!O_7\!-\!O_8\!-\!O_9\!-\!O_{10} \\
| \qquad\qquad\quad | \quad\ | \qquad | \\
| \qquad\qquad\quad | \quad\ | \qquad |
\end{array}
$$

A published study[11] illustrates a version of the equivalent time-samples design. Five subjects, identified as the most violently aggressive, were selected from a group of 46 retarded boys living in an institution dormitory. Their ages ranged from 12 to 16 (mean, 13.8); their IQs from 40 to 62 (mean, 50). Each subject was observed for ten weeks in ten randomly selected three-minute periods, during which time acts of aggressive behavior were recorded. Acts were classified as *motor aggressive* (throwing objects, kicking, fighting, scratching) and nonmotor aggressive (verbal abuse, screaming or shouting, insubordination).

The observations were scheduled in four periods:

1. Observation (baseline)   session 1

2. On-reinforcement   sessions 2,3,4,5

3. Off-reinforcement   sessions 6,7

4. On-reinforcement   sessions 9,10

Positive reinforcement as a reward for nonaggressive behavior consisted of candy, praise, or trips to the canteen. Negative reinforcement following aggressive acts consisted of withdrawal from group activities, taking away a favorite toy, or verbal reprimand. Two observers were employed, one observing motor-aggressive acts, the other, non-motor aggressive acts.

The researchers concluded that reinforcement affected the amount of aggressive output. Motor aggressive behavior was reduced more effectively than nonmotor aggressive behavior. To assess the permanence of behavior change after the conclusion of the experiment, a phase-out period of 89 days of observation was scheduled. The only reinforcement used was the posting of stars for nonaggressive behavior. Observations during the phase-out period indicated much more acceptable dormitory behavior.

Designs of this type have a number of limitations. While they may minimize the effect of history, it is possible that they may increase the influence of maturation, unstable instrumentation, testing, and experimental mortality.

---

[11] Harold V. Hall, A. Brent Price, Martin Shinedling, Sheldon B. Peizer, and Randall H. Massey, "Control of Aggressive Behavior in a Group of Retardates, Using Positive and Negative Reinforcement," *Training School Bulletin* 70 (Nov. 1973): 179–186.

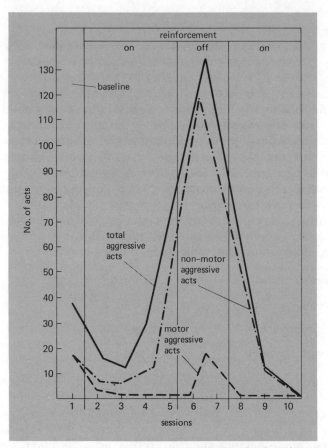

Fig. 3-1. Number of motor aggressive, nonmotor aggressive, and total aggressive acts during on-reinforcement and off-reinforcement experimental conditions.

The Equivalent Materials, Pretest, Posttest Design

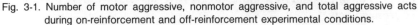

$$M_A \qquad O_1 \quad | \quad O_2 \qquad M_B \qquad O_3 \quad | \quad O_4$$

M_A = teaching method A $\qquad$ M_B = teaching method B

O_1 and O_3 are pretests $\qquad$ O_2 and O_4 are posttests

Another experimental design, using the same group or class for both experimental and control groups, involves two or more cycles. The class may be used as a control group in the first cycle and as an experimental group in the second. The order of exposure to experimental and control can be reversed—experimental first and control following.

Essential to this design is the selection of learning materials that are different, but as nearly equated as possible in interest to the students and in difficulty of comprehension. An example may help to clarify the procedure:

Ms. Smith hypothesized that the students in her class who were used to an atmosphere of background music while doing their homework would learn to spell more efficiently in the classroom if music were provided. Since she was unable to arrange a parallel group experiment, she decided to use her class both as an experimental and a control group.

To equate the words to be learned she randomly selected two sets of 100 words from an appropriate graded word list. For cycle I, the control cycle, she pretested the class on word list A. Then for twenty minutes each day the students studied the words, using drill and the usual spelling rules. At the end of two weeks she retested the class and computed the mean gain score in correct spelling.

For cycle II, the experimental cycle, she pretested the class on word list B. Then for twenty minutes each day, with soft, continuous music in the background (the independent variable), the students studied their word list, using the same drill and spelling rules. At the end of the second two-week period she retested the class and computed the mean gain score in correct spelling.

The mean gain score for the experimental cycle was significantly greater than the mean gain score for the control cycle. She concluded that the introduction of the experimental variable had indeed improved the effectiveness of the learning experience.

The apparent simplicity and logic of this design is somewhat misleading and when examined in light of the threats to experimental validity, the design's weaknesses become apparent.

1. It is often difficult to select equated materials to be learned. For types of learning other than spelling, finding learning materials equally interesting, difficult, and unfamiliar would be a serious problem.

2. As the students enter the second cycle, they are older and more mature.

3. Outside events (history) would be more likely to affect the experience in one cycle than in the other.

4. There would be an influence of prior treatment carrying over from the first cycle to the second.

5. The effects of testing would be more likely to have a greater impact on the measurement of gain in the second cycle.

6. Mortality, or loss of subjects from the experiment, would be more likely in an experimental design spread over a longer period of time.

7. When the experimenter's judgment was a factor in evaluation, contamination, the experimenter's knowledge of subject performance in the first cycle, could possibly influence evaluation of performance in the second.

Some of the limitations of the equivalent-materials, single-group, pretest-posttest design can be partially minimized by a series of replications in which the order of exposure to experimental and control treatments is reversed. This process, known as *rotation,* is illustrated by this pattern in a four-cycle experiment.

$$
\begin{array}{cccc}
\text{I} & \text{II} & \text{III} & \text{IV} \\
O_1 \ X \ O_2 & O_3 \ C \ O_4 & O_5 \ C \ O_6 & O_7 \ X \ O_8
\end{array}
$$

$$O_1 \quad O_3 \quad O_5 \quad O_7 = \text{pretests} \qquad O_2 \quad O_4 \quad O_6 \quad O_8 = \text{posttests}$$

If the experimental treatment yielded significantly greater gains regardless of the order of exposure, its effectiveness could be accepted with greater confidence. However, it is apparent that this design is not likely to equate materials, subjects, or experimental conditions.

All single-group experimental designs are sensitive to the influences of many of the threats to validity previously mentioned in this chapter: history, maturation, unstable instrumentation, testing and experimental mortality. Replication of the studies, using different units as subjects, is an effective way to improve their validity. However, single-group experiments should be performed only when randomly equated group designs cannot be arranged.

Pre-Experimental Designs

The *least adequate* of designs is characterized by:

a. the lack of a control group, or

b. a failure to provide for the equivalence of a control group

The one-shot case study

$$X \quad O$$

Carefully studied results of a treatment are compared with a general expectation of what would have happened if the treatment had not been applied. This design provides the weakest basis for generalization.

Mr. Jones used a 25-minute film on racial integration in his junior high school history class. In a test administered after the showing of the film, the mean score was 86 (a high score indicated a favorable attitude toward acceptance of all racial groups). Mr. Jones believes that the mean score was higher than it would have been had the film not been viewed, and, as he recalled, higher than the mean score of a test that he had administered to a similar class several years before. He concluded that the film had been effective in reducing racial prejudice.

How could he attribute what he believed to be a better attitude to the viewing of the film? What would it have been for a similar group in the same community that had not seen the film? Without a control group, this design is the poorest available.

The one-group, pretest-posttest design

$$O_1 \quad X \quad O_2$$

$$O_1 = \text{pretest} \qquad O_2 = \text{posttest}$$

This design provides some improvement over the first, for the effects of the treatment are judged by the difference between the pretest and the posttest scores. No comparison with a control group is provided.

In the same setting, Mr. Jones administered a pretest before showing the film and a posttest after the viewing. He computed the mean difference between the pretest and the posttest scores and found that the mean had increased from 52 to 80, a mean gain of 28 score points. He also apparently detected some temporary improvement in attitude toward racial integration. He concluded that there had been a significant improvement in attitude as a result of viewing the film. But what about the sensitizing effect of the pretest items that may have made the students aware of issues that they had not even thought of before? What would the gain have been if the pretest and the posttest had been administered to another class that had not viewed the film?

The static-group comparison design

$$X \quad O$$

$$C \quad O$$

This design compares the status of a group that has received an experimental treatment with one that has not. There is no provision for establishing the equivalence of the experimental and control groups, a very serious limitation.

A beginning researcher administered the 25-minute racial integration film to a group of elementary teachers in one school. He then administered the attitude scale and computed the mean score. At another elementary school he administered the attitude scale to teachers who had not viewed the film. A comparison of mean scores shows that the teachers who had viewed the film had a higher mean score than those who had not. He concluded that the film was an effective device in reducing racial prejudice.

What evidence did he have that the initial attitudes of groups were equivalent? Without some evidence of equivalence of the control and experimental groups, attributing difference to the experimental variable is unwarranted.

ETHICS IN HUMAN EXPERIMENTATION

Medical and psychological experimentation using human subjects involves some element of risk, however minor, and raises questions about the ethics of the process. Any set of rules or guidelines that attempts to define ethical limits for human experimentation raises controversy among scientists and other segments of society. Too rigid controls may limit the effectiveness of research, possibly denying science the answers to many important questions. On the other hand, without some restraints, experimental practices could cause serious injury and infringe upon human rights.

These issues go beyond courtesy or etiquette and concern the appropriate treatment of persons in a free society. Some of these questions have been dealt with by scientists and philosophers, by enactments of legislative bodies, by codes of ethics of professional organizations, or by guidelines established by educational institutions.

In 1974, the Congress of the United States established *The National Commission for the Protection of Human Subjects of Biomedical and Behavioral Research* to formulate guidelines for the research activities of the National Institute of Health and the National Institute of Mental Health.

The Commission's four-year, monthly deliberations, supplemented by discussions held at the Smithsonian Institution's Belmont Conference Center, resulted in the 1979 publication of the *Belmont Report: Ethical Principles and Guidelines for the Protection of Human Subjects of Research.*[12]

Many universities have established human experiment review committees to advise academic investigators about appropriate procedures

---

[12] *Belmont Report: Ethical Principles and Guidelines for the Protection of Human Subjects of Research* (Washington: Smithsonian Institution, Superintendent of Documents, U.S. Government Printing Office, 1979).

and to approve those studies that conform to their ethical guidelines. These may be ad hoc committees concerned with a particular study, or standing committees that deal with all experimental activities involving the institution or division. Some faculty researchers have complained that review committees have unduly restricted their experimental activities. It is possible in some cases that particular members of the committee did not have the technical background to make sound judgments outside their own fields of competence. Others have felt that, since the committee assignment demanded so much of their time, they could not contribute their best effort. However, since it is the primary function of the human experiment review committee to maintain the ethical standards of the institution and to supervise the ethical guidelines of the funding agencies, it serves a useful and necessary purpose.

In 1953, the American Psychological Association issued its first code of ethics for psychologists. In 1963, the code was revised and its preamble contained the following statement:

> The psychologist believes in the dignity and worth of the individual human being. He is committed to increasing man's knowledge of himself and others. While pursuing this endeavor he protects the welfare of any persons who may seek his services, or any subject, human or animal, that may be the object of his study. He does not use his professional position or relationship, nor does he knowingly permit his own services to be used by others, for purposes inconsistent with these values. While demanding for himself freedom of inquiry and communication, he accepts the responsibility this freedom confers; for competence where he claims it, for objectivity in the report of his findings, and for the consideration of the best interests of his colleagues and of society.[13]

In 1970, the Board of Directors appointed an Ad Hoc Committee on Ethical Standards in Psychological Research to bring the 1963 code up to date in light of the changes in the science, in the profession, and in the broader social context in which psychologists practice. The first draft of the committee report was circulated among 18,000 members of the association. About 5,000 responded with suggestions. In addition, journal editors, staff members of research review committees, directors of research organizations, writers on research ethics, and leaders in such special fields as hypnosis were interviewed. These contributions were supplemented by discussions at regional and national meetings of the association. Psychology departments of universities, hospitals, clinics, and government agencies, as well as anthropologists, economists, sociologists, lawyers, philosophers, and psychiatrists were consulted.

As a result of these conversations and correspondence with profes-

---

[13] *Ethical Standards of Psychologists* (Washington, D.C.: American Psychological Association, 1963): p. 2.

sionals from all scholarly disciplines, a final draft, submitted in 1972, was adopted and publication authorized.

Ten principles were formulated, dealing with the experimenter's responsibilities toward participants. In the published report, *Ethical Principles in the Conduct of Research with Human Participants*,[14] each principle is stated with discussion of issues, problems, situations, and recommendations for appropriate action. The meticulous care with which this code was developed attests to the concern of this professional organization for ethical practices in psychological research. Readers who are interested in a more complete discussion on ethics in human experimentation are urged to read this report.

The following discussion does not present a summary of the American Psychological Association code of ethics, but rather considers certain guidelines, not ethical absolutes, that characterize writing in the field of ethics and a number of professional codes that the author has examined. The guidelines deal with the following areas of concern.

1. *Informed consent.* Recruitment of volunteers for an experiment should always involve the subject's complete understanding of the purpose and nature of the experiment, the procedures employed, the risks involved, and the demands that may be made upon participants. When subjects are minors, senile persons, or those of limited intelligence, the informed consent of parents, guardians, or responsible agents should be secured. This freedom to participate or to decline to participate is basic and includes the freedom to withdraw from an experiment at any time without penalty. Coercion to participate or to remain as a participant should not be applied and any exploitation of participants is an unethical practice.

Some examples involving recruitment of participants in experiments raise questions of ethical practice:

a. Subjects who are inmates of penal institutions volunteer to participate because of a need for money or in anticipation of more favorable treatment or recommendation of earlier parole.

b. Medical students who need money are recruited for experiments by offers of financial reward.

c. Participants are recruited in institutions who do not have the competence to give rational consent: the senile, the illiterate, the disturbed, or those of low intelligence.

d. Members of a college class are required to participate in an experiment in order to meet a course requirement.

[14] American Psychological Association. *Ethical Principles and the Conduct of Research with Human Participants* (Washington, D.C.: Ad Hoc Committee on Ethical Standards, 1973).

2. *Invasion of privacy.* Ordinarily, it is justifiable to observe and record behavior that is essentially public, behavior that others normally would be in a position to observe. It is an invasion of privacy to observe and record intimate behavior that the subject has reason to believe is private. Concealed observers, cameras, microphones, or the use of private correspondence without the subject's knowledge and permission are invasions of privacy. If these practices are to be employed, the participant's understanding of the reasons should be explained and permission secured.

This statement is not to suggest that intimate behavior cannot be observed ethically. The sexual behavior studies of Doctors Masters and Johnson are based upon observation and recording of the most intimate acts, but subjects volunteer to participate with full knowledge of the purposes and procedures employed. The motivation is based upon confidence in the integrity of the researchers and the importance of their scientific contributions to human welfare.

3. *Confidentiality.* The ethical researcher holds all information that he or she may gather about the subject in strict confidence, disguising the participant's identity in all records and reports. No one should be in a position to threaten the subject's anonymity nor should any information be released without his or her permission.

4. *Protection from physical and mental stress, harm, or danger.* In using treatments that may have a temporary or permanent effect on the subjects, the researcher must take all precautions to protect their well-being. Treatments are administered under the direction of competent professional practitioners in clinical or research facilities where effective and thorough precautions and safeguards may be assured.

5. *Knowledge of outcome.* The participant has a right to receive an explanation for the reasons for the experimental procedures and the results of the investigation. The researcher may explain the results and their significance orally, by a written résumé, or by informing participants of the issue of the journal in which the report has been published.

Ethical researchers not only observe these ethical guidelines but take complete responsibility for the actions of their coexperimenters, colleagues, assistants, technical personnel, secretaries, and clerks involved in the project, constantly monitoring their research activities. Researchers have obligations to their subjects, their professional colleagues, and to the public. They do not discard unfavorable data that would modify the interpretation of their investigation. They make their data available to their professional peers so that they may verify the accuracy of the results. They honor promises made to subjects as a consideration for their participation in a study. They give appropriate credit to those who have aided them in their investigation, who have participated in the data analysis, or who have contributed to the preparation of the research report. They place scientific objectivity above personal advantage, and recognize their obligation to society for the advancement of knowledge.

Some researchers have been known to justify deception, coercion, invasion of privacy, breach of confidentiality, or risks to subjects in the name of science, but one might suspect that the prestige, ambition, or ego-involvement of the experimenter was the primary motivation.

This discussion, which has examined the many limitations of the experimental method in behavioral research, may convey a sense of futility. As is true in many other areas of significant human endeavor, researchers do not work under ideal conditions. They must do the best that they can under existing circumstances. They will find, however, that in spite of its limitations, the well-designed and well-executed experiment provides a legitimate method for testing hypotheses and making probability decisions about the relationships between variables.

Some variables cannot be manipulated. The ethical problems that would be raised if some others were manipulated indicates a place for such nonexperimental methods as *ex post factor* research. The researcher starts with the observation of dependent variables and goes back to the observation of independent variables that have previously occurred under uncontrolled conditions. Such studies are *not* experiments, for the researcher has had no control over the events; they occurred before he or she began the investigation. The description of cigarette-smoking cancer research in Chapter Four is an example of *ex post facto* research.

Throughout this chapter the author has avoided a description of factorial designs. The reader should not feel, however, that the experimental method is confined to the analysis of single-variable relationships. Most significant experimentation involves the analysis of the interaction of a number of variable relationships. However, the complexity of factorial designs preclude their discussion in an elementary treatment. Advanced students may wish to refer to such sources as Edwards, Kerlinger, or Winer, listed in the chapter bibliography.

SUMMARY

The experimental method provides a logical, systematic way to answer the question, "If this is done under carefully controlled conditions, what will happen?" To provide a precise answer, experimenters, manipulate certain influences, or variables, and observe how the condition or behavior of the subject is affected or changed. Experimenters control or isolate the variables in such a way that they can be reasonably sure that the effects they observe can be attributed to the variables they have manipulated, rather than to some other uncontrolled influences. In testing hypotheses, or evaluating tentative answers to questions, experimenters make decisions based upon probability rather than certainty. Experimentation, the classic method of the laboratory, is the most powerful method for discovering and developing a body of knowledge about the prediction and control of events. The experimental method has been used with some success in the school classroom, where, to some degree, variables can be controlled.

The early applications of experimental method, based upon John Stuart Mill's law of the single variable, have been replaced by the more effective applications of factorial designs made possible by the contributions of R. A. Fisher. His concept of equating groups by random selection of subjects and random assignment of treatments, and his development of the analysis of variance and the analysis of covariance, have made possible the study of complex multivariate relationships that are basic to the understanding of human behavior.

Experimenters must understand and deal with threats to the internal validity of the experiment so that the variable relationships they observe can be interpreted without ambiguity. They must also understand and deal with threats to the external validity of the experiment so that their findings can be extended beyond their experimental subjects and generalized to a wider population of interest.

Experimental design provides a plan or blueprint for experimentation. Three pre-experimental, three quasi-experimental, and three true experimental designs have been presented and their appropriate use, their advantages, and their disadvantages have been briefly discussed.

A brief discussion of the ethics of experimentation suggests some principles that should characterize the activities of the behavioral researcher.

Experimentation is a sophisticated technique for problem solving and may not be an appropriate activity for the beginning researcher. It has been suggested that teachers may make their most effective contribution to educational research by identifying important problems that they encounter in their classrooms and working cooperatively with research specialists in the conduct and interpretation of classroom experiments.

EXERCISES

1. In a classroom experiment, why is it more difficult to control extraneous variables than it would be in a pharmaceutical laboratory experiment?

2. What significant element distinguishes a quasi-experiment from a true experiment?
3. Why is an *ex post facto* study not an experiment?
4. A researcher, in proposing a research project, defines the dependent variable as achievement in mathematics. What is the difficulty that this definition presents? How would you improve it?
5. How could a double blind be applied in an educational experiment?
6. Under what circumstances could an independent variable in a study be a dependent variable in another study?
7. Why is randomization the best method for dealing with extraneous variables?
8. What effect could the Freedom of Information Act passed by Congress have upon experimental studies in education?
9. How could a high degree of experimental mortality seriously affect the validity of an experiment?
10. Read the report of an experiment in an educational research journal.
    a. Was the problem clearly stated?
    b. Were the variables defined in operational terms?
    c. Was the hypothesis clearly stated?
    d. Were the delimitations stated?
    e. Was the design clearly described?
    f. Were extraneous variables recognized? What provisions were made to control them?
    g. Were the population and the sampling method described?
    h. Were appropriate methods used to analyze the data?
    i. Were the conclusions clearly presented?
    j. Were the conclusions substantiated by the evidence presented?

BIBLIOGRAPHY

AMERICAN PSYCHOLOGICAL ASSOCIATION. *Ethical Principles and the Conduct of Research with Human Participants.* Washington, D.C.: Ad Hoc Committee on Ethical Standards, 1973.

BARBER, BERNARD ET AL. *Research on Human Subjects.* New York: Russell Sage Foundation, 1973.

BAUERNFEIND, ROBERT H. "The Need for Replication in Educational Research." *Phi Delta Kappan* 50 (October 1968): 126–128.

Belmont Report: Ethical Principles and Guidelines for the Protection of Human Subjects of Research. Washington, D.C.: Smithsonian Institution, Superintendent of Documents, U.S. Government Printing Office, 1979.

BIJOU, SIDNEY W., and DONALD M. BAER. "The Laboratory-Experimental Study of Child Behavior." Chapter 4 in *Handbook of Research Methods in Child Development,* Paul H. Mussen, ed. New York: John Wiley & Sons, 1960.

BLALOCK, H. M. *Causal Inferences in Nonexperimental Research.* Chapel Hill, N.C.: University of North Carolina Press, 1972.

BLOOM, BENJAMIN S. "The New Direction in Educational Research: Alterable Variables," *Phil Delta Kappan* 61:6 (Feb. 1980): 382–385.

BRACHT, GLENN H. and GENE V GLASS. "The External Validity of Experiments." *American Educational Research Journal* 5 (Nov. 1968): 437–474.

CAMPBELL, DONALD T. and THOMAS D. COOK. *The Design and Analysis of Quasi-Experiments for Field Settings.* Chicago: Rand McNally & Co., 1979.

CAMPBELL, DONALD T. and JULIAN C. STANLEY. *Experimental and Quasi-Experimental Designs for Research.* Chicago: Rand McNally & Co., 1966. Chapter 5 in *Handbook of Research on Teaching,* N. L. Gage, ed. Chicago: Rand McNally & Co., 1963.

COLLIER, RAYMOND and STANLEY ELAM, eds. *Research Design and Analysis.* Second Annual Phi Delta Kappa Symposium on Educational Research. Bloomington, Ind.: Phi Delta Kappa, 1961.

COMISKEY, R. J. "Use of Children for Medical Research." *Child Welfare* 57 (May 1978): 32–34.

CONROY, WILLIAM G. "Individual Privacy Rights and Research for Education." *Phi Delta Kappan* 56 (Feb. 1974): 415–418.

COOK, DESMOND L. "The Hawthorne Effect in Educational Research." *Phi Delta Kappan* 44 (Dec. 1962): 116–122.

COOK, DESMOND L. *The Impact of the Hawthorne Effect in Experimental Designs in Educational Research.* Final Report, Project No. 1757. Contract No. OE-3-10-041. Washington, D.C.: U.S. Office of Education, 1967.

DAYTON, C. M. *Design of Educational Experiments.* New York: McGraw-Hill Book Co., 1970.

EDWARDS, ALLEN L. "Experiments, Their Planning and Execution." Chapter 7 in *The Handbook of Social Psychology,* Vol. 1, Gardner Lindzey, ed., pp. 254–288. Cambridge, MA: Addison-Wesley, 1954.

EDWARDS, ALLEN L. *Experimental Design in Psychological Research.* New York: Holt, Rinehart & Winston, 1972.

"Ethical Aspects of Experimentation with Human Subjects." *Daedalus* (Spring 1969).

Ethical Standards of Psychologists. Washington, D.C.: American Psychological Association, 1963.

FIELDS, C. M. "Protecting the Subjects of Sensitive Research." *Chronicles of Higher Education* 17 (Dec. 1978): 7–11.

GARRETT, HENRY E. *Great Experiments in Psychology.* 3rd ed. New York: Appleton-Century-Crofts, 1951.

GEPHART, WILLIAM J. and DANIEL P. ANTONOPLOS. "The Effect of Expectancy and Other Research-Biasing Factors." *Phi Delta Kappan* 50 (June 1969) 579–583.

GLASS, GENE V "Evaluating Testing, Maturation, and Treatment Effects in a Pretest-Posttest Quasi-Experimental Design." *American Educational Research Journal* 2 (March 1965): 83–87.

KATZ, JAY. *Experimentation with Human Beings.* New York: Russell Sage Foundation, 1972.

KENNEDY, MARY M. "Findings from the Follow Through Planned Variation Study," *Educational Researcher* (June 1978): 3–11.

KERLINGER, FRED N. *Foundations of Behavioral Research.* 2d ed. New York: Holt, Rinehart & Winston, 1973.

KERLINGER, FRED N. *Scientific Behavioral Research: A Conceptual Primer.* New York: Holt, Rinehart & Winston, 1979.

KRATOCHWILL, THOMAS R. *Single Subject Research.* New York: Academic Press, 1978.

LINDQUIST, E. F. *Design and Analysis of Experiments in Psychology and Education.* Boston: Houghton-Mifflin Co., 1965.

O'LEARY, S. G. and K. D. O'LEARY. "Ethical Issues of Behavior Modification Research." *Psychology in the Schools* 14 (July 1977): 299–307.

ROSENTHAL, ROBERT and LENORE JACOBSON. *Pygmalion in the Classroom: Teacher Expectations and Pupils' Intellectual Development.* New York: Holt, Rinehart & Winston, 1968.

STANLEY, JULIAN C. "Controlled Experimentation in the Classroom." *Journal of Experimental Education* 25 (1957): 195–201.

STANLEY, JULIAN C. "A Common Class of Pseudo-Experiments." *American Educational Research Journal* 3 (March 1966): 78–87.

STANLEY, JULIAN C., ed. *Improving Experimental Design and Statistical Analysis.* Proceedings of the Seventh Annual Phi Delta Kappa Symposium on Educational Research. Chicago: Rand McNally & Co., 1967.

THORDIKE, ROBERT L. "Pygmalion in the Classroom by Robert Rosenthal and Lenore Jacobson, Book Review." *American Educational Research Journal* 5 (Nov. 1968): 708–711.

TOWNSEND, JOHN C. *Introduction to Experimental Method.* New York: McGraw-Hill Book Co., 1953.

UNDERWOOD, BENTON J. *Psychological Research.* New York: Appleton-Century-Crofts, 1957.

WEBB, EUGENE J. ET AL. *Unobtrusive Measures: Nonreactive Research in the Social Sciences.* Chicago: Rand McNally & Co., 1966.

WINER, B. J. *Statistical Principles in Experimental Design.* New York: McGraw-Hill Book Co., 1971.

WOLFENSBERGER, WOLF. "Ethical Issues in Research with Human Subjects." *Science* 155 (March 1967): 47–51.

FOUR

Assessment,

Evaluation,

and Descriptive

Research

A descriptive study describes and interprets what is. It is concerned with conditions or relationships that exist, opinions that are held, processes that are going on, effects that are evident, or trends that are developing. It is primarily concerned with the present, although it often considers past events and influences as they relate to current conditions.

The term *descriptive study* conceals an important distinction, for not all descriptive studies fall into the category of research. In Chapter One the similarities and differences between assessment, evaluation, and research were briefly discussed. We will restate those similarities and differences in this discussion of descriptive studies.

Assessment describes the status of a phenomenon at a particular time. It merely describes a situation that prevails without value judgment, attempts no explanation of underlying reasons, and makes no recommendations for action. It may deal with prevailing opinion, knowledge, practices, or conditions. As it is ordinarily used in education, assessment describes the progress students have made toward educational goals at a particular time. For example, in the National Assessment of Educational Progress program, the data are gathered by a testing program and a sampling procedure in such a way that no individual is tested over the entire test battery. It is not designed to determine the effectiveness of a particular process or program, but merely to estimate the degree of achievement of a large number of individuals who have been exposed to a great variety of educational and environmental influences. It does not propose or test hypotheses and does not deal with the many variables underlying the achievement or lack of achievement of those observed. It does not provide recommendations, but there may be some implied judgment as to the satisfactoriness of the situation or the fulfillment of society's expectations.

Evaluation adds the ingredient of value judgment of the social utility, desirability, or effectiveness of a process, product, or program, and it sometimes includes a recommendation for some course of action. School surveys are usually evaluation studies; educational products and programs are examined to determine their effectiveness in meeting accepted objectives, often with recommendations for constructive action.

Descriptive research, sometimes known as nonexperimental research, deals with the relationships between variables, the testing of hypotheses, and the development of generalizations, principles, or theories that have

93

universal validity. It is concerned with functional relationships. The expectation is that if variable A is systematically associated with variable B, prediction of future phenomena may be possible and the results may suggest additional or competing hypotheses to test.

In carrying on a descriptive research project, in contrast to an experiment, the researcher does not manipulate the variables or arrange for events to happen. In fact, the events that are observed and described would have happened even though there had been no observation or analysis. Descriptive research involves events that have already taken place and may be related to a present condition.

The method of descriptive research is particularly appropriate in the behavioral sciences, because many of the types of behavior that interest the researcher cannot be arranged in a realistic setting. Introducing significant variables may be harmful or threatening to human subjects. Ethical considerations often preclude exposing human subjects to potentially harmful manipulation. For example, it would be unthinkable to prescribe cigarette smoking to human subjects for the purpose of studying its possible relationship to throat or lung cancer, or to deliberately arrange auto accidents, except when manikins are used, in order to evaluate the effectiveness of seat belts or restraints in preventing serious injury.

Although some experimental studies of human behavior can be appropriately carried on, both in the laboratory and in the field, the prevailing research method of the behavioral sciences is descriptive. Under the conditions that naturally occur in the home, the classroom, the recreational center, the office, or the factory, human behavior can be systematically examined and analyzed.

The many similarities between these types of descriptive studies may have tended to cloud the distinctions between them. They are all characterized by disciplined inquiry, requiring expertise, objectivity, and careful execution. They all develop knowledge, adding to what is already known. They use similar techniques of observation, description, and analysis. The differences between them lie in the motivation of the investigator, the treatment of the data, the nature of the conclusions, and the use of the findings. Studies that illustrate these types of descriptive analysis are presented in this chapter.

ASSESSMENT STUDIES

The Survey

The survey method gathers data from a relatively large number of cases at a particular time. It is not concerned with characteristics of individuals *as* individuals. It is concerned with the generalized statistics that result when data are abstracted from a number of individual cases. It is essentially cross-sectional.

Ninety-four per cent of American homes have at least one television set. About three out of five students who enter the American secondary school remain to graduate. Fifty-six per cent of adult Americans voted in the 1972 presidential election. The average American consumes about 103 pounds of refined sugar annually. The ratio of female births to male births in the United States in 1974 was 946 to 1000. The population of Indiana, according to the 1970 census, was 5,194,000. Data like these result from many types of surveys. Each statement pictures a prevailing condition at a particular time.

In analyzing political, social, or economic conditions, one of the first steps is to get the facts about the situation—or a picture of conditions that prevail or that are developing. These data may be gathered from surveys of the entire population. Others are inferred from a study of a sample group, carefully selected from the total population. And, at times, the survey may describe a limited population which is the only group under consideration.

The survey is an important type of study. It must not be confused with the mere clerical routine of gathering and tabulating figures. It involves a clearly defined problem and definite objectives. It requires expert and imaginative planning, careful analysis and interpretation of the data gathered, and logical and skillful reporting of the findings.

Social Surveys

A significant social survey was made in the late 1930s under the direction of the Swedish sociologist, Gunnar Myrdal, and sponsored by the Carnegie Foundation. Myrdal and his staff of researchers made a comprehensive analysis of the social, political, and economic life of the American Negro, yielding a great mass of data on race relations in America.[1]

The late Alfred Kinsey of Indiana University made a comprehensive survey of the sexual behavior of the human male,[2] based on data gathered from more than 12,000 cases. His second study of the behavior of the human female was published five years later. Although these studies have raised considerable controversy, they represent a scientific approach to the study of an important social problem, and have many implications for jurists, legislators, social workers, and educators.

[1] Gunnar Myrdal, *An American Dilemma* (New York: Harper & Row, 1944).

[2] Alfred C. Kinsey *et al.*, *The Sexual Behavior of the American Male* (Philadelphia: W. B. Saunders Co., 1948); Alfred C. Kinsey et al., *The Sexual Behavior of the American Female* (Philadelphia: W. B. Saunders Co., 1953).

Paul Witty[3] has studied the television viewing habits of school children, and has published annual reports on his investigations since 1950. These studies were conducted in the Chicago area, and indicate the amount of time devoted to viewing and the program preferences of elementary and secondary students, their parents, and their teachers. An effort was made to relate television viewing to intelligence, reading habits, academic achievement, and other factors.

Clifford R. Shaw and Henry D. McKay[4] have made a study of juvenile delinquency in Chicago yielding significant data on the nature and extent of delinquency in large urban communities.

The National Safety Council conducts surveys on the nature, extent, and causes of automobile accidents in all parts of the United States. State high school athletic associations conduct surveys on the nature and extent of athletic injuries in member schools.

Public-Opinion Surveys

In our culture, where so many opinions on controversial subjects are expressed by well-organized special-interest groups, it is important to find out what the people think. Without a means of polling public opinion, the views of only the highly organized minorities are effectively presented through the printed page, radio, and television.

How do people feel about legalized abortion, the foreign aid program, busing to achieve racial integration in the public schools, or the adequacy of the public schools? What candidate do they intend to vote for in the next election? Such questions can be partially answered by means of the public-opinion survey. Many research agencies carry on these surveys and report their findings in magazines and in syndicated articles in daily newspapers.

Since it would be impracticable or even impossible to get an expression of opinion from every person, sampling techniques are employed in such a way that the resulting opinions of a limited number of people can be used to infer the reactions of the entire population.

The names Gallup, Roper, Harris, and Crossley are familiar to newspaper readers in connection with public-opinion surveys. These surveys of opinion are frequently analyzed and reported by such classifications as age groups, sex, educational level, occupation, income level, political affiliation, or area of residence. Researchers are aware of the existence of many publics, or segments of the public, who may hold conflicting

[3] Paul Witty, "Children of the TV Era," *Elementary English* 64 (May 1967): 528–535.

[4] Clifford R. Shaw and Henry D. McKay, *Juvenile Deliquency in Urban Areas* (Chicago: University of Chicago Press, 1942).

points of view. This further analysis of opinion by subgroups adds meaning to the analysis of public opinion in general.

Those who conduct opinion polls have developed more sophisticated methods of determining public attitudes through more precise sampling procedures and by profiting from errors that plagued early efforts. In prediction of voter behavior several well-known polls have proved to be poor estimators of election results.

In the 1948 election campaign a prominent poll predicted the election of Governor Thomas E. Dewey over President Harry S. Truman. Again the pollsters were wrong, possibly this time because they failed to recognize the shifting nature of public sentiment. Had the survey been made just prior to election day, a more accurate prediction might have resulted.

In addition to the limitations suggested, there is the hazard of careless responses, given in an off-hand way, that are sometimes at variance with the more serious opinions that are expressed as actual decisions.

Since 1969 the Gallup organization has conducted an annual nationwide opinion poll of public attitudes toward education. Using a stratified cluster sample of 1500 or more individuals over 18 years of age, the data have been gathered by personal interviews from seven geographic areas and four size-of-community categories. The responses were analyzed by age, sex, race, occupation, income level, political affiliation, and level of education. A wide range of problem areas has been considered; in the 1975 poll such problem areas confronting education were the use of drugs and alcohol; programs on drugs or alcohol; behavior standards in the schools; policies on suspension from school; work required of students, including amount of homework; requirements for graduation from high school; federal aid to public schools; the nongraded school program; open education; alternative schools; job training; right of teachers to strike; textbook censorship; and the role of the school principal as part of management.[5]

National Assessment of Educational Progress[6] This comprehensive educational survey was the first national assessment of educational achievement to be conducted in the United States. Originally financed by the Carnegie Foundation and the Fund for the Advancement of Education, with a supporting grant from the U.S. Office of Education, the Committee on Assessing the Progress of Education (CAPE) began its first survey in the spring of 1969. It gathered achievement test data

---

[5] Stanley M. Elam, *A Decade of Gallup Polls of Attitudes toward Education: 1969–78* (Bloomington, IN.: Phi Delta Kappan, 1979).

[6] *How Much Are Students Learning?* (Detroit: Committee on Assessing the Progress of Education, 1968).

by a sampling process such that no one individual was tested over the whole test battery or spent more than forty minutes in the process. Achievement was assessed every three years in four age groups (9, 13, 17, and young adults between 26 and 35), in four geographical areas (Northeast, Southeast, Central, and West), for four types of communities (large city, urban fringe, rural, and small city), and for several socioeconomic levels and ethnic groups.

Achievement has been assessed in art, reading, writing, social studies, science, mathematics, literature, citizenship, and music. Comparisons between individuals, schools, or school systems have never been made.

The agency now conducting the assessment is the National Assessment of Educational Progress (NAEP), financed by the National Center for Educational Statistics, a division of the Department of Education. Periodic reports are provided for educators, interested lay adults, and through press releases to periodicals for the general public.

Reports published by the National Assessment of Educational Progress in 1974 and 1975 indicated the decline in academic achievement in the following subject areas:

Science. Between 1969 and 1973, performance in science has declined on two-thirds of the test items with a total test score drop of two percentage points.[7] The gap between performance of whites and nonwhites, between males and females, and between inner-city and others has increased.

Politics and government.[8] Seventeen per cent of 13-year-olds and 49 per cent of 17-year-olds know that presidential candidates are nominated at national party conventions; 41 per cent of 17-year-olds and 44 per cent of young adults can correctly fill out a sample ballot, and 75 per cent of 13-year-olds and 90 per cent of 17-year-olds know that United States Senators are elected.

Consumer mathematics skills.[9] Of 34,000 17-year-olds and 4200 young adults, fewer than 50 per cent could determine the most economical size of a product, 1 per cent of 17-year-olds and 16 per cent of young

---

[7] J. Stanley Ahmann et al., "Science Achievement: The Trend Is Down," *Science Teacher* 42 (Sept. 1975): 23–25.

[8] Gaye Vandermyn, "Assessing Students' Political IQ," *American Education* 10 (June 1974): 21–25.

[9] Art Branscombe, "Checklist on Consumer Mathematics," *American Education* 11 (Oct. 1975): 21–24.

adults could correctly balance a checkbook, 60 per cent of 17-year-olds and 69 per cent of young adults could calculate the mean of three salaries, and 10 per cent of 17-year-olds and 20 per cent of young adults could correctly calculate a taxi fare. Males consistently outperformed females on exercises involving buying and household situations.

Writing.[10]   In 1974 both 13-year-olds and 17-year-olds used a simpler vocabulary and wrote less coherently than their counterparts in the survey four years earlier. The 17-year-olds showed an increase in awkwardness in writing and had a greater tendency to write as they spoke.

Observations of this type tend to paint a discouraging picture of the educational achievement of American youth and young adults. While the data may tend to convey a biased judgment, there does seem to be evidence that a relatively large number of Americans do not have the skill and knowledge necessary to function successfully in modern society.

A 1979 report[11] of the changes in average levels of achievement for 9-year-olds, 13-year-olds, and 17-year-olds indicates the following:

Science.   A general decline in science achievement with the decline in physical science more pronounced than that in biological science. The decline was greatest among the 17-year-olds, but there were small gains in biological science for 9-year-olds and 13-year-olds between 1972–73 and 1976–77.

Reading.   In composite levels in reading achievement there was a small gain among the 9-year-olds but no change for 13-year-olds or 17-year-olds.

Writing.   From 1969–70 to 1973–74, a slight gain for 9-year-olds, but an overall decline for 13-year-olds and 17-year-olds. In mechanics of writing (spelling, punctuation, etc.) no change was observed for any of the groups.

Political knowledge and attitudes.   While the achievement of 9-year-olds was not included in the report, there was a significant decline in all areas of knowledge and attitudes for 13-year-olds and 17-year-olds.

[10] George Neill, "Writing Skills Drop: 20% Can't Cope, Studies Show," *Phi Delta Kappan* 57 (Jan. 1976): 355.

[11] J. Stanley Ahmann, "Differential Changes in Levels of Achievement for Students in Three Age Groups," *Educational Studies* 10 (Winter 1979): 35–45.

In summary, there seems to be some evidence that the younger students showed the greatest gain or least loss over the period of the assessments.

International Assessment[12]   The International Association for the Evaluation of Educational Achievement, with headquarters in Stockholm, Sweden, has been carrying on an assessment program in a number of countries since 1964. The first study, *The International Study of Achievement in Mathematics,* compared achievement in twelve countries: Austria, Belgium, England, Finland, France, West Germany, Israel, Japan, the Netherlands, Scotland, Sweden, and the United States. Short answer and multiple choice tests were administered to 13-year-olds and to students in their last year of the upper secondary schools, prior to university entrance. More than 132,000 pupils and 5000 schools were involved in the survey. Japanese students excelled all others, regardless of their socioeconomic status, while the U.S. students ranked near the bottom.

While the purpose of assessment is not to compare school systems, the data lead observers to make such comparisons. Critics of the first assessment pointed out the inappropriateness of comparing 17-year-olds in the United States, where more than 75 per cent are enrolled in secondary schools, with 17-year-olds in other countries in which those enrolled in upper secondary schools comprise a small, highly selected population.

More recent assessments reveal that, while 10 per cent of the top United States students surpassed similar groups in all other countries in reading, in science they occupied seventh place.[13]

Other assessments have been carried out and the number of participating countries has been increased to twenty-two.

Activity Analysis

The analysis of the activities or processes that an individual is called upon to perform is important, both in industry and in various types of social agencies. This process of analysis is appropriate in any field of work and at all levels of responsibility. It is useful in the industrial plant, where needed skills and competencies of thousands of jobs are carefully studied, jobs ranging in complexity from that of unskilled laborer to that of plant manager.

In school systems the roles of the superintendent, the principal,

[12] Torsten Husen ed., *International Study of Achievement in Mathematics* (New York: John Wiley & Sons, 1967).

[13] Fred M. Hechinger and Grace Hechinger, "Are Schools Better in Other Countries?" *American Education* 10 (Feb. 1974): 6–8.

the teacher, and the custodian have been carefully analyzed to discover what these individuals do and need to be able to do. The Commonwealth Teacher Training Study,[14] made under the direction of W. W. Charters and Douglas Waples, described and analyzed the activities of several thousand teachers, and searched previous studies for opinions of writers on additional activities in which classroom teachers should engage.

This type of analysis may yield valuable information that would prove useful in:

1. Establishing the requirements for a particular job or position

2. Setting up a program for the preparation or training of individuals for various jobs or positions

3. Setting up an in-service program for improvement in job competence, or for upgrading of individuals already employed

4. Establishing equitable wage or salary schedules for various jobs or positions

Trend Studies

The trend, or predictive, study is an interesting application of the descriptive method. In essence, it is based upon a longitudinal consideration of recorded data, indicating what has been happening in the past, what the present situation reveals, and on the basis of these data, what will be likely to happen in the future. For example, if the population in an area shows consistent growth over a period of time, one might predict that by a certain date in the future the population will reach a given level. These assumptions are based upon the likelihood that the factors producing the change or growth will continue to exert their influence in the future. The trend study points to conclusions reached by the combined methods of historical and descriptive analysis, and is illustrated by *Problems and Outlook of Small Private Liberal Arts Colleges: Report to the Congress of the United States by the Comptroller General.*[15] In response to a questionnaire sent to 332 institutions, 283 furnished data on facility construction, loan repayments, enrollment, the effectiveness of methods used to attract more students, financial aid provided, and the general financial health of their institutions.

[14] W. W. Charters and Douglas Waples, *The Commonwealth Teacher Training Study* (Chicago: University of Chicago Press, 1929).

[15] *Problems and Outlook of Small Private Liberal Arts Colleges: Report to the Congress of the United States by the Comptroller General* (Washington, D.C.: United States General Accounting Office, 1978).

Based upon past and present experience, such influences as the growth of the community college, the effect of inflation on operating costs, tuition, living expenses and fees, and the decline in the number of college-age students were projected for the years 1978 to 1985, and their impact upon the financial stability of the small liberal arts college assessed.

The following trend study topics would also be appropriate:

1. The Growing Participation of Women in Intercollegiate Sports Programs

2. Trends in the Methods of Financial Support of Public Education

3. The Growth of Black Student Enrollment in Graduate Study Programs

4. The Minimum Competency Requirement Movement in American Secondary Education

EVALUATION STUDIES

School Surveys

What has traditionally been called a school survey is usually an assessment and evaluation study. Its purpose is to gather detailed information to be used as a basis for judging the effectiveness of the instructional facilities, curriculum, teaching and supervisory personnel, and financial resources in terms of best practices and standards in education. For example, professional and regional accrediting agencies send visitation teams to gather data on the characteristics of the institution seeking accreditation. Usually, following a self-evaluation by the school staff, the visiting educators evaluate the institution's characteristics on the basis of agency guidelines.

Many city, township, and county school systems have been studied by this method for the purpose of determining status and adequacy. These survey-evaluations are sometimes carried on by an agency of a university in the area. Frequently, a large part of the data is gathered by local educators, with the university staff providing direction and advisory services.

Assessment and Evaluation in Problem Solving

In solving a problem or charting a course of action, several sorts of information may be needed. These data may be gathered through the processes of assessment and evaluation methods.

The first type of information is based upon *present conditions.* Where are we now? From what point do we start? These data may be gathered by a systematic description and analysis of all the important aspects of the present situation.

The second type of information involves *what we may want.* In what direction may we go? What conditions are desirable or are considered to represent best practice? This clarification of objectives or goals may come from a study of what we think we want, possibly resulting from a study of conditions existing elsewhere, or of what experts consider to be adequate or desirable.

The third type of information is concerned with *how to get there.* This analysis may involve finding out about the experience of others who have been involved in similar situations. It may involve the opinions of experts, who presumably know best how to reach the goal.

Some studies emphasize only one of these aspects of problem solving. Others may deal with two, or even three, of the elements. Although a study does not necessarily embrace all the steps necessary for the solution of a problem, it may make a valuable contribution by clarifying only one of the necessary steps—from description of present status to the charting of the path to the goal.

Assessment and evaluation methods may supply some, or all, of the needed information. An example will illustrate how they can be used to help solve an educational problem.

Washington Township has a school building problem. Its present educational facilities seem inadequate, and if present developments continue, conditions may be much worse in the future. The patrons and educational leaders in the community know that a problem exists, but they realize that this vague awareness does not provide a sound basis for action. Three steps are necessary to provide such a basis.

The first step involves a systematic analysis of present conditions. How many school-age children are there in the township? How many children are of preschool age? Where do they live? How many classrooms now exist? How adequate are they? What is the average class size? How are these present buildings located in relation to residential housing? How adequate are the facilities for food, library, health, and recreational services? What is the present annual budget? How is it related to the tax rate and the ability of the community to provide adequate educational facilities?

The second step projects goals for the future. What will the school population be in five, ten, or twenty years? Where will the children live? How many buildings and classrooms will be needed? What provisions should be made for special school services, for libraries, cafeterias, gymnasiums, and play areas to take care of expected educational demands?

Step three considers how to reach those goals which have been established by the analysis of step two. What kind of buildings should be provided? Should schools be designed for grades one through eight, or should six-year elementary schools and separate three-year junior high schools be provided? How will the money be raised? When and how much should the tax rate be increased? When should the building program get under way?

Many of the answers to the questions raised in step three will be arrived at by analysis of practices of other townships, the expressed opinions of school patrons and local educational leaders, and the opinions of experts in the areas of school buildings, school organization, community planning, and public finance. Of course, this analysis of school building needs is but one phase of the larger educational problem of providing an adequate educational program for tomorrow's children. There remain problems of curriculum, pupil transportation, and school personnel. These problems can also be attacked by using similar methods of assessment and evaluation.

The Follow-up Study

The follow-up study investigates individuals who have left an institution after having completed a program, a treatment, or a course of study. The study is concerned with what has happened to them, and what has been the impact upon them of the institution and its program. By examining their status or seeking their opinions, one may get some idea of the adequacy or inadequacy of the institution's program. Which courses, experiences, or treatments proved to be of value? Which proved to be ineffective or of limited value? Studies of this type enable an institution to evaluate various aspects of its program in light of actual results.

Dillon's[16] study of early school leavers has yielded information that may lead to the improvement of the curriculum, guidance services, administrative procedures, and thus the holding power of the American secondary school.

Project Talent[17] was an educational survey conducted by the University of Pittsburgh with support from the Cooperative Research Program of the U.S. Office of Education, the National Institutes of Health, the National Science Foundation, and the Department of Defense. The survey consisted of the administration of a two-day battery of aptitude, ability,

[16] Harold J. Dillon, *Early School Leavers*. Pub. #401 (New York: National Child Labor Committee, 1949).

[17] U.S. Office of Education, *Progress towards the Goals of Project Talent* (Washington, D.C.: U.S. Government Printing Office, 1965).

and achievement tests, and inventories of the background characteristics of 440,000 students enrolled in 1353 secondary schools in all parts of the United States. Five basic purposes of the survey were stated:

1. To obtain an inventory of the capacities and potentialities of American youth

2. To establish a set of standards for educational and psychological measurement

3. To provide a comprehensive counseling guide indicating patterns of career success

4. To provide information on how youth choose their life work

5. To provide better understanding of the educational experiences which prepare students for their life work.

In addition to the testing program, questionnaire follow-up studies have been conducted, and are planned at regular intervals, to relate the information gathered to patterns of aptitude and ability required by various types of occupations. The vast amount of data stored in the data bank, now available in the computer files, will make significant educational research possible and may provide a basis for possible changes in the educational patterns of American secondary schools.

Project Talent, described as an example of an educational survey, also provides an illustration of a follow-up study. One phase of the longitudinal study, conducted in 1964 and reported by Janet Combs and William W. Cooley,[18] involved the follow-up of the ninth grade group who failed to complete the high school program. This group, which represented a random sample of the ninth grade secondary school population, provided an estimate of the characteristics of the dropout population, compared with those of a random sample of students who graduated but did not enter a junior college or four-year institution of higher learning. These two samples were compared on a number of characteristics, such as academic achievement, participation in extra-curricular activities, work experiences, hobbies, contacts with school counselors, and self-reported personal qualities.

The students who graduated scored significantly higher on most of the characteristics, except self-reported qualities of leadership and impulsiveness. One unusual finding indicated that the dropouts earned as much as those who had finished high school and had been earning it longer. It was pointed out, however, that the study concerned students who were about 19 years of age, and that the economic advantages of

[18] Janet Combs and William S. Cooley, "Dropouts: In High School and after School," *American Educational Research Journal* 5 (May 1968): 343–363.

finishing high school could not be adequately evaluated until later in life.

Project Talent, now funded by the National Institute of Education, has maintained contact with the original students and has completed the eleventh-year follow-up survey. Many of the students expressed dissatisfaction with their schooling, and regretted that they had not gone on to college or vocational school and that they had married too early. More than half still live within 30 miles of their high schools, a surprising observation in a society that is believed to be extremely mobile. The more mobile half were the high academic achievers. Eighty per cent of the men, but only 65 per cent of the women, expressed satisfaction with their jobs as meeting their long-range goals.

DESCRIPTIVE RESEARCH

The examples discussed up to this point in the chapter have been designated as assessment studies and evaluation studies. Descriptive research studies have characteristics that distinguish them from the types previously described.

1. They are nonexperimental, for they deal with the relationships between nonmanipulated variables in a natural, rather than artificial, setting. Since the events or conditions have already occurred or exist, the researcher selects the relevant variables for an analysis of their relationships.

2. They involve hypothesis formulation and testing.

3. They use the logical methods of inductive-deductive reasoning to arrive at generalizations.

4. They often employ methods of randomization so that error may be estimated when inferring population characteristics from observations of samples.

5. The variables and procedures are described as accurately and completely as possible so that the study can be replicated by other researchers.

Document or Content Analysis

Documents are an important source of data in many areas of investigation, and the methods of analysis are similar to those used by historians. The analysis is concerned with the explanation of the status of some phenomenon at a particular time or its development over a period of time. The activity may be classified as descriptive research, for problem identification, hypothesis formulation, sampling, and systematic observation of variable relationships may lead to generalizations. It serves a useful purpose in adding knowledge to fields of inquiry and in explaining certain social events. Its application to educational research is suggested in some of the studies listed as examples.

In documentary analysis, the following may be used as sources of data: records, reports, printed forms, letters, autobiographies, diaries, compositions, themes or other academic work, books, periodicals, bulletins or catalogues, syllabi, court decisions, pictures, films, and cartoons.

When using documentary sources, one must bear in mind the fact that data appearing in print are not necessarily trustworthy. Documents used in descriptive research must be subjected to the same careful types of criticism employed by the historian. Not only is the authenticity of the document important, but the validity of its contents is crucial. It is the researcher's obligation to establish the trustworthiness of all data that he or she draws from documentary sources.

The following purposes may be served through documentary analysis (examples of actual studies are given as illustrations):

1. To describe prevailing practices or conditions.
   Entrance Requirements of Ohio Colleges as Revealed by an Analysis of College Bulletins
   Criteria for Primary Pupil Evaluation Used on Marion County Report Cards

2. To discover the relative importance of, or interest in, certain topics or problems.
   Public Information on Education as Measured by Newspaper Coverage in Three Indianapolis Daily Newspapers during the Month of December, 1958
   Statistical Concepts Presented in College Textbooks in Educational Research Published since 1940

3. To discover level of difficulty of presentation in textbooks or in other publications.
   The Vocabulary Level of Intermediate Science Textbooks
   Abstract Concepts Found in First Grade Readers

4. To evaluate bias, prejudice, or propaganda in textbook presentation.
   The Soviet Union as Presented in High School History Textbooks
   The Free Enterprise System as Pictured in High School Social Problems Textbooks
   Racial and Religious Stereotypes in Junior High School Literature Textbooks

5. To analyze types of errors in students' work.
   Typing Errors of First Semester Typing Students at Shortridge High School

Errors in English Usage Found in Letters of Application for Admission to the University of Wisconsin

6. To analyze the use of symbols representing persons, political parties or institutions, countries, or points of view.
   Great Britain as a Symbol, as Represented in New York City Newspaper Cartoons in the Decade, 1930–1940
   The New Dealer as Depicted in the American Press from 1932 to 1942

7. To identify the literary style, concepts, or beliefs of a writer.
   Shakespeare's Use of the Metaphor
   Alexander Campbell's Concept of the Trinity, as Revealed in His Sermons
   John Dewey's Interpretation of Education as Growth

8. To explain the possible causal factors related to some outcome, action, or event.
   The Effect of Media Coverage upon the Outcome of the 1976 Presidential Election
   The Influence of Newspaper Editorials upon the Action of the State Assembly on Sales Tax Legislation

Content or document analysis should serve a useful purpose in yielding information that is helpful in evaluating or explaining social or educational practices. Since there are so many significant areas to be investigated, setting up studies for the pure joy of counting and tabulating has little justification. "The Uses of Shall and Will in the Spectator Papers," or "The Use of Too, Meaning Also, in the Works of Keats" would seem to add little useful knowledge to the field of literature.

The Case Study

The case study is a way of organizing social data for the purpose of viewing social reality. It examines a social unit as a whole. The unit may be a person, a family, a social group, a social institution, or a community. The purpose is to understand the life cycle or an important part of the life cycle of the unit. The case study probes deeply and analyzes interaction between the factors that explain present status or that influence change or growth. It is a longitudinal approach, showing development over a period of time.

The element of typicalness, rather than uniqueness, is the focus of attention, for an emphasis upon uniqueness would preclude scientific abstraction and generalization of findings.

Data may be gathered by a wide variety of methods, including:

1. Observation by the researcher or his or her informants of physical characteristics, social qualities, or behavior

2. Interviews with the subject(s), relatives, friends, teachers, counselors, and others

3. Questionnaires, opinionnaires, psychological tests and inventories

4. Recorded data from newspapers, schools, courts, clinics, government agencies, or other sources.

A single case study emphasizes analysis in depth. Though it may be fruitful in developing hypotheses to be tested, it is not directed toward broad generalizations. Someone has observed that one cannot generalize from an N of 1. To the extent that a single case may represent an atypical situation, the observation is sound. But if the objective analysis of an adequate sample of cases leads researchers to consistent observations of significant variable relationships, hypotheses may be confirmed, leading to valid generalizations.

The individual case study has been a time-honored procedure in the field of medicine and medical research. Sigmund Freud[19] was a pioneer in using case study methods in the field of psychiatry. In an effort to treat his psychoneurotic patients, he began to discover consistent patterns of experience. Under his careful probing, patients recalled long-forgotten, traumatic, sex-related incidents in their childhood and youth. Freud hypothesized that these incidents probably explained their neurotic behavior.

His famous case history of Sergei Petrov, "the Wolf Man," published in 1918 under the title "From the History of an Infantile Neurosis," is one of the classic examples of Freud's use of the case study. He believed that these case studies confirmed his hypothesis, leading to psychoanalysis as a method of treatment. He also used them to demonstrate how theoretical models could be used to provide concrete examples.

Case studies are not confined to the study of individuals and their behavioral characteristics. Case studies have been made of all types of communities from hamlet to great metropolis. Case studies have been made of types of individuals—alcoholics, drug addicts, juvenile delinquents, migratory workers, sharecroppers, industrial workers, members of professions, executives, army wives, trailer court residents, members of social classes, Quakers, Amish, members of other religious sects and denominations, Negroes, American Indians, Chinese-Americans, Hispanics, and many other social and ethnic groups. Such institutions as

[19] James Strachey, *The Complete Psychological Works of Sigmund Freud,* Vol. XVII (London: Hogarth Press, 1964).

colleges, churches, corrective institutions, welfare agencies, fraternal organizations, and business groups have been studied as cases. These
studies have been conducted for the purpose of understanding the culture and the development of variable relationships.

For example, a community study is a thorough observation and
analysis of a group of people living together in a particular geographic
location in a corporate way. The study deals with such elements of community life as location, appearance, prevailing economic activity, climate
and natural resources, historical development, mode of life, social structure, goals or life values and patterns, the individuals or power groups
that exert the dominant influence, and the impact of the outside world.
It also evaluates the social institutions that meet the basic human needs
of health, protection, making a living, education, religious expression,
and recreation.

The early community studies made by Robert and Helen Lynd are
well known. The first, reported in 1929, *Middletown*,[20] and the second,
Middletown in Transition,[21] in 1937, described the way of life in Muncie,
Indiana, a typical midwestern, average-size city, tracing its development
from the gas boom of the 1890s through World War I, the prosperity
of the twenties, and the depression of the thirties. James West described
the nature of a very small community in the Ozark region in *Plainville*,[22]
USA. Sherman and Henry have studied the way of life in five "hollow"
communities, hidden in the Blue Ridge Mountains, in *Hollow Folk*.[23]

Some community studies have singled out particular aspects for
special investigation. St. Clair Drake and H. R. Cayton have described
life in the Black section of Chicago in *Black Metropolis*.[24] August B. Hollingshead has portrayed the life of adolescents in a small Illinois community in *Elmtown's Youth*.[25] W. Lloyd Warner and his associates developed
a hypothesis of social class structure in a New England community in
their study of Newburyport, Massachusetts, in *Social Life in a Modern
Community*.[26] Rex A. Lucas has compared the way of life in three Canadian

[20] Robert S. Lynd and Helen M. Lynd, *Middletown* (New York: Harcourt, Brace & Co.,
1929).

[21] Robert S. Lynd and Helen M. Lynd, *Middletown in Transition* (New York: Harcourt, Brace
& World, 1937).

[22] James West, *Plainville, USA* (New York: Columbia University Press, 1945).

[23] Mandel Sherman and Thomas R. Henry, *Hollow Folk* (New York: Thomas Y. Crowell,
1933).

[24] St. Claire Drake and H. R. Cayton, *Black Metropolis* (New York: Harcourt, Brace & World,
1945).

[25] August B. Hollingshead, *Elmtown's Youth* (New York: John Wiley & Sons, 1949).

[26] W. Lloyd Warner and Paul S. Lunt, *Social Life in a Modern Community*, Vol. I, "Yankee
City Series" (New Haven, CT.: Yale University Press, 1941).

communities in *Minetown, Milltown, Railtown: Life in Canadian Communities of Single Industry.*[27]

While the case study is a useful method of organizing research observations, there are certain precautions that should be considered:

1. The method may look deceptively simple. To use it effectively, the researcher must be thoroughly familiar with existing theoretical knowledge of the field of inquiry, and skillful in isolating the significant variables from many that are irrelevant. There is a tendency to select variables because of their spectacular nature, rather than for their crucial significance.

2. Subjective bias is a constant threat to objective data-gathering and analysis. The danger of selecting variable relationships based upon preconceived convictions and the apparent consistency of a too limited sample of observations may lead the researcher to an unwarranted feeling of certainty about the validity of his or her conclusions.

3. Effects may be wrongly attributed to factors that are merely associated, rather than cause-and-effect related. While the case study process is susceptible to this *post hoc* fallacy, it is a hazard associated with other types of nonexperimental studies.

Ethnographic Studies

Ethnography, sometimes known as cultural anthropology, is a *method of field study observation* that became popular in the latter part of the nineteenth century. It has continued to show significant development, suggesting promising techniques for the study of behavior in an educational situation. In its early application, it consisted of participant observation, conversation, and the use of informants to study the cultural characteristics of primitive people; African, South Sea Island, and American Indian tribes. These groups were small in number, geographically and culturally isolated, with little specialization in social function and with simple economies and technology. Such cultural features as language, marriage and family life, child-rearing practices, religious beliefs and practices, social relations and rules of conduct, political institutions, and methods of production were analyzed.

The data gathered consisted of observation of patterns of action, verbal and nonverbal interaction between members of the tribe as well as between the subjects and the researcher and his or her informants, and the examination of whatever records or artifacts were available.

[27] Rex A. Lucas, *Minetown, Milltown, Railtown: Life in Canadian Communities of Single Industry* (Toronto: University of Toronto Press, 1970).

Many of the early studies were subsequently criticized on the grounds that the anthropologist spent too little time among the people of the tribe to get more than a superficial view, didn't learn the native language and had to depend too much on the reports of poorly trained informants, relied too much on his or her own cultural perspective, reaching ethnocentric, judgmental conclusions, which resulted in stereotyped theories of the development of the primitive society.

Later investigators realized that studies of this type would be invalid unless the observer:

1. lived for a much more extensive period of time among the tribe and became an integrated member of the social group;

2. learned the native language, enabling him or her to develop the sensitivity to think, feel, and interpret observations in terms of the tribe's concepts, feelings, and values, while at the same time supplementing his or her own objective judgment in interpreting observations;

3. trained his or her informants to systematically record field data in their own language and cultural perspective.

This refinement of participant observation resulted in more objective and valid observation and analysis. Some studies were directed toward the examination of the total way of life of a group. Other studies singled out a particular phase of the culture for intensive analysis, taking into account those elements that were relevant to the problem.

In her study *Coming of Age in Samoa*,[28] Margaret Mead observed the development of 53 adolescent girls in a permissive Samoan society. She concluded that there were no differences in the physical processes of adolescent growth between Samoan and American girls: the differences were differences in response. The difficulties of this period of development, a troublesome feature of American life, do not occur in Samoa. She attributed the difference to Samoa's more homogeneous culture, a single set of religious and moral beliefs, and a wider kinship network that conferred authority and affection. She attributed the difficulties of American girls to the restraints of the culture, not to nature.

Her study of *Antler*, an alias for a South Dakota Plains Indian tribe, was published under the title, *The Changing Culture of an Indian Tribe*.[29] This study examined the total way of life of a group.

Many of the time-honored techniques of the ethnographic study

[28] Margaret Mead, *Coming of Age in Samoa* (New York: William Morrow & Co., 1928).

[29] Margaret Mead, *The Changing Culture of an Indian Tribe* (New York: William Morrow & Co., 1931).

involving integration into the group and using participant observation are being applied to research in sociology, psychology, social psychology, and education. Some of the assumptions and characteristics of the method may be described.

The ethnographic study is a qualitative approach, employing few, if any, quantitative data-gathering instruments. Using the methods of participant observation, the researcher observes, listens to, and converses with the subjects in as free and natural an atmosphere as possible. The assumption is that the most important behavior of individuals in groups is a dynamic process of complex interactions and consists of more than a set of facts, statistics, or even discrete incidents. The strength of this kind of study lies in the observation of natural behavior in a real-life setting, free from the constraints of more conventional research procedures.

Another assumption is that human behavior is influenced by the setting in which it occurs. The researcher must understand that setting, the nature of the social structure, its traditions, values, and norms of behavior. It is important to observe and interpret as an outside observer, but also to observe and interpret in terms of the subjects—how they view the situation, how they interpret their own thoughts, words, and activities, as well as those of others in the group. The researcher gets inside the minds of the subjects, while at the same time interpreting the behavior from his or her own perspective.

The relationship of researchers to their subjects is based upon trust and confidence. Researchers do not allow themselves to be aligned with either the authority figures or the subjects. A position of neutrality is essential to objective participant observation.

Unlike conventional deductive quantitative research, participant observers begin without preconceptions and hypotheses. Using inductive logic, they build their hypotheses as they are suggested by observations. They periodically reevaluate them on the basis of new observations, modifying them when they appear to be inconsistent with the evidence. They look for negative evidence to challenge their temporary hypotheses. In a sense, this type of research has the characteristics of a series of consecutive studies. Unlike the conventional research study, the interpretation is not deferred to the conclusion, but is a constant ongoing process of testing tentative hypotheses against additional observations in a real situation.

Ethnographic methods of research have been used to investigate such problems as:

1. Student Leadership Roles in an Urban, Racially Integrated High School

2. Pupil-Teacher Relationships in a Suburban Junior High School

3. Social Relationships in a Class of Emotionally Disturbed Children

4. Changes in Attitudes and Behavior in a Drug Abuse Rehabilitation Center

5. The Social Class Structure of a Florida, Cuban-American Community

Ex Post Facto or Explanatory Observational Studies

Descriptive research seeks to find answers to questions through the analysis of variable relationships. What factors seem to be associated with certain occurrences, outcomes, conditions, or types of behavior? Since it is often impracticable to arrange occurrences, an analysis of past events may be the only feasible way to study causation.

For example, one would not arrange automobile accidents in order to study their causes. The automobile industry, police departments, safety commissions, and insurance companies study the conditions associated with accidents that have occurred. Such factors as mechanical faults or failures, excessive speed, driving under the influence of alcohol and others have been identified as causal.

Seat Belt Research   Seat belt research has had an important influence upon auto-safety equipment. Federal legislation requires that all new cars sold after January 1, 1968, be equipped with lap and shoulder belts. A Detroit news release cites research evidence that supports the effectiveness of safety belts.[30]

> Now that U.S. autos are being equipped with a maze of belts and harnesses for drivers and passengers, this question is being asked by many car buyers: Are they really useful, or are they more trouble than they are worth?
>
> The answer, from the best available evidence, seems to be: The new harnesses can be an important factor in reducing injuries and death from accidents.
>
> The widest research done to date on this subject was a Swedish survey of 28,780 accidents, showing how the use or non-use of shoulder harnesses affected the drivers and passengers. Main results of the survey were made public late in 1967. The survey by the manufacturers of Volvo autos also showed this: Use of a combined shoulder-lap belt reduced skull damage by 69 per cent for drivers and 88 per cent for passengers. Facial injuries dropped by 73 per cent for drivers and 83 per cent for passengers.
>
> The U.S. auto industry has accepted the Federal Government edict that it provide the belts and harnesses—a total of 16 straps in each new

[30] *US News and World Report* (January 29, 1968), copyrighted article, p. 12.

auto. Now being worked on are plans to make them less unsightly and less awkward to use.

But dealers are finding a number of buyers unenthusiastic about all the belts. Some dealers asked if they could remove the belts at the request of the customers. The answer from manufacturers: No. The dealer, it was explained, might be breaking the law if he did so.

Some industry officials have also raised the question of whether the belts, themselves, can cause injury in case of accident. So far there has been no broad study in the United States to back this theory. The Swedish survey, however, did show this: In the 28,780 accidents studied, safety belts caused 34 injuries to drivers, 25 to front seat passengers. Most were minor injuries.

Figures below show results of 28,780 traffic accidents in Sweden. In these accidents 98 per cent of the cars were equipped with lap and shoulder belts. But only 25 per cent of the drivers and 30 per cent of the front seat passengers were using the belts. This is what happened:

	Killed	Severely injured	Slightly injured
DRIVERS			
Among 6870 using belts	2	51	175
Among 21,910 not using belts	37	263	835
FRONT SEAT PASSENGERS			
Among 2699 using belts	1	22	109
Among 6032 not using belts	12	160	439

While these statistics may appear to present convincing evidence in favor of the use of lap and shoulder belts in reducing fatalities and serious injuries, one might speculate that motorists who are prudent enough to wear them are likely to be more careful drivers than those who do not.

Studies of juvenile delinquency may compare the social and educational backgrounds of delinquents and nondelinquents. What factors, if any, were common to the delinquent group? What factors, if any, were common to the nondelinquent group? Any factors common to one group, but not to the other, might serve as a possible explanation of the underlying causes of delinquency.

Some efforts have been made to associate good or poor teaching with the type of educational institution in which the teachers prepared. Those studies have proved inconclusive, possibly for a number of reasons. In addition to the difficulty of finding valid and satisfactory criteria of good and poor teaching, many factors other than type of college attended seem to be significant. Such variables as quality of scholarship, socioeconomic status, personality qualities, types of nonschool experiences, attitudes toward the teaching profession, and a host of others have possible relevancy.

Sesame Street studies   Minton[31] studied the effect of viewing the children's television program, "Sesame Street," on the reading readiness of kindergarten children. Of three sample groups, a 1968, a 1969, and a 1970 group, only the 1970 group had viewed the program.

Reading Readiness and "Sesame Street"

Sample group	N	White	Black	Spanish-Speaking
1968	482	431	51	18
1969	495	434	61	9
1970	524	436	88	25

Scores on the Metropolitan Reading Readiness Test battery, consisting of six subtests (word meaning, listening, matching, alphabet letter recognition, numbers, and copying text) were used to measure readiness. Using pretest-posttest design, the mean gain scores of the 1970 group were compared with those of the 1968 and 1969 groups.

No significant differences at the .05 level were observed in total scores. On only one of the subtests, letter recognition, was a significant difference observed, favoring the 1970 group. When classified by socio-economic status, advantaged children watched more and scored higher than disadvantaged children. The hypothesis that viewing "Sesame Street" would help to close the gap between advantaged and disadvantaged children was not supported; rather, the gap was widened.

Anderson and Levin[32] studied the effect of age on the viewing attention of small children to a 57-minute taped "Sesame Street" program, consisting of 41 bits, each ranging in length from 10 to 453 seconds. Six groups of 5 boys and 5 girls, ages 12, 18, 24, 30, 36, 42, and 48 months were observed by video tape recordings. In a viewing room, in the presence of parents, toys were provided as alternatives to viewing. The following observations were reported:

1. Length of attention increased with age. The younger children appeared to be more interested in the toys and interacting with their mothers.

2. Length of attention decreased as bit length increased.

3. Attention to animals increased to 24 months, but dropped thereafter.

[31] J. M. Minton, "Impact of Sesame Street on Reading Readiness," *Sociology of Education* 48 (Spring 1975): 141–151.

[32] Daniel B. Anderson and Stephen B. Levin, "Young Children's Attention to Sesame Street," *Child Development* 47 (Sept. 1976): 806–811.

4. Children showed more interest in the presence of women, lively music, puppets, peculiar voices, rhyming repetition, and motion.

5. Children showed less interest in the presence of adult men, animals, inactivity, and still drawings.

Replication and Secondary Analysis

Replication, a combination of the terms *repeat* and *duplicate*, has been described as an important method of challenging or verifying the conclusions of a previous study. Using different subjects at a different time and in a different setting, arriving at conclusions that are consistent with those of the previous study would strengthen its conclusions and justify more confidence in its validity. Replication is essential to the development and verification of new generalizations and theories.

Another useful procedure, known as *secondary analysis,* consists of reanalyzing the data gathered by a previous investigator, and may involve different hypotheses, different experimental designs, or different methods of statistical analysis. The subjects are the same and the data are the same. The difference is that of alternative methods of analysis.

The method of secondary analysis has a number of advantages that command its use:

1. The new investigator may bring an objectivity, a fresh point of view, to the investigation and may think of better questions to be raised or hypotheses to be tested. For example, the viewpoint of a psychologist rather than that of a sociologist (or vice versa) may find greater meaning in the data already available.

2. Secondary analysis may bring greater expertise to the area of investigation and greater skill in experimental design and statistical analysis.

3. The reanalysis would involve less expense in both time and money. Because the data are already available, a more modest appropriation of funds would be possible. It would not be necessary to intrude upon the time of subjects (teachers and students) whose primary activities had been diverted in the original investigation.

4. Secondary analysis may provide useful experience for students of research methodology by enabling them to use real data, rather than simulated or inferior data for the purposes of the exercise.

Secondary analysis has played an important part in educational research. No investigation has been subjected to as great a degree of secondary analysis as the *Equality of Educational Opportunity* study, described in the following pages of this chapter.

118   *Research in Education*

Equality of Educational Opportunity Study   In 1964, the Congress of the United States passed the Civil Rights Act that directed the United States Commissioner of Education to carry out a study of "the lack of educational opportunity by reason of race, color, religion or national origin in public educational institutions at all levels in the United States, its territories and possessions, and the District of Columbia."

This authorization assumed that educational opportunity for members of minority groups was unequal to that available for white students. This study was one of the largest of its type ever conducted. The report of its findings, commonly known as the Coleman Report, was titled *Equality of Educational Opportunity*,[33] written by James S. Coleman, a distinguished sociologist.

The nationwide investigation selected, by a two-stage probability sample, 640,000 public school pupils in grades 1, 3, 6, 9, and 12, and 60,000 teachers in more than 4,000 schools. Data were also gathered from parents, school principals, school district superintendents, and prominent community members. In addition, case studies of individual cities were conducted by educators, lawyers, and sociologists. The data were organized for comparative purposes by geographic location as northern, northern metropolitan, southern and southwestern, southern metropolitan, and midwestern and western. Individuals were classified as White, Negro, Oriental, Indian, Mexican-American, and Puerto Rican.

Data gathering instruments, distributed by mail, consisted of questionnaires, opinionnaires, tests, scales, and inventories. Pupils in grades 1, 3, 6, 9, and 12 provided data on:

1. Reading comprehension

2. Work-study skills

3. Verbal ability

4. Nonverbal ability

5. Mathematics achievement

6. Self-concept

7. General information

8. Socioeconomic status

Teachers and administrators provided information on:

[33] James S. Coleman et al., *Equality of Educational Opportunity* (Washington, D.C.: U.S. Government Printing Office, 1965).

1. Socioeconomic status
2. Degrees held
3. Type of academic preparation
4. Attitudes toward minorities
5. Length of teaching service

Information on the schools and facilities included:

1. School buildings—age and condition
2. Special facilities—auditoriums, gymnasiums, cafeterias
3. Accreditation—state and regional
4. Length of school day and school year
5. Courses offered
6. Extracurricular activities
7. Library—full-time librarian
8. Art and music teachers
9. Health services—school nurse—psychological services
10. Guidance services
11. Special education programs for academically talented, physically handicapped, mentally retarded
12. Adequacy of textbooks
13. Free kindergarten
14. Free milk—free lunch programs
15. Provision for standardized test, inventory programs
16. Per-pupil money expenditures

Some information was gathered concerning the parents:

1. Socioeconomic status
2. Occupation
3. Educational level
4. Father and mother at home
5. Attitudes toward educational achievement of children.

As far as possible, data-gathering instruments were checked for validity and reliability. Methods of data analysis included multiple correlation and factorial analysis of variance and covariance.

While it would not be feasible to present a detailed account of the findings of the study, a few of the major conclusions are included:

1. The report rejected the assumption that the educational opportunities provided for minority children were unequal. There seemed to be little difference in almost all school facilities that would relate to equality of opportunity. In some areas, minority schools seemed to be more adequate than predominantly White schools.

2. Family background, rather than the characteristics of the school, appeared to be the major influence on school achievement. It was apparent that, over the years, the school experience did little to narrow the initial achievement gap.

3. The socioeconomic composition of the student body was more highly related to achievement than any school factor.

4. The achievement level in rank order was White, Oriental-American, American Indian, Mexican-American, Puerto Rican, and Negro. While White students scored significantly higher than any other group, Oriental-Americans excelled in nonverbal and mathematics achievement.

5. Inequalities of educational opportunity were more closely related to regional differences, rather than to differences between predominantly Negro and White schools. Schools in the North, Midwest, and West seemed to have better facilities than those in the South and Southwest.

6. Social class differences within all groups appeared to be more significant than the differences between ethnic groups.

The Coleman Report has been subjected to criticism, both by experienced researchers and by members of special interest groups. The findings were unacceptable to some who pointed out flaws in the gathering of data and their interpretation. Others found procedural defects in sampling and statistical analysis of the data.

Of 900,000 pupils solicited, only about 640,000, or about two-thirds of the invited sample, were tested. Twenty-one Northern metropolitan school districts refused to participate in the study, including such large cities as Boston, Chicago, Indianapolis, and Los Angeles. In addition, twenty-three other school districts, who participated to a limited degree, refused to test their pupils. The provision for an equal number of white and nonwhite participants in the sample introduced a possible element of invalidity in the statistical analysis of the data.

The questionnaires were criticized for their lack of what has been termed a "qualitative bite," the effort to get beneath the surface for more meaningful responses. There was also a high degree of nonresponse to the questionnaires, particularly on some items of an emotional or controversial nature. For example, one-third of the principals failed to answer questions on the racial composition of their faculties.

Some critics believed that the report did not make a highly significant contribution to education, but most agreed that it did stimulate interest in further research concerning the relationship of the family, the school, and the community.

The fact that no previous study has generated so much controversy is not surprising, for the complexity of the problems involved, the sensitive nature of the issues, and the defensive attitudes of special interest groups were inevitable sources of disagreement. For example, both advocates and opponents of school busing viewed the data in the light of their own established positions.

A number of studies, using secondary analysis, were authorized by various government agencies, special commissions, and philanthropic foundations. Using the Coleman Report data, various aspects of the problem were examined more closely, using different statistical procedures and raising different questions. Some confined their investigations to data relating to a single geographic area while others considered a wider range of data analysis. Helpful résumés of several of these studies are included in the publication, *On Equality of Educational Opportunity*,[34] edited by Frederick Mosteller and Daniel P. Moynihan.

Genetic Studies of Genius   A classic series of studies, entitled *Genetic Studies of Genius*, are landmarks in the investigation of giftedness, providing important information and suggesting a number of hypotheses that subsequently have been examined, using a variety of methods. These studies, conceived by Lewis M. Terman, illustrate a variety of types of investigation: survey, document analysis, case study, follow-up study, evaluation, and causal comparative study.

The first study, *The Mental and Physical Traits of a Thousand Gifted Children*,[35] compared the characteristics of a gifted group with those of a nongifted group. The second, *The Early Mental Traits of Three Hundred*

[34] Frederick Mosteller and Daniel P. Moynihan, eds., *On Equality of Educational Opportunity* (New York: Random House, Vintage Books, 1972).

[35] Lewis M. Terman et al., *The Mental and Physical Traits of a Thousand Gifted Children*, Vol. 1 (Stanford, CA.: Stanford University Press, 1926).

Geniuses,[36] using documentary evidence, analyzed the characteristics in childhood and youth of historically eminent men and women who lived between the years 1450 to 1850. The third, *The Promise of Youth*,[37] was a follow-up study of the original group of gifted children after a period of six years. The fourth, *The Gifted Child Grows Up*,[38] described their status twenty-five years later, and the fifth, *The Gifted Group at Midlife*,[39] thirty-five years later. The sixth was "The Fulfillment of Promise: Forty-Year Follow-Up of the Terman Gifted Group,[40] the seventh, "Sources of Life Satisfaction of the Terman Gifted Men,"[41] and the eighth, "Career and Life Satisfaction Among Terman's Gifted Women in *The Gifted and the Creative: Fifty-Year Perspective*.[42]

This longitudinal series of studies, spanning more than a half century, enabled the researchers to examine the characteristics of gifted individuals and to follow them from childhood through adulthood, evaluating some of the influences of giftedness upon their development as individuals and as creative contributors to society.

THE *POST HOC* FALLACY

One of the most serious dangers of *ex post facto* research is the *post hoc* fallacy, the conclusion that, because two factors go together, one is the cause and the other the effect. Because there seems to be a high relationship between the number of years of education completed and earned income, many educators have argued that staying in school will add an *x* number of dollars of income over a period of time for each additional year of education completed. Although there may be such a

[36] Catherine M. Cox, *The Early Mental Traits of Three Hundred Geniuses*, Vol. 2 (Stanford, CA.: Stanford University Press, 1926).

[37] Barbara S. Burks, Dorthea W. Jensen, and Lewis M. Terman, *The Promise of Youth*, Vol. 3 (Stanford, CA.: Stanford University Press, 1930).

[38] Lewis M. Terman and Melita H. Oden, *The Gifted Child Grows Up*, Vol. 4 (Stanford, CA.: Stanford University Press, 1947).

[39] Lewis M. Terman and Melita H. Oden, *The Gifted Group at Midlife*, Vol. 5 (Stanford, CA.: Stanford University Press, 1959).

[40] Melita H. Oden, "The Fulfillment of Promise: Forty-Year Follow-Up of the Terman Gifted Group," *Genetic Psychology Monographs* 7 (1968): 3–93.

[41] Robert R. Sears, "Sources of Life Satisfaction of the Terman Gifted Men," *American Psychologist* 32 (1977): 119–128.

[42] Pauline S. Sears and Ann H. Barbee, "Career and Life Satisfaction Among Terman's Gifted Women" in *The Gifted and the Creative: Fifty-Year Perspective* (Baltimore: Johns Hopkins University Press, 1978).

relationship, it is also likely that some of the factors that influence young people to seek additional education are more important than the educational level completed. Such factors as socioeconomic status, persistence, desire, willingness to postpone immediate gratification, and intelligence level are undoubtedly significant factors in vocational success. Staying in school may be a symptom rather than the prevailing cause.

Some critics of cigarette-cancer research have advanced a similar argument. The case that they propose follows this line of reason: Let us suppose that certain individuals with a type of glandular imbalance have a tendency toward cancer. The imbalance could induce a certain amount of nervous tension. Since excessive cigarette smoking is a type of nervous-tension release, these individuals would tend to be heavy smokers. The cancer could result from the glandular imbalance, rather than from the smoking which is a type of symptom. This error of confusing symptoms or merely associated factors with cause could lead researchers to deduce a false cause-and-effect relationship.

This illustration is not presented to discredit this type of cancer research. Substantial evidence does seem to suggest a significant relationship. Laboratory experiments have supported the relationship between the coal-tar products that are distilled from cigarette combustion and malignant growth in animals. The association explanation, however, is one that should always be examined carefully.

Ex post facto research is widely and appropriately used, particularly in the behavioral sciences. In education, since it is impossible, impracticable, or unthinkable to manipulate such variables as aptitude, intelligence, personality traits, cultural deprivation, teacher competence, and some variables that might present an unacceptable threat to human beings, this method will continue to be used.

However, its limitations should be recognized:

1. The independent variables cannot be manipulated.

2. Subjects cannot be randomly assigned to treatment groups.

3. Causes are often multiple rather than single.

It is for these reasons that scientists are reluctant to use the expression *cause and effect* in nonexperimental studies in which the variables have not been carefully manipulated. They prefer to observe that when variable A appears, variable B is consistently associated, possibly for reasons not completely understood or explained.

Since there is a danger of confusing symptoms with causes, *ex post facto* research should test not one, but other logical alternate or competing hypotheses. Properly employed and cautiously interpreted, it will continue to provide a useful methodology for the development of knowledge.

Students who have completed a course in research methods should be sensitive to the operation of extraneous variables that threaten the validity of conclusions. In "Educational Piltdown Men," Gene V Glass[43] cautions educators of the need for critical analysis of reported research. He cites a number of interesting examples of carelessly conducted studies that resulted in completely false conclusions. Unfortunately, these conclusions were accepted by gullible readers and widely reported in popular periodicals and some educational psychology textbooks.

The author trusts that the experience of the introductory course in educational research will help students and educators to read research reports more carefully and to apply more rigorous standards of judgment.

SUMMARY

The term *descriptive studies* has been used to classify a number of different types of activity. This chapter points out the distinctions between three major categories: assessment, evaluation, and descriptive research.

Assessment describes the status of a phenomenon at a particular time *without* value judgment, explanation of reasons or underlying causes, or recommendations for action.

Evaluation adds to the description of status the element of value judgment, in terms of effectiveness, desirability, or social utility, and may suggest a course of action. No generalizations are extended beyond the situation evaluated.

Descriptive research is concerned with the analysis of the relationships between nonmanipulated variables and the development of generalizations, extending its conclusions beyond the sample observed.

Assessment types of studies described are surveys, public opinion polls, the *National Assessment of Educational Progress,* the *International Assessment of Educational Achievement,* activity analysis, and trend studies.

Evaluation studies included are school surveys and follow-up studies. The application of evaluation findings to social problem solving is discussed.

Descriptive research studies include document or content analysis, case studies, community studies, ethnographic studies, and *ex post facto* or explanatory observational studies. These methods have been de-

[43] Gene V Glass, "Educational Piltdown Men," *Phi Delta Kappan* 50 (Nov. 1968): 148–151.

scribed and examples provided. The hazards of the *post hoc* fallacy have been emphasized.

EXERCISES

1. Why is it sometimes difficult to distinguish between an assessment study, an evaluation study, and a descriptive research project? Illustrate with an example.
2. Public opinion polls base their conclusions on a sample of approximately 1500 respondents. Is this an adequate sample for a nationwide survey?
3. In a 1974 study, the West Virginia State Department of Education reported that counties with the highest per-pupil expenditure were the counties with the highest level of academic achievement, and that this "shows for the first time the clearest possible relationship between student achievement and the amount of money invested in the public schools." Can you suggest several competing hypotheses that might account for high academic achievement?
4. What is the difference between a study and a research project?
5. In what ways do conducting longitudinal studies run the risk of the violation of confidentiality of personal information?
6. How can a study of money and investment trends help you provide for your future financial security?
7. Draw up a proposal for a follow-up study of your high school graduating class of five years ago. Indicate what information you believe would be helpful in improving the curriculum of the school.
8. Of what value are the findings of the annual Gallup poll of public attitudes toward education?
9. How could the survey type of study be helpful in arriving at solutions to the crime problem in large cities?

BIBLIOGRAPHY

AHMANN, J. STANLEY ET AL. "Science Achievement: The Trend Is Down." *Science Teacher* 42 (Sept. 1975): 23–25.

ANDERSON, C. ARNOLD. "The International Comparative Study of Achievement in Mathematics." *Comparative Education Review* 11 (June 1967): 182–196.

BACKSTROM, CHARLES H. and GERALD D. HURSH. *Survey Research.* Evanston, IL.: Northwestern University Press, 1963.

BRANSCOMBE, ART. "Checkout on Consumer Mathematics." *American Education* 11 (Oct. 1975): 21–24.

BURSTEIN, LEIGH. "Secondary Analysis: An Important Resource for Educational Research and Evaluation." *Educational Researcher* (May 1978): 9–12.

CHALL, JEANNE. *Learning to Read: The Great Debate.* New York: McGraw-Hill Book Co., 1967.

COLEMAN, JAMES S. ET AL. *Equality of Educational Opportunity.* Washington, D.C.: U.S. Office of Education, Government Printing Office, 1966.

COLEMAN, JAMES S. "International Assessment for Evaluation of Schools." *Review of Educational Research* 45 (Summer 1975): 355–386.

COLEMAN, JAMES S. "Racial Segregation in the Schools: New Research With New Policy Implications." *Phi Delta Kappan* 57 (Oct. 1975): 75–77.

COLEMAN, JAMES S. "Social Research and Advocacy: A Response to Young and Bress." *Phi Delta Kappan* 57 (Nov. 1975): 66–69.

COMBS, JANET and WILLIAM W. COOLEY. "Dropouts: In High School and after School." *American Educational Research Journal* 5 (May 1968): 343–363.

COOLEY, WILLIAM W. "Explanatory Observational Studies." *Educational Researcher* 7 (Oct. 1978): 9–15.

COOLEY, WILLIAM and PAUL R. LOHNES. *Evaluation Research in Education.* New York: Irvington Publishers, 1976.

COPPERMAN, PAUL. "The Achievement Decline of the 1970s." *Phi Delta Kappan* 60 (June 1979): 736–739.

DILLON, HAROLD J. *Early School Leavers.* New York: National Child Labor Committee, 1949.

ENNIS, ROBERT H. "On Causality." *Educational Researcher* 2 (June 1973): 4–16.

FLANNIGAN, JOHN C. *The American High School Student.* Pittsburgh: Project Talent Office, 1964.

GLASS, GENE V "Educational Piltdown Men." *Phi Delta Kappan* (Nov. 1968): 148–151.

GLASS, GENE V and BLAINE R. WORTHEN. "Educational Evaluation and Research: Similarities and Differences." *Curriculum Theory Network* (Fall 1971).

GLASS, GENE V and BLAINE R. WORTHEN. "Educational Inquiry and the Practice of Education," in *Conceptual Frameworks for Viewing Educational Research: Development, Dissemination and Evaluation,* H. D. Schalock and G. R. Sell, eds. Monmouth, OR.: Oregon College of Education, 1972.

GOLEMAN, DANIEL. "1528 Little Geniuses and How They Grew: Still

Learning From Terman's Children," *Psychology Today* 13:9 (Feb. 1980): 28–53.

GREELEY, ANDREW M. and PETER H. ROSSI. *The Education of Catholic Americans.* Chicago: Aldine Publishing Co., 1966.

HARRIS, DALE B. *Children's Drawings as Measures of Intellectual Maturity.* New York: Harcourt, Brace & World, 1963.

HENDERSON, KENNETH B. and JOHN E. GOERTWITZ. *How to Conduct a Follow-up Study.* Illinois Secondary School Curriculum Program Bulletin No. 11, Springfield, IL.: Superintendent of Public Instruction, 1950.

HESS, ROBERT D. and JUDITH V. TORNEY. *The Development of Political Attitudes in Children.* Chicago: Aldine Publishing Co., 1967.

HIRSCHI, TRAVIS and HANAN C. SELVIN. *Delinquency Research: An Appraisal of Analytical Methods.* New York: Free Press, 1967.

HUSÉN, TORSTEN, ed. *International Study of Achievement in Mathematics.* 2 vols. New York: John Wiley & Sons, 1967.

HUSÉN, TORSTEN. *The School in Question: A Comparative Study of the School and its Future in Western Societies.* New York: Oxford University Press, 1979.

HYMAN, HERBERT H. *Survey Design and Analysis.* Beverly Hills, CA.: Glencoe Press, 1955.

International Association for the Evaluation of Educational Achievement. "Bibliography of Publications, 1962–1974." *Comparative Education Review* 18 (June 1974): 327–329.

JACKSON, GREGG. Reanalysis of Coleman's "Recent Trends in School Integration." *Educational Researcher* (Oct. 1975): 21–25.

JENCKS, CHRISTOPHER ET AL. *Who Gets Ahead? The Determinants of Economic Success in America.* New York: Basic Books, 1979.

LESSER, GERALD S. *Children Learn Lessons from Sesame Street.* New York: Random House, 1974.

MELLON, JOHN C. *National Assessment and the Teaching of English.* Urbana, IL.: National Council of Teachers of English, 1974.

MINTON, J. H. "Impact of Sesame Street on Reading Readiness." *Sociology of Education* 48 (Spring 1975): 141–145.

MOSTELLER, FREDERICK and DANIEL P. MOYNIHAN, eds. *On Equality of Educational Opportunity: Papers Deriving from the Harvard Faculty Seminar on the Coleman Report.* New York: Random House, Vintage Books, 1972.

National Association of Science. *A Capsule Description of Changes in Science Achievement.* Science Report 04500. Washington, D.C.: Government Printing Office, 1975.

NEUWEIN, REGINALD A., ed. *Catholic Schools in Action: The Notre Dame Study of Catholic Elementary and Secondary Schools in the United States.* Notre Dame, IN.: University of Notre Dame Press, 1966.

OVERHOLT, GEORGE E. and WILLIAM M. STALLINGS. "Ethnographic and Experimental Hypotheses in Educational Research." *Educational Researcher* (May 1977): 12–14.

PIAGET, JEAN. *Biology and Knowledge.* Chicago: University of Chicago Press, 1971.

POLSKY, RICHARD M. *Getting to Sesame Street.* New York: Praeger, 1974.

POPHAM, W. JAMES. *Educational Evaluation.* Englewood Cliffs, N.J.: Prentice-Hall, 1975.

Problems and Outlook of Small Private Liberal Arts Colleges: Report to the Congress of the United States. Washington, D.C.: U.S. General Accounting Office, 1978.

RAPH, JANE B., MERIAM L. GOLDBERG, and A. HARRY PASSOW. *Bright Underachievers: Studies of Scholastic Underachievement among Intellectually Superior High School Students.* New York: Teachers College Press, 1966.

ROGERS, JANET M. "A Summary of Literature on Sesame Street." *Journal of Special Education* 6 (Spring 1972): 270–272.

RYANS, DAVID G. *Characteristics of Teachers: Their Description, Comparison, and Appraisal.* Washington, D.C.: American Council on Education, 1966.

ST. JOHN, NANCY. *School Desegregation: Outcomes for Children.* New York: John Wiley & Sons, 1975.

SCOTT, W. RICHARD. "Field Methods in the Study of Organizations," in *Handbook of Organizations,* James G. March, ed. Chicago: Rand McNally & Co., 1965, pp. 261–304.

STAKE, ROBERT E. "The Case Method in Social Inquiry," *Educational Researcher* (Feb 1978): 5–8.

STRACHEY, JAMES, ed. and trans. *The Complete Psychological Works of Sigmund Freud.* Volume XVII. London: Hogarth Press, 1964.

WILSON, STEPHEN. "The Use of Ethnographic Techniques in Educational Research." *Review of Educational Research* 47 (Spring 1977): 245–265.

WORTHEN, BLAINE R. and JAMES R. SANDERS. *Educational Evaluation: Theory and Practice.* Worthington, OH.: Charles A. Jones Publishing Co., 1973.

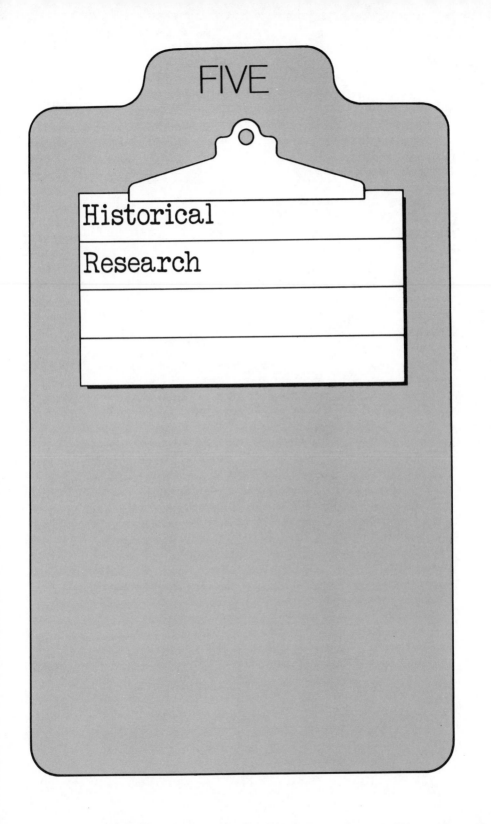

FIVE

Historical

Research

History is a meaningful record of human achievement. It is not merely a list of chronological events, but a truthful integrated account of the relationships between persons, events, times, and places. We use history to understand the past, and to try to understand the present in light of past events and developments. Historical analysis may be directed toward an individual, an idea, a movement, or an institution. However, none of these objects of historical observation can be considered in isolation. People cannot be subjected to historical investigation without some consideration of their interaction with the ideas, movements, or institutions of their times. The focus merely determines the points of emphasis toward which historians direct their attention.

Table 5-1 illustrates several such historical interrelationships, taken from the history of education. For example, no matter whether the historian chooses for study the Jesuit Society, religious teaching orders, the Counter-Reformation, or Ignatius of Loyola, each of the other elements appears as a prominent influence or result and as an indispensable part of the account.

THE HISTORY OF AMERICAN EDUCATION

Historical studies deal with almost every aspect of American education. Such investigations have pointed out the important contributions of both educators and statesmen. They have examined the growth and development of colleges and universities, elementary and secondary schools, educational organizations and associations, the rise and decline of educational movements, the introduction of new teaching methods, and the issues that have persistently confronted American education.

An understanding of the history of education is important to professional workers in this field. It helps them to understand the *how* and the *why* of educational movements that have appeared and, in some cases, continue to prevail in the schools. It helps them to evaluate not only lasting contributions, but also the fads and "bandwagon" schemes that have appeared on the educational scene only to be discarded.

An examination of many developments of the past seems to confirm the observation that there is little in education that is really new. Practices hailed as innovative are often old ideas that have previously been tried

TABLE 5-1 Some Examples of the Historical Interrelationship between Men, Movements, and Institutions

Men	Movements	General Type	Institutions Name
Ignatius of Loyola	Counter-Reformation	Religious Teaching Order	Society of Jesus, 1534 (Jesuit Society)
Benjamin Franklin	Scientific Movement Education for Life	Academy	Philadelphia Academy, 1751
Daniel Coit Gilman G. Stanley Hall Wm. Rainey Harper	Graduate Study and Research	University Graduate School	Johns Hopkins University, 1876 Clark University, 1887 University of Chicago, 1892
John Dewey	Experimentalism Progressive Education	Experimental School	University of Chicago Elementary School, 1896
W. E. B. Dubois Walter White	Racial Integration in the Public Schools	Persuasion Organization	National Assn. for the Advancement of Colored People, 1909
B. R. Buckingham	Scientific Research in Education	Research Periodical, Research Organization	Journal of Ed. Research, 1920 American Educational Research Assn., 1931

and replaced by something new. Innovators should examine the reasons why such practices were discarded and consider whether their own proposals are likely to prove more successful. Several studies, briefly described, illustrate the historical background of some contemporary educational movements and issues.

Organized programs of individualized instruction introduced in a number of school systems in the 1960s seem to be similar in many respects to those introduced in a number of schools in the 1890s and in the first quarter of the twentieth century. First introduced at Pueblo, Colorado, and known as the Pueblo Plan, later modified and known as the Winnetka and Dalton Plans, these programs do seem to have common elements. Dispensing with group class activity in academic courses, students were given units of work to complete at their own rate before proceeding to more advanced units. Individual progress, based upon mastery of subject matter units, was the criterion for promotion or completion of a course. Preston W. Search[1] advocated this plan, and his influence upon Carleton Washburn in the elementary schools of Winnetka, Illinois, and Helen Parkhurst in the secondary schools at Dalton, Massachusetts, is generally recognized. Whether the Pueblo, Winnetka, or Dalton plans were fads or sound programs, the fact remains that they disappeared from the schools before reappearing in the 1960s.

The place of religion in public education is an issue that concerns many people. In the period following World War II, in a series of Supreme Court decisions, religious instruction and religious exercises within the schools have been declared unconstitutional and in violation of the First Amendment of the United States Constitution. In 1963, in the case of *School District of Abington Township, Pennsylvania, v. Schempp,* the Court held that a Pennsylvania law requiring daily Bible reading was in violation of the First Amendment. Much resentment and criticism of the Supreme Court followed this decision and several efforts have been made to introduce amendments to the Constitution to permit religious exercises in the public schools.

The Bible reading issue was a bitter one more than 100 years ago. The "Philadelphia Bible Riots of 1840,"[2] resulted in the deaths of about 45 soldiers and civilians, serious injury to about 140, and property damage to homes and churches valued at nearly $500,000. Nativist–foreign-born, and Catholic-Protestant conflicts produced the tense atmosphere,

---

[1] Preston W. Search, *An Ideal School: Looking Forward* (New York: Appleton-Century-Crofts, 1901).

[2] Vincent L. Lannie and Bernard C. Diethorn, "For the Honor and Glory of God: The Philadelphia Bible Riots of 1840," *History of Education Quarterly* 8 (Spring 1968) pp.: 44–106.

but the Bible reading issue precipitated the riots. It is apparent that Bible reading is not an issue of recent origin, and that an understanding of previous conflicts places the issue in clearer perspective.

The contributions of Thomas Jefferson, Benjamin Franklin, Calvin Stowe, Horace Mann, Henry Barnard, William Holmes McGuffey, Daniel Coit Gilman, John Dewey, and many other eminent educators have been carefully examined in many studies and their impact on American education noted.

Richard E. Thursfield[3] studied Henry Barnard's *American Journal of Education*, published in 31 massive volumes between 1855 and 1881. He points out the *Journal's* vital contribution to the development of American education. Through its comprehensive treatment of all aspects of education it provided a readily available medium for the presentation and exchange of ideas of many of the great educators of the period. It has been stated that almost every educational reform adopted in the last half of the nineteenth century was largely due to the influence of the *Journal*. Among its contributors were Henry Barnard, Horace Mann, Bronson Alcott, Daniel Coit Gilman, William T. Harris, Calvin Stowe, and Herbert Spencer, in addition to many prominent foreign contributors.

Lawrence Cremin[4] examined the reasons for the rise and decline of the Progressive Education movement, including the major changes in philosophy and practices that transformed American education and the forces that brought the movement to a halt in the 1950s. Although some historians differ with some of his conclusions, Cremin's analysis is the definitive history of Progressive Education in America.

These historical studies are but a few of the thousands of books, monographs, and periodical articles that depict the story of American education. In addition to examining these works, students are urged to consult the *History of Education Quarterly*, in which scholarly book reviews and critical analyses of contemporary historical research are presented.

HISTORY AND SCIENCE

There is some difference of opinion on the question of whether or not the activities of the historian can be considered scientific or whether there is such a thing as historical research.

[3] Richard E. Thursfield, *Henry Barnard's American Journal of Education* (Baltimore: Johns Hopkins Press, 1945).

[4] Lawrence Cremin, *The Transformation of the School: Progressivism in American Education* (New York: Alfred A. Knopf, 1961).

Those who take the negative position may point out the following limitations:

1. Although the purpose of science is prediction, the historian cannot always generalize on the basis of past events. Because past events were often unplanned or didn't develop as planned, because there were so many uncontrolled factors, and because the influence of one or a few individuals was so crucial, the same pattern of factors is never repeated.

2. The historian must depend upon the reported observations of others, often witnesses of doubtful competence and sometimes of doubtful objectivity.

3. The historian is much like a person trying to complete a complicated jig-saw puzzle with many of the parts missing. On the basis of what is often incomplete evidence, he must fill in the gaps by inferring what has happened and why it happened.

4. History does not operate in a closed system such as may be created in the physical science laboratory. The historian cannot control the conditions of observation nor manipulate the significant variables.

Those who contend that historical investigation may have the characteristics of scientific research activity present these arguments:

1. The historian delimits a problem, formulates hypotheses or raises questions to be answered, gathers and analyzes primary data, tests the hypotheses as consistent or inconsistent with the evidence, and formulates generalizations or conclusions.

2. Although the historian may not have witnessed an event or gathered data directly, he may have the testimony of a number of witnesses who have observed the event from different vantage points. It is possible that subsequent events have provided additional information not available to contemporary observers. The historian rigorously subjects the evidence to critical analysis in order to establish its authenticity, truthfulness, and accuracy.

3. In reaching conclusions, the historian employs principles of probability similar to those used by physical scientists.

4. Although it is true that the historian cannot control the variables directly, this limitation also characterizes most behavioral research, particularly nonlaboratory investigations in sociology, social psychology, and economics.

5. The observations of historians are usually described in *qualitative,* rather than *quantitative,* terms. This absence of quantitative measurement does not preclude the application of scientific methodology in the historian's activities, for the application of both quantitative and qualitative description are appropriately employed in scientific investigations.

Historical Generalization

There is some difference of opinion, even among historians, as to whether or not historical investigations can establish generalizations. Most historians would agree that some generalizations are possible, but they disagree on the validity of applying them to different times and places. Louis Gottschalk states the case of the comparative historian in this way:

> Sooner or later one or more investigators of a period or area begin to suspect some kind of nexus within the matter of their historical investigation. Though such "hunches," "insights," "guesses," "hypotheses"— whatever you may call them—may be rejected out of hand by some of them, the bolder or rasher among them venture to examine the possibility of objective reality of such a nexus, and then it is likely to become a subject of debate, and perhaps of eventual refinement to the point of wide recognition in the learned world. The process is not very different from the way analytical scholars in other fields proceed—Darwin, for example, or Freud. If this process serves no other purpose, it at least may furnish propositions upon which to focus future investigations and debates. . . .
>   But do not these historical syntheses, no matter what their author's intention, invariably have a wider applicability than to any single set of data from which they rose? If Weber was right, isn't it implicit in this concept of the Protestant ethic that where a certain kind of religious attitude prevails, there the spirit of capitalism will, or at least may, flourish? . . . If Mahan was right, couldn't victory in war (at least before the invention of the airplane) be regarded as dependent on maritime control? If Turner was right, won't his frontier thesis apply to some extent to all societies that have frontiers to conquer in the future, as well as it has applied to American society in the past?[5]

M. I. Finley comments on generalization:

> Ultimately the question at issue is the nature of the historian's function. Is it only to recapture the individual, concrete events of a past age, as

[5] Louis Gottschalk, "Categories of Historical Generalization," in *Generalization in the Writing of History,* Louis Gottschalk, ed. (Chicago: University of Chicago Press, 1963), pp. 121–122.

in a mirror, so that the progress of history is merely one of rediscovering lost data and of building bigger and better reflectors? If so, then the chronicle is the only correct form for his work. But if it is to understand— however one chooses to define the word—then it is to generalize, for every explanation is, or implies, one or more generalizations.[6]

William O. Aydelotte states the argument for generalization:

Certainly the impossibility of final proof of any historical generalization must be at once conceded. Our knowledge of the past is both too limited and too extensive. Only a minute fraction of what has happened has been recorded, and only too often the points on which we need most information are those on which our sources are most inadequate. On the other hand, the fragmentary and incomplete information we do have about the past is too abundant to prevent our coming to terms with it; its sheer bulk prevents its being easily manipulated, or even easily assimilated, for histori- cal purposes. Further, historians deal with complex problems, and the pattern of the events they study, even supposing it to exist, seems too intricate to be easily grasped. Doubtless, finality of knowledge is impossible in all areas of study. We have learned through works of popularization how far this holds true even for the natural sciences, and, as Crane Brinton says, the historian no longer needs to feel that "the uncertainties and inaccuracies of his investigation leave him in a position of hopeless inferior- ity before the glorious certainties of physical science."[7]

The foregoing quotations are presented in support of the position that the activities of the historian are not different from those of the scientist. Historical research, as defined in this chapter, includes the delimitation of a problem, formulating hypotheses or generalizations to be tested or questions to be answered, gathering and analyzing data, and arriving at probability-type conclusions or at generalizations based upon deductive-inductive reasoning.

The Historical Hypothesis

Allan Nevins[8] illustrates the use of hypotheses in the historical re- search of Edward Channing in answering the question: Why did the Confederacy collapse in April 1865? Channing formulated four hypothe- ses and tested each one in the light of the evidence gathered from letters,

[6] M. I. Finley, "Generalizations in Ancient History," in *Generalization in the Writing of History*, Louis Gottschalk, ed. (Chicago: University of Chicago Press, 1963), p. 34.

[7] William O. Aydelotte, "Notes on the Problem of Historical Generalization," in *Generalization in the Writing of History*, Louis Gottschalk, ed. (Chicago: University of Chicago Press, 1963), pp. 156–157.

[8] Allan Nevins, *The Gateway to History*, Copyright © 1962, by D. C. Heath and Company, Lexington, Mass. (Boston: Raytheon Education Co., 1962), pp. 238–242.

diaries, and official records of the army and the government of the Confederacy. He hypothesized that the Confederacy collapsed because of:

1. The military defeat of the Confederate army

2. The dearth of military supplies

3. The starving condition of the Confederate soldiers and the people

4. The disintegration of the will to continue the war

Channing produced evidence that seemed to refute the first three hypotheses. More than 200,000 well-equipped soldiers were under arms at the time of the surrender, the effective production of powder and arms provided sufficient military supplies to continue the war, and enough food was available to sustain fighting men and civilians.

Channing concluded that hypothesis number 4, *the collapse of morale and the will to fight,* was substantiated by the excessive number of desertions of enlisted men and officers. Confederate military officials testified that they had intercepted many letters from home urging the soldiers to desert. Although the hypothesis sustained was not specific enough to be particularly helpful, the rejection of the first three did claim to dispose of some commonly held explanations. This example illustrates a historical study in which hypotheses were explicitly stated.

Hypotheses in Educational Historical Research   Hypotheses may be formulated in historical investigations of education. Several examples are listed.

1. The educational innovations of the 1950s and 1960s were based upon practices that previously have been tried and discarded.

2. Christian countries whose educational systems required religious instruction have had lower church attendance rates than those countries in which religious instruction was not provided in the schools.

3. The observation of European school systems by American educators during the nineteenth century had an important effect upon American educational practices.

4. The monitorial system had no significant effect upon American education.

Although hypotheses are not always *explicitly* stated in historical investigations, they are usually implied. The historian gathers evidence and carefully evaluates its trustworthiness. If the evidence is compatible with the consequences of the hypothesis, it is confirmed. If the evidence is not compatible, or negative, the hypothesis is not confirmed. It is through such synthesis that historical generalizations are established.

The activities of the historian, when education is his or her field of inquiry, are no different from those employed in any other field. The sources of evidence may be concerned with schools, educational practices and policies, movements, or individuals, but the historical processes are the same.

Difficulties Encountered in Historical Research

The problems involved in the process of historical research make it a somewhat difficult task. A major difficulty is delimiting the problem so that a satisfactory analysis is possible. Too often, beginners state a problem much too broadly; the experienced historian realizes that historical research must be confined to a penetrating analysis of a limited problem, rather than involve only a superficial examination of a broad area. The weapon of research is the rifle, not the shotgun.

Since historians may not have lived during the time they are studying and may be removed from the events that they investigate, they must often depend upon inference and logical analysis, using the recorded experience of others, rather than upon direct observation. To ensure that their information is as trustworthy as possible, they must rely on primary, or first-hand, accounts. Finding appropriate primary sources of data requires imagination, hard work, and resourcefulness.

SOURCES OF DATA

Historical data are usually classified into two main categories:

1. *Primary sources* are eyewitness accounts. They are reported by an actual observer or participant in an event.

2. *Secondary sources* are accounts of an event that were not actually witnessed by the reporter. He or she may have talked with an actual observer or read an account by an observer, but his or her testimony is not that of an actual participant or observer. Secondary sources may sometimes be used, but because of the distortion in passing on information, the historian uses them only when primary data are not available.

Primary Sources of Data

Documents, or the records kept and written by actual participants in, or witnesses of, an event. These sources are produced for the purpose of transmitting information to be used in the future. Documents classified as primary sources are constitutions, charters, laws, court decisions, official minutes or records, autobiographies, letters, diaries, genealogies, contracts, deeds, wills, permits, licenses, affidavits, depositions, declarations, proclamations, certificates, lists, handbills, bills, receipts, newspaper and magazine accounts, advertisements, maps, diagrams, books, pamphlets, catalogs, films, pictures, paintings, inscriptions, recordings, transcriptions, and research reports.

Remains or relics associated with a person, group, or period. Fossils, skeletons, tools, weapons, food, utensils, clothing, buildings, furniture, pictures, paintings, coins, and art objects are examples of those relics and remains that were not deliberately intended for use in transmitting information or as records. However, these sources may provide clear evidence about the past. The contents of an ancient burial place, for instance, may reveal a great deal of information about the way of life of a people—their food, clothing, tools, weapons, art, religious beliefs, means of livelihood, and customs.

Oral testimony, or the spoken account of a witness of, or participant in, an event. This evidence is obtained in a personal interview and may be recorded or transcribed as the witness relates his or her experiences.

Primary Sources of Educational Data   Many old materials provide primary evidence that may be useful in studying the history of education. Although it would be impossible to list all the types of historical evidence, a number are listed.

Official records and other documentary materials.   Included in this category are records and reports of legislative bodies and state departments of public instruction, city superintendents, principals, presidents, deans, department heads, educational committees, minutes of school boards and boards of trustees, surveys, charters, deeds, wills, professional and lay periodicals, school newspapers, annuals, bulletins, catalogs, courses of study, curriculum guides, athletic game records, programs (for graduation, dramatic, musical, and athletic events), licenses, certificates, textbooks, examinations, report cards, pictures, drawings, maps, letters, diaries, autobiographies, teacher and pupil personnel files, samples of student work, and recordings.

Oral testimony.   Included here are interviews with administrators, teachers and other school employees, students and relatives, school patrons or lay citizens, and members of governing bodies.

Relics.   Included in this category are buildings, furniture, teaching materials, equipment, murals, decorative pictures, textbooks, examinations, and samples of student work.

Secondary Sources of Data

Secondary sources are the reports of a person who relates the testimony of an actual witness of, or participant in, an event. The writer of the secondary source was not on the scene of the event, but merely reports what the person who *was* there said or wrote. Secondary sources of data are usually of limited worth for research purposes because of the errors that may result when information is passed on from one person to another. Most history textbooks and encyclopedias are examples of secondary sources, for they are often several times removed from the original, first-hand account of events.

Some types of material may be secondary sources for some purposes and primary sources for another. For example, a high school textbook in American history is ordinarily a secondary source. But if one were making a study of the changing emphasis on nationalism in high school American history textbooks, the book would be a primary document or source of data.

HISTORICAL CRITICISM

It has been noted that the historian does not often use the method of direct observation. Past events cannot be repeated at will. Since he or she must get much of the data from the reports of those who witnessed or participated in these events, the data must be subjected to careful analysis to sift the true from the false, irrelevant, or misleading.

Trustworthy, usable data in historical research are known as *historical evidence.* It is that body of validated facts and information that can be accepted as trustworthy, as a proper basis for the testing and interpretation of a hypothesis. Historical evidence is derived from historical data by the process of criticism, which is of two types: *external* and *internal.*

External Criticism

External criticism establishes the authenticity or genuineness of data. Is the relic or document a true one rather than a forgery, a counterfeit, or a hoax? Various tests of genuineness may be employed.

The problem of establishing age or authorship of documents may involve intricate tests of signature, handwriting, script, type, spelling, language usage, documentation, knowledge available at the time, and consistency with what is known. It may involve physical and chemical tests of ink, paint, paper, parchment, cloth, stone, metals, or wood. Are these elements consistent with known facts about the person, the knowledge available, and the technology of the period in which the remain or the document originated?

Internal Criticism

After the authenticity of historical documents or relics have been established, there is still the problem of evaluating their accuracy or worth. Although they may be genuine, do they reveal a true picture? What of the writers or creators? Were they competent, honest, unbiased, and actually acquainted with the facts, or were they too antagonistic or too sympathetic to give a true picture? Did they have any motives for distorting the account? Were they subject to pressure, fear, or vanity? How long after the event did they make a record of their testimony, and were they able to remember accurately what happened? Were they in agreement with other competent witnesses?

These questions are often difficult to answer, but the historian must be sure that the data are authentic and accurate. Only then may he or she introduce them as historical evidence, worthy of serious consideration. The following examples illustrate how the processes of historial criticism were used to expose a hoax and to establish the authenticity of an important historical discovery.

The Cardiff Giant An amazing series of events concerning the authenticity of a historical remain is related in "The Real Story of the Cardiff Giant," by Alan Hynd.[9] The Cardiff Giant was a 10′ 4½″ figure of a man, weighing about 3000 pounds, found in 1869, buried three feet beneath the surface of a farmer's field, near Cardiff, New York, about 13 miles south of Syracuse.

The huge figure was examined by two scientists from Yale University, who pronounced it a fossilized human figure. A delegation of archaeologists from the New York State Museum were of the opinion that the figure was an ancient statue. Ralph Waldo Emerson called it a bona fide petrified human being, while Dr. Oliver Wendell Holmes, the celebrated Harvard anatomist and father of the great jurist, declared that it was a statue of great antiquity. Scores of clergymen who came to see it enthusiastically claimed that the figure was a fossilized man of biblical times, proving the story of Genesis to be literally true.

The local owners turned down an offer by P. T. Barnum to buy the figure, whereupon Barnum commissioned a sculptor to make an exact replica of the Giant, which he later exhibited in his museum on Broadway in New York City, advertising it as the one, the only, the

[9] Alan Hynd, "The Real Story of the Cardiff Giant," originally published in *True, The Man's Magazine*, later anthologized in *Grand Deception*, Alexander Klein, ed. (Philadelphia: J. B. Lippincott Co., 1955), 126–135. Used here with permission of Fawcett Publications.

original Cardiff Giant. When the Cardiff owners sought an injunction against Barnum, the judge denied it, saying that the original was only a fake.

An unknown newspaper reporter, prompted by the growing feeling that the giant was a hoax, traced the shipment of a huge box labeled "machinery" to the farm near Cardiff, nearly a year before the Giant's discovery. Carefully tracing back detail upon detail, he discovered that a Mr. Hull had acquired a huge block of gypsum at Ft. Dodge, Iowa, and had shipped a box labeled "machinery," weighing exactly what the block of gypsum had weighed, to Chicago. From hotel, railroad, and drayage company records, he traced the shipment to a barn in the 900 block of North Clark Street in Chicago. The owner of the barn confessed his part in the scheme and implicated Hull, a stonecutter and an artist, who had fashioned the figure.

It was revealed that Hull, while visiting his sister in Ft. Dodge, Iowa, had gone to hear an evangelist who, while preaching about the sixth chapter of Genesis, had described in some detail and with much enthusiasm the "giants in the earth" mentioned there. Seeing a chance to make some easy money, Hull planned to have one of these giants fabricated, aged with sulphuric acid, secretly planted in the ground on his cousin's New York farm, and accidentally discovered by some well-diggers, ostensibly hired to dig a new well.

The rest was easy. Hull made no claims. The clergymen and the experts made the claims for him, and the controversy between them only added to the fame (and money-drawing power) of his stone figure.

Although this story does not actually illustrate scholarly research, the activities of the reporter represent a simple example of external criticism, for by following his hunch or hypothesis that the figure was recently manmade and not an ancient statue or a fossilized man, he tracked down and exposed the facts. This is quite remarkable in the light of the fact that prominent archaeologists, anatomists, and scholars had been completely fooled by the hoax.

The following example describes historical criticism of a more scholarly type, carried on by scientists and biblical scholars, in which historic documents were proven to be genuine.

The Dead Sea Scrolls   One of the most interesting and significant historical discoveries of the past century was the finding of the Dead Sea Scrolls. This collection of ancient manuscripts was discovered in 1947 by a group of Bedouins of the Ta'amere tribe. Five leather scrolls were found, sealed in tall earthenware jars in the Qumran caves near Aim Feshkha, on the northwest shore of the Dead Sea.[10]

[10] A. Powell Davies, *The Meaning of the Dead Sea Scrolls* (New York: New American Library of World Literature, 1956), p. 9. Used with permission of the publisher.

The Bedouins took the scrolls to Metropolitan Mar Athanesius Yeshue Samuel, of St. Mark's monastery in Jerusalem, who purchased them after discovering that they were written in ancient Hebrew. A consultation with biblical scholars confirmed the fact that they were very old and possibly valuable. They were later purchased by Professor Sukenik, an archaeologist of Hebrew University at Jerusalem, who began to translate them. He also had portions of the scrolls photographed to send to other biblical scholars for evaluation. Upon examining some of the photographs, Dr. William F. Albright of Johns Hopkins University pronounced them "the greatest manuscript discovery of modern times."

A systematic search of the Wadi Qumran area caves in 1952 yielded other leather scrolls, many manuscript fragments, and two additional scrolls of copper, so completely oxidized that they could not be unrolled without being destroyed. By 1956, scientists at the University of Manchester, England, had devised a method of passing a spindle through the scrolls, spraying them with aircraft glue, baking them, and then sawing them across their rolled-up length to yield strips which could be photographed.[11]

There has been some question about the origin, the age, and the historic value of the scrolls. By careful and systematic external and internal criticism, however, certain facts have been established and are quite generally accepted by biblical scholars and scientists.

The scrolls are very old, probably dating back to the first century A.D. They are written in ancient Hebrew, and probably originated in a pre-Christian monastery of one of the Jewish sects. The writings contain two versions (one complete and one incomplete) of the Book of Isaiah, a commentary or *Midrash* on the Book of Habakkuk, a set of rules of the ancient Jewish monastery, a collection of about twenty psalms similar to those of the Old Testament, and several scrolls of apocalyptic writings, similar to the Book of Revelation.[12]

The contents of the copper scrolls and other fragments have now been translated. It is possible that more scrolls and writings may be discovered in the area, and it is likely that these ancient documents may throw new light on the Bible and the origins of Christianity.

It is interesting to note how these documents were authenticated, dated, and evaluated by:

1. Paleography, an analysis of the Hebrew alphabet forms used. These written characters were similar to those observed in other documents known to have been written in the first century.

[11] *Ibid.*, p. 18.

[12] *Ibid.*, p. 19.

2. A radiocarbon test of the age of the linen scroll coverings, conducted by the Institute of Nuclear Research at the University of Chicago. All organic matter contains radiocarbon 14, introduced by the interaction of cosmic rays from outer space with the nitrogen in the earth's atmosphere. The radioactivity constantly introduced throughout the life of the specimen ceases at death and disintegrates at a constant known rate. At the time of death, all organic matter yields 15.3 disintegrations per minute per gram of carbon content. The number of disintegrations is reduced by one-half after 5568, plus or minus 30 years. By measuring disintegrations by the use of a Geiger-type counter, it is possible to estimate the age of specimens within reasonable limits of accuracy. By the use of this technique the date of the scrolls was estimated at A.D. 33, plus or minus 200 years.

3. Careful examination of the pottery form in which the scrolls were sealed. These jars, precisely shaped to fit the manuscripts, were the type commonly used during the first century.

4. Examination of coins found in the caves with the scrolls. These dated Roman coins provided convincing evidence of the age of the scrolls.

5. Translation of the scrolls compared to other writings, both biblical and nonbiblical, of known antiquity.

Although external criticism has now produced convincing evidence of the genuineness and age of the Dead Sea Scrolls, internal criticism of their validity and relevance will be pursued by biblical scholars for many years to come, and may provide many new hypotheses concerning biblical writings and the early history of Christianity and the pre-Christian Jewish sects.

Modern approaches to historical research have applied advanced technology, emphasizing the usefulness of both qualitative and quantitative data. The previous study employed the radiocarbon 14 test to verify the authenticity of the scrolls. Another study illustrates the use of the computer in archaeological and historical research.

Stonehenge (Hanging Stones) For centuries a controversy has interested historians and archaeologists concerning the origin and purpose of Stonehenge, a curious arrangement of stones and archways, each weighing more than forty tons, located on the Salisbury Plain, about ninety miles southwest of London. From the beginning of recorded history, writers have speculated about the stones. Their construction and arrangement have been attributed to many tribes and national groups who invaded or inhabited England. Modern radiocarbon dating of a deer antler found in the stone fill seems to place their time of erection at about 1900 to 1600 B.C. Their purpose has been explained in many legends that have developed—a city of the dead, a place of human sacrifice, a temple of the sun, a pagan cathedral, and a Druid ceremonial place.

More recently some scientists and historians have suggested that Stonehenge was a type of astronomical computer calendar used by early Britons who were apparently sophisticated enough to compute the position of the sun and the moon at their various stages. Using an IBM 704 computer, Gerald S. Hawkins, an astronomer at the Smithsonian Astrophysical Observatory at Cambridge, Massachusetts, entered into the computer 240 stone alignments, translated into celestial declinations. Accomplishing in less than a minute a task that would have required more than four months of human calculator activity, the computer compared the alignments with the precise sun/moon extreme positions as of 1500 B.C. and indicated that they matched with amazing accuracy.

Hawkins suggests that the stone arrangements may have been created for several possible reasons: they made a calendar that would be useful for planting crops; they helped to create and maintain priestly power, by enabling the priest to call out the people to see the rise and setting of the midsummer sun and moon over the heel stone and midwinter sunset through the great trilithon; or possibly they served as an intellectual exercise. He concludes:

> In any case, for whatever reasons those Stonehenge builders built as they did, their final completed creation was a marvel. As intricately aligned as an interlocking series of astronomical instruments (which indeed it was) and yet architecturally perfectly simple, in function subtle and elaborate, in appearance stark, imposing, awesome, Stonehenge was a thing of surpassing ingenuity of design, variety of usefulness and grandeur—in concept and construction an eighth wonder of the world.[13]

The account of this interesting historical-archaeological controversy illustrates the use of sophisticated computer technology to test a hypothesis related to the nature of Stonehenge.

WRITING THE HISTORICAL REPORT

No less challenging than research itself is the writing of the report, which calls for creativity in addition to the qualities of imagination and resourcefulness already illustrated. Research reports should be written

[13] Gerald S. Hawkins with John B. White, *Stonehenge Decoded* (Garden City, N.Y.: Doubleday Co., 1965; London Souvenir Press, 1966), pp. 117–118. Used by permission of Doubleday Co., and Souvenir Press.

in a style that is dignified and objective. However, the historian is permitted a little more freedom in reporting. Homer Carey Hockett suggests that "the historian is not condemned to a bald, plain, unattractive style," and that "for the sake of relieving the monotony of statement after statement of bare facts, it is permissible, now and then, to indulge in a bit of color." He concludes, however, by warning that "above all, embellishments must never become a first aim, or be allowed to hide or distort the truth."[14]

An evaluation of graduate students' historical-research projects generally reveals one or more of the following faults:

1. Problem too broadly stated

2. Tendency to use easy-to-find secondary sources of data, rather than sufficient primary sources, which are harder to locate, but usually more trustworthy

3. Inadequate historical criticism of data, due to failure to establish authenticity of sources and trustworthiness of data. For example, there is often a tendency to accept a statement as necessarily true when several observers agree. It is possible that one may have influenced the other, or that all were influenced by the same inaccurate source of information

4. Poor logical analysis resulting from:
   a. Oversimplification—failure to recognize the fact that causes of events are more often multiple and complex than single and simple
   b. Overgeneralization on the basis of insufficient evidence, and false reasoning by analogy, basing conclusions upon superficial similarities of situations
   c. Failure to interpret words and expressions in the light of their accepted meaning in an earlier period
   d. Failure to distinguish between significant facts in a situation and those that are irrelevant or unimportant

5. Expression of personal bias, as revealed by statements lifted out of context for purposes of persuasion, assuming too generous or uncritical an attitude toward a person or idea (or being too unfriendly or critical), excessive admiration for the past (sometimes known as the "old oaken bucket" delusion), or an equally unrealistic admiration for the new or contemporary, assuming that all change represents progress

[14] Homer C. Hockett, *Introduction to Research in American History* (New York: Macmillan Co., 1948), p. 139. Used with permission.

6. Poor reporting in a style that is dull and colorless, too flowery or flippant, too persuasive or of the "soap-box" type, or improper in usage.

It is apparent that historical research is difficult and demanding. The gathering of historical evidence requires long hours of careful examination of such documents as court records, records of legislative bodies, letters, diaries, official minutes of organizations, or other primary sources of data. Historical research may involve traveling to distant places to examine the necessary documents or relics. In fact, any significant historical study would make demands that few students have the time, the financial resources, the patience, or the expertise to meet. For these reasons, good historical studies are not often attempted for the purpose of meeting academic degree requirements.

SUMMARY

History, the meaningful record of human achievement, helps us to understand the present and, to some extent, to predict the future. Historical research is the application of scientific method to the description and analysis of past events.

Historians ordinarily draw their data from the observations and experiences of others. Since they are not likely to have been at the scene of the event, they must use logical inferences to supplement what is probably an incomplete account.

Primary sources may be "unconscious" testimony, not intended to be left as a record—relics or remains such as bones, fossils, clothing, food, utensils, weapons, coins, and art objects are useful. Conscious testimony, in the form of records or documents, is another primary source of information—examples are constitutions, laws court decisions, official minutes, autobiographies, letters, contracts, wills, certificates, newspaper and magazine accounts, films, recordings, and research reports.

Historical criticism is the evaluation of primary data. External criticism is concerned with the authenticity or genuineness of remains or documents. Internal criticism is concerned with the trustworthiness or relevance of materials. The story of the Cardiff Giant and the accounts of the Dead Sea Scrolls and Stonehenge illustrate the processes of historical criticism.

The historical research studies of graduate students often reveal serious limitations. Frequently encountered are such faults as stating the problem too broadly, inadequate primary sources of data, unskillful historical criticism, poor logical analysis of data, personal bias, and ineffective reporting.

EXERCISES

1. Write a proposal for a historical study in a local setting. You may select a community, a school, a church, a religious or ethnic group, or an individual.

   State an appropriate title, present your hypothesis, indicate the primary sources of data that you would search, and indicate how you would evaluate the authenticity and validity of your data.
2. Select a master's thesis of the historical type from the university library and analyze it in terms of:
   a. hypothesis proposed or questions raised
   b. primary and secondary sources of data used
   c. external and internal criticism employed
   d. logical analysis of data relationships
   e. soundness of conclusions
   f. documentation.

BIBLIOGRAPHY

BARZUN, JACQUES, and HENRY F. GRAFF. *The Modern Researcher.* 2nd ed. New York: Harcourt Brace Jovanovich, 1977.

BILLINGTON, RAY A. *Allan Nevins on History.* New York: Charles Scribner's Sons, 1975.

BRICKMAN, WILLIAM W. *Guide to Research in Educational History.* New York: New York University Bookstore, 1949.

CARR, EDWARD H. *What Is History?* New York: Alfred A. Knopf, 1962.

CREMIN, LAWRENCE. *The Transformation of the School: Progressivism in American Education.* New York: Alfred A. Knopf, 1961.

EDGERTON, HAROLD E. "Stonehenge: New Light on an Old Riddle." *National Geographic,* 117 (June 1960): 846–866.

GARRAGHAN, GILBERT J. *A Guide to Historical Method.* New York: Fordham University Press, 1946.

GOTTSCHALK, LOUIS R. *Understanding History.* New York: Alfred A. Knopf, 1950.

GOTTSCHALK, LOUIS R., ed. *Generalization in the Writing of History. Report of the Committee on Historical Analysis of the Social Science Research Council.* Chicago: University of Chicago Press, 1963.

HAWKINS, GERALD S. with JOHN B. WHITE. *Stonehenge Decoded.* Garden City, N.Y.: Doubleday & Co., 1965.

HOCKETT, HOMER CAREY. *Introduction to Research in American History.* New York: Macmillan Co., 1948.

HOCKETT, HOMER CAREY. *The Critical Method in Historical Research and Writing.* New York: Macmillan Co., 1955.

KLEIN, ALEXANDER, ed. *Grand Deception.* Philadelphia: J. B. Lippincott Co., 1955.

LANNIE, VINCENT L. and BERNARD C. DIETHORN. "For the Honor and Glory of God: The Philadelphia Bible Riots of 1840." *History of Education Quarterly* 8 (Spring 1968): 44–106.

MOEHLMAN, ARTHUR ET AL. *A Guide to Computer Assisted Historical Research in American Education.* Austin: The Center for the History of Education, University of Texas, 1969.

NEVINS, ALLAN. *The Gateway to History.* Rev. ed. Boston: Raytheon Education Co., 1962.

NORDIN, VIRGINIA D. and WILLIAM LLOYD TURNER, "More Than Segregation Academies: The Growing Protestant Fundamentalist Schools," *Phi Delta Kappan* 61 (Feb. 1980): 391–394.

PETERSON, CLARENCE S. *America's Rune Stone.* New York: Hobson Book Press, 1946.

SEARCH, PRESTON W. *An Ideal School: Looking Forward.* New York: Appleton-Century-Crofts, 1901.

STEBBINS, CATHERINE L. *Here I Shall Finish My Voyage: The Death Site of Father Jacques Marquette.* Onema, MI.: Solle's Press, 1960.

THURSFIELD, RICHARD E. *Henry Barnard's American Journal of Education.* Baltimore: Johns Hopkins University Press, 1945.

ZIRKEL, PERRY A. *A Digest of Supreme Court Decisions Affecting Education.* Bloomington, IN.: Phi Delta Kappa, 1979.

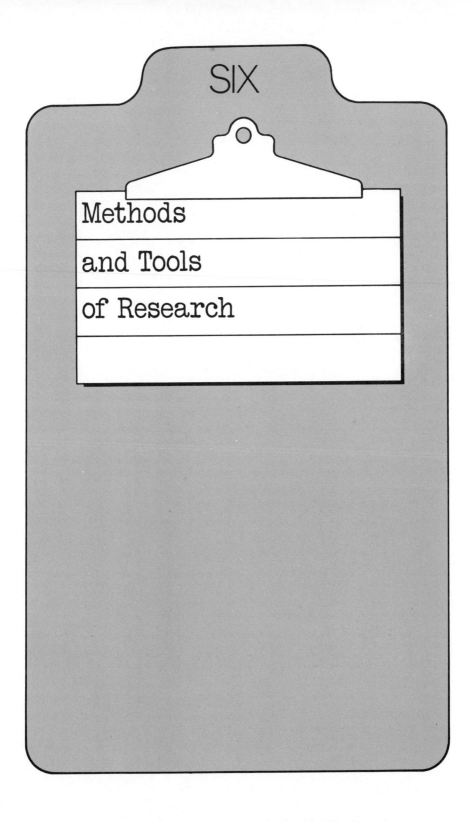

SIX

Methods

and Tools

of Research

To carry out any of the types of research investigation described in the preceding chapters, data are gathered with which the hypothesis may be tested. A great variety of methods and procedures have been developed to aid in the acquisition of data. These tools are of many kinds and employ distinctive ways of describing and quantifying the data. Each is particularly appropriate for certain sources of data, yielding information of the kind and in the form that would be most effectively used.

Many writers have argued the superiority of the interview over the questionnaire, or the use of the psychological test over the interview. The late Arvil S. Barr, University of Wisconsin teacher and researcher, resolved discussions of this sort by asking, "Which is better, a hammer or a handsaw?" Like the tools in the carpenter's chest, each is appropriate in a given situation.

Some researchers have become preoccupied with one method of inquiry that leads to a neglect of the potentiality of others. An examination of the publications of some authors shows many studies using the same method applied to many different problems, possibly indicating that they may have become attached to the one particular method, choosing problems that were appropriate to its use.

There is probably too much dependence upon single methods of inquiry. Because each data-gathering procedure or device has its own particular weakness or bias, there is merit in using multiple methods, supplementing one with others to counteract bias and generate more adequate data. Students of research should familiarize themselves with each of these tools of research and attempt to develop skill in their use and sensitivity to their effectiveness in specific situations.

THE VALIDITY AND RELIABILITY OF RESEARCH TOOLS AND METHODS

Validity and *reliability* are qualities that are essential to the effectiveness of any data-gathering procedure. These terms are defined here in the most general terms. A more detailed discussion of the various types is presented later in the chapter.

Validity is that quality of a data-gathering instrument or procedure that enables it to determine what it was designed to determine. *Reliability* is the quality of consistency that the instrument or procedure demonstrates over a period of time. Whatever it determines, it does so consistently.

It is quite feasible through a variety of statistical treatments to quantitatively assess the validity and reliability of psychological tests and inventories. It is much more difficult to determine these qualities for such other data-gathering instruments or procedures as observation, interview, or the use of the questionnaire, in which the responses are more qualitative than quantitative, yielding data that are not ordinarily measurable. One can speculate about ways to improve the validity and reliability of these procedures, but precise determination of the degree to which they are achieved is elusive.

A brief consideration of the problems of validity and reliability follows the discussion of each type of data-gathering procedure.

QUANTITATIVE STUDIES

Quantification has been defined as a numerical method of describing observations of materials or characteristics. When a defined portion of the material or characteristic is used as a standard for measuring any sample, a valid and precise method of data description is provided. Scientists distinguish among four levels of measurement, listed and described as:

A nominal scale. A nominal scale is the lowest level method of quantification. A nominal scale indicates "telling apart" or describing differences between things by assigning them to such categories as professors, associate professors, assistant professors, instructors, or lecturers, and to such subsets as males or females.

Nominal data are counted data. Each individual can be a member of only one set and all other members of the set have the same defined characteristic. Such categories as nationality, gender, educational level, occupation, or religious affiliation provide other examples. Nominal

TABLE 6-1   Academic Rank of Members of the Instructional Staff of Southland College

	Male	Female	Total
Professors	20	4	24
Associate professors	34	22	56
Assistant professors	44	30	74
Instructors	26	14	40
Lecturers	17	5	22
Totals	141	75	216

scales are nonorderable, but in some situations this simple enumeration or counting is the only feasible method of quantification and may provide an acceptable basis for statistical analysis.

An ordinal scale. Sometimes it is possible not only to indicate that things differ, but also to indicate that they differ in amount or degree. Ordinal scales permit ordering into *more than* or *less than* adjacent things. The criterion for highest to lowest ordering is expressed as relative position or rank in a group: 1st, 2nd, 3rd, 4th, 5th, . . . , *n*th. Ordinal measures have no absolute values and the differences between adjacent ranks may not be equal. Ranking spaces them equally though they may not be equally spaced. The following example illustrates this limitation:

Subject	Height in Inches	Difference in Inches	Rank
Jones	76		1st
Smith	68	8	2nd
Brown	66	2	3rd
Porter	59	7	4th
Taylor	58	1	5th

An interval scale. An arbitrary scale based on equal units of measurement indicates how much of a given characteristic is present. The difference in amount of the characteristic possessed by persons with scores of 90 and 91 is assumed to be equivalent to that between persons with scores of 60 and 61.

The interval scale represents a decided advantage over nominal and ordinal scales because it indicates the relative amount of a trait or characteristic. Its primary limitation is the lack of a true zero. It does not have the capacity to measure the complete absence of the trait, and a measure of 90 is not double that of 45. Psychological tests and inventories are interval scales and have this limitation.

A ratio scale. A ratio scale has the equal interval properties of an interval scale but has two additional features:

1. The ratio scale has a true zero. It is possible to indicate the complete absence of a property. For example, the zero point on a centimeter scale indicates the complete absence of length or height.

2. The numerals of the ratio scale have the qualities of real numbers and can be added, subtracted, multiplied, and divided and expressed in ratio relationships. Five grams is one-half of ten grams, fifteen grams is three times five grams, and on a laboratory weighing scale, two one-gram weights will balance a two-gram weight. One of the

advantages enjoyed by practitioners in the physical sciences is the ability to describe variables in ratio scale form. The behavioral sciences are limited to describing variables in interval scale form, a less precise type of measurement.

Proceeding from the nominal scale (the least precise type) to ratio scale (the most precise), increasingly relevant information is provided. If the nature of the variables permits, the scale that provides the most precise description should be used.

In behavioral research, most of the qualities or variables of interest are abstractions and cannot be observed directly. It is necessary to define them in terms of observable acts, from which the existence and amount of the variables are inferred. This operational definition tells what the researcher must do to measure the variable. For example, intelligence is an abstract quality that cannot be observed directly. Intelligence may be defined operationally as scores achieved on an intelligence test.

Operational definitions have limited meaning. Their interpretation is somewhat subjective, which may lead experts to disagree about their validity. The fact that numerical data are generated does not insure valid observation and description, for ambiguities and inconsistencies are often represented quantitatively.

Some behavioral scientists feel that excessive emphasis on quantification may result in the measurement of fragmentary qualities not relevant to real behavior. The temptation to imitate the descriptive measures of the physical scientist has led some behavioral researchers to focus their attention on trivial, easy-to-measure elements of behavior, resulting in pretentious studies of little value.

The limitations that have been mentioned are not intended to minimize the significance of quantitative methods. Progress is being made in developing more valid operational definitions and better observation techniques. The quantitative approach is not only useful, but may be considered indispensable in most types of research. It has played an essential role in the history and development of science as it progressed from pure philosophical speculation to modern empirical, verifiable observation.

QUALITATIVE STUDIES

Qualitative studies are those in which the description of observations is not ordinarily expressed in quantitative terms. It is not suggested that numerical measures are never used, but that other means of description are emphasized. For example, in the ethnographic studies described in Chapter Four, when the researcher gathers data by participant observation, interviews, and the examination of documentary materials, little measurement may be involved. However, observations may be classified into discrete categories, yielding nominal level data.

Piaget, a scientist with a distinguished biological research career of more than forty years, came to the conclusion that a nonquantitative search for explanations would be fruitful in the study of human development. His qualitative approach, known as *genetic epistemology*, has suggested another method of observing learning behavior and the nature of human growth and development. He built his logic of operations upon what he observed when children of different age levels were confronted with tasks that required reasoning for their solution.

In some types of investigation, events and characteristics may appropriately be described qualitatively. Topics such as these may serve as examples:

The Effect of Diplomatic Failure upon a Presidential Election

Types of Political Leaders and Their Influence upon Social Unrest

The Terrorist as an Agent of Social Change

The Extended Tribal Family and its Influence upon Child-Rearing Practices

The Influence of Tribal Religious Beliefs upon Attitudes to·ₐ·rd Death and Dying

The Influence of the Socioeconomic Status of a Group of High School Students in the Selection of Career Goals

The Influence of the Home on Pupil-Teacher Relationships

To conclude this discussion on quantitative and qualitative studies, several observations may be appropriate. It may be unwise to try to draw a hard-and-fast distinction between qualitative and quantitative studies. The difference is not absolute but one of emphasis. One emphasis should not be considered superior to the other. The appropriate approach would depend upon the nature of the variables under consideration and the objectives of the researcher.

Traditionally, educational research has emphasized the quantitative approach. A substantial number of researchers feel that qualitative studies have, for too long, remained outside the mainstream of educational research. Some investigations could be strengthened by supplementing one approach with the other.

OBSERVATION

From the earliest history of scientific activity, observation has been the prevailing method of inquiry. Observing natural phenomena, aided by systematic classification and measurement, led to the development of theories and laws of nature's forces. Observation continues to characterize all research; experimental, descriptive, and historical. The use of the technique of participant observation in ethnological research has been described in Chapter Four.

As a data-gathering device, direct observation may make an important contribution to descriptive research. Certain types of information can best be obtained through direct examination by the researcher. When the information concerns aspects of material objects or specimens, the process is relatively simple, and may consist of classifying, measuring, or counting. But when the process involves the study of a human subject in action, it is much more complex.

One may study the characteristics of a school building by observing and recording such aspects as materials of construction, number of rooms for various purposes, size of rooms, amount of furniture and equipment, presence or absence of certain facilities, and other relevant aspects. Adequacy could then be determined by comparing these facilities with reasonable standards, previously determined by expert judgment and research.

In university athletic departments or professional football organizations, observation has been used effectively to scout the performance of the teams that will be encountered in football competition. Careful observation and recording of the skills and procedures of both team and individual players are made, and defenses and offenses are planned to cope with them. What formations or patterns of attack or defense are employed? Who carried the ball? Who does the passing, and where and with what hand does he pass? Who are the likely receivers, and how do they pivot and cut?

During a game a coaching assistant may sit high in the stands, relaying strategic observations by phone to the coach on the bench. At the same time, every minute of play is being recorded on film for careful study by the coaching staff and players. Who missed his tackle when that play went through for twenty yards? Who missed his block when play number two lost six yards? Careful study of these films provides valuable data on weaknesses to be corrected before the following game. Through the use of binoculars, the phone, the motion picture camera, and the video tape recorder, observations can be carefully made and recorded.

Although this example may seem inappropriate in a discussion of observation as a research technique, improving the performance of a football team is not altogether different from the problem of analyzing learning behavior in a classroom. The difference is one of degree of complexity. The objectives of the football team are more concretely identifiable than are the more complex purposes of the classroom. Yet some of the procedures of observation so effective in football coaching may also be systematically employed in studying classroom performance. In some schools, teachers make short periodic classroom or playground observations of pupil behavior, which are filed in the cumulative folder. These recorded observations, known as anecdotal reports, may provide useful data for research studies.

The method of laboratory experimentation seeks to describe action or behavior that will take place under carefully arranged and controlled conditions. But many important aspects of human behavior cannot be profitably observed under the contrived conditions of the laboratory. The method of descriptive research seeks to describe behavior under less rigid controls, under more naturally occurring conditions. The behavior of children in a classroom situation cannot be effectively analyzed by observing their behavior in a laboratory. It is necessary to observe what they actually do in a real classroom.

This does not suggest that observation is haphazard or unplanned. On the contrary, observation as a research technique must always be expert, directed by a specific purpose, systematic, carefully focused, and thoroughly recorded. Like other research procedures, it must be subject to the usual checks for accuracy, validity, and reliability.

The observer must know just what to look for. He or she must be able to distinguish between the significant aspects of the situation and factors that have little or no importance to the investigation. Of course, objectivity is essential, and careful and accurate methods of measuring and recording may be employed when appropriate.

Since human behavior is complex and important traits and characteristics are difficult, if not impossible, to observe directly, they must be defined in precise operational form. Perhaps interest in a subject can be operationally defined as the number of times a student volunteers to participate in discussion by raising his or her hand within a time sample period. Lack of concentration during a study period can be operationally defined by the number of times the student looks around, talks to another student, fiddles with a book, pen, or paper, or engages in other distractive acts within a time sample period. These examples of operational definitions may be unsatisfactory, but they do illustrate the kinds of behavior that can be directly observed.

Instruments such as the stopwatch, mechanical counter, camera, lightmeter, audiometer, audio and video tape recorders, and other devices make possible observations that are more precise than mere sense observations.

Systematic observations of human behavior in natural settings are, to some degree, an intrusion into the dynamics of the situation. This intervention may produce confounding effects that cannot be ignored. It is widely believed that individuals do not behave typically when they know that they are being observed. The situation may become too artificial, too unnatural, to provide for a valid series of observations.

Concealing the observer has been used to minimize this reactive effect. Cameras and one-way screens were used by Gesell[1] to make unobtrusive observations of infant behavior. One-way glass and concealed microphones and video tape recorders have been used in observing the behavior of children in natural group activities so that the observers could see and hear without being seen and heard.

Some authorities believe that the presence of an outside observer in the classroom over a period of time will be taken for granted, viewed as a part of the natural setting, and have little effect on the behavior observed. Others feel that introducing observers as active participants in the activities of the group will minimize the reactive effect more efficiently.

Should the research responsibilities of the participant observers be made known to the members of the group observed? There are those who feel that concealing the intentions of the participant observers may raise ethical questions of invasion of privacy and the establishment of a false, hypocritical, interpersonal relationship with the individuals in the group. Do the ends of science justify the means of deception? In a society that increasingly questions the ethics of science, this issue must be confronted.

Validity and Reliability of Observation

To achieve a satisfactory degree of validity, those critical incidents of behavior that are truly significant must be identified. Supplementing the knowledge and skill of the researcher, the judgment of experts in the field may help in selecting a limited number of observable incidents whose relationship to the qualities of interest is based upon sound, established theories.

The reactive effect of the intrusion of the observer as a threat to the validity of the process has been mentioned. When researchers are sole observers, they unconsciously tend to see what they expect to see

[1] Arnold Gesell, *Studies in Child Development* (New York: Harper & Brothers, 1948): 103–105.

and to overlook those incidents that do not fit their theory. Their own values, feelings, and attitudes, based upon past experience, may distort their observations. It may be desirable to engage several others who are well-prepared as observers, restricting the researchers' role to that of interpreter of the observations. Independent observers should be prepared by participation in:

1. the development of the procedures for observing and recording observations

2. the try-out or dry run phase of the procedure

3. the critique of the results of the try-out phase.

If researchers wish to be participant observers, they may pool their observations with those of the other independent observers.

Randomly selected time samples of frequently occurring incidents may help to yield more representative samples of behavior. A *time-on-task* study, described in a previous chapter, involved randomly selected five-second observations of each student per class period for nine weeks. Some types of behavior would require longer time periods for each observation, perhaps at different times of the day. This method of selecting observation periods would enhance both reliability and validity of observation.

Recording Observations

If it does not distract or create a barrier between observer and those observed, simultaneous recording of observations is recommended. This practice minimizes the errors that result from faulty memory. There are other occasions when recording would more appropriately follow some time after observation. The recording of observations should be done as soon as possible, while the details are still fresh in the mind of the observer. But many authorities agree that objectivity is more likely when the interpretation of the meaning of the behavior described is deferred until a later time, for simultaneous recording and interpretation often interfere with objectivity.

Systematizing Data Collection

To aid in the recording of information gained through observation, a number of devices have been extensively used. Check lists, rating scales, score cards, and scaled specimens provide systematic means of summarizing or quantifying data collected by observation or examination.

Check List   The check list, the simplest of the devices, consists of a prepared list of items. The presence or absence of the item may be indicated by checking *yes* or *no*, or the type or number of items may be indicated by inserting the appropriate word or number. This simple "laundry-list" type of device systematizes and facilitates the recording of observations, and helps to ensure the consideration of the important aspects of the object or act observed. Readers are familiar with check lists prepared to help buyers purchase a used car, choose a home site, or buy an insurance policy, indicating characteristics or features that one should bear in mind before making a decision.

Appendix E illustrates a check list for the evaluation of a research report.

Rating Scale   The rating scale involves qualitative description of a limited number of aspects of a thing, or of traits of a person. The classifications may be set up in five to seven categories in such terms as:

superior	above average	average	fair	inferior
excellent	good	average	below average	poor
always	frequently	occasionally	rarely	never

Another procedure establishes positions in terms of behavioral or situational descriptions. These statements may be much more specific, and enable the judge to identify more clearly the characteristic to be rated. Instead of deciding whether the individual's leadership qualities are superior or above average, it may be easier to decide between "Always exerts a strong influence on his associates," and "Sometimes is able to move others to action."

One of the problems in constructing a rating scale lies in the difficulty of conveying to the rater just what quality one wishes evaluated. It is likely that a brief behavioral statement is more objective than an adjective that may have no universal meaning in the abstract.

Rating scales have several limitations. In addition to the difficulty of clearly defining the trait or characteristic to be evaluated, the halo effect causes raters to carry qualitative judgment from one aspect to another. Thus, there is a tendency to rate a person who has a pleasing personality high on other traits like intelligence or professional interest. This halo effect is likely to appear when the rater is asked to rate many factors, on a number of which he has no evidence for judgment. This suggests the advisability of keeping at a minimum the number of characteristics to be rated.

Another limitation of rating is the tendency of raters to be too generous. A number of studies have verified the tendency to rate 60 to 80 per cent of an unselected group above average in all traits. Rating scales should carry the suggestion that raters omit the rating of characteristics that they have had no opportunity to observe.

Score Card The score card, similar in some respects to both the check list and the rating scale, usually provides for the appraisal of a relatively large number of aspects. In addition, the presence of each characteristic or aspect, or the rating assigned to each, has a predetermined point value. Thus, the score-card rating may yield a total weighted score that can be used in the evaluation of the object observed. Score cards are frequently used in evaluating communities, building sites, schools, or textbooks. Accrediting agencies sometimes use the score card in arriving at an overall evaluation of a school.

Score cards have been designed to help in estimating the socioeconomic status of a family. Such aspects as type of neighborhood, home (owned or rented), number of rooms, ownership of a piano, number of books in the library, number and type of periodicals subscribed to, telephone, occupation of father, and organizations parents belong to are all considered significant and have appropriate point values assigned.

The limitations of the score card are similar to those of the rating scale. In addition to the difficulty of choosing, identifying, and quantifying the significant aspects of the factor to be observed, there is the suspicion that the whole of a thing may be greater than the sum of its parts.

Colleges and universities are frequently evaluated in terms of such elements as size of endowment, proportion of faculty members holding the earned doctoral degree, pupil-teacher ratio, and number of volumes in the library. Although these aspects are important, the effectiveness of an institution may not be accurately appraised by their summation, for certain important intangibles do not lend themselves to score card ratings.

The Scaled Specimen The scaled specimen, although not frequently encountered in behavioral research, provides a method for evaluating certain observed levels of performance or measures of a quality in question. Testing a solution for acidity in a chemistry laboratory involves a pH test. A drop of color indicator is introduced into a sample of the solution. The resulting color of the solution is matched with the color of one of a set of display vials, indicating the percentage of acidity of the solution.

One of the early scaled specimens developed in the field of education was the handwriting scale developed by Thorndike. From a large sample of handwriting exhibits taken at different ages and grade levels, norms were established. The handwriting to be evaluated was then matched with the exhibit sample, yielding a measure of handwriting quality.

The Goodenough-Harris Drawing Test[2] provides a 71-point scale with examples for comparing various details of a child's drawing of a man, a woman, or a self-portrait. Each point is scored + or 0, indicating the presence or absence of a part of body detail in the figure drawn. The total of + scores is equated with separate age norms, established for boys and girls. The scale is based on the assumption that as individuals mature intellectually, they perceive greater detail in the human figure that they reveal in their drawings. Variations of the test include *Draw a Man, Draw a Woman,* and *Draw Yourself.* Studies have reported correlations as high as +.60 to +.72 with the Stanford-Binet Intelligence Scale.

Observation, as a research data-gathering process, demands rigorous adherence to the spirit of scientific inquiry. The following standards should characterize observers and their observations:

Observation is carefully planned, systematic, and perceptive. Observers know what they are looking for, and what is irrelevant in a situation. They are not distracted by the dramatic or the spectacular.

Observers are aware of the wholeness of what is observed. Although they are alert to significant details, they know that the whole is often greater than the sum of its parts.

Observers are objective. They recognize their likely biases, and they strive to eliminate their influence upon what they see and report.

Observers separate the facts from the interpretation of the facts. They observe the facts, and make their interpretation at a later time.

Observations are checked and verified, whenever possible, by repetition, or by comparison with those of other competent observers.

Observations are carefully and expertly recorded. Observers use appropriate instruments to systematize, quantify, and preserve the results of their observations.

THE INTERVIEW

The interview is, in a sense, an oral questionnaire. Instead of writing the response, the subject or interviewee gives the needed information verbally in a face-to-face relationship.

With a skillful interviewer, the interview is often superior to other data-gathering devices. One reason is that people are usually more willing to talk than to write. After the interviewer gains rapport, or estab-

---

[2] Dale B. Harris, *Children's Drawings as Measures of Intellectual Maturity* (New York: Harcourt, Brace & World, 1963).

lishes a friendly, secure relationship with the subject, certain types of confidential information may be obtained that an individual might be reluctant to put in writing. The interviewer can explain the purpose of the investigation, and can explain more clearly just what information he or she wants. If the subject misinterprets the question, the interviewer may follow it with a clarifying question. At the same time, he or she may evaluate the sincerity and insight of the interviewee. It is also possible to seek the same information, in several ways, at various stages of the interview, thus providing a check of the truthfulness of the responses.

Through the interview technique the researcher may stimulate the subject to greater insight into his or her own experiences, and thereby explore significant areas not anticipated in the original plan of investigation. The interview is also particularly appropriate when dealing with young children, illiterates, those with language difficulties, and those of limited intelligence.

If one were to study what junior high school students like and dislike in teachers, some sort of written schedule would probably be satisfactory. In order to conduct a similar study with first grade pupils, the interview would be the only feasible method of getting responses.

The preparation for the interview is a critical step in the procedure. Interviewers must have a clear conception of just what information they need. They must clearly outline the best sequence of questions and stimulating comments that will systematically bring out the desired responses. A written outline, schedule, or check list will provide a set plan for the interview, precluding the possibility that the interviewer will fail to get important and needed data.

An open-form question, in which the subject is encouraged to answer in his or her own words at some length, is likely to provide a greater depth of response. In fact, this penetration exploits the advantage of the interview in getting beneath-the-surface reactions. However, distilling the essence of the reaction is difficult and interviewer bias may be a hazard. The closed-form question in the pattern of a multiple-choice response is easier to record, but may yield more superficial information.

Leading questions that unconsciously imply a specific answer should be avoided. The question, "Do you think that the United Nations has failed in its peace-keeping function?" is perhaps an exaggerated example, but it does illustrate the danger of eliciting agreement to an idea implanted in the question. It would be preferable to phrase it, "How effective do you feel the United Nations has been in its peace-keeping function?" This form is neutral and doesn't suggest a particular response. A question of this type would appropriately be followed by the question, "Could you explain how you reached this conclusion?"

The nature of the personal relationship between interviewer and subject requires an expertness and sensitivity that might well be called an art. The initial task of securing the confidence and cooperation of the subject is crucial. Talking in a friendly way about a topic of interest to the subject will often dispel hostility or suspicion and, before he or she realizes it, the subject is freely giving the desired information. As is true in the use of the questionnaire, the interviewer must be able to assure the subject that responses will be held in strict confidence. When interviews are not recorded by tape or other electronic device, it will be necessary for the interviewer to take written notes, either during the interview or immediately thereafter. It is suggested that the actual wording of the responses be retained. It is advisable to make the interpretation later, separating this phase of analysis from the actual recording of responses.

Recording interviews on tape is convenient and inexpensive, and obviates the necessity of writing during the interview, which may be a distracting influence, both to interviewer and to subject. Interviews recorded on tape may be replayed as often as necessary for complete and objective analysis at a later time. In addition to the words, the tone of voice and emotional impact of the response is preserved by the tapes. It is generally considered unethical to record interviews without the knowledge and permission of the subject.

Validity and Reliability of the Interview

The key to effective interviewing is the extent to which the interviewer can establish rapport. This skill is a somewhat intangible quality that may be both a personality quality and a developed ability. Researchers have studied the effect of interviewer status on ability to achieve this confidence. Many studies have been conducted in which interviewers of different status have interviewed the same respondents. The responses were often significantly different, both in how much the subject was willing to reveal and the nature of the attitudes expressed.

Ethnic origin seems to be an important factor. Those of the same ethnic background seem to be more successful in establishing rapport. When there is an ethnic difference, a certain amount of suspicion and even resentment may be encountered. The same relationship seems to prevail when the social status of the interviewer and respondent is different. Even the type of clothing worn may have an inhibiting effect. Younger interviews seem to be more successful than older, particularly when middle-aged respondents are involved. Women seem to have a slight advantage over men in getting candid responses. Of course, experience tends to improve interviewing skill.

Validity is achieved to a greater degree when the interview is based upon a carefully designed structure, to ensure that the significant information is elicited. The critical judgment of experts in the field of inquiry is helpful in selecting those questions that are essential to the purposes of the investigation.

Reliability, the consistency of response, may be evaluated by restating a question in slightly different form at a later time in the interview. Repeating the interview at another time may provide another estimate of the consistency of response. The use of more than one interviewer may also contribute to greater reliability.

As a data-gathering technique, the interview has unique advantages. In areas where human motivation as revealed in reasons for actions, feelings, and attitudes is concerned, the interview can be most effective. In the hands of a skillful interviewer, a depth of response is possible, a penetration quite unlikely to be achieved through any other means.

This technique is time consuming, however, and one of the most difficult to employ successfully. The danger of interview bias is constant. Since the objectivity, sensitivity, and insight of the interviewer are crucial, this procedure is one that requires a level of expertness not ordinarily possessed by inexperienced researchers.

INQUIRY FORMS

The general category of inquiry forms includes data-gathering instruments through which respondents answer questions or respond to statements in writing. A questionnaire is used when factual information is desired. When opinions rather than facts are desired, an opinionnaire or attitude scale is used.

The Questionnaire

Questionnaires administered personally to groups of individuals have a number of advantages. The person administering the instrument has an opportunity to establish rapport, to explain the purpose of the study, and to explain the meaning of items that may not be clear. The availability of a number of respondents in one place makes possible an economy of time and expense and provides a high proportion of usable responses. It is likely that a principal would get completely usable responses from teachers in the building, or a teacher from students in the classroom. However, individuals who have the desired information cannot always be contacted personally without the expenditure of a great deal of time and money in travel. It is in such situations that the mailed questionnaire may make a useful contribution. The mailed questionnaire is probably both the most used and most criticized data-gathering device. It has been referred to as the lazy person's way of gaining information, although the careful preparation of a good questionnaire takes a great deal of time, ingenuity, and hard work. There is little doubt that the poorly constructed questionnaires that flood the mails have created a certain amount of contempt. This is particularly true when the accompanying letter pleads that the sender needs the information to complete the requirements for a graduate course, a thesis, or a dissertation. The recipient's reaction may be, "Why should I go to all this trouble to help this person get a degree?"

Filling out lengthy questionnaires takes a great deal of time and effort, a favor that few senders have any right to expect of strangers. The unfavorable reaction is intensified when the questionnaire is long, the subject trivial in importance, the items vaguely worded, and the form poorly organized. The unfavorable characteristics of so many questionnaires help to explain why so small a proportion of mailed questionnaires are returned. As a result of this sparse response, often as low as 40 percent to 50 percent, the data obtained are often of limited validity. The information in the unreturned questionnaires might have changed the results of the investigation materially. The very fact of no response might imply certain types of reactions, reactions that can never be included in the summary of data.

Unless one is dealing with a group of respondents who have a genuine interest in the problem under investigation, who know the sender, or who have some common bond of loyalty to a sponsoring institution or organization, the rate of returns is frequently disappointing, and provides a flimsy basis for generalization.

Although the foregoing discussion may seem to discredit the questionnaire as a respectable research technique, the attempt has been to consider the abuse or misuse of the device. Actually, the questionnaire has unique advantages and, properly constructed and administered, it may serve as a most appropriate and useful data-gathering device in a research project.

The Closed Form Questionnaires that call for short, check responses are known as the *restricted,* or *closed-form,* type. They provide for marking a *yes* or *no,* a short response, or checking an item from a list of suggested responses. The following example illustrates the closed-form item:

> Why did you choose to do your graduate work at this university? Kindly indicate three reasons in order of importance, using number 1 for the most important, 2 for the 2nd most important, and 3 for the 3rd most important.

	Rank
(a) Convenience of transportation	_____
(b) Advice of a friend	_____
(c) Reputation of institution	_____
(d) Expense factor	_____
(e) Scholarship aid	_____
(f) Other _____	_____
(kindly specify)	

Even when using the closed form, it is well to provide for unanticipated responses. Providing an "other" category permits respondents to indicate what might be their most important reason, one that the questionnaire builder had not anticipated. Note the instruction "(kindly specify)," which enables the tabulator to properly classify all responses.

For certain types of information the closed-form questionnaire is entirely satisfactory. It is easy to fill out, takes little time, keeps the respondent on the subject, is relatively objective, and is fairly easy to tabulate and analyze.

The Open Form   The *open-form,* or *unrestricted,* type of questionnaire calls for a free response in the respondent's own words. The following open-form item seeks the same type of information as the previous closed-form item:

Why did you choose to take your graduate work at this unversity?

Note that no clues are given. The open form probably provides for greater depth of response. The respondents reveal their frame of reference and possibly the reasons for their responses. Since it requires greater effort on the part of the respondents, returns are often meager. This type of item is sometimes difficult to interpret, tabulate, and summarize in the research report.

Many questionnaires include both open- and closed-type items. Each type has its merits and limitations, and the questionnaire builder must decide which type is more likely to supply the information he or she wants.

Improving Questionnaire Items   Inexperienced questionnaire makers are likely to be naïve about the clarity of their questions. The author recalls a brilliant graduate student who submitted a questionnaire for the professor's approval. She seemed somewhat irritated and impatient at the subsequent questions and suggestions, and remarked that anyone with any degree of intelligence should know what she meant. At the advisor's suggestion she duplicated some copies and personally administered the questionnaire to a graduate class in research.

She was literally swamped with questions of interpretation, many that she could not answer clearly. There was considerable evidence of confusion about what she wanted to know. After she had collected the completed copies and had tried to tabulate the responses, she began to see the questionnaire's faults. Even her directions and explanation in class had failed to clarify the ambiguous intent of her questionnaire. Her second version was a much-improved instrument.

Many beginning researchers aren't really sure what they want to know. They use a shotgun approach, attempting to cover their field broadly in the hope that some of the responses will provide the answers for which they are groping. Unless researchers know exactly what they want, however, they are not likely to ask the right questions, or to phrase them properly.

In addition to the problem of knowing what one wants, there is the difficulty of wording the questionnaire clearly. The limitations of words are particular hazards in the questionnaire. The same words mean different things to different people. Questionnaire makers have their own interpretation—the respondents may have many different interpretations. In the interview, or in conversation, we are able to clear up misunderstanding by restating our question, by inflection of the voice, by suggestions, and by a number of other devices. But the written question stands by itself, often ambiguous and misunderstood.

A simple example illustrates the influence of voice inflection alone. Consider the following question. Read it over, each time emphasizing the underlined word, noting how the change in inflection alters the meaning.

> Were you there last night?
> Were you there last night?
> Were you there last night?
> Were you there last night?
> Were you there last night?

Questionnaire makers must depend on written language alone. It is apparent that they cannot be too careful in phrasing questions to insure their clarity of purpose. Although there are no certain ways of producing fool-proof questions, certain principles can be employed to make items more precise. A few are suggested here, with the hope that students constructing questionnaires and opinionnaires will become critical of their first efforts and strive to make each item as clear as possible.

Define or qualify terms that could easily be misinterpreted.

What is the value of your house?

The meaning of the term *value* is not clear. It could mean the assessed value for tax purposes, what it would sell for on the present market, what you would be willing to sell it for, what it would cost to replace, or what you paid for it. These values may differ considerably. It is essential to frame specific questions such as, "What is the present market value of your house?"

As simple a term as *age* is often misunderstood. When is an individual twenty-one? Most people would say that a person is twenty-one from the day of the twenty-first birthday until the day of the twenty-second. An insurance company would consider the person twenty-one from the twenty-year, six-months date until the twenty-first-year, six-months date. Perhaps this question could be clarified by asking *age to nearest birthday,* or *date of birth.*

Hundreds of words are ambiguous because of their many interpretations. One has only to think of such words and phrases as *curriculum, democracy, progressive education, cooperation,* and *integration*—even such simple words as *how much* and *now.* To the question, "What work are you doing now?" the respondent might be tempted to answer, "Filling out your foolish questionnaire."

Be careful in using descriptive adjectives and adverbs that have no agreed-upon meaning. This fault is frequently found in rating scales as well as in questionnaires. *Frequently, occasionally,* and *rarely* do not have the same meanings to different persons.[3] One respondent's *occasionally* may be another's *rarely.* Perhaps a stated frequency—*times per week, times per month*—would make this classification more precise.

Beware of double negatives. Underline negatives for clarity.

Are you opposed to <u>not</u> requiring students to take showers after gym class?
Federal aid should <u>not</u> be granted to those states in which education is <u>not</u> equal regardless of race, creed, or color.

Be careful of inadequate alternatives.

Married? Yes _____No_____

Does this question refer to present or former martial status? How would the person answer who is widowed, separated, or divorced?

How late at night do you permit your children to watch television?

[3] Milton D. Hakel, "How Often Is Often?" *American Psychologist* 23 (July 1968): 533–534.

There may be no established family policy. If there is a policy, it may differ for children of different ages. It may be different for school nights, or for Friday and Saturday nights when the late, late show may be permitted.

Avoid the double-barreled question.

Do you believe that gifted students should be placed in separate groups for instructional purposes and assigned to special schools?

One might agree on the advisability of separate groups for instructional purposes, but be very much opposed to the assignment of gifted students to special schools. Two questions are needed.

Underline a word if you wish to indicate special emphasis.

A parent should not be told his child's IQ score.
Should all schools offer a modern foreign language?

When asking for ratings or comparisons a point of reference is necessary.

How would you rate this student teacher's classroom teaching?
Superior _____ Average _____ Below Average _____

With whom is the student teacher to be compared—an experienced teacher, other student teachers, former student teachers—or should the criterion be what a student teacher is expected to be able to do?

Avoid unwarranted assumptions.

Are you satisfied with the salary raise that you received last year?

A *no* answer might mean that I didn't get a raise, or that I did get a raise, but I'm not satisfied.

Do you feel that you benefited from the spankings that you received as a child?

A *no* response might mean that the spankings did not help me, or that my parents did not administer corporal punishment. These unwarranted assumptions are nearly as bad as the classic, "Have you stopped beating your wife?"

Phrase questions so that they are appropriate for all respondents.

What is your monthly teaching salary?

Some teachers are paid on a nine-month basis, some ten, some eleven, and some twelve. Three questions would be needed.

     Your salary per month? _____
     Number of months in school term? _____
     Number of salary payments per year? _____

Design questions that will give a complete response.

     Do you read the *Indianapolis Star?*   Yes _____No _____

A *yes* or *no* answer would not reveal much information about the reading habits of the respondent. The question might be followed with an additional item, as in Figure 6.1.

Provide for the systematic quantification of responses.   One type of question that asks respondents to check a number of items from a list is difficult to summarize, especially if all respondents do not check the same number. One solution is to ask respondents to rank, in order of preference, a specific number of responses.

If your answer is *Yes,* kindly check *how often* and *what sections* of the *Star* you read.

Section	Always	Usually	Seldom	Never
National and inter- national news				
State and local news				
Editorial				
Sports				
Comic				
Society				
Financial				
Advertising				
Want ad				
Syndicated features				
Special features				
Other (specify)				

Fig. 6-1

What are your favorite television programs? Rank in order of preference your first, second, third, fourth, and fifth choices.

The items can then be tabulated by inverse weightings.

1st choice	5 points
2nd choice	4 points
3rd choice	3 points
4th choice	2 points
5th choice	1 point

The relative popularity of the programs could be described for a group in terms of total weighted scores, the most popular having the largest total.

Consider the possibility of classifying the responses yourself, rather than having the respondent choose categories. If students were asked to classify their father's occupation in one of the following categories, the results might be quite unsatisfactory.

Unskilled labor	_____
Skilled labor	_____
Clerical work	_____
Managerial work	_____
Profession	_____
Proprietorship	_____

It is likely that by asking the children one or two short questions about their father's work, it could be classified more accurately.

1. At what place does your father work?
2. What kind of work does he do?

The student should bear in mind these few suggestions in constructing questionnaire items. There is no recipe or set of easy directions. It is a difficult job, one that requires a great deal of hard work, imagination, and ingenuity. (See reference by Stanley Payne listed in chapter bibliography.)

1. Male _____ Female _____
2. Age _____
3. Marital status: single _____ married _____ divorced/separated _____
4. Number of dependent children _____; their ages _____
5. Number of other dependents _____
6. Highest degree held _____
7. Years of teaching experience _____
8. Years of teaching at present school _____
9. Teaching level; primary _____ intermediate _____ upper grades _____ Jr. H.S. _____ Sr. H.S. _____; If secondary, your major teaching area _____
10. Enrollment of your school _____
11. Your average class size _____

12. Population of your community or school district _____
13. Your principal is: male _____ female _____
In the following questions kindly check the appropriate column:

	a	b	c	d
a. *excellent* b. *good* c. *fair* d. *poor*				
14. How does your salary schedule compare with those of similar school districts?				
15. How would you rate your principal on these traits?				
competence				
friendliness				
helpfulness				
ability to inspire				
16. How would you rate the consulting or advisory services that you receive? encourage creativity				
availability				
17. Provision made for teacher free time				
relaxation				
preparation				
lunch				
conferences				
18. How would you rate your faculty lounge?				
19. How would you rate your faculty professional library? books				
periodicals				
references				
20. How would you evaluate the adequacy of teaching materials and supplies? textbooks				
references				
AV aids				
supplies				
21. How would you evaluate the assignment of your nonteaching duties? (leave blank if item *does not apply*)				
reports				
meetings				
halls				
lunchroom				
supervision of: { playground				
study hall				
extra-class				
organizations				
22. How would you rate the compatibility of your faculty?				
23. How would you rate the parent support of your school?				
24. How would you rate your morale as a teacher?				

25. Kindly *rank in order of importance to you* at least *five* factors that you would consider most important in increasing your morale or satisfaction with your

working conditions: Rank 1, most important, 2 next in importance, etc.

_____ a. higher salary
_____ b. smaller class size
_____ c. more free time
_____ d. more adequate faculty lounge
_____ e. more compatible faculty
_____ f. more adequate teaching materials
_____ g. more effective principal
_____ h. better consulting services
_____ i. more effective faculty meetings
_____ j. assistance of a teacher aide
_____ k. more attractive classroom/building
_____ l. fewer reports to make out
_____ m. fewer nonteaching duties
_____ n. better provision for atypical students
_____ o. more participation in policy making
_____ p. fewer committee meetings
_____ q. teaching in a higher socioeconomic area
_____ r. teaching in a lower socioeconomic area
_____ s. other (kindly specify)

On the back of this sheet kindly add any comments that you believe would more adequately express your feelings of satisfaction or dissatisfaction with teaching.

Fig. 6-2. Teacher Morale Questionnaire—Opinionnaire

Characteristics of a Good Questionnaire

1. It deals with a significant topic, one the respondent will recognize as important enough to warrant spending his or her time on. The significance should be clearly and carefully stated on the questionnaire, or in the letter that accompanies it.
2. It seeks only that information which cannot be obtained from other sources such as school reports or census data.
3. It is as short as possible, only long enough to get the essential data. Long questionnaires frequently find their way into the wastebasket.
4. It is attractive in appearance, neatly arranged, and clearly duplicated or printed.
5. Directions are clear and complete, important terms are defined, each question deals with a single idea, all questions are worded as simply and as clearly as possible, and the categories provide an opportunity for easy, accurate, and unambiguous responses.
6. The questions are objective, with no leading suggestions as to the responses desired. Leading questions are just as inappropriate on a questionnaire as they are in a court of law.
7. Questions are presented in good psychological order, proceeding from general to more specific responses. This order helps respondents to organize their own thinking, so that their answers are logical and objective. It may

be well to present questions that create a favorable attitude before proceeding to those that may be a bit delicate or intimate. If possible, annoying or embarrassing questions should be avoided.
8. It is easy to tabulate and interpret. It is advisable to preconstruct a tabulation sheet, anticipating how the data will be tabulated and interpreted, before the final form of the question is decided upon. This working backward from a visualization of the final analysis of data is an important step in avoiding ambiguity in questionnaire form.

If mechanical tabulating equipment is to be used, it is important to allow code numbers for all possible responses to permit easy transference to machine-tabulation cards.

Preparing and Administering the Questionnaire

1. Get all the help you can in planning and constructing your questionnaire. Study other questionnaires, and submit your items for criticism to other members of your class or your faculty, especially those who have had experience in questionnaire construction.
2. In the process of designing an inquiry form (questionnaire or opinionnaire) it is advisable to use a separate card or slip for each item. As the instrument is being developed items may be refined, revised, or replaced by better items without recopying the entire instrument. This procedure also provides desirable flexibility in arranging items in the most appropriate psychological order before the instrument is finally transferred to the stencil or ditto sheet for duplication.
3. Try out your questionnaire on a few friends and acquaintances. When you do this personally, you may find that a number of your items are ambiguous. What may seem perfectly clear to you may be confusing to a person who does not have the frame of reference that you have gained from living with and thinking about an idea over a long period.
   This "dry run" will be well worth the time and effort it takes. It may reveal defects that can be corrected before the final form is printed and committed to the mails. Once the instrument has been sent out, it is too late to remedy its defects.
4. Choose respondents carefully. It is important that questionnaires be sent only to those who possess the desired information—those who are likely to be sufficiently interested to respond conscientiously and objectively. A preliminary card, asking whether the individual would be willing to participate in the proposed study, is recommended by some research authorities. This is not only a courteous approach, but a practical way of discovering those who will cooperate in furnishing the desired information.
   In a study on questionnaire returns, Harold W. See[4] discovered that a greater proportion of returns was obtained when the original request was sent to the administrative head of an organization, rather than directly to the person who had the desired information. It is possible that when a superior officer turns over a questionnaire to a staff member to fill out, there is an implied feeling of obligation.

[4] Harold W. See, "Send It to the President," *Phi Delta Kappan* 38 (Jan. 1957): 130.

5. If questionnaires are planned for use in a public school, asking for the responses of teachers or pupils, it is essential that approval of the project be secured from the principal, who may then wish to secure approval from the superintendent of schools. Schools are understandably sensitive to public relations. One can understand the possibilities of unfavorable publicity that may result from certain types of studies made by individuals not officially designated to conduct research.

   School officials may also want to prevent the exploitation of teachers and pupils by amateur researchers, whose activities would require an excessive amount of time and effort in activities not related to the purposes of the school.

6. If the desired information is delicate or intimate in nature, consider the possibility of providing for anonymous responses. The anonymous instrument is most likely to produce objective responses. There are occasions, however, for purposes of classification, when the identity of the respondents is necessary. If a signature is needed, it is essential to convince the respondents that their responses will be held in strict confidence, and that their answers will in no way jeopardize the status and security of their position.

7. Try to get the aid of sponsorship. Recipients are more likely to answer if a person, organization, or institution of prestige has endorsed the project. Of course, it is unethical to claim sponsorship unless it has been expressly given.

8. Be sure to include a courteous, carefully constructed cover letter to explain the purpose of the study. The letter should promise some sort of inducement to the respondent for compliance with the request. Commercial agencies furnish rewards in goods or money. In educational circles a summary of questionnaire results is considered an appropriate reward, a promise that should be scrupulously honored after the study has been completed.

   The cover letter should assure the respondent that delicate information will be held in strict confidence. The explanation of sponsorship might well be mentioned. Of course, a stamped, addressed return envelope should be included. To omit this courtesy would be practically to guarantee that many of the questionnaires would go into the wastebasket. It has been suggested that two copies of the questionnaire be sent, one to be returned when completed, and the other for the respondent's own file.

9. Recipients are often slow to return completed questionnaires. To increase the number of returns, a vigorous follow-up procedure may be necessary. A courteous post card reminding the recipient that the completed questionnaire has not been received will bring in some additional responses. This reminder will be effective with those who have just put off or forgotten to fill out or mail the document. A further step in the follow-up process may involve a personal letter of reminder. In extreme cases a telegram, phone call, or personal visit may bring additional responses.

   It is difficult to estimate, in the abstract, what percentage of questionnaire responses is to be considered adequate or satisfactory. The importance of the project, the quality of the questionnaire, the care used in selecting recipients, the time of year, and many other factors may be significant in determining the proportion of responses. In general, the smaller the percentage of responses, the smaller the degree of confidence one may place in the adequacy of the data collected. Of course, objectivity of reporting requires that the proportion of responses received should always be included in the research report.

Validity and Reliability of Questionnaires   Infrequently do questionnaire designers and administrators deal consciously with the extent of validity or reliability of their instrument. Perhaps this is one reason why so many questionnaires are lacking in these qualities. It must be recognized, however, that questionnaires, unlike psychological tests and inventories, have a very limited purpose. They are often one-shot data-gathering devices with a very short life, administered to a limited population. However, there are ways to improve both validity and reliability of questionnaires that deserve careful consideration.

Basic to the validity of a questionnaire are the right questions phrased in the least ambiguous way. The question of content validity is: Do the items sample a significant aspect of the purpose of the investigation?

The meaning of all terms must be clearly defined so that they have the same meaning to all respondents. The researcher needs all the help that he or she can get; suggestions from colleagues and experts in the field of inquiry may reveal some ambiguities that can be removed and some items that do not contribute to its purpose. The panel of experts may rate the instrument in terms of how effectively it samples significant aspects of its purpose, providing estimates of content validity.

It is possible to estimate the predictive validity of a questionnaire by a follow-up observation of respondent behavior at the present time or at some time in the future.

There are some situations in which overt behavior can be observed without invasion of the privacy of respondents. A correlation of questionnaire responses with voting data on a campus or community election or issue may provide a basis for the computation of a coefficient of predictive validity.

Reliability of questionnaires may be inferred by a second administration of the instrument, comparing the responses with those of the first. Reliability may also be estimated by comparing responses of an alternate form with the original form.

The Opinionnaire, or Attitude Scale

The information form that attempts to measure the attitude or belief of an individual is known as an *opinionnaire,* or *attitude scale.* Since the terms *opinion* and *attitude* are not synonymous, a clarification is necessary.

How people feel, or what they believe, is their attitude. But it is difficult, if not impossible, to describe and measure attitude. Researchers must depend upon what people *say* are their beliefs and feelings. This is the area of opinion. Through the use of questions, or by getting people's expressed reaction to statements, a sample of their opinions is obtained. From this statement of opinion, one may infer or estimate their attitudes—what they *really* believe.

The process of inferring attitude from expressed opinion has many limitations. People may conceal their attitudes and express socially acceptable opinions. They may not really know how they feel about a social issue; they may never have given the idea serious consideration. People may be unaware of their attitude about a situation in the abstract. Until confronted with a real situation, they may be unable to predict their reaction or behavior.

Even behavior itself is not always a true indication of attitude. When politicians kiss babies, their behavior may not be a true expression of affection toward infants. Social custom or the desire for social approval makes many overt expressions of behavior mere formalities, quite unrelated to people's inward feelings. Even though there is no sure method of describing and measuring attitude, the description and measurement of opinion, in many instances, may be closely related to people's real feelings or attitudes.

With these limitations in mind, psychologists and sociologists have explored an interesting area of research, basing their data upon people's expressed opinions. Several methods have been employed:

1. Asking people directly how they feel about a subject. This technique may employ a schedule or questionnaire of the open or closed form. It may employ the interview process, in which the respondents express their opinions orally.

2. Asking people to check in a list the statements with which they agree.

3. Asking people to indicate their degree of agreement or disagreement with a series of statements about a controversial subject.

4. Inferring their attitudes from reactions to projective devices, through which they may reveal attitudes unconsciously. (A projective device is a data-gathering instrument which conceals its purpose in such a way that the subjects cannot guess how they should respond to appear in their best light. Thus, their real characteristics are revealed.)

Two of these procedures for eliciting opinion have been used extensively in opinion research, and warrant a brief description.

Thurstone Technique   The first method of attitude assessment is known as the Thurstone Technique of Scaled Values.[5] A number of statements, usually twenty or more, that express various points of view

[5] L. L. Thurstone and E. J. Chave, *The Measurement of Attitudes* (Chicago: University of Chicago Press, 1929).

toward a group, institution, idea, or practice are gathered. They are then submitted to a panel of a number of judges, who each arranges them in eleven groups, ranging from one extreme to another in position. This sorting by each judge yields a composite position for each of the items. When there has been marked disagreement between the judges in assigning a position to an item, that item is discarded. For items that are retained, each is given its median scale value, between one and eleven, as established by the panel.

The list of statements is then given to the subjects, who are asked to check the statements with which they agree. The median value of the statements that they check establishes their score, or quantifies their opinion.

Likert Method The second method, the Likert Method of Summated Ratings, which can be carried out without the panel of judges, has yielded scores very similar to those obtained by the Thurstone method. The coefficient of correlation between the two scales was reported as high as +.92 in one study.[6] Since the Likert-type scale takes much less time to construct, it offers an interesting possibility for the student of opinion research.

The first step in constructing a Likert-type scale consists of collecting a number of statements about a subject. The correctness of the statements is not important. If they express opinions held by a substantial number of people, they may be used. It is important that they express definite favorableness or unfavorableness to a particular point of view. The number of favorable and unfavorable statements should be approximately equal.

After the statements have been gathered, a trial test should be administered to a number of subjects. Only those items that correlate with the total test should be retained. This testing for internal consistency will help to eliminate statements that are ambiguous or that are not of the same type as the rest of the scale.

The attitude or opinion scale may be analyzed in several ways. The simplest way to describe opinion is to indicate percentage responses for each individual statement. For this type of analysis by item, three responses are preferable to the usual five: agree, undecided, and disagree. If a Likert-type scale is used it may be possible to report percentage responses by combining the two outside categories: strongly agree and agree; disagree and strongly disagree.

strongly agree	undecided	disagree
agree		strongly disagree

[6] Allen L. Edwards and Katherine C. Kenney, "A Comparison of the Thurstone and Likert Techniques of Attitude Scale Construction," *Journal of Applied Psychology* 30 (Feb. 1946): 72–83.

For example, 70 percent of the male respondents agree with the statement, "Merit rating will tend to encourage conformity and discourage initiative."

The Likert scaling technique assigns a scale value to each of the five responses. Thus, the instrument yields a total score for each respondent and a discussion of each individual item, while possible, is not necessary. Starting with a particular point of view, all statements favoring this position would be scored:

	Scale value
a. strongly agree	5
b. agree	4
c. undecided	3
d. disagree	2
e. strongly disagree	1

For statements opposing this point of view, the items are scored in the opposite order:

	Scale value
a. strongly agree	1
b. agree	2
c. undecided	3
d. disagree	4
e. strongly disagree	5

The opinionnaire illustrated in Figure 6.3 below attempts to measure Christian religious orthodoxy or conservatism. It is apparent that this type of instrument could be used to measure opinion in many controversial areas: racial integration, merit rating of teachers, universal military training, and many others.

The test scores obtained on all the items would then measure the respondent's favorableness toward the given point of view.

Opinionnaire

The following statements represent opinions, and your agreement or disagreement will be determined on the basis of your particular beliefs. Kindly check your position on the scale as the statement first impresses you. Indicate what you believe, rather than what you think you should believe.

   a. I strongly agree
   b. I agree
   c. I am undecided
   d. I disagree
   e. I strongly disagree

	a	b	c	d	e
1. Heaven does *not* exist as an actual place or location. ____					
2. God sometimes sets aside natural law, performing miracles. _____					
3. Jesus was born of a virgin, without a human father. ____					
4. Hell does *not* exist as an actual place or location. _____					
5. The inspiration that resulted in the writing of the Bible was no different from that of any other great religious literature. _____					
6. There is a final day of judgment for all who have lived on earth. _____					
7. The devil exists as an actual person. _____					
8. Prayer directly affects the lives of persons, whether or not they know that such prayer has been offered. _____					
9. There is another life after the end of organic life on earth. _____					
10. When on earth, Jesus possessed and used the power to restore the dead to life. _____					
11. God is a cosmic force, rather than an actual person. ____					
12. Prayer does *not* have the power to change such conditions as a drought. _____					
13. The creation of the world did *not* literally occur in the way described in the Old Testament. _____					
14. After Jesus was dead and buried, he actually rose from the dead, leaving an empty tomb. _____					
15. Everything in the Bible should be interpreted as literally true. _____					

Fig. 6-3. A Likert-type Opinionnaire.

Figure 6-4 below illustrates an instrument that was used to seek the opinions of a group of classroom teachers toward merit rating.

MERIT RATING OPINIONNAIRE

Male _____ Female _____ Age _____
Teaching level: elementary _____ secondary _____
Marital status: single _____ married _____ divorced/separated _____
widowed _____
Years of teaching experience _____ years.

The following statements represent opinions, and your agreement or disagreement will be determined on the basis of your particular convictions. Kindly check your position on the scale as the statement first impresses you. Indicate what you believe, rather than what you think you should believe.

> a. I strongly agree
> b. I agree
> c. I am undecided

    d. I disagree
    e. I strongly disagree

1. It is possible to determine what constitutes merit, or effective teaching. _____
2. A valid and reliable instrument can be developed to measure varying degrees of teaching effectiveness. _____
3. Additional remuneration will _not_ result in improved teaching. _____
4. Merit rating destroys the morale of the teaching force by creating jealousy, suspicion, and distrust. _____
5. Mutual confidence between teachers and administrators is impossible if administrators rate teachers for salary purposes. _____
6. Merit salary schedules will attract more high-quality young people to the teaching profession.
7. Merit salary schedules will hold quality teachers in the profession. _____
8. Parents will object to having their children taught by nonmerit teachers. _____
9. Merit rating can be as successful in teaching as it is in industry. _____
10. The hidden purpose of merit rating is to hold down salaries paid to most teachers by paying only a few teachers well. _____
11. There is no justification for paying poor teachers as well as good teachers are paid. _____
12. Apple-polishers will profit more than superior teachers from merit rating. _____
13. Merit rating will encourage conformity and discourage initiative. _____
14. The way to make teaching attractive is to reward excellence in the classroom. _____
15. Most administrators _do not_ know enough about teaching to rate their faculty members fairly.
16. Salary schedules based on education and experience only encourage mediocre teaching. _____

a	b	c	d	e

Fig. 6-4. A Likert-type Opinionnaire on Merit Rating

If the opinionnaire consisted of 30 statements or items, the following score values would be revealing:

$$30 \times 5 = 150 \quad \text{Most favorable response possible}$$
$$30 \times 3 = 90 \quad \text{A neutral attitude}$$
$$30 \times 1 = 30 \quad \text{Most unfavorable attitude}$$

The scores for any individual would fall between 30 and 150; above 90, if opinions tended to be favorable, and below 90, if opinions tended to be unfavorable to the given point of view.

The author has used this device in a course which includes a unit dealing with intercultural relations. It is interesting to note whether information about minority groups tends to alter an individual's attitude or opinion toward those groups. Before the unit is begun, the students respond to a 30-statement opinionnaire devised by the author. The papers are filled out anonymously, and students are instructed to mark their paper with some symbol known only to them, so that they can identify it at a later date.

Upon the completion of the unit several weeks later, the students respond to another copy of the same opinionnaire, again marking it with the symbol previously used. After the papers are scored, the instructor has a device which indicates possible changes in attitude or, at least, in expressed opinions. Invariably, there has been consistent growth in favorableness toward minority groups. Although the measure is crude, it does seem to support the hypothesis that knowledge about minority groups brings about a more favorable attitude toward them—in the classroom, at least. It is possible that the change in score is more significant than the magnitude of the score itself, for the validity of the instrument has not been, and cannot be, established.

This example of opinion analysis demonstrates how a teacher may use this technique to create class interest, even though it may fail to achieve the rigorous standards of fundamental research procedures.

It would be unwise to conclude this discussion without a recognition of limitations of this type of opinion measurement. Obviously, it is somewhat inexact, and fails to measure opinion with the precision one would desire.

There is no basis for belief that the five positions indicated on the scale are equally spaced. The interval between "tend to agree" and "agree" may not be equal to the interval between "tend to agree" and "cannot say." It is also unlikely that the statements are of equal value in "for-ness" or "against-ness." That the respondent can validly react to a short statement on a printed form, in the absence of real-life qualifying situations, is unlikely. That equal scores obtained by several individuals indicate equal favorableness toward the given position is unlikely. Actually, different combinations of positions can yield equal score values, without necessarily indicating equivalent positions of attitude or opinion. Even though the opinionnaire provides for anonymous response, there is a possibility that people may answer according to what they think they *should* feel, rather than how they *really* feel.

In spite of these limitations, the process of opinion measurement has merit, and until more precise measures of attitude are developed, this technique may serve a useful purpose in social research.

Q METHODOLOGY

Q methodology, devised by William Stephenson[7] is a technique for scaling objects or statements. It is a method of ranking attitudes or judgments and is particularly effective when the number of items to be ranked is large. The procedure is known as a *Q*-sort, in which cards or slips bearing the statements or items are arranged in a series of numbered piles. Usually nine or eleven piles are established, representing relative positions on a standard scale. Some examples of simple polarized scales are illustrated.

most important	least important
most approve	least approve
most liberal	least liberal
most favorable	least favorable
most admired	least admired
most like me	least like me

The respondent is asked to place a specified number of items on each pile, usually on the basis of an approximately normal or symmetrical distribution. If nine piles were established, the assignment of slips or cards would be based upon an approximate stanine percentage distribution. From 50 to 100 items should be used.

Most like me								*Least like me*
#	1	2	3	4	5	6	7	8	9
%	4	7	12	17	20	17	12	7	4

Self-concept *Q*-sort   Let us assume that a *Q*-sort has been designed to measure the before-and-after therapy status of a subject. A few examples of appropriate traits are presented to be placed on the scale.

afraid	ignored	discouraged
suspicious	admired	energetic
successful	disliked	loved
enthusiastic	cheerful	hated
friendly	happy	stupid

A change in position of items from before-therapy to after-therapy would indicate possible change or improvement in self-esteem. Computing the coefficient of correlation between the pile positions of items before and after therapy would provide a measure of change. If no

---

[7] William Stephenson, *The Study of Behavior*, (Chicago: University of Chicago Press, 1953).

change in item placement had occurred the coefficient of correlation would be +1.00. If a completely opposite profile appeared the coefficient would be −1.00. While perfect +1.00 or −1.00 coefficient would be improbable, a high positive coefficient would indicate little change, whereas a high negative coefficient would indicate significant change.

Another type of *Q*-sort solicits the composite judgment of a selected panel of experts (in this case, professors of educational research). The criterion of judgment involves the relative importance of research concepts that should be included in the introductory course in educational research. One hundred slips, each listing a concept, were to be sorted into nine piles, ranging from most important to least important. A few of the concepts that were considered are listed:

hypothesis	historical method
probability	survey
dependent variable	null hypothesis
coefficient of correlation	preparing a questionnaire
sources of reference materials	deductive method
preparing the research report	descriptive method
randomization	sampling
post hoc fallacy	intervening variables
experimental method	independent variable
interviewing	*Q*-sorts
level of significance	standard deviation
the research proposal	nonparametric statistics
attitude studies	action research

The mean value of the positions assigned each item indicates the composite judgment of the panel as to its relative importance.

Two applications of the *Q*-sort technique have been illustrated in our simplified discussion. The first attempted to measure change in the attitude of an individual toward himself or herself, the second the composite judgment of a group of individuals. Many types of analysis may be carried on in the area of attitudes by the use of *Q* methodology. Researchers contemplating the use of this technique should carefully consider the theoretical assumptions underlying the criteria and the items selected.

Sociometry[8]

Sociometry is a technique for describing social relationships that exist between individuals in a group. In an indirect way it attempts to describe attractions or repulsions between individuals by asking them

---

[8] J. L. Moreno, *Who Shall Survive?* 2nd ed. (New York: Beacon Press, 1953).

188 Research in Education

to indicate whom they would choose or reject in various situations. Children in a school classroom may be asked to name the child, or several children, in order of preference (usually two or three) that they would invite to a party, eat lunch with, sit next to, work on a class project with, or have as a close friend.

There is an extensive body of research, using the sociometric method of analysis, on classroom groups from kindergarten through college, fraternities and sororities, dormitory residents, camp groups, factory and office workers, military combat units, and entire communities. The United States Air Force has used sociometry to study the nature of leadership in various situations. For example, the following question was used in a study of air combat crews: "What member of the crew would you select, disregarding rank, as the most effective leader if your plane were forced down in a remote and primitive area? Name three, in order of your preference."

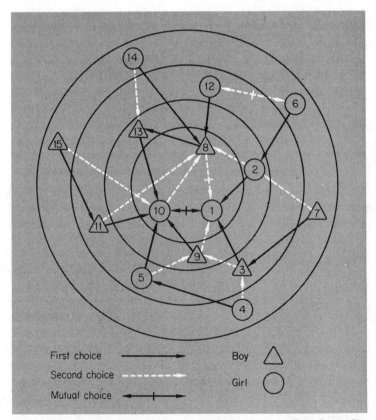

Fig. 6-5. Sociogram Showing First and Second Choices in a Third Grade Class

Although some researchers object to the method, negatively phrased questions have been used: "If you were to work on a class project with another student, who would you prefer *not* to work with?"

Scoring Sociometric Choices One widely used procedure is to count the number of times an individual is chosen, disregarding the order of choice. This is the most simple method and is widely used. The objection has been raised that it is insensitive, for it does not distinguish between a first and third choice.

Another procedure is to score a first choice three points, a second choice two points, and a third choice one point. The weakness of this scoring plan is that it suggests that the difference between a third choice and no choice at all is identical to the differences between third, second, and first choices. This is an assumption that is difficult to defend.

A third scoring plan is based upon the concept of the normal curve standard score distribution, which can be roughly translated into the following scheme, depending upon the size of the group of participants:

| | Size of group | | |
Rank	10	30	70
1st	10	11	12
2nd	7	8	10
3rd	5	6	9
not chosen	0	0	0

An example of the scoring of ten subjects:

| | Score | | | |
Subject	1st (10)	2nd (7)	3rd (5)	Total Score
a	2	3	1	46
b	1	0	2	20
c	3	1	1	42
d	1	2	1	29
e	0	2	0	14
f	0	1	3	22
g	0	0	2	10
h	0	0	0	0
i	0	2	2	24
j	0	0	0	0

The scores for each individual in the group can be related to such measures as intelligence or other traits that can be measured by tests, or to such categories as sex, race nationality, religious affiliation, economic status, birth order, family size, grade point average, teacher or employment supervisor judgment, or other characteristics that may be of interest to the researcher.

The Sociogram   Sociometric choices may be represented graphically on a chart known as a sociogram. There are many variations of pattern, and the reader is urged to consult specialized references on sociometry. A few observations will illustrate the nature of the sociogram.

In consulting a sociogram, boys may be represented by triangles and girls by circles. A choice may be represented by a single-pointed arrow, a mutual choice by an arrow pointing in opposite directions. Those chosen most often are referred to as stars, those not chosen by others as isolates. Small groups made up of individuals who choose one another are cliques.

Identifying numbers are placed within the symbols. Numbers of those chosen most often are placed nearest the center of the diagram, with those chosen less often progressively outward. Those not chosen are, literally, on the outside. (See Figure 6-5, on page 188.) It must be remembered that the relationship between individuals in a group is a changeable thing. Children's choices are most temporary, for stability tends to develop only with age.

Students of group relationships and classroom teachers may construct a number of sociograms over a period of time to measure changes that may have resulted from efforts to bring isolates into closer group relationships, or to transform cliques into more general group membership. The effectiveness of socializing or status-building procedures can thus be measured by the changes revealed in the sociogram. Since sociometry is a peer rating, rather than a rating by superiors, it adds another dimension to the understanding of members of a group.

"Guess-who" Technique

A process of description closely related to sociometry is the "guess-who" technique. Developed by Hugh Hartshorne and Mark A. May,[9] the process consists of description of the various roles played by children in a group.

Children are asked to name the individuals who fit certain verbal descriptions.

> This one is always happy.
> This one is always picking on others.
> This one is always worried.
> This one never likes to do anything.
> This one will always help you.

[9] Hugh Hartshorne and Mark A. May, *Studies in Deceit* (New York: Macmillan Co., 1929).

Items of this type yield interesting and significant peer judgments, and are useful in the study of individual roles. Of course, the names of children chosen should not be revealed.

Social-distance scale

Another approach to the description and measurement of social relationships is the social-distance scale, developed by E. S. Bogardus[10] at the University of Southern California. This device attempts to measure to what degree an individual, or a group of individuals, is accepted or rejected by another individual or group.

Various scaled situations, with score values ranging from acceptance to rejection, are established. The individual checks his or her position by choosing one of the points on the scale. For example, in judging acceptance of different minority groups, the choices might range between these extremes:

Complete acceptance	I wouldn't object to having a member of this group become a member of my family by marriage.
Partial acceptance	I wouldn't mind sitting next to a member of this group on a bus.
Rejection	I don't think that members of this group should be admitted into our country.

When applied to an individual in a classroom situation, the choices might range between these extremes:

Complete acceptance	I'd like to have this student as my best friend.
Partial acceptance	I wouldn't mind sitting near this student.
Rejection	I wish this student weren't in my room.

Of course, in the real social-distance scale, illustrated by the sample items above, there would be a larger number of evenly spaced scaled positions (usually seven in number), giving a more precise measure of acceptance or rejection.

Devices of the type described here have many possibilities for the description and measurement of social relationships and, in this important area of social research, may yield interesting and useful data.

---

[10] E. S. Bogardus, "A Social Distance Scale," *Sociology and Social Research* 17 (Jan. 1933): 265–271.

PSYCHOLOGICAL TESTS AND INVENTORIES

As data-gathering devices, psychological tests are among the most useful tools of educational research, for they provide the data for most experimental and descriptive studies in education. Since we are able here to examine only limited aspects of the nature of psychological testing, students of educational research should consult other volumes for a more complete discussion.[11]

A psychological test is an instrument designed to describe and measure a sample of certain aspects of human behavior. Tests may be used to compare the behavior of two or more persons at a particular time, or one or more persons at different times. Psychological tests yield objective and standardized descriptions of behavior, quantified by numerical scores. Under ideal conditions, achievement or aptitude tests measure the best performance of which individuals are capable. Under ideal conditions, inventories attempt to measure typical behavior. Tests and inventories are used to describe status (or a prevailing condition at a particular time), to measure changes in status produced by modifying factors, or to predict future behavior on the basis of present performance.

In the simple classroom experiment described in the chapter on experimental research (Chapter Three), test scores were used to equate the experimental and control groups, to describe status in achievement before the application of teaching methods, to measure pupil mean gain resulting from the application of experimental and control teaching methods, and to evaluate the relative effectiveness of teaching methods. This example of classroom experimentation illustrates how experimental data may be gathered through the application of tests.

In descriptive research studies, tests are frequently used to describe prevailing conditions at a particular time. How does a student compare with those of his or her own age or grade in school achievement? How does a particular group compare with other groups in other schools, or in other cities?

In school surveys for the past forty years, achievement tests have been used extensively in the appraisal of instruction. Because tests yield quantitative descriptions or measure, they make possible more precise analysis than can be achieved through subjective judgment alone.

There are many ways of classifying psychological tests. One distinction is made between *performance tests* and *paper-and-pencil tests.* Performance tests, usually administered individually, require that the subjects manipulate objects or mechanical apparatus while their actions are ob-

[11] Lee J. Cronbach, *Essentials of Psychological Testing,* 3rd ed. (New York: Harper & Row, 1970); Ann Anastasia, *Psychological Testing,* 3rd ed. (New York: Macmillan Co., 1968).

served and recorded by the examiner. Paper-and-pencil tests, usually administered in groups, require the subjects to mark their response on a prepared sheet.

Two other classes of tests are *power* versus *timed* or *speed* tests. Power tests have no time limit, and the subjects attempt progressively more difficult tasks until they are unable to continue successfully. Timed or speed tests usually involve the element of power, but in addition, limit the time that the subjects have in which to complete certain tasks.

Another distinction is that made between *nonstandardized,* teacher-made tests and *standardized* tests. The test that the classroom teacher constructs is likely to be less expertly designed than that of the professional, although it is based upon the best logic and skill that the teacher can command, and is usually "tailor-made" for a particular group of pupils.

By contrast, the standardized test is designed for more general use. Each item and the total scores have been carefully analyzed, and validity and reliability established by careful statistical controls. Norms have been established, based upon the performance of many subjects of various ages living in many different types of communities and geographic areas. Not only has the content of the test been standardized, but the administration and scoring have also been set in one pattern so that those subsequently taking the tests will take them under like conditions. As far as possible, the interpretation has also been standardized.

Although it would be inaccurate to claim that all standardized tests meet optimum standards of excellence, these instruments have been made as sound as possible in the light of the best that is known by experts in test construction, administration, and interpretation.

Psychological tests may also be classified in terms of their purposes— the types of psychological traits that they describe and measure.

Achievement Tests

Achievement tests attempt to measure what an individual has learned—his or her present level of performance. Most tests used in schools are achievement tests. They are particularly helpful in determining individual or group status in academic learning. Achievement test scores are used in placing, advancing, or retaining students at particular grade levels. They are used in diagnosing strengths and weaknesses, and as a basis for awarding prizes, scholarships, or degrees.

Frequently, achievement test scores are used in evaluating the influences of courses of study, teachers, teaching methods, and other factors considered to be significant in educational practice. In using tests for evaluative purposes it is important not to generalize beyond the specific elements measured. For example, to identify effective teaching exclusively with the limited products measured by the ordinary achievement test would be to define effective teaching too narrowly. It is essential that researchers recognize that the elements of a situation under appraisal need to be evaluated on the basis of a number of criteria, not merely on a few limited aspects.

Aptitude Tests

Aptitude tests attempt to predict the degree of achievement that may be expected from individuals in a particular activity. To the extent that they measure past learning, they are similar to achievement tests. To the extent that they measure nondeliberate or unplanned learning, they are different. Aptitude tests attempt to predict an individual's capacity to acquire improved performance with additional training.

Actually, capacity (or aptitude) cannot be measured directly. Aptitude can only be inferred on the basis of present performance, particularly in areas where there has been no deliberate attempt to teach the behaviors to be predicted.

Intelligence, which is generally thought of as inborn potentiality, is really measured by present ability. Whether one's achievement is relatively high, average, or low, we assume that it is a measure of how effectively one has profited from one's informal opportunities for learning. To the extent that others have had similar opportunities, we predict one's capacity or potentiality on the basis of how one's ability compares with that of others one's own age. This is a matter of inference rather than of direct measurement. Since it has proved useful in predicting future achievement, particularly in academic pursuits, we consider this concept of intelligence measurement a valid application.

Aptitude tests have been similarly designed to predict improved performance with further training in many areas. These inferred measurements have been applied to mechanical and manipulative skills, musical and artistic pursuits, and many professional areas involving many types of predicted ability.

In music, for example, ability to remember and discriminate between differences in pitch, rhythm pattern, intensity, and timbre seems to be closely related to future levels of development in musicianship. Present proficiency in these tasks provides a fair predictive index of an individual's ability to profit from advanced instruction, particularly when the individual has had little formal training in music prior to the test.

Aptitude tests may be used to divide students into relatively homogeneous groups for instructional purposes, to identify students for scholarship grants, to screen individuals for particular educational programs, or help guide individuals into areas where they are most likely to succeed.

Aptitude tests, particularly those that deal with academic aptitude, used for purposes of placement and classification have become highly controversial, and their use has been prohibited in many communities. The fact that some individuals with culturally different backgrounds do not score well on these tests has led to charges of discrimination against members of minority groups. The case has been made that most of these tests do not accurately predict academic achievement since their contents are culturally biased. Efforts have been, and are being, made to develop culture-free tests that eliminate this undesirable quality.

Interest Inventories

Interest inventories attempt to yield a measure of the types of activities that an individual has a tendency to like and to choose. One kind of instrument has compared the subject's pattern of interest to the interest patterns of successful practitioners in a number of vocational fields. A distinctive pattern has been discovered to be characteristic of each field. The assumption is that an individual is happiest and most successful working in a field most like his or her own measured profile of interests.

Another inventory is based on the correlation between a number of activities from the areas of school, recreation, and work. These related activities have been identified by careful analysis with mechanical, computational, scientific, persuasive, artistic, literary, musical, social-service, and clerical areas of interest. By sorting the subject's stated likes and dislikes into various interest areas, a percentile score for each area is obtained. It is then assumed that the subject will find his or her area of greatest interest where the percentile scores are relatively high.

Interest blanks or inventories are examples of self-report instruments in which individuals note their own likes and dislikes. These self-report instruments are really standardized interviews in which the subjects, through introspection, indicate feelings that may be interpreted in terms of what is known about interest patterns.

Personality Measures

Personality scales are usually self-report instruments. The individual checks responses to certain questions or statements. These instruments yield scores which are assumed or have been shown to measure certain personality traits or tendencies.

Because of the difficulty, inability, or unwillingness of individuals to report their own reactions accurately or objectively, these instruments may be of limited value. Part of this limitation may be due to the inadequate theories of personality upon which some of these inventories have been based. At best, they provide data useful in suggesting the need for further analysis. Some have reasonable empirical validity with particular groups of individuals, but prove to be invalid when applied to others. For example, one personality inventory has proven valuable in yielding scores that correlate highly with the diagnoses of psychiatrists in clinical situations. But when applied to college students, its diagnostic value has proved disappointing.

The development of instruments of personality description and measurement is relatively recent, and it is likely that continued research in this important area will yield better theories of personality and better instruments for describing and measuring its various aspects.

The Mooney Problems Check List[12] is an inventory to be used by students in reporting their own problems of adjustment. The subjects are asked to indicate on the check list the problems that trouble them. From a list of these items, classified into different categories, a picture of the students' problems, from their own viewpoint, is drawn. Although the most useful interpretation may result from an item analysis of personal problems, the device does yield a quantitative score which may indicate the degree of difficulty that students feel they are experiencing in their adjustment. This instrument has been used as a research device to identify and describe the nature of the problems facing individuals and groups of individuals in a school.

The tendency to withhold embarrassing responses and to express those that are socially acceptable; the emotional involvement of individuals with their own problems; and lack of insight—all these limit the effectiveness of personal and social-adjustment scales. Some psychologists believe that the projective type of instrument offers greater promise, for these tests attempt to disguise their purpose so completely that the subject is unable to know how to appear in the best light.

The most commonly used projective tests involve the subject's interpretation of the meaning of various standardized ink-blot figures or pictured situations.

Projective Devices

A projective instrument enables subjects to project their internal feelings, attitudes, needs, values, or wishes to an external object. Thus, the subjects may unconsciously reveal themselves as they react to the external object. The use of projective devices is particularly helpful in

---

[12] Ross L. Mooney, *Problem Check List, High School Form* (Columbus: Bureau of Educational Research, Ohio State University, 1941).

counteracting the tendency of subjects to try to appear in their best light, to respond as they believe they are expected to respond.

Projection may be accomplished through a number of techniques:

1. *Association.* The respondent is asked to indicate what he or she sees, feels, or thinks when presented with a picture, cartoon, ink blot, word, or phrase. The Thematic Apperception Test, the Rorschach Ink Blot Test, and various word-association tests are familiar examples.

2. *Completion.* The respondent is asked to complete an incomplete sentence or task. A sentence-completion instrument may include such items as:
   My greatest ambition is
   My greatest fear is
   I most enjoy
   I dream a great deal about
   I get very angry when
   If I could do anything I wanted it would be to

3. *Role-playing.* Subjects are asked to improvise or act out a situation in which they have been assigned various roles. The researcher may observe such traits as hostility, frustration, dominance, sympathy, insecurity, prejudice, or their absence.

4. *Creative or constructive.* Permitting subjects to model clay, finger paint, play with dolls, play with toys, or draw or write imaginative stories about assigned situations may be revealing. The choice of color, form, words, the sense of orderliness, evidence of tensions, and other reactions may provide opportunities to infer deep-seated feelings.

QUALITIES OF A GOOD TEST

Validity

In general, a test is valid to the extent that it measures what it claims to measure. However, there are several types of validity. *Content validity* refers to the degree to which the test actually measures, or is specifically related to, the traits for which it was designed. It shows how adequately the test samples the universe of knowledge, attitudes, and skills that a student is expected to master. Content validity is based upon careful examination of course textbooks, syllabi, objectives, and the judgments of subject matter specialists. The criterion of content validity is often assessed by a panel of experts in the field who judge its adequacy, but there is no numerical way to express it.

Construct validity is the degree to which scores on a test can be accounted for by the explanatory constructs of a sound theory. If one were to study such a construct as dominance, one would hypothesize that people who have this characteristic will perform differently from those who do not. Theories can be built describing how dominant people behave in a distinctive way. If this is done, dominant people can be identified by observation of their behavior, rating or classifying them in terms of the theory. A test could then be designed to have construct validity to the degree that the test scores are systematically related to the judgments made by observation of behavior identified by the theory as dominant.

Criterion-related validity is a broad term that refers to two different criteria of time frame in judging the usefulness of a test.

1. Predictive validity refers to the usefulness of a test in predicting some future performance such as the degree of usefulness of the Scholastic Aptitude Test taken in high school in predicting college grade point averages.

2. Concurrent validity refers to the usefulness of a test in closely relating to such other measures as present academic grades, teacher ratings, or scores on another test of known validity. If a test is designed to pick out good candidates for appointment as shop foremen, and test scores show a high positive correlation with actual success on the job, the test has a high degree of predictive validity, whatever factors it actually measures. It predicts well. It serves a useful purpose.

But before a test can be evaluated on the basis of predictive validity, success on the job must be accurately described and measured. The criteria of the production of the department, the judgment of supervisors, or measures of employee morale might serve as evidence. Since these criteria might not be entirely satisfactory, however, predictive validity is not easy to assess. It is often difficult to discover whether the faults of prediction lie in the test, in the criteria of success, or in both.

Tests are often validated by comparing their results with a test of known validity. A well-known scale of personal adjustment, the Minnesota Multiphasic Personality Inventory, involved sorting nearly 500 cards into three categories, *yes, no,* and *cannot say.* The test equipment was expensive, and it could not be easily administered to large groups at the same time. A paper-and-pencil form was devised, using the simple process of checking responses to printed items on a test form. This form could be administered to a large group at one time and then scored by machine, all with little expense. The results were so similar to the more time-consuming, expensive card-sorting process, that the latter has been largely replaced. This is the process of establishing *concurrent validity;* in this case, by comparing an expensive individual test with an easy-to-administer group test.

In like manner, performance tests have been validated against paper-and-pencil tests, and short tests against longer tests. Through this process, more convenient and more appropriate tests can be devised to accomplish the measurement of behavior more effectively.

The validity of a test is expressed as a coefficient of validity (coefficient of correlation). Criterion-related validity is expressed as the coefficient of correlation between test scores and some measure of future performance, or between test scores and scores on another test or measure of known validity. The subject of correlation is explained in detail in Chapter Seven.

Reliability

A test is reliable to the extent that it measures consistently, from one time to another. In tests that have a high coefficient of reliability, errors of measurement have been reduced to a minimum. Reliable tests, whatever they measure, yield comparable scores upon repeated administration. An unreliable test would be comparable to a stretchable rubber yardstick that yielded different measurements each time it was applied.

A test may be reliable, even though it is not valid. A valid test is always reliable.

The reliability of a test is expressed as a coefficient of correlation. There are a number of methods used to compute various coefficients of reliability.

1. Test of stability—test retest. The scores on a test may be correlated with scores on a second administration of the test at a later date.

2. Equivalent or parallel forms. The scores on a test may be correlated with scores on an alternative form of the test—scores on *form A* with scores on *form B*.

3. Internal consistency.
    a. Split halves—odd vs. even items. The scores on the odd-numbered items are correlated with the scores on the even-numbered items. Since this is actually comparing scores on two shorter tests, the coefficient is modified by the application of the Spearman-Brown formula, explained in Chapter Seven.
    b. Split halves—first half with second half. On some, but not on all types of tests, it may be feasible to correlate the scores on the first half with those of the second half.
    c. A combination of a. and b., which is an estimate of the average reliability of such possible combinations of split halves—first half vs. second half, odd vs. even items, etc. The Kuder-Richardson formula is used for this purpose.

The reliability of a test may be raised by increasing the number of items of equal quality to the other items. Carefully designed directions for the administration of the test with no variation from group to group, providing an atmosphere free from distractions and one that minimizes boredom and fatigue will also improve the reliability of the testing instrument.

Objectivity

A test should yield a clear score value for each performance, the score being independent of the personal judgment of the scorer.

Economy

Tests that can be given in a short period of time are likely to gain the cooperation of the subject, and to conserve the time of all those involved in test administration. The matter of expense of administering a test is often a significant factor, if the testing program is being operated on a limited budget.

Simplicity of Administration, Scoring, and Interpretation

Ease of administration, scoring, and interpretation is an important factor in selecting a test, particularly when expert personnel or an adequate budget are not available. Many good tests are easily and effectively administered, scored, and interpreted by the classroom teacher, who may not be an expert.

Interest

Tests that are interesting and enjoyable help to gain the cooperation of the subject. Those that are dull or seem silly may discourage or antagonize the subject. Under these unfavorable conditions, the test is not likely to yield useful results.

Fig. 6-6. A Target Analogy of Reliability and Validity

It is important in selecting a test to recognize the fact that a good test does not necessarily possess all the desirable qualities for all subjects or for all levels of performance. Within a certain range of age, maturity, or ability, a test may be suitable. For other individuals outside that range, the test may be quite unsatisfactory and a more appropriate one needed.

The selection should be made after careful examination of the standardizing data contained in the test manual and extensive analysis of published evaluations of the instrument. Research workers should select the most appropriate standardized tests available. Detailed reports of their usefulness and limitations are usually supplied in the manual furnished by the publisher. The considered judgments of outside experts are also available. *The Mental Measurements Yearbook,*[13] the best single reference on psychological tests, contains many critical evaluations of published tests, each contributed by an expert in the field of psychological measurement. Usually, several different evaluations are included for each test. Since the reports are not duplicated from one volume to another, it is advisable to consult *Tests in Print* or previous *Yearbooks* for additional reports not included in the current volume. In addition to the reviews and evaluations, the names of test publishers, prices, forms, and appropriate uses are included. Readers are also urged to consult the listings and reviews of newly published psychological tests in the *Journal of Educational Measurement.*

When psychological tests are used in educational research, it is important to recognize that standardized test scores are only approximate measures of the traits under consideration. This limitation is inevitable, and may be ascribed to a number of possible factors:

1. The choice of an inappropriate test for the specific purpose in mind

2. Errors inherent in any psychological test; no test is completely valid or reliable

3. Errors that result from poor test conditions, inexpert or careless administration or scoring of the test, or faulty tabulation of test scores

4. Inexpert interpretation of test results.

SIMPLE DATA ORGANIZATION

The following discussion is directed to the beginner and does not suggest appropriate procedures for the advanced researcher. Theses, dissertations, and advanced research projects usually involve sophisticated ex-

---

[13] Oscar K. Buros, ed. *Eighth Mental Measurements Yearbook* (Highland Park, N.J.: Gryphon Press, 1978).

perimental designs and statistical analysis. The use of the computer has become standard procedure. Because it can effectively process complex variable relationships, it has made a significant contribution to research. However, for the simple studies of the beginner, the use of the computer may not be justified.

When the results of an observation, interview, questionnaire, opinionnaire, or test are to be analyzed, the problems of organization confront the researcher. The first problem is to designate appropriate logical and mutually exclusive categories for tabulation of the data. At times the hypothesis or question to be answered may suggest the type of organization. If the hypothesis involved the difference between the attitudes of men and women toward teacher merit rating, the categories *male* and *female* would be clearly indicated. In other instances the categories are not determined by the hypothesis and other subdivisions of the group under investigation may be desirable.

When the responses or characteristics of a group are analyzed, it is sometimes satisfactory to describe the group as a whole. In simple types of analysis, when the group is sufficiently homogeneous, no breakdown into subgroups is necessary. But in many situations the picture of the whole group is not clear. The heterogeneity of the group may yield data that have little meaning. One tends to get an unreal picture of a group of subjects that are actually very different from one another, and the differences are concealed by a description of a nonexistent or unreal average. In such cases it may be helpful to divide the group into more homogeneous subgroups or categories that have in common some distinctive characteristics that may be significant for the purpose of the analysis. Distinguishing between the responses of men and women, between elementary and secondary teachers, between gifted and slow-learning children may reveal significant relationships.

For example, a new type of classroom organization may seem to have little impact on a group of students. But, after dividing the group into two subgroups, the gifted and the slow learners, some interesting relationships may become clear. The grouping may be effective for the bright students, but most ineffective for the slow learners.

Many studies employ the classification of data into dichotomous, or twofold, categories. When the categories are established on the basis of test scores, rankings, or some other quantitative measure, it may be advisable to compare those at the top with those at the bottom, omitting from the analysis those near the middle of the distribution. It is possible to compare the top third with the bottom third, or the top 25 per cent with the bottom 25 per cent. This eliminates those cases near the midpoint that tend to obscure the differences that may exist. By eliminating the middle portion, sharper contrast is achieved, but the risk of the regression effect is increased.

Comparisons are not always dichotomous. At times it is desirable to divide a large group into more than two categories, depending on the nature of the variables that are to be considered.

Outside Criteria for Comparison

In addition to the comparisons that may be made between subgroups, or *within* the larger group, the group may be analyzed in terms of some *outside criteria*. Of course, it must be assumed that reasonably valid and reliable measuring devices are available for making such comparisons. These "measuring sticks" may consist of standardized tests, score cards, rating scales, frequency counts, and physical as well as psychological measuring devices. Some of these outside criteria are:

1. *Prevailing conditions, practices, or performance* of a different but comparable unit, or comparable units. This comparison may be made with another community or other communities, school or schools, and class or classes. Comparisons may be made with groups representing best conditions or practices, typical or average status, or equated groups that have been matched in terms of certain variables, leaving one or a limited number of variables for comparison.

2. *What experts believe to constitute best conditions or practices.* These experts may comprise a specially selected panel, chosen for the purpose. A group of practitioners in the field who are assumed to be most familiar with the characteristics under consideration, or the survey staff itself, may constitute the body of experts. The judgments of recognized authorities who publish their opinions are frequently selected as criteria.

3. *What a professional group, a commission, an accrediting agency, or another scholarly deliberative body establishes as appropriate standards.* These standards may be expressed as lists of objectives, or may be quantitative measures of status for accreditation or approval. The *American Medical Association's* standards for accreditation of medical schools, the *North Central Association of Secondary Schools and Colleges* accreditation standards, or the standards of the *National Commission on Teacher Education and Professional Standards* for programs of teacher education are examples of evaluative criteria.

4. *Laws or rules that have been enacted or promulgated by a legislative or quasilegislative body.* The areas of teacher certification regulations, school building standards, or health and safety regulations provide appropriate criteria for comparison.

5. *Research evidence.* The factors to be analyzed may be examined in the light of principles confirmed by scholarly research that has been published and generally accepted.

6. *Public opinion.* Although not always appropriate as a criterion of what
   should be, the opinions or views of "the man on the street" are
   sometimes appropriate as a basis for comparison.

Sorting and Tabulating Data

Tabulation is the process of transferring data from the data-gathering instruments to the tabular form in which they may be systematically
examined. This process may be performed in a number of ways. In
simple types of research, hand-tabulating procedures are usually employed. In more extensive investigations a card-tabulating process may
be used, possibly including machine methods.

Most simple research studies employ the method of hand-sorting
and recording, with tabulations written on tabulation sheets. To save
time and to ensure greater accuracy, it is recommended that one person
read the data while the other records them on the tabulation sheet.
Marks are best recorded by fence tallies, ( ) with a cross line every
five tallies. In constructing tally form sheets it is important to provide
enough space to record the tallies in each category.

The following discussion on hand tabulation emphasizes the importance of careful planning before the sorting and tabulation begin.

Without careful planning, inexperienced researchers may waste effort when tabulating responses on a set of questionnaires filled out by
a group of teachers. After completing the tabulation, they may decide
to compare the responses of elementary teachers with secondary teachers. This would involve retabulating the responses of the questionnaire.
It might then occur to them that it would be interesting to compare
the responses of the men with those of the women. Another handling
of the questionnaires would be necessary.

If they had decided upon their categories before tabulation, one
handling of the questionnaires would have been sufficient. Sorting the
questionnaires into two piles, one for elementary teachers and another
for secondary teachers, then sorting each of these into separate piles
for men and for women, would have yielded four stacks. Then by tabulating the responses of each of the piles separately, one planned operation
would have yielded the same amount of information as three unplanned
operations.

	ELEMENTARY	*SECONDARY*
men		
women		

	AGREE	CANNOT SAY	DISAGREE
Freshmen			
Sophomores			
Juniors			
Seniors			

Fig. 6-7. Tabulation Form Providing for the Analysis of 12 Possible Response Categories Based upon Question 1 on an Opinionnaire

Before tabulating questionnaires or opinionnaires, it is always important to decide upon the categories that are to be established for analysis. It has been shown that if this decision is delayed, it may be necessary to retabulate the items a number of times, needlessly consuming a great deal of time and effort.

If the data-gathering device called for a larger number of responses, the system of presorting would be similar. It would be advisable, however, to set up a separate tabulation sheet for each of the categories, because a single sheet would become unwieldy.

Figure 6-7 illustrates how a three-item opinionnaire response could be tabulated for a question such as the following:

An honor system would eliminate cheating in examinations.

I agree _____ .
I cannot say _____ .
I disagree _____ .

Students may apply these procedures to classify and tabulate similar types of data. These data sheets are not ordinarily presented in the report, but they may suggest ways in which some of the data may be presented as tables or graphic figures.

Tables and Figures

The process of tabulation which has just been described is the first step in the construction of the tables that are included in a research report. It is likely that the beginning researcher thinks of tables purely as aids to understanding. Displaying data in rows and columns, according to some logical plan of classification, they may serve an even more important purpose in helping researchers to see the similarities and relationships of their data in bold relief.

A discussion of the construction and use of tables and figures is presented in some detail in Chapter Ten.

Percentage Comparisons

Presenting data by frequency counts has a number of limitations. If the groups to be compared are unequal in size, the frequency count may have little meaning. Converting to percentage responses enables the researcher to compare subgroups of unequal size meaningfully. Translating frequency counts into percentages indicates the number-per-hundred compared. The provision of a common base makes the comparison clear.

There are several limitations that should be recognized in using percentage comparisons. Unless the number of frequencies is reasonably large, a percentage may be misleading and may seem to suggest a generalization that is unwarranted. It may be appropriate to indicate that, of four physicians interviewed, one believed that a particular medication would be harmful. To indicate that 25 per cent of physicians interviewed believed that the medication would be harmful creates an image of a larger sample of physicians than was actually interviewed. It is essential that both frequency counts and percentage responses be included in the presentation and analysis of data.

In converting frequency counts to percentages, rounding to the nearest percentage point is preferable. Because the type of data presented in educational research is not too precise, there is little value in expressing percentages in decimal values. In other situations, however, such as the drug industry, where ratio scales of measurement are often used, it would be extremely important to carry a percentage reported to four or five decimal places, particularly when a trace of an element would be harmful if exceeded.

When using percentages in dichotomous comparisons it is only necessary to state the percentage in one of the categories. If 65 per cent of the respondents are men, it is not necessary to indicate that 35 per cent are women. Unnecessary duplication is evidence of poor reporting.

Crossbreaks

A crossbreak is a graphic way of presenting observations and is a useful device in organizing and describing a data relationship. An example of an opinionnaire response follows: A legal abortion, during the first trimester, should be the right of any woman.

	Agree	No Opinion	Disagree
Roman Catholic	8 (14)	10 (17)	40 (69)
Protestant	30 (61)	7 (14)	12 (24)
Jewish	25 (69)	9 (25)	2 (6)

Numbers are expressed frequencies of response
Numbers in parentheses are expressed as percentages

Ranking and Weighting Items

There are times when response categories are not mutually exclusive. Preferences for certain things or reasons for an act are usually explained in terms of a number of factors, rarely single ones. It would be unrealistic to expect respondents to indicate their favorite type of recreation or the single reason they decided to attend a particular university. In such instances it would be appropriate to ask the respondents to indicate two or three responses in order of importance or preference. This ranking of items makes possible a useful method of analysis. Items may be weighted in inverse order. For example, if three items are to be ranked, it would be appropriate to assign weightings as follows:

1st choice	3 points
2nd choice	2 points
3rd choice	1 point

A composite judgment of the importance of the items could be determined by the weighted totals or averages for all the respondents.

It should be remembered that when items are ranked in order, the differences between ranked items may not be equal. Ranking is not the most refined method of scaling.

THE COMPUTER

The electronic digital computer is one of the most versatile and ingenious developments of the technological age. It is unlikely that complex modern institutions of business, finance, and government would have developed without the contributions of the computer. Making out payrolls, keeping stock inventories, maintaining credit balances, recording security transactions, reporting pupil data, providing individualized instruction, verifying tax returns, maintaining subscription lists, navigating ships, piloting sophisticated aircraft, aiming intercontinental missiles, predicting earthquakes and tornados, retrieving relevant legal decisions, and diagnosing diseases are some nonresearch applications.

To the researcher, the use of the computer in the search for related literature and the analysis of complex data have made complicated research designs practicable. Performing calculations almost at the speed of light, the computer has become one of the most useful tools of research in the humanities and in the physical and behavioral sciences.

An early predecessor of the modern computer was a mechanical device developed by Charles Babbage, a nineteenth-century English mathematician. Late in that century, Herman Hollerith, a director of the United States Census Bureau, devised a hole-punched card to aid in the more efficient processing of census data. The punched card was a significant development, for it is a very important part of modern computer data processing.

In the mid-1940s, an electrical impulse computer was devised with circuits employing thousands of vacuum tubes. These computers were very large and cumbersome and required a great deal of space. The heat generated by the vacuum tubes required extensive air-conditioning equipment to prevent heat damage, and the uncertain life of the vacuum tubes caused frequent malfunction.

With the development of transistorized components, replacement of the vacuum tubes, smaller space requirements, increased component reliability, elimination of heat dissipation considerations, and other improvements, the computer has become a much more effective device for the storage, processing, and retrieval of information.

The most advanced current models have incorporated micro-circuitry of even more compact size, improved storage capacity, and greater processing speed. Functions can be processed in nanoseconds, or billionths of a second.

Computer technology involves a number of functions:

1. *Input.* Information or data are entered into the computer through the use of punched cards, mark sense cards, or optical scanning readers that translate printed page information to punched cards or magnetic tape.

2. *Storage.* Information is stored in magnetic cores, tapes, or disks, available for processing upon the demand of the program.

3. *Control.* The program written in computer language directs the computer to perform a series of operations in a designated sequence written by the programmer. FORTRAN IV (FORmula TRANslator) is a modified version of the original FORTRAN. Such directions as *do, go to, read, punch, call,* and *write* are FORTRAN language terms. FORTRAN IV is the prevailing language used for statistical calcula-

tions. ALGOL (ALGorithmic Oriented Language) and COBOL (COmmon Business Oriented Language) are other widely used computer languages. Library and computer centers have many "canned" or prepared programs to perform a variety of statistical procedures so that the researcher need not always write his or her own.

4. *Output.* The output or retrieval process transfers the processed information or data from the computer to the researcher, using one of a number of devices to communicate the results. The output may be displayed on a screen, recorded on magnetic tape, or printed on paper by a rapid typing machine that can print as many as 1100 lines of up to 30 characters per minute.

The computer can perform many statistical calculations easily and quickly. Computation of means, standard deviations, coefficients of correlation, *t* tests, analysis of variance, and multivariate and factor analysis are some of the programs that are available at computer centers. However, simple calculations using small samples and few variables may not justify the use of the computer.

It has been said that the computer makes no mistakes; but program writers do make mistakes and any directions given the computer are faithfully executed. The computer doesn't think; it can only execute the directions of a thinking person. If poor data or faulty programs are introduced into the computer, the data analysis will lead to invalid conclusions. The expression "garbage in, garbage out" describes the problem quite well.

The author recognizes that it would be impracticable to attempt to present a comprehensive explanation of the functions of the computer in a brief discussion. For complete understanding of computers and their application to data-processing, instruction in computer programming, some actual experience with computers, and careful study of the literature in the field would be required.

SUMMARY

From the instruments and procedures that provide for the collection and analysis of data upon which hypotheses may be tested, the researcher chooses the most appropriate.

The data-gathering devices that have proven useful in educational research include: questionnaires, opinionnaires, *Q* methodology, observation, check lists, rating scales, score cards, scaled specimens, document or content analyses, interviews, psychological tests and inventories, sociograms, "guess-who" techniques, and social-distance scales.

Some research investigations use but one of these devices. Others
employ a number of them in combination. Students of educational research should make an effort to familiarize themselves with the strengths
and limitations of these tools, and should attempt to develop skill in
constructing and using them effectively.

The analysis and interpretation of data represent the application
of deductive and inductive logic to the research process. The data are
often classified by division into subgroups, and are then analyzed and
synthesized in such a way that hypotheses may be verified or rejected.
The final result may be a new principle or generalization. Data are examined in terms of comparisons between the more homogeneous segments
within the whole group, and by comparison with some outside criteria.

The processes of classification, sorting, and tabulation of data are
important parts of the research process. In extensive studies, mechanical
methods of sorting and tabulating are used to save time and effort and
to minimize error. In smaller projects, hand-sorting and hand-tabulating
processes are usually employed.

The researcher must guard against the limitations and sources of
error inherent in the processes of analysis and interpretation of data.

What are some of the limitations and sources of error in the analysis
and interpretation of data that would jeopardize the success of an investigation?

Confusing Statements with Facts.   A common fault is the acceptance of statements as facts. What individuals report may be a sincere
expression of what they believe to be the facts in a case, but these
statements are not necessarily true. Few people observe skillfully, and
many forget quickly. It is the researcher's responsibility to verify all
statements as completely as possible before they are accepted as facts.

Failure to Recognize Limitations.   The very nature of research
implies certain restrictions or limitations about the group or the situation
described—its size, its representativeness, and its distinctive composition. Failure to recognize these limitations may lead to the formulation
of generalizations that are not warranted by the data collected.

Careless or Incompetent Tabulation.   When one is confronted
with a mass of data, it is easy to make simple mechanical errors. Placing
a tally in the wrong cell or incorrectly totaling a set of scores can easily
invalidate carefully gathered data. Errors sometimes may be attributed
to clerical helpers with limited ability and little interest in the research
project.

Inappropriate Statistical Procedures.   The application of the
wrong statistical treatment may lead to invalid conclusions. This error
may result from a lack of understanding of statistics or the limitations
inherent in a particular statistical application.

Computational Errors.   Since the statistical manipulation of data often involves large numbers and many separate operations, there are many opportunities for error. Readers may be familiar with the story of the engineer who, after witnessing the collapse of his bridge, remarked, "I must have misplaced a decimal point." There is no way to eliminate completely human fallibility, but the use of either mechanical or electronic tabulating devices will help to reduce error.

Faulty Logic.   This rather inclusive category may embrace a number of the sources of error in the thought processes of the researcher. Invalid assumptions, inappropriate analogies, inversion of cause and effect, confusion of a simple relationship with causation, failure to recognize that group phenomena may not be used indiscriminately to predict individual occurrences or behavior, failure to realize that the whole may be greater than the sum of its parts, belief that frequency of appearance is always a measure of importance, and many other errors are limitations to accurate interpretation.

The Researcher's Unconscious Bias.   Although objectivity is the ideal of research, few individuals achieve it completely. There is great temptation to omit evidence unfavorable to the hypothesis, and to overemphasize favorable data. Effective researchers are aware of their feelings and the likely areas of their bias, and constantly endeavor to maintain the objectivity that is essential.

Lack of Imagination.   The quality of creative imagination distinguishes the true researcher from the compiler. Knowledge of the field of inquiry, skill in research procedures, experience, and skill in logical thinking are qualities that enable the adroit researcher to see relationships leading to possible generalizations that would escape the less skillful analyst. It is this ability to see all the implications in the data that produces significant discoveries.

EXERCISES

1. For what type of problem and under what circumstances would you find the following data-gathering techniques most appropriate:
    a. Schedule
    b. Questionnaire
    c. Interview
    d. Observation
    e. Q-sort.
2. Construct a short schedule that could be administered in class. The following topics are suggested:
    a. Leisure Interests and Activities

    b. Reasons for Selecting Teaching as a Profession
    c. Methods of Dealing with School Discipline
    d. Political Interests and Activities.
3. Construct a Likert-type opinionnaire dealing with a controversial problem. One of the following topics may be appropriate:
    a. Teacher Affiliation with Professional Organizations
    b. Teacher Strikes and Sanctions
    c. Religious Activities in the School Program
    d. The Nongraded School.
4. Construct a short rating scale to be used for the evaluation of the teaching performance of a probationary teacher.
5. To what extent is the administration of personal and social adjustment inventories an invasion of a student's privacy?

BIBLIOGRAPHY

ALEVIZOS, P. N. ET AL. "Behavior Observation Instrument; a Method of Direct Observation for Program Evaluation." *Journal of Applied Behavior Analysis* 11 (Summer 1978): 243–257.

ALVERSON, L. G. "Comparison of Indirect Measures for Long Duration Behavior." *Journal of Applied Behavior Analysis* 11 (Winter 1978): 530.

American Psychological Association Standards for Educational and Psychological Tests. Washington, D.C.: APA, 1974.

ANASTASI, ANN. *Psychological Testing.* New York: Macmillan Co., 1968.

BONNEY, MERLE F. "Sociometric Methods," in *Encyclopedia of Educational Research.* New York: Macmillan Co., 1960, pp. 1319–1323.

CARTWRIGHT, CAROL A. and G. PHILLIP CARTWRIGHT. *Developing Observation Skills.* New York: McGraw-Hill Book Co., 1974.

CONRAD, HERBERT S. "Clearance of Questionnaires with Respect to Invasion of Privacy, Public Sensitivities, Ethical Standards, Etc." *Journal of Educational Measurement* (Spring 1967): 22–28.

CRONBACH, LEE J. *Essentials of Psychological Testing.* New York: Harper & Row, 1970.

DALE, EDGAR and JEANNE CHALL. "A Formula for Predicting Readability." *Educational Research Bulletin* 27 (Jan. 1, 1948): 11–20.

EBEL, ROBERT L. *Essentials of Educational Measurement.* Englewood Cliffs, N.J.: Prentice-Hall, 1972.

EDWARDS, ALLEN L. and KATHERINE C. KENNEY. "A Comparison of the Thurston and Likert Techniques of Attitude Scale Construction." *Journal of Applied Psychology* 30 (Feb. 1946): 72–78.

FENLASON, ANN, *Essentials of Interviewing.* New York: Harper & Row, 1952.

FESTINGER, LEON and DANIEL KATZ. *Research Methods in the Behavioral*

Sciences. New York: Holt, Rinehart & Winston, 1953. Chapters 2, 4, 6, 8, and 9.

FLESCH, RUDOLPH. *How to Test Readability.* New York: Harper & Row, Publishers, 1951.

GOODE, WILLIAM J. and PAUL K. HATT. *Methods in Social Research.* New York: McGraw-Hill Book Co., 1952. Chapters 10, 11, 13, 16, and 20.

GRONLUND, NORMAN E. *Sociometry in the Classroom.* New York: Harper & Brothers, 1959.

GUTTMAN, LOUIS. "The Principal Components of Scalable Attitudes," in Paul F. Lazarsfeld, *Mathematical Thinking in the Social Sciences.* Beverly Hills, CA.: Glencoe Press, 1954.

HARRIS, A. J. and M. D. JACOBSON. "Framework for Readability Research: Moving Beyond Herbert Spencer." *Journal of Reading* 22 (Feb. 1979): 390–398.

HERRIOTT, ROBERT E. "Survey Research Method," in *Encyclopedia of Educational Research.* New York: Macmillan Co., 1960, pp. 1400–1410.

HOPKINS, KENNETH D. and JULIAN C. STANLEY. *Educational and Psychological Measurement and Evaluation.* 5th ed. Englewood Cliffs, N.J.: Prentice-Hall, 1972.

HYMAN, HERBERT H. *Survey Design and Analysis.* Beverly Hills, CA.: Glencoe Press, 1975.

HYMAN, HERBERT H. ET AL. *Interviewing in Social Research.* Chicago: University of Chicago Press, 1954.

Interview Manual. Ann Arbor, MI.: Institute for Social Research, University of Michigan, 1969.

KAHN, ROBERT L. and CHARLES F. CANNELL. *The Dynamics of Interviewing.* New York: John Wiley & Sons, 1957.

KERLINGER, FRED N. *Foundations of Behavioral Research.* New York: Holt, Rinehart & Winston, 1973. Chapters 22–24, 28–34.

KISH, L. *Survey Sampling.* New York: John Wiley & Sons, 1965.

LINDZEY, GARDNER, ed. *The Handbook of Social Psychology.* Cambridge, MA: Addison-Wesley, 1954. Chapters 9–13.

McCALL, GEORGE J. and J. L. SIMMONS. *Issues in Participant Observation.* Reading, MA.: Addison-Wesley, 1969.

MEHRENS, WILLIAM A. and IRVIN J. LEHMANN. *Standardized Tests in Education.* New York: Holt, Rinehart & Winston, 1975.

MORENO, JACOB L. *Sociometry: Experimental Method and the Science of Society.* New York: Beacon Press, 1951.

MORENO, JACOB L. *The Sociometry Reader.* New York: Free Press, 1960.

MORENO, JACOB L. *Who Shall Survive?* New York: Beacon Press, 1953.

MURSTEIN, BERNARD I., ed. *Handbook of Projective Techniques.* New York: Basic Books, 1966.

MUSSEN, PAUL H., ed. *Handbook of Research Methods in Child Development.* New York: John Wiley & Sons, 1960. Chapters 3, 14–16, 18.

NOLL, VICTOR H. *Introduction to Educational Measurement.* Boston: Houghton Mifflin Co., 1979.

NUNNALY, JUM C. *Educational Measurement and Evaluation.* New York: McGraw-Hill Book Co., 1972.

OPPENHEIM, A. N. *Questionnaire Design and Attitude Measurement.* New York: Basic Books, 1966.

PARTEN, M. B. *Surveys, Polls and Samples: Practical Procedures.* New York: Harper & Row, 1950.

PAYNE, STANLEY. *The Art of Asking Questions.* Princeton, N.J.: Princeton University Press, 1951.

REMMERS, H. H. *Introduction to Opinion and Attitude Measurement.* New York: Harper & Row, 1954.

"School Surveys," in *Encyclopedia of Educational Research.* New York: Macmillan Co., 1960, pp. 1211–1216.

SELLTIZ, CLAIRE, MARIE JAHODA, MORTON DEUTSCH and STUART W. COOK. *Research Methods in Social Relations.* New York: Holt, Rinehart & Winston, 1961. Chapters 5–8, 10, Appendix C.

SHAW, MARVIN E. and JACK M. WRIGHT. *Scales for the Measurement of Attitudes.* New York: McGraw-Hill Book Co., 1967.

STANLEY, JULIAN C. *Measurement in Today's Schools.* Englewood Cliffs, N.J.: Prentice-Hall, 1970.

STEPHENSON, WILLIAM. *The Study of Behavior: Q Technique and Its Methodology.* Chicago: University of Chicago Press, 1953.

SUMMERS, GENE F., ed. *Attitude Measurement.* Chicago: Rand McNally & Co., 1970.

THURSTONE, LOUIS L. "The Measurement of Values." *Psychological Review* 41 (Jan. 1954): 47–58.

TORGERSON, WARREN S. *Theory and Methods of Scaling.* New York: John Wiley & Sons, 1958.

WEBB, EUGENE J., DONALD T. CAMPBELL, RICHARD D. SCHWARTZ, and LEE SECHREST. *Unobtrusive Measures: Nonreactive Research in the Social Sciences.* Chicago: Rand McNally & Co., 1966.

YOUNG, PAULINE V. *Scientific Social Surveys and Research.* Englewood Cliffs, N.J.: Prentice-Hall, 1966.

Computers

BORKO, HAROLD, ed. *Computer Applications in the Behavioral Sciences.* Englewood Cliffs, N.J.: Prentice-Hall, 1962.

DAVIS, GORDON B. *An Introduction to Electronic Computers.* New York: McGraw-Hill Book Co., 1965.

LABBETT, B. "Case Studies and the Computer." *New York Times Educational Supplement* 3309 (Dec. 1, 1978): 39.

LEE, R. M. *A Short Course in FORTRAN IV Programming.* New York: McGraw-Hill Book Co., 1967.

MARKER, R. W. P. MCGRAW and F. D. STONE, eds. *Computer Concepts and Educational Information.* Iowa City, IA.: Educational Information Center, 1966.

MCCRACKEN, D. A. *Guide to FORTRAN Programming.* New York: John Wiley & Sons, 1961.

Personnel and Guidance Journal 49 (Nov. 1970) (entire issue devoted to technology in guidance).

SAXON, JAMES A. *COBOL, A Self-Instruction Manual.* Englewood Cliffs, N.J.: Prentice-Hall, 1970.

Scientific American 215 (Sept. 1966) (entire issue devoted to computers).

SIPPLE, CHARLES J. and CHARLES P. SIPPLE. *Computer Dictionary.* Indianapolis: Howard Sams Co., 1974.

VELDMAN, DONALD J. *FORTRAN Programming for the Behavioral Sciences.* New York: Holt, Rinehart & Winston, 1967.

YASAKI, Ed. "Educational Data Processing," *Datamation* 9 (June 1963): 24–27.

SEVEN

Descriptive

Data

Analysis

Since the following discussion is only a part of a general textbook on educational research, the treatment of statistical analysis is in no sense complete or exhaustive. Some of the most simple and basic concepts are presented. Students whose mathematical experience includes high school algebra should be able to understand the logic and the computational processes involved and should be able to follow the examples without difficulty.

The purpose of this discussion is twofold:

1. To help the student, as a consumer, develop an understanding of statistical terminology and the concepts necessary to read with understanding some of the professional literature in educational research

2. To help the student develop enough competence and know-how to carry on research studies using simple types of analysis.

The emphasis is upon intuitive understanding and practical application rather than on the derivation of mathematical formulas. Those who expect and need to develop real competence in educational research will need to take some of the following steps:

1. Take one or more courses in behavioral statistics and experimental design

2. Study more specialized textbooks in statistics, particularly those dealing with statistical inference (see Glass and Stanley, Guilford and Fruchter, Popham, Siegel, cited in the bibliography)

3. Read research studies in professional journals extensively and critically

4. Carry on research studies involving some serious "digging for oneself" in the use of statistical procedures.

WHAT IS STATISTICS?

Statistics is a body of mathematical techniques or processes for gathering, organizing, analyzing, and interpreting numerical data. Since research yields such quantitative data, statistics is a basic tool of measurement, evaluation, and research.

The word *statistics* is sometimes used to describe the numerical data that are gathered. Statistical data describe group behavior or group characteristics abstracted from a number of individual observations which are combined to make generalizations possible.

Everyone is familiar with such expressions as the average family income, the typical white-collar worker, or the representative city. These are statistical concepts and, as group characteristics, may be expressed in measurement of age, size, or any other traits that can be described quantitatively. When we say that the average fifth grade boy is ten years old, we are generalizing about all fifth grade boys, not any particular boy. Thus the statistical measurement is an abstraction that may be used in place of a great mass of individual measures.

The research worker who uses statistics is concerned with more than the manipulation of data. Statistical method goes to the fundamental purposes of description and analysis, and its proper application involves answering the following questions:

1. What facts need to be gathered to provide the information necessary to answer the question or to test the hypothesis?

2. How are these observations to be selected, gathered, organized, and analyzed?

3. What assumptions underlie the statistical methodology to be employed?

4. What conclusions can be validly drawn from the analysis of the data?

Research consists of systematic observation and description of the characteristics or properties of objects or events for the purpose of discovering relationships between variables. The ultimate purpose is to develop generalizations that may be used to explain phenomena and to predict future occurrences. To conduct research, principles must be established so that the observation and description have a commonly understood meaning. Measurement is the most precise and universally accepted process of description, assigning quantitative values to the properties of objects and events.

Parametric and Nonparametric Data

In the application of statistical treatments, two types of data are recognized.

1. *Parametric data.* Data of this type are measured data, and parametric statistical tests assume that the data are normally or nearly normally

TABLE 7-1 Levels of Quantitative Description[1]

Level	Scale	Process	Data Treatment	Some Appropriate Tests
4	Ratio	measured equal intervals true zero ratio relationship	parametric	*t* test analysis of variance analysis of covariance factor analysis Pearson's *r*
3	Interval	measured equal intervals no true zero		
2	Ordinal	ranked in order	nonparametric	Spearman's *rho* (ρ) Mann-Whitney Wilcoxon
1	Nominal	classified and counted		chi square median sign

[1] Refer to Chapter Six for a discussion of the four levels of measurements.

distributed. Parametric tests are applied to both interval and ratio scaled data.

2. *Nonparametric data.* Data of this type are either counted or ranked. Nonparametric tests, sometimes known as distribution-free tests, do not rest upon the more stringent assumption of normally distributed populations.

Table 7-1 presents a graphic summary of the levels of quantitative description and the types of statistical analysis appropriate for each level; the concepts will be developed further later in the discussion.

Descriptive and Inferential Analysis

To this point no reference has been made to the limits to which statistical analysis may be generalized. Two types of statistical application are relevant.

Descriptive analysis. Descriptive statistical analysis limits generalization to the particular group of individuals observed. No conclusions are extended beyond this group and any similarity to those outside the group cannot be assumed. The data describe one group and that group only. Much simple action research involves descriptive analysis and provides valuable information about the nature of a particular group of individuals.

Inferential analysis. Inferential statistical analysis always involves the process of sampling, and the selection of a small group that is assumed to be related to a larger group from which it is drawn. The small group is known as the sample; the large group the population. Drawing conclusions about populations based upon observations of samples is the purpose of inferential analysis.

A *statistic* is a measure based on observations of the characteristics of a *sample.* A statistic computed from a sample may be used to estimate a *parameter,* the corresponding value in the population from which the sample is selected.

Before any assumptions can be made, it is essential that the individuals selected be chosen in such a way that the small group, or sample, approximates the larger group, or population. Within a margin of error, which is always present, and by the use of appropriate statistical techniques, this approximation can be assumed, making possible the estimation of population characteristics by an analysis of the characteristics of the sample.

It should be emphasized that when data are derived from a group without careful sampling procedures, the researcher should carefully state that his or her findings apply only to the group observed and may not apply to or describe other individuals or groups. The statistical theory of sampling is complex and involves the estimation of error of inferred measurements, error that is inherent in estimating the relationship between a random sample and the population from which it is drawn. The discussion of inferential data analysis is presented later in the discussion.

THE ORGANIZATION OF DATA

The list of test scores in a teacher's grade book provides an example of unorganized data. Since the usual method of listing is alphabetical, the scores are difficult to interpret without some other type of organization.

Alberts, James	60
Brown, John	78
Davis, Mary	90
Smith, Helen	70
Williams, Paul	88

The array. Arranging the same scores in descending order of magnitude produces what is known as an array.

$$90$$
$$88$$
$$78$$
$$70$$
$$60$$

TABLE 7-2   Scores of 37 Students on a Semester Algebra Test

98	85	80	76	67
97	85	80	76	67
95	85	80	75	64
93	84	80	73	60
90	82	78	72	57
88	82	78	70	
87	82	78	70	
87	80	77	70	

Range $= 98 - 57 = 41 + 1 = 42$.

The array provides a more convenient arrangement. The highest score (90), the lowest score (60), and the middle score (78) are easily identified. Thus the range (the difference between the highest and lowest scores, plus one) can easily be determined.

Illustrated in Table 7-2 is an ungrouped data arrangement in array form.

Grouped Data Distributions

Data are more clearly presented when scores are grouped with a frequency column included. Data can be presented in frequency tables with different class intervals, depending on the number and range of the scores.

TABLE 7-3   Scores on Algebra Test Grouped in Intervals of Five

Score Interval	Tallies	Frequency (f)	Includes
96–100	||	2	(96 97 98 99 100)
91–95	||	2	(91 92 93 94 95)
86–90	||||	4	etc.
81–85	ⅲ| ||	7	
76–80	ⅲ| ⅲ| |	11	
71–75	|||	3	
66–70	ⅲ|	5	
61–65	|	1	
56–60	||	2	
		$N = 37$	

A score interval with an odd number of units may be preferable because its midpoint is a whole number rather than a fraction. Since all scores are assumed to fall at the midpoint (for purposes of computing the mean) the computation is less complicated.

Even interval of four: 8 9 10 11 (midpoint 9.5)
Odd interval of five: 8 9 10 11 12 (midpoint 10)

There is no rule that rigidly determines the proper score interval, and intervals of ten are frequently used.

STATISTICAL MEASURES

Several basic types of statistical measures are appropriate in describing and analyzing mass data in a meaningful way.

Measures of central tendency or averages
   Mean
   Median
   Mode
Measures of spread or dispersion
   Range
   Variance
   Standard deviation
Measures of relative position
   Percentile rank
   Percentile score
   Standard scores
Measures of relationship
   Coefficient of correlation

Describing characteristics of groups by using averages is understood by nonstatisticians. Climate of an area is often noted by average temperature or average amount of rainfall. We may describe students by grade point averages or by average age. Socioeconomic status of groups is directed by average income and the return on an investment portfolio may be judged in terms of average income return on investment. But to the statistician, the term *average* is unsatisfactory, for there are a number of types of averages, only one of which may be appropriate to use in describing given characteristics of a group. Of the many averages that may be used, three have been selected as most useful in educational research: the mean, the median, and the mode.

Measures of Central Tendency

The Mean *(M)* The mean of a distribution is commonly understood as the arithmetic average. The term *grade point average,* familiar to students, is a mean value. It is computed by dividing the sum of all the scores by the number of scores. In formula form:

$$M = \frac{\Sigma X}{N}$$

where M = mean
$\quad\quad\Sigma$ = sum of
$\quad\quad X$ = scores in a distribution
$\quad\quad N$ = number of scores

Example

X
6
5
4
3
2
1

$\Sigma X = \overline{21}$
$N = \ 6$
$M = \frac{21}{6} = 3.50$

The mean is probably the most useful of all statistical measures, for, in addition to the information that it provides, it is the base from which many other important measures are computed.

The Median *(Md)* The median is a point (not necessarily a score) in an array, above and below which one-half of the scores fall. It is a measure of position rather than of magnitude and is frequently found by inspection rather than by calculation.

7	
6	3 scores fall above
5	
4 —median	
3	
2	3 scores fall below
1	

When the number of scores is odd, the midscore is the median. When the number of scores is even, the median is the midpoint between the two middle scores.

```
6
5                               3 scores above
4
   —median = 3.50
3                               3 scores below
2
1
```

The median is not influenced by extreme scores at either end of a distribution. In the following examples the medians are identical.

```
        A                 B
        7                 50
        6                 49
        5                 30
        4 —Md             4 —Md
        3                 3
        2                 2
        1                 0
```

In certain types of data distributions, the median may be a more realistic measure of central tendency than the mean.

In a small school with five faculty members, the salaries are:

```
                    Teacher A   $30,000
                          B      16,000
                          C      15,400 Md
                          D      15,000
                          E      13,600
                                 $90,000
        M = 90,000 / 5 = 18,000
```

$$M = \frac{90,000}{5} = 18,000$$

The average salary of the group is represented with a different emphasis by the median salary ($15,400) than by the mean salary ($18,000), which is substantially higher than that of four of the five faculty members. Thus, the median is less sensitive than the mean to extreme values at either end of a distribution.

The Mode *(Mo)*

```
6
5
4 ⎫
4 ⎬—Mode
3
2
1
```

The mode is that score that occurs most frequently in a distribution. It is located by inspection rather than by computation. In grouped data distribution, the mode is assumed to be the midscore of the interval in which the greatest frequency occurs.

The modal age of fifth grade children is ten years. There are more ten-year-old fifth graders than any other age. A menswear salesman will verify the fact that there are more sales of size 40 suits than of any other size. Consequently, a larger number of size 40 suits are ordered and stocked, 40 being the mode.

In some distributions there may be more than one mode. A two-mode distribution is bimodal, more than two, multimodal. If the number of auto accidents on the streets of a city were tabulated by hours of occurrence, it is likely that two modal periods would become apparent— between 7 and 8 A.M. and between 5 and 6 P.M., the hours when traffic to and from stores and offices was heaviest and when drivers were in the greatest hurry. In a normal distribution of data there is one mode, and it falls at the midpoint. However, in some unusual distributions, the mode may fall at some other point. When the mode or modes reveal such unusual behavior, they do not serve as measures of central tendency, but they do reveal useful information about the nature of the distribution.

Measures of Spread or Dispersion

Measures of central tendency describe location along an ordered scale. These are characteristics of data distributions that call for additional types of statistical analysis. The following scores were made by two groups of students.

	Group I			Group II	
Pupil	*Score*	*Academic grade*	*Pupil*	*Score*	*Academic grade*
Arthur	100	A	John	82	C
Betty	90	B	Katherine	81	C
Charles	80	C	Larry	80	C
Donna	70	D	Nancy	79	C
Edward	60	F	Mary	78	C
	$\Sigma\ X = \overline{400}$			$\Sigma\ X = \overline{400}$	
	$N = \ 5$			$N = \ 5$	
	$M = \frac{400}{5} = 80$			$M = \frac{400}{5} = 80$	
	$Md = \ 80$			$Md = \ 80$	

The mean and the median are identical for both groups. It is apparent that averages do not fully describe the differences in achievement between students in Group I or those in Group II. To contrast their performance it is necessary to use a measure of score spread or dispersion.

Group II is homogeneous with little difference between adjacent scores. Group I is decidedly heterogeneous with performances ranging from superior to very poor.

The Range   The range, the simplest measure of dispersion, is the difference between the highest and lowest score, plus one. For Group I the range is 41 (100 − 60 + 1). For Group II the range is 5 (82 − 78 + 1).

The Deviation from the Mean (small *x*)   A score expressed as its distance from the mean is called a deviation score. Its formula is:

$$x = (X - M)$$

If the score falls above the mean the deviation score is positive (+), if it falls below the mean the deviation score is negative (−).

Using the same example, comparing Groups I and II:

	Group I			Group II	
Pupil	X	(X − M)	*Pupil*	X	(X − M)
		x			x
Arthur	100	+20	John	82	+2
Betty	90	+10	Katherine	81	+1
Charles	80	0	Larry	80	0
Donna	70	−10	Nancy	79	−1
Edward	60	−20	Mary	78	−2
	$\Sigma X = 400$	$\Sigma x = 0$		$\Sigma X = 400$	$\Sigma x = 0$
	$N = 5$			$N = 5$	
	$M = 80$			$M = 80$	

It is interesting to note that the sum of the score deviations from the mean equals zero.

$$\Sigma (X - M) = 0$$
$$\Sigma x = 0$$

In fact, an alternative definition of the mean is:

The mean is that value in a distribution about which the sum of the deviation scores equals zero.

The Variance (σ^2)   The sum of the squared deviations from the mean, divided by *N*, is known as the variance. We have noted that the sum of the deviations from the mean equals zero ($\Sigma x = 0$). From a mathematical point of view it would be impossible to find a mean value to describe these deviations (unless the signs were ignored). Squaring each deviation score yields a positive score. They can then be summed, divided by *N*, and the mean of the squared deviations computed.

$$x^2 = + \text{values}$$

Example

x	x^2
-2	$+4$
$+2$	$+4$

The variance formula is:

$$\sigma^2 = \frac{\Sigma (X - M_x)^2}{N} \quad \text{or} \quad \frac{\Sigma x^2}{N} \qquad x = (X - M_x)$$

Thus the variance is a value that describes how all of the scores in a distribution are dispersed or spread about the mean. This value is very useful in describing the characteristics of a distribution and will be employed in a number of very important statistical tests.

The Standard Deviation (σ)   The standard deviation is the positive square root of the variance and is also used as a measure of the spread or dispersion of scores in a distribution. The formula for standard deviation is:

$$\sigma = \sqrt{\frac{\Sigma (X - M)^2}{N}} \quad \text{or} \quad \sqrt{\frac{\Sigma x^2}{N}}$$

In the following example the variance and the standard deviation are computed.

	x	x^2
82	$+2$	$+4$
81	$+1$	$+1$
80	0	0
79	-1	$+1$
78	-2	$+4$
	$\Sigma x^2 =$	10

variance $\sigma^2 = \dfrac{10}{5} = 2$ $\qquad$ standard deviation $\sigma = \sqrt{\dfrac{10}{5}} = \sqrt{2} = 1.414$

While the deviation approach provides a clear example of the meaning of variance and standard deviation, in actual practice the deviation method is too awkward to use in computing the variances or standard deviations for large score distributions. A much less complicated method uses the raw scores instead of the deviation scores. The number values tend to be large, but the use of a calculator facilitates the computation.

$$\text{variance } \sigma^2 = \frac{N \Sigma X^2 - (\Sigma X)^2}{N^2}$$

$$\text{standard deviation } \sigma = \sqrt{\frac{N \Sigma X^2 - (\Sigma X)^2}{N^2}}$$

The following example demonstrates the process of computation, using the raw score method:

X	X^2
90	8100
85	7225
83	6889
80	6400
70	4900
68	4624
68	4624
68	4624
65	4225
65	4225
61	3721
$\Sigma X = 803$	$\Sigma X^2 = 59{,}557$
$N = 11$	

$$\sigma^2 = \frac{11(59{,}557) - (803)^2}{(11)(11)}$$

$$\sigma^2 = \frac{655{,}127 - 644{,}809}{121}$$

$$\sigma^2 = \frac{10{,}318}{121} = 85.27$$

$$\sigma = \sqrt{85.27} = 9.24$$

The standard deviation is a very useful device for comparing characteristics that may be quite different or that may be expressed in different units of measurement. The discussion that follows indicates that when the normality of distributions can be assumed, it is possible to compare the proverbial oranges and bananas. The standard deviation is independent of the magnitude of the mean and provides a common unit of measurement. To use a rather far-fetched example, imagine a man whose height is one standard deviation below the mean, and whose weight is one standard deviation above the mean. Since we assume that there is a normal relationship between height and weight (or that both characteristics are normally distributed) we have a picture of a short, overweight individual. His height, expressed in inches, is in the lowest 16 per cent of the population, his weight, expressed in pounds, in the highest 16 per cent.

This concept is developed later, but before the discussion of the use of the standard deviation as a means of describing status or position in a group, an examination of the normal distribution is appropriate.

The Normal Distribution

The earliest mathematical analysis of the theory of probability dates back to the eighteenth century. Abraham DeMoivre, a French mathematician, discovered that a mathematical relationship explained the probabilities associated with various games of chance. He developed the equation and the graphic pattern that describes it. During the nineteenth century, a French astronomer, LaPlace, and a German mathematician, Gauss, independently arrived at the same principle and applied it more broadly to areas of measurement in the physical sciences. From the limited applications made by these early mathematicians and astronomers, the theory of probability or the curve of distribution of error has been applied to data gathered in the areas of biology, psychology, sociology, and other sciences. It has been found to describe the fluctuations of chance errors of observation and measurement. Some understanding of the theory of probability and the nature of the curve of normal distribution is necessary for comprehension of many important statistical concepts, particularly in the area of standard scores, the theory of sampling, and inferential statistics.

The law of probability and the normal curve that illustrates it are based upon the law of chance or the probable occurrence of certain events. When any body of observations conforms to this mathematical form, it can be represented by a bell-shaped curve with definite characteristics (see Figure 7-1).

1. It is symmetrical around its vertical axis.

2. The terms cluster around the center (the mean).

3. The mean, median, and the mode of the distribution have the same value.

4. The curve has no boundaries in either direction, for the curve never touches the base line, no matter how far it is extended. The curve is a curve of probability, not of certainty.

The operation of chance prevails in the tossing of coins or dice. It is believed that many human characteristics respond to the influence of chance. For example, if certain limits of age, race, and gender were kept constant, such measures as height, weight, intelligence, and even longevity would approximate the normal distribution pattern. But the

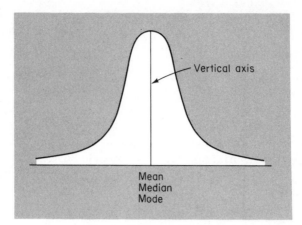

Fig. 7-1. The Normal Curve

normal distribution does not appear in data based upon observations of samples. There just are not enough observations. The normal distribution is based upon an infinite number of observations beyond the capability of any observer; thus, there is usually some observed deviation from the symmetrical pattern. But for purposes of statistical analysis, it is assumed that many characteristics do conform to this mathematical form within certain limits, providing a convenient reference.

The concept of measured intelligence is based upon the assumption that this trait is normally distributed throughout limited segments of the population. Tests are so constructed (standardized) that scores are normally distributed in the large group that is used for the determination of norms or standards. Insurance companies determine their premium rates by the application of the curve of probability. Basing their expectation on observations of past experience, they can estimate the probabilities of the survival of a man from age 45 to 46. They do not purport to predict the survival of a particular individual, but from a large group they can predict the mortality rate of all insured risks.

The total area under the normal curve may be considered to approach 100 per cent probability. Interpreted in terms of standard deviations, areas between the mean and various standard deviation distances from the mean under the curve show these percentage relationships (Figure 7-2).

Note the graphic conformation of the characteristics of the normal curve.

1. The curve is symmetrical. The percentage of frequencies is the same for equal intervals below or above the mean.

Fig. 7-2. Percentage of Frequencies in a Normal Distribution Falling Within a Range of a
Given Number of Standard Deviations from the Mean

2. The terms cluster or crowd around the mean. Note how the percentages in a given standard deviation distance are greatest around the
   mean and decrease as one moves away from the mean.

M to $\pm 1.00z$	34.13%	$z =$ standard deviation distance from the mean
± 1.00 to $\pm 2.00z$	13.54%	
± 2.00 to $\pm 3.00z$	2.15%	

3. The curve is highest at the mean. The mean, median, and mode
   have the same value.

4. The curve has no boundaries. A small fraction of 1 per cent of the
   space falls outside of ± 3.00 standard deviations from the mean.

   The normal curve is a curve that also describes probabilities. For
example, if height is normally distributed for a given segment of the
population, the chances are 34.13/100 that a person selected at random
will be between the mean and one standard deviation above the mean
in height, or 34.13/100 that the person selected will be between the
mean and one standard deviation below the mean in height, or 68.26/
100 that the selected person will be within one standard deviation (above
or below) the mean in height. Another interpretation would be that
68.26 per cent of this population segment would be between the mean
and one standard deviation above or below the mean in height.

234 Research in Education

For practical purposes the curve is usually extended to ±3 standard deviations from the mean (±3z). Most events or occurrences (or probabilities) will fall between these limits. The probability is 99.97/100 that these limits account for observed or predicted occurrences. This statement does not suggest that events or measures could not fall more than three standard deviations from the mean, but that the likelihood would be too small to consider when making predictions or estimates based upon probability. Statisticians deal with probabilities, not certainty, and there is always a degree of reservation in making any prediction. Statisticians deal with the probabilities that cover the normal course of events, not the extremely deviant events outside the normal range of experience.

The normal probability table provides a basis for estimating probabilities; an understanding of its interpretation is essential for students of statistics.

Interpreting the Normal Probability Table   The values presented in the normal probability table (Appendix B) provide data for normal distributions that may be interpreted in these ways (Figure 7-3):

1. The percentage of total space included between the mean and a given sigma distance (z) from the mean

2. The percentage of cases or the number, when N is known, that fall between the mean and a given sigma distance from the mean

3. The probability that an event will occur between the mean and a given sigma distance (z) from the mean.

$$z = \text{number of standard deviations from the mean}$$

$$z = \frac{X - M}{\sigma}$$

In a normal distribution:

1. The space included between the mean and +1.00z is .3413 of the total area under the curve.

2. The percentage of cases that fall between the mean and +1.00z is .3413.

3. The probability of an event occurring (observation) between the mean and +1.00z is .3413.

Since the normal probability curve is symmetrical, the shape of the right side (above the mean) is identical to the shape of the left side

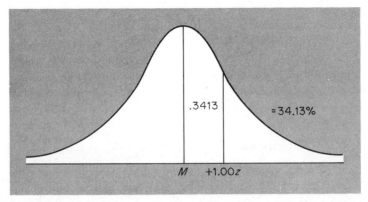

Fig. 7-3. The Space Included under the Normal Curve between the Mean and ±1.00z.

(below the mean). Since the values for each side of the curve are identical, only one set of values is presented in the probability table, expressed to one hundredths of a sigma (standard deviation) unit.

What is the probability that a score falls

		Probability
above the mean	.5000	50/100
below the mean	.5000	50/100
above + 1.96z	.5000 − .4750 = .0250	2½/100
below + .32z	.5000 + .1255 = .6255	62½/100
below − .32z	.5000 − .1255 = .3745	37½/100

Practical Applications of the Normal Curve   In the field of educational research there are a number of practical applications of the normal curve, among which are:

1. To calculate the percentile rank of scores in a normal distribution

2. To normalize a frequency distribution, an important process in standardizing a psychological test or inventory

3. To test the significance of observed measures in experiments, relating them to the chance fluctuations or errors that are inherent in the process of sampling, and generalizing about populations from which the samples are drawn.

Measures of Relative Position; Standard Scores

Standard scores provide a method of expressing any score in a distribution in terms of its distance from the mean in standard deviation units. The utility of this conversion of a raw score to a standard score will become clear as each type is introduced and illustrated. Three types of standard scores are considered.

1. Sigma Score *(z)*
2. Standard Score *(Z or T)*
3. College Board Score *(Z_{eb})*

The reader is reminded that an assumption of the normality of the distribution is made when using any type of standard score.

The Sigma Score *(z)* In describing a score in a distribution, its deviation from the mean, expressed in standard deviation units, is often more meaningful than the score itself. The unit of measurement is the standard deviation.

$$z = \frac{X - M}{\sigma} \quad \text{or} \quad \frac{x}{\sigma}$$

where X = raw score
  M = mean
  σ = standard deviation
  $x = (X - M)$ score deviation from the mean

Example A	*Example B*
$X = 66$	$X = 57$
$M = 60$	$M = 62$
$\sigma = 4$	$\sigma = 5$
$z = \frac{66-60}{4} = +\frac{6}{4} = +1.50$	$z = \frac{57-62}{5} = \frac{-5}{5} = -1.00$

The raw score of 66 in Example A may be expressed as a sigma score of +1.50, indicating that 66 is 1.5 standard deviations above the mean. The score of 57 in Example B may be expressed as a sigma score of −1.00, indicating that 57 is one standard deviation below the mean.

In comparing or averaging scores on distributions where total points may differ, the use of raw scores may create a false impression or basis for comparison. A sigma score *(z)* makes possible a realistic comparison of scores and may provide a basis for equal weighting of the scores. On the sigma scale, the mean of any distribution is converted to zero and the standard deviation equal to 1.

A teacher wished to get a student's equally weighted average (mean) achievement on an algebra test and an English test.

Subject	Test score	Mean	Highest possible score	Standard deviation
Algebra	40	47	60	5
English	84	110	180	20

It is apparent that the mean of the two raw test scores would not provide a valid summary if the student's performance for the mean would weight overwhelmingly in favor of the English test score. The conversion of each test score to a sigma score makes them equally weighted and comparable, for both test scores have been expressed on a scale with a mean of zero and a standard deviation of 1.

$$z = \frac{X - M}{\sigma}$$

$$\text{Algebra test score} = \frac{40 - 47}{5} = \frac{-7}{5} = -1.40$$

$$\text{English test score} = \frac{84 - 110}{20} = \frac{-26}{20} = -1.30$$

$$M = \frac{\Sigma X}{N} = \frac{-2.70}{2}$$

$$M = -1.35$$

The mean sigma score of -1.35 shows that, on an equally weighted basis, the performance of the student was fairly consistent: 1.40 standard deviations below the mean in algebra and 1.30 standard deviations below the mean in English.

Since the normal probability table describes the percentage of area lying between the mean and successive standard deviation units under the normal curve (see Appendix B), the use of sigma scores has many other useful applications to hypothesis testing, determination of percentile ranks, and probability judgments.

The Standard Score (Z)

$$Z = 50 + 10 \frac{(X - M)}{\sigma} \quad \text{or} \quad 50 + 10z$$

Another version of a standard score, sometimes called a Z or T score, has been devised to avoid some confusion resulting from negative z scores (below the mean) and also to eliminate decimal values.

Adding 50 to the mean and multiplying the z score by 10 results in a scale of positive whole number values or convenient conversion. Using the scores in the previous example: $Z = 50 + 10z$

Algebra $Z = 50 + 10(-1.40) = 50 + (-14) = 36$

English $Z = 50 + 10(-1.30) = 50 + (-13) = 37$

Z scores are always rounded to the nearest whole number. A sigma score of $+1.27$ would be converted to a Z score of 63.

$$Z = 50 + 10(+1.27) = 50 + (+12.70) = 50 + 12.70 = 62.70 = 63$$

The College Board Score (Z_{cb}) The College Entrance Examination Board and several other testing agencies use another conversion that provides a more accurate measure by spreading out the scale (see Figure 7-4).

$$Z_{cb} = 500 + 100 \frac{(X - M)}{\sigma} = 500 + 100z$$

The mean of this scale is 500.
The standard deviation is 100.
The range is 200–800.

Percentile Rank   Often useful to describe a score in relation to other scores, the percentile rank is the point in the distribution below which a given percentage of scores fall. If the 80th percentile rank is a score of 65, 80 per cent of the scores fall below 65. The median is the 50th percentile rank, for 50 per cent of the scores fall below it.

When N is small, the definition needs an added refinement. To be completely accurate, the percentile rank is the score in the distribution

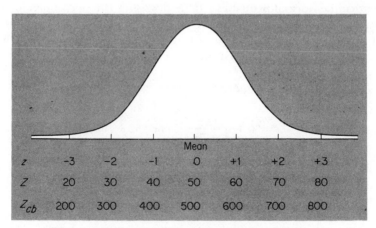

Fig. 7-4. A Comparison of Three Types of Standard Scores

below which a given percentage of the scores fall, plus one-half the percentage of space occupied by the given score.

This point can be demonstrated by a rather extreme example.

Scores

50
47
<u>43</u>
39
30

Upon inspection it is apparent that 43 is the median or 43 occupies the 50th percentile rank. Fifty per cent of the scores should fall below it, but only two out of five scores fall below 43. That would indicate 43 has a percentile rank of 40. But by adding the phrase, "plus one-half the percentage of space occupied by the score," we reconcile the calculation:

40% of scores fall below 43: each score occupies 20% of
the total space

40% + 10% = 50 (true percentile rank)

When N is large this qualification is unimportant because percentile ranks are rounded to the nearest whole number, ranging from the highest percentile rank of 99 to the lowest of zero.

High schools frequently rate their graduating seniors in terms of rank in class. Because schools vary so much in size, colleges find these rankings of limited value unless they are converted to some common basis for comparison. The percentile rank provides this basis by converting class rank into a percentile rank.

$$\text{Percentile rank} = 100 - \frac{(100\,RK - 50)}{N}$$

where $RK =$ rank from the top

Jones ranks 27th in his senior class of 139 students. Twenty-six rank above him, 112 below him. His percentile rank is:

$$100 - \frac{(2700 - 50)}{139} = 100 - 19 = 81$$

Measures of Relationship

Correlation Correlation is the relationship between two or more paired variables, between two or more sets of data. The degree of relationship may be measured and represented by the coefficient of correlation. This coefficient may be identified by either the Greek letter *rho* (ρ), the symbol *r*, or other symbols, depending upon certain assumptions about the data distributions and the way the coefficient has been calculated.

Teachers observe that students who have high intelligence quotients tend to receive high scores in mathematics tests, whereas those with low *IQ*'s tend to score low. When this type of relationship is obtained, the factors of measured intelligence and scores on mathematics tests are said to be positively correlated.

Sometimes variables are negatively correlated when a large amount of one variable is associated with a small amount of the other. As one increases the other tends to decrease.

When the relationship between two sets of variables is a pure chance relationship, we say that there is no correlation.

−1.00	0	+1.00
high in one trait	pure chance	high in one trait
low in the other	relationship	high in the other

These pairs of variables are usually positively correlated; as one increases the other tends to increase.

a. intelligence	academic achievement
b. productivity per acre	value of farm land
c. height	shoe size
d. family income	value of family home

These variables are usually negatively correlated. As one increases the other tends to decrease.

a. total corn production	price per bushel
b. time spent in practice	number of typing errors
c. prime interest rate	Dow Jones Industrial Average
d. age of an automobile	trade-in value

There are other traits that probably have no correlation.

a. body weight	intelligence
b. shoe size	monthly salary

The degree of linear correlation can be represented quantitatively by the coefficient of correlation. A perfect positive correlation is +1.00. A complete lack of relationship is zero(0). Rarely, if ever, are perfect coefficients of correlations of +1.00 or −1.00 encountered, particularly in relating human traits. Although some relationships tend to appear fairly consistently, there are variations or exceptions that reduce the measured coefficient from either a −1.00 or a +1.00 toward zero.

A definition of perfect positive correlation specifies that for every unit increase in one variable there is a proportional unit increase in the other. The perfect negative correlation specifies that for every unit increase in one variable there is a proportional unit decrease in the other. That there can be no exceptions explains why coefficients of correlation of +1.00 or −1.00 are not encountered in relating human traits. The sign of the coefficient indicates the direction of the relationship, and the numerical value its strength.

The scattergram and linear regression line. When the relationship between two variables is plotted graphically, paired variable values are plotted against each other on the X and Y axis.

The line drawn through, or near, the coordinate points is known as the line of best fit or the regression line. It is the line from which the sum of the deviations of all the coordinate points has the smallest possible value. As the coefficient approaches zero (0) the coordinate points fall further from the regression line.

When the coefficient of correlation is either +1.00 or −1.00, all of the coordinate points fall on the regression line, indicating that, when r = +1.00, for every increase in X there is a proportional increase in Y, and when r = −1.00, for every increase in X there is a proportional decrease in Y. There are no individual exceptions.

The slope of the regression line, or line of best fit, is not determined by guess or estimation but by a geometric process described later.

There are actually two regression lines. When r = +1.00 or −1.00 the lines are superimposed and appear as one line. As r approaches zero the lines separate further.

Only one of the regression lines is described in this discussion, the Y on X (or Y from X) line. It is used to predict unknown Y values from known X values. The X values are known as the predictor variable, the Y values, the predicted variables.

Plotting the slope of the regression line. The slope of the regression (Y from X) line is a geometric representation of the coefficient of correlation and is expressed as a ratio of the magnitude of the *rise* (if r is +)

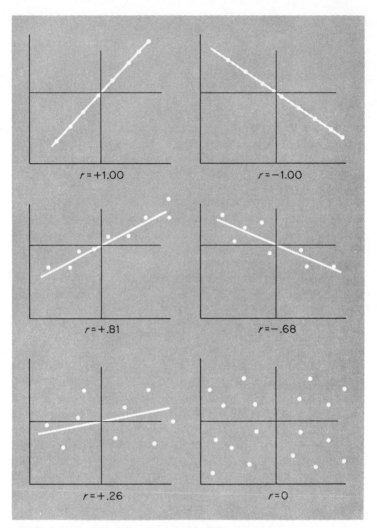

Fig. 7-5. Scatter Diagrams Illustrating Different Coefficients of Correlation

to the run, or as a ratio of the *fall* (if *r* is −) to the run, expressed in standard deviation units.

For example, if $r = +.60$, for every sigma unit increase (run) in X, there is a .60 sigma unit increase (rise) in Y.

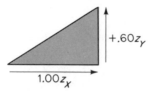

If $r = -.60$, for every sigma unit increase (run) in X, there is a .60 sigma unit decrease (fall) in Y.

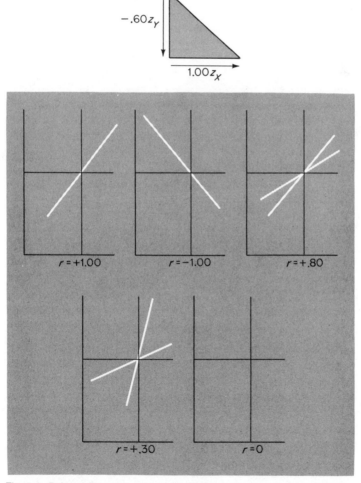

Fig. 7-6. Pairs of Regression Lines for Different Coefficients of Correlation

The geometric relationship between the two legs of the right triangle determines the slope of the hypotenuse or the regression line.

Since all regression lines pass through the intersection of the mean of X and the mean of Y lines, only one other point is necessary to determine the slope. By measuring one standard deviation of the X distribution on the X axis and a .60 standard deviation of the Y distribution on the Y axis, the second point is established.

The regression line (r) involves one awkward feature: all values must be expressed in sigma scores (z) or standard deviation units. It would be more practicable to use actual scores to determine the slope of the regression line. This can be done by converting to a slope known as b. The slope of the b regression line Y on X is determined by the formula:

$$b = r\frac{\sigma_Y}{\sigma_X}$$

For example, if $r = +.60$

$$\sigma_Y = 6$$

and

$$\sigma_x = 5$$

$$b = +.60\,\frac{6}{5} = \frac{3.60}{5} = +.72$$

Fig. 7-7. A Positive Regression Line, $r = +.60$

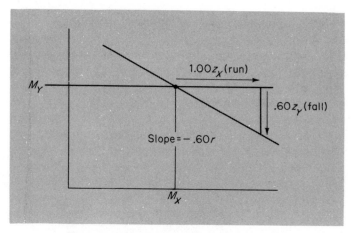

Fig. 7-8. A Negative Regression Line, $r = -.60$

Thus an r of $+.60$ becomes $b = +.72$. Now the ratio of the rise to the run has another value and indicates a different slope of the regression line (Figure 7-9).

Rank Order Correlation (σ)

The simplest type of correlation analysis is known as the Spearman rank order coefficient of correlation. The paired variables are expressed as ordinal values (ranked) rather than as interval or ratio values. It lends itself to an interesting graphic demonstration.

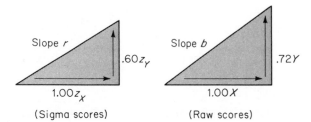

Fig. 7-9. Two Regression Lines, r and b. An r of $+.60$ Is Converted to a b of $+.72$ by the Formula:

$$b = r\frac{\sigma_Y}{\sigma_X}$$

Pupil	IQ rank	Achievement in mathematics rank
A	1 —————————	1
B	2 —————————	2
C	3 —————————	3
D	4 —————————	4
E	5 —————————	5

Perfect positive coefficient of correlation

$$\rho = +1.00$$

Student ranking highest in IQ ranks highest in mathematics, lowest in IQ, lowest in mathematics achievement.

Pupil	Time spent in practice rank	Number of typing errors rank
A	1	5
B	2	4
C	3	3
D	4	2
E	5	1

Perfect negative coefficient of correlation

$$\rho = -1.00$$

Student ranking highest in amount of time spent in practice ranks lowest in number of errors.

Pupil	Height rank	IQ rank
A	1	3
B	2	4
C	3	2
D	4	1
E	5	5

Very low coefficient of correlation

$$\rho = +.10$$

There is probably little more than a pure chance relationship between height and intelligence.

To compute the nonparametric Spearman rank order coefficient of correlation, this rather simple formula is used:

$$\rho = 1 - \frac{6\Sigma\, D^2}{N(N^2 - 1)}$$

where D = the difference between paired ranks
        $\Sigma\,D^2$ = the sum of the squared differences between ranks
        N = number of paired ranks

Judges Jones and Smith ranked ten pupils in a speech contest. The coefficient of correlation indicated the extent to which their judgments were in agreement.

Pupil	Jones' rank	Smith's rank	D	D²
A	1	1	0	0
B	3	2	1	1
C	4	5	1	1
D	7	9	2	4
E	6	6	0	0
F	9	8	1	1
G	8	10	2	4
H	10	7	3	9
I	2	4	2	4
J	5	3	2	4
$N = 10$				$\Sigma\,D^2 = 28$

$$\rho = 1 - \frac{6(28)}{10(100 - 1)} = 1 - \frac{168}{10(99)}$$

$$\rho = 1 - \frac{168}{990} = 1 - .17$$

$$\rho = +.83$$

A coefficient of correlation of +.83 shows a high degree of agreement between the judges.

The Spearman rank order coefficient of correlation computation is quick and easy. It is an acceptable method if data are available only in ordinal form, or if the number of paired variables is more than 9 or fewer than 30, with not more than a few ties in ranks. Teachers will find this method of computation useful when conducting studies using a single classroom group of students as subjects.

Pearson's Product-Moment Coefficient of Correlation

The most often used and most precise coefficient of correlation is known as the Pearson product-moment coefficient. It may be used when:

1. The data are expressed in interval or ratio score form.

2. The distributions of X and Y have a linear relationship.

3. The variances are approximately equal.

4. The distributions have no more than one mode.

The coefficient may be calculated by converting the raw scores to sigma scores and finding the mean value of their cross products.

$$r = \frac{\Sigma \, (z_X)(z_Y)}{N}$$

z_X	z_Y	$(z_X)(z_Y)$
+1.50	+1.20	+1.80
+2.00	+1.04	+2.08
−.75	−.90	+.68
+.20	+.70	+.14
−1.00	+.20	−.20
−.40	+.30	−.12
+1.40	+.70	+.98
+.55	+.64	+.35
−.04	+.10	−.00
−.10	+.30	−.03

$$\Sigma \, (z_X)(z_Y) = 5.68$$

$$r = \frac{+5.68}{10} = +.568$$

If most of the negative z values of X are associated with negative z values of Y, and positive z values of X with positive z values of Y, the correlation coefficient will be positive. If most of the paired values are of opposite signs, the coefficient will be negative.

positive correlation $(+)(+) = +$ high on X, high on Y

$(-)(-) = +$ low on X, low on Y

negative correlation $(+)(-) = -$ high on X, low on Y

$(-)(+) = -$ low on X, high on Y

The z score method is not often used in actual computation because it involves the conversion of each score into a sigma score. A raw score method computation is more convenient and is most often used when a calculator or computer is available.

$$r = \frac{N \Sigma \, XY - (\Sigma \, X)(\Sigma \, Y)}{\sqrt{N \Sigma \, X^2 - (\Sigma X)^2} \, \sqrt{N \Sigma \, Y^2 - (\Sigma \, Y)^2}}$$

The process involves setting up a table with five columns.

where $\Sigma X =$ sum of the X scores
 $\Sigma Y =$ sum of the Y scores
 $\Sigma X^2 =$ sum of the squared X scores
 $\Sigma Y^2 =$ sum of the squared Y scores
 $\Sigma XY =$ sum of the products of paired X and Y scores
 $N =$ number of paired scores

Variable X	Variable Y	X^2	Y^2	XY
24	13	576	169	312
20	9	400	81	180
18	12	324	144	216
17	20	289	400	340
15	11	225	121	165
12	16	144	256	192
10	5	100	25	50
8	2	64	4	16
6	7	36	49	42
4	1	16	1	4
$\Sigma X = 134$	$\Sigma Y = 96$	$\Sigma X^2 = 2174$	$\Sigma Y^2 = 1250$	$\Sigma XY = 1517$

$$r = \frac{10(1517) - (134)(96)}{\sqrt{10(2174) - (134)^2} \sqrt{10(1250) - (96)^2}}$$

$$r = \frac{15,170 - 12,864}{\sqrt{(21,740 - 17,956)} \sqrt{(12,500 - 9216)}}$$

$$r = + \frac{2306}{\sqrt{(3784)} \sqrt{(3284)}}$$

$$r = + \frac{2306}{\sqrt{12,426,656}} = + \frac{2306}{3525.15} = +.65$$

$$r = +.65$$

Prediction[2] An important inferential use of the coefficient of correlation and the Y on X regression line is for prediction of unknown Y values from known X values.

Let us assume that a college admissions officer wishes to predict the likely academic performance of students considered for admission or for scholarship grants. He or she has built up a body of data based upon the past records of a substantial number of admitted college students over a period of several years. He or she has calculated the coeffi-

---

[2] Because it is a method for estimating future performance of individuals on the basis of past performance of a sample, prediction is an inferential application of correlational analysis. It has been included in this chapter to illustrate one of the most useful applications of correlation.

cient of correlation between their high school grade point averages and their college freshman grade point averages. He or she now can construct a regression line and predict the future college freshman GPA for any prospective student, based upon his or her high school GPA.

Let us assume that he or she found the coefficient of correlation to be +.52. The slope of the line could be used to determine any *Y* values for any *X* value. This process would be quite inconvenient, however, for all grade point averages would have to be entered as sigma *(z)* values.

A more practicable procedure would be to construct a regression line with a slope of *b* so that any college grade point average *(Y)* could be predicted directly from any high school grade point average. The *b* regression line and a carefully drawn graph would provide a quick method for prediction. For example:

$$r = +.52 \qquad b = r \frac{(\sigma_Y)}{(\sigma_X)}$$

$$\sigma_y = .50 \qquad b = +.52 \frac{(.50)}{(.60)}$$

$$\sigma_x = .60 \qquad b = +.43$$

X_A student A's high school GPA, Y_A his predicted college GPA

X_B student B's high school GPA, Y_B her predicted college GPA

Fig. 7-10. A Regression Line Used to Predict College Freshman GPA from High School GPA

Another, and perhaps more accurate, alternative for predicting unknown Y's from known X's would be to use the regression equation rather than the graph. The formula for predicting Y from X is:

$$\tilde{Y} = r\left(\frac{\sigma_y}{\sigma_x}\right)(X - M_x) + M_y$$

Several examples using the following data will illustrate the computation.

$r = +.52$ coefficient of correlation between X and Y

$\sigma_x = .60$ standard deviation of X distribution

$\sigma_Y = .50$ standard deviation of Y distribution

$M_x = 2.10$ mean of X distribution

$M_y = 2.40$ mean of Y distribution

$X =$ student's high school GPA

$\tilde{Y} =$ student's college freshman GPA

$b = \quad +.52\dfrac{(.50)}{(.60)}$

$b = +.43$

Prediction for student A:

$$\tilde{Y} = r\left(\frac{\sigma_y}{\sigma_x}\right)(X - M_x) + M_y$$

$$\tilde{Y}_A = .52\left(\frac{.50}{.60}\right)(2.00 - 2.10) + 2.40$$

$$\tilde{Y}_A = .43(-.10) + 2.40$$

$$\tilde{Y}_A = -.04 + 2.40$$

$$\tilde{Y}_A = 2.36 \text{ student A's predicted college GPA}$$

Prediction for student B:

$$X_B = 3.10$$

$$\tilde{Y} = r\left(\frac{\sigma_y}{\sigma_x}\right)(X - M_x) + M_y$$

$$\tilde{Y}_B = +.52\frac{.50}{.60}(3.10 - 2.10) + 2.40$$

$$\tilde{Y}_B = .43(1.00) + 2.40$$

$$\tilde{Y}_B = .43 + 2.40$$

$$\tilde{Y}_B = 2.83 \text{ student B's predicted college GPA}$$

For student A, whose high school GPA was below the mean, the predicted college GPA was also below the mean. For student B, whose high school GPA was well above the mean, the predicted GPA was substantially above the mean. These results are consistent with a positive coefficient of correlation—high in X, high in Y; low in X, low in Y.

Errors in Prediction

When the coefficient of correlation based upon a sufficient body of data has been determined as ±1.00, there would be no error of prediction. Perfect correlation indicates that for every increase in X, there was a proportional increase (when $+$) or proportional decrease (when $-$) in Y. There were no exceptions. But when r is less than $+1.00$ or -1.00, error of prediction is inherent since there have been exceptions to a consistent, orderly relationship. The regression line does not coincide or pass through all of the coordinate values used in determining the slope.

A measure for estimating this prediction error is known as the standard error of estimate (σ_{est}).

$$\sigma_{est_y} = \sigma_y \sqrt{1 - r^2}$$

As the coefficient of correlation increases, the prediction error decreases. When $r = \mp1.00$

$$\sigma_{est_y} = \sigma_y \sqrt{1 - r^2} = \sigma_y \sqrt{1 - (1)^2} = \sigma_y(0) = 0$$

When $r = 0$

$$\sigma_{est_y} = \sigma_y \sqrt{1 - (0)^2} = \sigma_y(1) = \sigma_y$$

When $r = 0$ (or when the coefficient of correlation is unknown) the best blind prediction of any Y from any X is the mean of Y. This is true because we know that most of the scores in a normal distribution cluster around the mean and that about 68 percent of them would probably fall within one standard deviation from the mean. In this situation the standard deviation of Y may be thought of as the standard error of estimate. When $r = 0$, $\sigma_{est_y} = \sigma_y$.

If the coefficient of correlation is more than zero, this blind prediction can be improved upon in two ways:

1. By plotting Y from a particular X from the regression line

2. By reducing the error of prediction of Y by calculating how much σ_y is reduced by the coefficient of correlation.

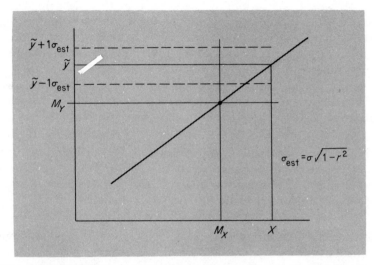

Fig. 7-11. A Predicted Y Score from a Given X Score, Showing the Standard Error of Estimate

For example; when $r = \pm.60$

$$\sigma_{est_y} = \sigma_y \sqrt{1 - (r)^2} = \sigma_y \sqrt{1 - (.60)^2} = \sigma_y \sqrt{1 - .36}$$
$$= \sigma_y \sqrt{.64} = .80\sigma_y$$

Thus the estimate error of Y has been reduced from σ_Y to $.80\sigma_Y$. Interpretation of the standard error of estimate is similar to the interpretation of the standard deviation. If $r = \pm.60$, the standard error of estimate of Y would be $.80\sigma_Y$. An actual performance score of Y would probably fall within a band of $\pm.80\sigma_Y$ from the predicted Y in about 68 of 100 predictions. In other words, the probability is that the predicted score would not be more than one standard error of estimate from the actual score in about 68 per cent of the predictions.

In addition to the applications described, the coefficient of correlation is indispensable to psychologists who construct and standardize psychological tests and inventories. A few of the basic procedures are briefly described.

Standardization of Psychological Instruments

Computing the coefficient of correlation is the procedure used to evaluate the degree of validity and reliability of psychological tests and inventories.

The coefficient of validity.   A test is said to be valid to the degree that it measures what it claims to measure, or to the extent that it predicts accurately such types of behavior as academic success or failure, job success or failure, or stability or instability under stress. Tests are usually validated by correlating test scores against some outside criteria which may be scores on tests of accepted validity, successful performance or behavior, or the expert judgment of recognized authorities.

The coefficient of reliability.   A test is said to be reliable to the degree that it measures accurately and consistently, yielding comparable results when administered a number of times. There are a number of ways of using the process of correlation to evaluate reliability:

1. Test-retest, correlating the scores on two or more successive administrations of the test (administration #1 vs. administration #2)

2. Equivalent forms, correlating the scores when groups of individuals take equivalent forms of the test (form L vs. form N)

3. Split halves, correlating the scores on the odd items of the test (numbers 1, 3, 5, 7, etc.) against the even items (numbers 2, 4, 6, 8, etc). This method yields lower correlations because of the reduction in size to two tests of half the number of items. This may be correlated by the application of the Spearman-Brown prophecy formula.

$$r = \frac{2r}{1 + r}$$

If $r = +.60$,

$$r = \frac{1.20}{1 + .60} = +.75$$

Partial and Multiple Correlation

It is possible to measure the relationship between more than two variables through the process of partial correlation. This is done by holding certain of the variables constant, or momentarily eliminating them from consideration, thus "partialling out" the influence of an independent factor. Partial correlation makes possible multiple correlations, useful in establishing the relative influence or weight of each of the factors in the relationship. For example, a university has computed a multiple regression equation (a prediction index) involving three weighted factors closely related to academic success in college:

1. Rank in high school graduating class

2. High school grade point average

3. Scores on college entrance examination board tests.

These three, combined in proper proportion, have proved to be more accurate for predictive purposes than any one or two of the factors.

Frequently, textbook authors present a crude criterion for the evaluation of a coefficient:

Coefficient (r)			Relationship
.00	to	.20	negligible
.20	to	.40	low
.40	to	.60	moderate
.60	to	.80	substantial
.80	to	1.00	high to very high

The foregoing table's crude analysis may be somewhat misleading. The significance of the coefficient of correlation depends upon the nature of the variables, the number of observations, the range of scores, and the purpose of the application. A test of the statistical significance of a coefficient is based upon the concept of sampling error, described in the next chapter.

Misinterpretation of the Coefficient of Correlation

Several fallacies and limitations should be considered in interpreting the meaning of a coefficient of correlation. The coefficient does not imply a cause-and-effect relationship between variables. High positive correlations have been observed between the number of stork's nests and the number of births in northwestern Europe, and between the number of ordinations of ministers in the New England colonies and the consumption of gallons of rum.

These are inappropriate comparisons, for they may be merely symptoms of a common situation. As population increases both good things and bad things are likely to increase in frequency. Technological and social change may underlie the developments of many variables that have no logical relationship. Before a causal relationship between variables can be accepted, it must be established by logical analysis. The process of correlation merely quantifies a relationship. Confusing association with cause leads one to the *post hoc* fallacy.

A NOTE OF CAUTION

Statistics is an important tool of the research worker, and an understanding of statistical terminology, methodology, and logic is important for the consumer of research. There are a number of limitations, however, that should be recognized in using statistical processes, and in drawing conclusions from statistical evidence.

1. Statistical process is the servant of logic and only has value if it verifies, clarifies, and measures relationships that have been established by clear, logical analysis. Statistics is a means, never an end, of research.

2. A statistical process should not be employed in the analysis of data unless the basic assumptions and limitations underlying its uses are clearly understood.

3. The conclusions derived from statistical analysis will be no more accurate or valid than the original data. To use an analogy, no matter how elaborate the mixer, a cake made of poor ingredients will be a poor cake. All the refinement of elaborate statistical manipulation will not yield significant truths if the data result from crude or inexact measurement.

4. All treatment of data must be checked and double-checked frequently to minimize the likelihood of errors in measurement, recording, tabulation, and analysis.

5. There is a constant margin of error wherever measurement by human beings is involved. The error is increased when qualities or characteristics of human personality are subjected to measurement, or when inferences about the population are made from measurements derived from statistical samples.

   When comparisons or contrasts are made, a mere number difference is, in itself, not a valid basis for any conclusion. A test of statistical significance should be employed to weigh the possibility that chance in sample selection could have yielded the apparent difference. To apply these measures of statistical significance is to remove some of the doubt from the conclusions.

6. Statisticians and liars are often equated in humorous quips. There is little doubt that statistical processes can be used to prove nearly anything that one sets out to prove. Starting with false assumptions, using inappropriate procedures, or omitting relevant data, the biased investigator can arrive at false conclusions. These conclusions are often particularly dangerous because of the authenticity that the statistical treatment seems to confer.

Distortion may be deliberate or unintentional. In research, omitting certain facts or choosing only those facts favorable to one's position is as culpable as actual distortion, which has no place in research. The reader must always try to evaluate the manipulation of data, particularly when the report seems to be persuasive.

Research reports, particularly in the behavioral sciences, sometimes include elaborate statistical processes that serve no useful purpose, but are apparently included to lend an air of scholarship and dignity to a superficial, barren study. No statistical technique should be employed unless it adds clarity or meaning to the analysis of data. Never should it be used as window dressing to impress the reader.

SUMMARY

This chapter deals with only the most elementary statistical concepts. For a more complete treatment the reader is urged to consult one of the references listed at the end of Chapter Eight.

Statistical analysis is the mathematical process of gathering, organizing, analyzing, and interpreting numerical data, and is one of the basic phases of the research process. Descriptive statistical analysis involves the description of a particular group. Inferential statistical analysis leads to judgments about the whole population, to which the sample at hand is presumed to be related.

Data are organized in arrays in ascending or descending numerical order. Data are often grouped into class intervals, so that analysis is simplified and characteristics more readily noted.

Measures of central tendency (mean, median, and mode) describe data in terms of some sort of average. Measures of position, spread, or dispersion describe data in terms of relationship to a point of central tendency. The range, deviation, variances, standard deviation, percentile, sigma score, and standard score are useful measures of position, spread, or dispersion.

Measures of relationship describe the relationship of paired variables, quantified by a coefficient of correlation. The coefficient is useful in educational research in standardizing tests and in making predictions when only some of the data are available. It should be noted that a high coefficient does not imply a cause-and-effect relationship, but merely quantifies a relationship that has been logically established prior to its measurement.

Statistics is the servant, not the master, of logic, a means rather than an end of research. Unless basic assumptions are valid, unless the right data are carefully gathered, recorded, and tabulated, and unless

the analysis and interpretations are logical, statistics can make no contribution to the search for truth.

EXERCISES

1. More than half the families in a community can have an annual
   income that is lower than the mean income for that community.
   Do you agree or disagree? Why?
2. The median is the midpoint between the highest and the lowest
   scores in a distribution. Do you agree or disagree? Why?
3. Compute the mean and the median of this distribution:
       74
       72
       70
       65
       63
       61
       56
       51
       42
       40
       37
       33
4. Determine the mean, the median, and the range of this distribution:
       88
       86
       85
       80
       80
       77
       75
       71
       65
       60
       58
5. Compute the variance (σ^2) and the standard deviation (σ) of this
   distribution:
       27
       27
       25
       24

20
18
16
16
14
12
10
7

6. The distribution with the larger range is the distribution with the larger standard deviation. Do you agree or disagree? Why?

7. If five points were added to each score in a distribution how would it change:
    a. the range
    b. the mean
    c. the median
    d. the mode
    e. the variance
    f. the standard deviation.

8. John Brown ranked 27th in a graduating class of 367. What was his percentile rank?

9. A coin-tossing experiment where $N = 144$ and $P = .50$,

$$\sigma_{DV} = \sqrt{\frac{N}{4}}$$

Draw the curve depicting the distribution of probable outcomes of heads appearing for an infinite number of repetitions of this experiment. Indicate the number of heads for the mean, and at 1, 2, and 3 standard deviations from the mean, both positive and negative.

10. Assuming the distribution to be normal with a mean of 61 and a standard deviation of 5, calculate the following standard score equivalents:

X	x	z	Z
66			
58			
70			
61			
52			

11. Using the normal probability table in Appendix B, calculate the following values:

    a. below $-1.25z$ _____%

    b. above $-1.25z$ _____%

    c. between $-1.40z$ and $+1.67z$ _____%

    d. between $+1.50z$ and $+2.50z$ _____%

    e. 65th percentile rank   _____z

    f. 43rd percentile rank   _____z

    g. top 1% of scores   _____z

    h. middle 50% of scores   _____z to _____z

    i. not included between $-1.00z$ and $+1.00z$ _____%

    j. 50th percentile rank   _____z

12. Assuming a normal distribution of scores, a test has a mean score of 100 and a standard deviation of 15. Compute the following scores:

    a. score that cuts off the top 10%   _____

    b. score that cuts off the lower 40%   _____

    c. percentage of scores above 90   _____%

    d. score that occupies the 68th percentile rank _____

    e. score limits of the middle 68%   _____ to _____

13.

	Mean	*s*	*Tom*	*Dick*	*Harry*
Algebra	90	30	60	100	85
History	20	4	25	22	19

who had:

    a. the poorest score on either test   _____

    b. the best score on either test   _____

    c. the most consistent scores on both tests _____

    d. the least consistent scores on both tests _____

    e. the best mean score on both tests   _____

    f. the poorest mean score on both tests   _____

14. The coefficient of correlation measures the magnitude of the cause-and-effect relationship between paired variables. Do you agree or disagree? Why?

15. Using the Spearman rank order coefficient of correlation method, compute (ρ).

	X variable	*Y variable*
Mary	1	3
Peter	2	4
Paul	3	1
Helen	4	2
Ruth	5	7
Edward	6	5
John	7	6

16. Two sets of paired variables are expressed in sigma scores. Compute the coefficient of correlation between them.

z_X	z_Y
+.70	+.55
−.20	−.32
+1.50	+2.00
+1.33	+1.20
−.88	−1.06
+.32	−.40
−1.00	+.50
+.67	+.80
−.30	−.10
+1.25	+1.10
+.50	−.20

17. Using the Pearson product-moment raw score method, compute the coefficient of correlation between these paired variables:

X	Y	X^2	Y^2	XY
66	42			
50	55			
43	60			
8	24			
12	30			
35	18			
24	48			
20	35			
16	22			
54	38			

18. A class took a statistics test. The students completed all of the questions. The coefficient of correlation between the number of correct and the number of incorrect responses for the class was

_____.

19. There is a significant difference between the slope of the regression line r and that of the regression line b. Do you agree? Why?

20. Compute the standard error of estimate of Y from X when:

$$S_y = 6.20$$
$$r = +.60$$

21. Given the following information, predict the Y score from the given X, when $X = 90$, and:

   a. $r = +.60$
      $M_x = 80$ $S_x = 12$
      $M_y = 40$ $S_y = 8$
   b. $r = −.60$

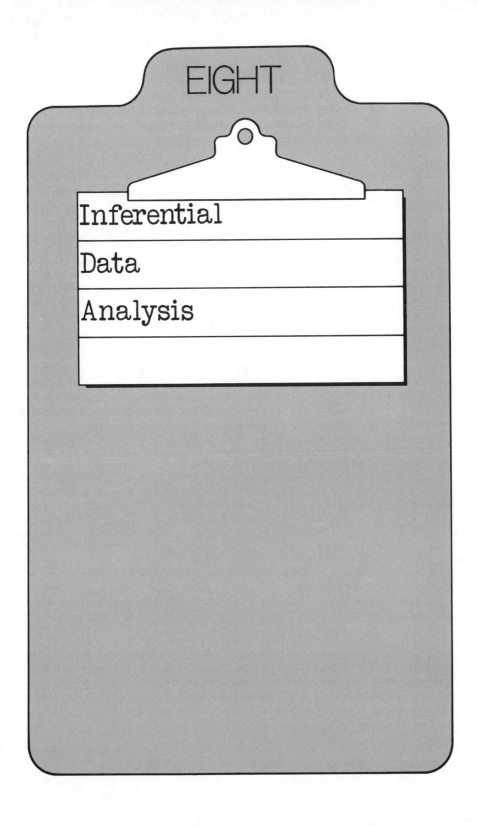

EIGHT

Inferential

Data

Analysis

In Chapter One the ultimate purpose of research was described as the discovery of general principles based upon observed relationships between variables. If it were necessary to observe all of the individuals in the population about which one wished to generalize, the process would be never-ending and prohibitively expensive. The practicable solution is to select samples that are representative of the population of interest and, through observations and analysis of the sample data, the researcher may infer characteristics of the population.

The reader may wish to refer to the discussion of types of samples and sampling procedures presented in Chapter One.

STATISTICAL INFERENCE

The belief that an adequate sample is a small carbon copy of or has the identical characteristics of the population is a misconception shared by many laymen. If a large number of researchers selected random samples of 100 teachers from the population of all teachers in California, the mean weight of the samples would not be identical. A few would be relatively high, a few relatively low, but most of them would tend to cluster around the population mean. This variation of sample means is due to what is known as sampling error. The term does not suggest any fault or mistake in the *sampling process,* it merely describes the chance variations that are inevitable when a number of randomly selected sample means are computed.

Estimating or inferring a population characteristic (parameter) of a random sample (statistic) is not an exact process. It has been noted that successive means of randomly selected samples from the same population are not identical. Thus, if these means are not identical, it would be logical to assume that any one of them probably differs from the population mean. This would seem to present an insurmountable obstacle to statisticians, for they have only a sample to use as a basis for generalizations about a population. Fortunately, since the nature of the variations of sample means is known, it is possible to estimate the degree or variation of sample means on a probability basis.

The Central Limit Theorem

An important principle, known as the central limit theorem, describes the characteristics of sample means.

If a large number of equal-sized samples (greater than 30 in size) is selected at random from an infinite population:

1. The means of the samples will be normally distributed.

2. The mean value of the sample means will be the same as the mean of the population.

3. The distribution of sample means will have its own standard deviation. Known as the standard error of the mean, it is computed from this formula:

$$s_M = \frac{s}{\sqrt{N}}$$

where s = the standard deviation of individual scores
N = the size of the sample
s_M = the standard error of the mean

To illustrate the operation of the central limit theorem, let us assume that the mean of a population is 180 and the standard deviation is 12. Figure 8-1 illustrates the relationship between the distribution of individual scores and the distribution of sample means when the sample size is 36. If $M = 180$, $N = 36$, and $s = 12$:

$$s_M = \frac{s}{\sqrt{N}} = \frac{12}{\sqrt{36}} = \frac{12}{6} = 2$$

The standard error of the mean has a smaller value than the standard deviation of individual scores. This is understandable, because in computing the means of samples, the extreme scores are not represented, for means are middle score values. Note the difference between the range and standard deviation of individual scores and those of the sample means.

From the formula, $$s_M = \frac{s}{\sqrt{N}}$$

it is apparent that as the size of the sample increases, the standard error of the mean decreases. To cite extreme cases as illustrations; as

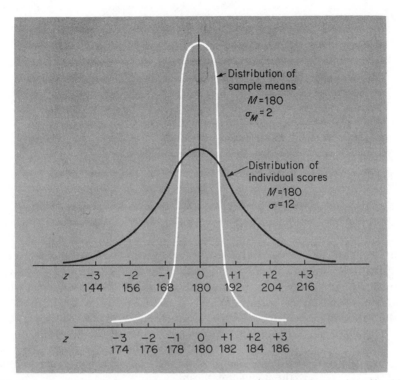

Fig. 8-1. Normal Distribution of Individual Scores and of Sample Means when $N = 36$

the sample N approaches infinity, the mean approaches the population mean and the standard error of the mean approaches zero.

$$s_M = \frac{s}{\sqrt{\infty}} = \frac{s}{\infty} \doteq 0$$

As the sample is reduced in size and approaches one, the standard error of the mean approaches the standard deviation of the individual scores.

$$s_M = \frac{s}{\sqrt{1}} = \frac{s}{1} = s$$

As sample size increases the magnitude of the error decreases. Sample size and sampling error are negatively correlated (see Figure 8-2).

It may be generalized that as the number of independent observations increases, the error involved in generalizing from sample values to population values decreases, and accuracy of prediction increases.

To the statistician who must estimate the population mean from a

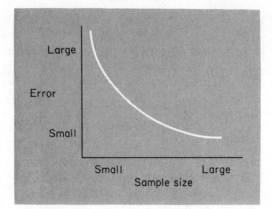

Fig. 8-2. The Relationship between Sample Size and the Magnitude of Sampling Error

sample mean, his or her obtained sample mean would not be too far away from the unknown population mean. One might say that the population mean is "known only to God," but a particular mean calculated from a randomly selected sample can be related to the population mean in the following way.

The chances or probabilities are approximately:

> 68/100 that the sample mean will not be farther than 1 s_M from the population mean
>
> 95/100 that the sample mean will not be farther than 1.96 s_M from the population mean
>
> 99/100 that the sample mean will not be farther than 2.58 s_M from the population mean.

Thus the value of a population mean, inferred from a randomly selected sample mean, can be estimated on a probability basis. In the example presented in Figure 8.1, since $s_M = 2$ points, there is a 68/100 probability that the mean of any randomly selected sample of 36 would not be more than 2 points away from the population mean, and 95/100 probability that the sample mean would not be more than 4 points away.

PARAMETRIC TESTS

Parametric tests are considered to be the most powerful tests and should be used if their basic assumptions can be met. These assumptions are based upon the nature of the population distribution, and on the way the type of scale is used to quantify the data observations.

268

1. The observations are independent. The selection of one case is not dependent upon the selection of any other case.

2. The samples have equal or nearly equal variances. This condition is particularly important to determine when samples are small.

3. The variables described are expressed in interval or ratio scales. Nominal measures (frequency counts) and ordinal measures (ranking) do not qualify for parametric treatment.

TESTING STATISTICAL SIGNIFICANCE

The Significance of the Difference Between the Means of Two Independent Groups

Since a mean is probably the most satisfactory measure for characterizing a group, researchers find it important to determine whether the difference between means of samples is significant. To illustrate the point an example might be helpful.

Let us assume that an experiment is set up to compare the effectiveness of two methods of teaching reading. Two groups are selected at random from the same population, one designated by random assignment as the experimental group and the other as the control group. The experimental group is taught by the initial alphabet method, and the control group by the traditional alphabet. At the end of a year a standardized reading test is administered and the mean score of each group is computed. The effectiveness of the experimental group method as compared to the effectiveness of the control group method is the issue, with the end-of-year mean scores of each group the basis for comparison.

A mere quantitative superiority of the experimental group mean score over the control group mean score is not conclusive proof of its superiority. Since we know that the means of two groups randomly drawn from the same population were not necessarily identical, any difference that appeared at the end of the experimental cycle could possibly be attributed to sampling error or chance. To be statistically significant, the difference must be greater than that reasonably attributed to sampling error. Determining whether a difference is significant always involves discrediting a sampling error explanation. The test of the significance of the difference between two means is known as a *t* test. It involves the computation of the ratio between experimental variance (observed difference between two sample means) and error variance (the sampling error factor).

$$t = \frac{M_1 - M_2}{\sqrt{\dfrac{S_1^2}{N_1} + \dfrac{S_2^2}{N_2}}}$$

$M_1 =$ mean of experimental sample
$M_2 =$ mean of control sample
$N_1 =$ number of cases in experimental sample
$N_2 =$ number of cases in control sample
$S_1^2 =$ variance of experimental sample
$S_2^2 =$ variance of control sample

If the value of the numerator in this ratio is not significantly greater than the denominator, it is likely that sampling error, and not the effect of the treatment or experimental variable, is indicated. But before the discussion of the quantitative criteria determining statistical significance of the difference between means, two additional concepts should be considered:

1. the null hypothesis (H_0)
2. the level of significance.

The Null Hypothesis (H_0)

A null hypothesis states that there is no significant difference or relationship between two or more parameters. It concerns a judgment as to whether apparent differences or relationships are true differences or relationships or whether they merely result from sampling error. The experimenter formulates a null hypothesis, a no-difference or relationship hypothesis. What he or she hypothesizes is that any apparent difference between the mean achievement of the experimental and control sample groups at the end of the experimental cycle is simply the result of sampling error, as explained by the operation of the central limit theorem.

The use of the null hypothesis is not restricted to experimental studies. It may be used as appropriately when inferring generalizations about populations from sample data in descriptive research studies.

Students have complained that the statement of a null hypothesis sounds like double talk. They are understandably puzzled about the reasons for the negative statement that the researcher attempts to reject. The explanation is somewhat involved, but the logic is sound. Verification of one consequence of a positive hypothesis does not prove it to be true. Observed consequences that may be consistent with a positive hypothesis may also be compatible with equally plausible but competing hypotheses. Verifying a positive hypothesis provides a rather inconclusive test.

Rejecting a null or negative hypothesis provides a stronger test of logic. Evidence that is inconsistent with a particular negative hypothesis provides a strong basis for its rejection. Before a court of law, a defendant is assumed to be not guilty until the not-guilty assumption is discredited or rejected. In a sense, the not-guilty assumption is comparable to the null hypothesis.

If the difference between the mean achievement of the experimental and the control groups is too great to attribute to the normal fluctuations that result from sampling error, the experimenter may fail to accept the null hypothesis, saying, in effect, that it is probably not true that the difference is merely the result of sampling error. The means no longer behave as random sample means from the same population. Something has happened to, or affected, the experimental group in such a way that it behaves like a random sample from a different or changed population. Thus the researcher may conclude that the experimental variable or treatment probably accounted for the difference in performance, as measured by the mean test scores. The experimenter is using a statistical test to discount chance or sampling error as an explanation for the difference.

If the difference between means was not great enough to reject the null hypothesis, the researcher fails to reject it. He or she concludes that there was no significant difference, and that chance or sampling error probably accounted for the apparent difference.

The Level of Significance

The rejection or acceptance of a null hypothesis is based upon some level of significance (alpha level) as a criterion. In psychological and educational circles, the 5 per cent (.05) alpha level of significance is often used as a standard for rejection. Rejecting a null hypothesis at the .05 level indicates that a difference in means as large as that found between experimental and control group would not likely have resulted from sampling error in more than 5 out of 100 replications of the experiment. This suggests a 95 per cent probability that the difference was due to the experimental treatment rather than to sampling error.

A more rigorous test of significance is the 1 per cent (.01) alpha level. Rejecting a null hypothesis at the .01 level would suggest that as large a difference between experimental and control mean achievement would not likely have resulted from sampling error in more than 1 in 100 replications of the experiment.

When samples are large (more than 30 in size) the t critical value is expressed as a z (sigma score). If the z value equals or exceeds 1.96,

we may conclude that the difference between means is significant at
the .05 level. If the z value equals or exceeds 2.58 we may conclude
that the difference between means is significant at the .01 level.

Using the example of the reading experiment previously described,
let us supply the data and test the null hypothesis that there was no
significant difference between the mean reading achievement of the initial teaching alphabet experimental group and the traditional alphabet
control group.

Experimental *i t a group*	*Control* *traditional alphabet group*
$N_1 = 32$	$N_2 = 34$
$M_1 = 87.43$	$M_2 = 82.58$
$S_1^2 = 39.40$	$S_2^2 = 40.80$

$$t = \frac{M_1 - M_2}{\sqrt{\dfrac{S_1^2}{N_1} + \dfrac{S_2^2}{N_2}}} = \frac{87.43 - 82.58}{\sqrt{\dfrac{39.40}{32} + \dfrac{40.80}{34}}}$$

$$= \frac{4.85}{\sqrt{1.23 + 1.20}} = \frac{4.85}{\sqrt{2.43}} = \frac{4.85}{1.56} \qquad t = 3.11$$

Since a t value of 3.11 exceeds 2.58, the null hypothesis may be
rejected at the .01 level of significance. If this experiment were replicated
with random samples from the same population, the probability is that
a difference between mean performance as great as that observed would
result from sampling error in fewer than 1 out of 100 replications. This
test would indicate rather strong evidence that the treatment would
probably make a difference in the teaching of reading when applied to
similar populations of pupils.

Decision Making

Statistical decisions about parameters based upon evidence observed
in samples always involve the possibility of error. Statisticians do not
deal with decisions based upon certainty. They merely estimate the probability or improbability of occurrences of events.

Rejection of a null hypothesis when it is really true is known as a
Type I error. The level of significance selected determines the probability
of a Type I error. For example, when the researcher rejects a null hypothesis at the .05 level, he or she is taking a 5 per cent risk of rejecting
what should be a sampling error explanation when it is probably true.

Accepting a null hypothesis when it is really false is known as a
Type II error. This decision errs in accepting a sampling error explanation when it is probably false.

Setting a level of significance as high as the .01 level minimizes the risk of a Type I error. But this high level of significance is more conservative and increases the risk of a Type II error.

Two-Tailed and One-Tailed Tests of Significance

If a null hypothesis were established that there was no difference (other than a sampling error difference) between the mean IQ's of athletes and nonathletes, we would be concerned only with a difference, and not with the superiority or inferiority of either group.

There is no difference between the mean IQ's of athletes and nonathletes. In this situation we apply a two-tailed test.

If we changed the null hypothesis to indicate the superiority or inferiority of either group it might be stated:

Athletes do not have higher IQ's than nonathletes.
Athletes do not have lower IQ's than nonathletes.

Each of these hypotheses indicates a direction of difference. When researchers are hypothesizing a direction of difference, rather than the mere existence of a difference, they use a one-tailed test.

For a large sample two-tailed test, the 5 per cent area of rejection is divided between the upper and lower tails of the curve (2½ per cent at each end), and it is necessary to go out to ±1.96 on the sigma scale to reach the area of rejection (Figure 8-3).

For a one-tailed test, since the 5 per cent area of rejection is either at the upper tail or at the lower tail of the curve, the t critical value is lower, for it is not necessary to go as far out on the sigma scale to reach the area of rejection (Figure 8–4). The t critical value in such a case is ±1.645.

Fig. 8-3. A Two-tailed Test at the .05 Level (2½ Per Cent at Each End)

Fig. 8-4. A One-tailed Test at the .05 Level (5 Per cent at One End or 5 Per cent at the Other End)

Large Sample *t* Critical Values for Rejection of the Null Hypothesis

	.05 level	*.01 level*
Two-tailed test	1.96	2.58
One-tailed test	1.64	2.33

A similar pair of curves would illustrate the difference between *t* critical areas of rejection at the 1 per cent level of significance. The *t* values must equal or exceed these *t* critical values for the rejection of a null hypothesis.

The test of the significance of the difference between two independent means to this point has concerned large samples, and the critical *t* values for rejection of the null hypothesis have been found in the normal probability table.

When small samples are used to infer population differences, a different set of *t* critical values is used. But before discussing small sample tests, an important concept known as degrees of freedom should be considered.

Degrees of Freedom

The number of degrees of freedom in a distribution is the number of observations or values that are independent of each other, that cannot be deduced from each other. While this concept has been puzzling to students of statistics, several analogies and their application to estimation or prediction may help to clarify it.

1. Let us assume that a coin is tossed in the air. The statistician predicts

that a head will turn up. If a head comes up, he or she has made one correct, independent prediction. But if the statistician predicted that a head would turn up and a tail would face down, he or she has made two predictions. Only one prediction, however, is an independent prediction, for the other can be deduced from the first. The second added no new information. In this case there was one degree of freedom, not two.

The strength of a prediction is increased as the number of independent observations or degrees of freedom is increased.

2. When a mean is computed from a number of terms in a distribution, the sum is calculated and divided by N.

$$M = \frac{\Sigma X}{N}$$

But in computing a mean, 1 degree of freedom is used up or lost, and subsequent calculations of the variance and the standard deviation will be based on $N - 1$ independent observations or $N - 1$ degrees of freedom. An example of the loss of a degree of freedom follows.

A *original distribution*	*B* *altered distribution*	
+5	15	These four terms can be al-
+4	8	tered in any way.
+3	5	
+2	7	
+1	−20	This term is dependent on, or
$\Sigma X = +15$	$\Sigma X = +15$	determined by, the other four
$N = 5$	$N = 5$	terms.
$M = +3$	$M = +3$	

In the altered distribution, the fifth term must have a value of -20 for the sum to equal $+15$; the mean to be $+3$, and the sum of the deviations from the mean to equal zero. Thus four terms are independent and can be altered, but one is dependent or fixed and is deduced from the other four. There are $N - 1$ $(5 - 1)$ or 4 degrees of freedom.

When the variance or standard deviation of a sample is used to estimate a population variance or standard deviation, the denominator of the formula is $N - 1$, rather than N.

The variance or standard deviation calculated this way is known as *unbiased estimate* of the corresponding population value.

$$S^2 = \frac{\Sigma x^2}{N - 1} \qquad \text{an unbiased estimate of the variance of a population estimate from a sample}$$

$$S = \sqrt{\frac{\Sigma x^2}{N-1}} \quad \text{an unbiased estimate of the standard deviation of a population estimate from a sample}$$

Note that the symbols S^2 and S are used, rather than σ^2 and σ when sample calculations (statistics) are used to estimate population values (parameters). The denominator is always $N-1$ in such calculations.

The computation using the number of degrees of freedom ($N-1$), rather than N in the denominator of the fraction, increases the magnitude of the quotient. This correction for the number of independent observations, or degrees of freedom, is particularly important when the sample is small. When N is large, the correction is negligible.

For example, when N is small, if $N=5$ and $\Sigma x^2 = 80$:

$$\sigma^2 = \frac{\Sigma x^2}{N} \qquad\qquad x = (X-M)$$

$$\sigma = \sqrt{\frac{\Sigma x^2}{N}}$$

$$\sigma^2 = \tfrac{80}{5} = 16.00 \qquad \sigma = \sqrt{\tfrac{80}{5}} = \sqrt{16} = 4.00$$

$$S^2 = \frac{\Sigma x^2}{N-1} \qquad\qquad S = \sqrt{\frac{\Sigma x^2}{N-1}}$$

$$S^2 = \tfrac{80}{4} = 20.00 \qquad S = \sqrt{\tfrac{80}{4}} = \sqrt{20} = 4.48$$

Notice that the correction for the number of degrees of freedom makes a substantial difference in the calculated variance and standard deviation. When N is large, the correction for $N-1$ degrees of freedom has little effect. If $N=50$ and $\Sigma x^2 = 400$

$$\sigma^2 = \tfrac{400}{50} = 8.00 \qquad \sigma = \tfrac{400}{50} = 8.00 = 2.83$$

$$S^2 = \frac{\Sigma x^2}{N-1} \qquad\qquad S = \sqrt{\frac{\Sigma x^2}{N-1}}$$

$$S^2 = \tfrac{400}{49} = 8.16 \qquad S = \sqrt{\tfrac{400}{49}} = \sqrt{8.16} = 2.86$$

The correction for calculating the variance and standard deviation is important because unless the loss of a degree of freedom is considered, the calculated sample variance or standard deviation is likely to underestimate the population variance or standard deviation. This is true because the mean of the squared deviations from the mean of any distribution is the smallest possible value, and probably would be smaller than the mean of the squared deviation from any other point in the distribution. Since the mean of the sample is not likely to be identical to the population mean (because of sampling error), the use of the number of degrees of freedom, rather than N in the denominator, tends to correct for this underestimation of the population variance or standard deviation.

The strength of a prediction or the accuracy of an inferred value increases as the number of independent observations (sample size) is increased. Since large samples may be biased, sample size is not the only important determinant, but if unbiased samples are selected randomly from a population, large samples will provide a more accurate basis than will smaller samples for inferring population values.

Student's Distribution *(t)*

When small samples (fewer than 30 observations in number) are involved, the *t* table, rather than the normal probability table, is used to determine statistical significance. This concept of small sample size was developed around 1915 by William Seely Gosset, a consulting statistician for Guinness Breweries of Dublin, Ireland. Since his employer's rules prohibited publication under the researcher's name, he signed the name "Student" when he published his findings.

Gosset determined that the distribution curves of small sample means were somewhat different from the normal curve. Small sample distributions were observed to be lower at the means and higher at the tails or ends of the distributions.

Gosset's *t* critical values, carefully calculated for small samples, are reproduced in the *t* distribution table in Appendix C. The *t* critical values necessary for rejection of a null hypothesis are higher for small samples at a given level of significance (see Figure 8-5). Each *t* critical value for rejection is based upon the appropriate number of degrees of freedom.

As the sample sizes increase, the *t* critical values necessary for rejec-

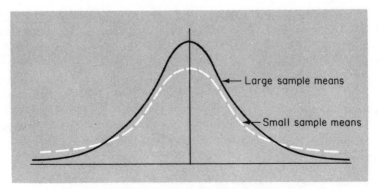

Fig. 8-5. Distribution of Large and Small Sample Means

tion of a null hypothesis diminish and approach the z values of the normal probability table.

Significance of the difference between two small sample independent means. When the samples are small and their variances are equal or nearly equal, the method of pooled variances provides the appropriate test of the significance of the difference between two independent means.

The formula is a bit more involved than the one previously illustrated, but it provides a more powerful test of significance. The appropriate t critical value for rejection of the null hypothesis would be found for $N + N - 2$ degrees of freedom, using the t distribution table.

$$t = \frac{M_1 - M_2}{\sqrt{\frac{(N-1)\,S_1^2 + (N-1)\,S_2^2}{N_1 + N_2 - 2}\left(\frac{1}{N_1} + \frac{1}{N_2}\right)}}$$

For example, in comparing the significance of the mean IQ difference between samples of 8 athletes and 10 nonathletes, the number of degrees of freedom would be $N + N - 2 = 8 + 10 - 2 = 16$. From the t distribution table at 16 degrees of freedom, the t critical values necessary for the rejection of the null hypothesis would be:

	Level of significance	
16 degrees of freedom	*.05*	*.01*
Two-tailed test	2.120	2.921
One-tailed test	1.746	2.583

Homogeneity of Variances

In t tests for small samples there is one condition that must be met to justify the method of pooled variances. This condition is known as equality or *homogeneity of variances*. It does not literally mean that the variances of the samples to be compared must be identical, but only that they do not differ by an amount that is statistically significant. Differences that would be attributed to sampling error do not impair the validity of the process.

To determine whether the samples meet the criterion of equality of variances an F test is used.

$$F = \frac{S^2 \text{ (larger variance)}}{S^2 \text{ (smaller variance)}}$$

TABLE 8-1   Distribution of F (.05 level)

		9	10	11	12
		span			

Degrees of Freedom for Larger $S^2(N-1)$

		9	10	11	12
Degrees of	9	3.18	3.13	3.10	3.07
freedom for	10	3.02	2.97	2.94	2.91
smaller S^2	11	2.90	2.86	2.82	2.79
$(N-1)$	12	2.80	2.76	2.72	2.69

This F ratio is never less than one, for the larger variance is always divided by the smaller. To test for homogeneity of variances an F distribution table is used in much the same way as the t distribution table. F critical values are presented for determining the statistical significance of the calculated F critical ratio, based upon the appropriate rows and columns, each at $N-1$ degrees of freedom.

A few .05 level of significance values from the F distribution table are presented. The complete table may be found in many statistics textbooks.

Unless the calculated F equals or exceeds the appropriate F critical value, it may be assumed that the variances are homogeneous and the difference is not significant.

For example, if two samples with 10 degrees of freedom (greater variance 38.40) and 12 df (smaller variance 18.06) were subjected to the test of homogeneity:

$$F = \frac{38.40}{18.06} = 2.13$$

An F critical value of 2.76 must be equaled or exceeded to determine that the difference between variances is significant at the .05 level. In this example, since $2.13 < 2.76$, the researcher would conclude that the variances fulfilled the condition of homogeneity and that the method of pooled variances is appropriate. An example using small samples illustrates the process.

The mean score of 10 delinquent boys on a personal adjustment inventory was compared with the mean score of 12 nondelinquent boys, both groups selected at random. Test the null hypothesis that there is no statistically significant difference between the mean test scores at the .01 level of significance.

Delinquent boys	*Nondelinquent boys*
$M_2 = 9$	$M_1 = 14$
$S_2^2 = 20.44$	$S_1^2 = 19.60$
$N_2 = 10$	$N_1 = 12$

$df = 10 + 12 - 2 = 20$ (the variances are homogeneous)

$$F = \frac{20.44}{19.60} = 1.04$$

$$t = \frac{M_1 - M_2}{\sqrt{\dfrac{(N-1)S_1^2 + (N-1)S_2^2}{N_1 + N_2 - 2}\left(\dfrac{1}{N_1} + \dfrac{1}{N_2}\right)}}$$

$$t = \frac{14 - 9}{\sqrt{\dfrac{11(19.60) + 9(20.44)}{12 + 10 - 2}\left(\dfrac{1}{12} + \dfrac{1}{10}\right)}}$$

$$t = \frac{5}{\sqrt{\dfrac{215.60 + 183.96}{20}\left(\dfrac{11}{60}\right)}}$$

$$t = \frac{5}{\sqrt{19.98\,(\frac{11}{60})}} = \frac{5}{\sqrt{3.66}}$$

$$t = \frac{5}{1.96} = 2.62$$

Since this is a two-tailed test, the t critical value for rejection of the null hypothesis at the .01 level of significance for 20 degrees of freedom is 2.831.

Since the calculated value is 2.62, it does not equal or exceed the t critical value necessary for rejection of the null hypothesis at the .01 level for 20 degrees of freedom; the hypothesis is not rejected and we conclude that there is no significant difference.

Had we used the .05 level of significance for 20 degrees of freedom, the t critical value necessary for rejection would be 2.086, and we could have rejected the null hypothesis, for our calculated t critical ratio of 2.62 exceeds the 2.086 t table value.

Significance of the difference between the means of two matched or correlated groups. The two previous examples of testing the significance of the difference between two independent means assumed that the individuals were randomly assigned to the control and experimental groups. There are situations when it is appropriate to determine the significance of the difference between means of groups that are not randomly assigned. Two such situations are:

a. When the pairs of individuals who make up the groups have been matched by one or more characteristics—IQ, reading achievement, identical twins, or on some other basis for equating the individuals.

b. When the same group of individuals takes a pretest, is exposed to a treatment, and then is retested to determine whether the influence of the treatment has been statistically significant, as determined by mean gain scores.

In such cases it is necessary to calculate the coefficient of correlation between:

a. The posttest scores of the matched pairs sample, or

b. The pretest and posttest scores of the participants in the experiment.

Using the coefficient of correlation, the appropriate t test would be based upon this formula:

$$t = \frac{M_1 - M_2}{\sqrt{\dfrac{S_1^2}{N_1} + \dfrac{S_2^2}{N_2} - 2r\left(\dfrac{S_1}{\sqrt{N_1}}\right)\left(\dfrac{S_2}{\sqrt{N_2}}\right)}}$$

The number of degrees of freedom would be the number of pairs minus one. Two examples illustrate situations a and b:

Example a.

Two groups, each made up of 20 fifth grade students, were matched on the basis of IQ's. The use of film strips was the method used to teach the experimental group; the control group was exposed to a conventional "read and discuss" method.

The research wished to test the null hypothesis that there was no difference between the mean achievement of the two groups (a two-tailed test) at the .05 level.

$$F = 1.30 \text{ (variances are equal}$$

X	C
$N_1 = 20$	$N_2 = 20$
$S_1^2 = 54.76$	$S_2^2 = 42.25$
$M_1 = 53.20$	$M_2 = 49.80$
$r = +.60$	$df = 19$

$$t = \frac{53.20 - 49.80}{\sqrt{\dfrac{54.76}{20} + \dfrac{42.85}{20} - 2(+.60)\left(\dfrac{7.40}{4.47}\right)\left(\dfrac{6.50}{4.47}\right)}}$$

$$t = \frac{3.40}{\sqrt{2.74 + 2.14 - 1.20(1.66)(1.45)}}$$

$$t = \frac{3.40}{\sqrt{4.84 - 2.89}}$$

$$t = \frac{3.40}{\sqrt{1.95}} = \frac{3.40}{1.40} = 2.43$$

Since the t value of 2.43 exceeds the t critical value of 2.093 for a two-tailed test at the .05 level at 19 degrees of freedom, the null hypothesis may be rejected.

Example b.

A typing teacher wished to determine the effectiveness of ten minutes of transcendental meditation upon the speed and accuracy of his class of 30 students. He administered a timed speed/accuracy test and recorded the score for each student. The next day, after ten minutes of class participation in a TM exercise, he administered a similar timed speed/accuracy test.

He computed the mean scores for the pretest and the scores obtained after the TM experience and calculated the coefficient of correlation between the pairs of scores to be +.84.

He then tested the hypothesis that the TM experience would not improve the proficiency in speed and accuracy of typing of his class. He chose the .01 level of significance, using a one-tailed test.

$$F = \frac{37.21}{36.10} = 1.03 \text{ (variances are equal)}$$

Pretest   *Test after TM*

$N_2 = 30$ $N_1 = 30$
$S_2^2 = 37.21$ $S_1^2 = 36.10$
$M_2 = 44.80$ $M_1 = 49.10$
$r = +.84$ $df = 29$

$$t = \frac{49.10 - 44.80}{\sqrt{\frac{37.21}{30} + \frac{36.10}{30} - 2(+.84)\left(\frac{6.10}{5.48}\right)\left(\frac{6.01}{5.48}\right)}}$$

$$t = \frac{4.30}{\sqrt{1.24 + 1.20 - 1.68(1.11)(1.10)}}$$

$$t = \frac{4.30}{\sqrt{2.44 - 2.05}} = \frac{4.30}{\sqrt{.39}}$$

$$t = \frac{4.30}{.62} = 6.94$$

Since the t value of 6.94 exceeds the t critical value of 2.462 for a one-tailed test at the .01 level for 29 degrees of freedom, he rejected the null hypothesis, concluding that the meditation experience did improve performance proficiency.

Analysis of Variance (ANOVA)

We have noted that the critical ratio z and t tests were employed to determine, after treatment, whether the means of two random samples were too different to attribute to chance or sampling error. The analysis of variance is an effective way to determine whether the means of *more than two samples* are too different to attribute to sampling error.

It would be possible to use a number of t tests to determine the significance of the difference between five means, two at a time, but it would involve ten separate tests. The number of necessary pair-wise comparisons of N things is determined by the formula:

$$\frac{N(N-1)}{2}$$

If $N = 5$

$$\frac{5(5-1)}{2} = \frac{20}{2} = 10$$

An analysis of variance makes this determination possible with a single test, rather than ten. Another advantage lies in the fact that computing a number of separate t tests, by chance alone, may appear to yield significant differences.

In *single classification*, or *one-way analysis of variance, the relationship between one independent and one dependent variable is examined.* For example, a test of abstract reasoning was administered to four randomly selected groups of students in a large state university majoring in mathematics, physics, philosophy, and chemistry. Were the mean test scores of each of the four groups significantly different from one another?

The analysis of variance consisted of these operations:

1. The variance of the scores for four groups combined into one composite group is known as the *total groups variance* (V_t).

2. The mean value of the variances of each of the four groups, computed separately, is known as the *within groups variance* (V_w).

3. The difference between the total groups variance and the within groups variance is known as the *between groups variance* ($V_t - V_w = V_b$).

4. The F ratio is computed:

$$F = \frac{V_b}{V_w} = \frac{\text{between groups variance}}{\text{within groups variance}}$$

The logic of the F ratio is as follows. The within groups variance represents the sampling error in the distributions. The between groups variance represents the influence of the variable of interest or the experimental variable. If the *between groups variance* is not substantially greater than the *within groups variance,* the researcher would conclude that the difference between the means is probably only a reflection of sampling error. If the *F* ratio were substantially greater than one, it would seem that the ratio between the *between groups variance* and the *within groups variance* was probably too great to attribute to sampling error.

The significance of the *F* ratio (so named for Sir Ronald Fisher) is found in an *F* table, which indicates the critical values necessary to test the null hypothesis at selected levels of significance.

In *multiple classification,* or *factorial analysis of variance, both the independent and interactive effects of two or more independent variables on one dependent variable may be analyzed.* Not only may the effect of several independent variables be tested, but their interaction (how they may combine in a significant way) may be examined. Since human behavior and the factors influencing it are complex and can rarely be explained by single independent variable influences, this method of analysis is a powerful statistical tool of the behavioral researcher.

Analysis of covariance (ANCOVA)

In classroom research, it would be desirable to select and assign subjects to experimental and control groups by randomization. However, because of administrative limitations, at times intact groups must be used. Analysis of covariance is a method of analysis that enables the researcher to equate the pre-experimental status of the groups in terms of relevant variables. The initial status of the groups may be determined by pretest scores in a pretest-posttest study, or in posttest only studies, by such measures as intelligence, reading scores, grade point average, or previous knowledge of subject matter. Differences in the initial status of the groups can be removed statistically so that they can be compared as though their initial status had been equated. The scores that have been corrected by this procedure are known as *residuals,* for they are what remain after the inequalities have been removed.

Analysis of covariance, used with one or more independent variable and one dependent variable, is an important method of analyzing experiments carried on under conditions that otherwise would be unacceptable. The mathematical procedures are rather complicated and there are many steps in computing their values. However, when data are transferred to data-processing cards, with the use of standard computer programs, the analysis of complex studies can be processed almost instantaneously.

Only the basic purposes have been described in this section. The volume by Hopkins and Glass, listed in the chapter bibliography, is recommended for a more complete explanation.

CORRELATION

Correlation is the relationship between two or more sets of paired variables. The degree of the relationship is measured and described by the
coefficient of correlation.

Both the parametric Pearson product-moment method and the
Spearman nonparametric method have been presented and explained
in Chapter Seven. Methods of determining their statistical significance
are considered in the following pages.

Statistical Significance of a Coefficient of Correlation

Throughout this chapter on inferential data analysis, the idea of
statistical significance and its relationship to the null hypothesis have
been emphasized. An observed coefficient of correlation may result from
chance or sampling error, and a test to determine its statistical significance is appropriate. In small sample correlations, chance could yield
what might appear to be evidence of a genuine relationship.

The null hypothesis (H_0) states that the coefficient of correlation
is zero. Only when chance or sampling error has been discredited on
a probability basis can a coefficient of correlation be accepted as statistically significant. The test of the significance of r is determined by the
use of the formula:

$$t_r = \frac{r\sqrt{N-2}}{\sqrt{1-r^2}}$$

With $N-2$ degrees of freedom a coefficient of correlation is judged
as statistically significant when the t value equals or exceeds the t critical
value of the t distribution table.

If $r = .40$

$N = 25$

$$t = \frac{.40\sqrt{23}}{\sqrt{1-(.40)^2}} = \frac{1.92}{.92} = 2.09$$

On a two-tailed test at the .05 level with 23 degrees of freedom, the
null hypothesis is rejected, exceeding the t critical value of 2.07. As
sample size is decreased, sampling error increases. For a smaller sample,
the coefficient must be larger to be statistically significant.

If $r = .40$

$N = 18$

$$t = \frac{.40\sqrt{16}}{\sqrt{1-(.40)^2}} = \frac{1.60}{.92} = 1.74$$

At 16 degrees of freedom the observed value of 1.74 fails to equal or exceed the t critical value of 2.12 at the .05 level of significance, and the null hypothesis would be accepted. With a sample N of 18, a coefficient of correlation of .40 would not be large enough for the rejection of the null hypothesis, a sampling error explanation.

Practical Significance

The criteria for statistical significance and for practical significance are different. A test of significance may not be the final measure of the finding's usefulness in reaching a practical decision. The test of significance merely indicates whether or not a variable relationship $= 0$, the result of chance or sampling error.

Some professional practitioners have deprecated significance tests, pointing out that they are of little value, particularly in large sample studies. It is true that when samples are large, sampling error is small. Thus, if the size of the sample is large enough, almost any coefficient of correlation or difference between means, however small or apparently inconsequential, will pass the test of statistical significance. When N = 400, a coefficient of correlation of .10 is significant at the .05 level, a coefficient of .13 at the .01 level. Such coefficients may be too small to be of practical value for making certain decisions.

The test of significance is the primary concern of the researcher, but the professional practitioner has other judgments to make. He or she must consider the nature of the variables and the strength of the variable relationship in terms of risk, cost, or benefits that a given course of action may involve. In crucial situations, the application of very expensive medical procedures would be justified if they offered the probability of saving even a small percentage of patients that otherwise would have been lost. In such less critical situations as an academic classroom, a new and expensive teaching procedure might not be justified if the probability of more effective learning was small.

NONPARAMETRIC TESTS

Nonparametric or distribution-free tests are used when:

1. The nature of the population distribution from which samples are drawn is not known to be normal.
2. The variables are expressed in nominal form (classified in categories and represented by frequency counts).

3. The variables are expressed in ordinal form (ranked in order, expressed as 1st, 2nd, 3rd, etc.).

Nonparametric tests, because they are based upon counted or ranked data rather than on measured values, are less precise, have less power than parametric tests, and are not as likely to reject a null hypothesis when it is false.

Many statisticians suggest that parametric tests be used if possible, and that nonparametric be used only when parametric assumptions cannot be met. Others argue than nonparametric tests have greater merit than is often attributed to them because their validity is not based upon assumptions about the nature of the population distribution, assumptions that are so frequently ignored or violated by researchers employing parametric tests.

Of the many nonparametric tests, six of the most frequently used are described and illustrated here.

1. Chi square (χ^2) test

2. Median test

3. Mann-Whitney test

4. Sign test

5. Wilcoxon matched-pairs signed ranks test

The Chi Square Test (χ^2)

The χ^2 test applies only to discrete data, counted rather than measured values. The test is a test of independence, the idea that one variable is not affected by, or related to, another variable. The χ^2 is not a measure of the degree of relationship. It is merely used to estimate the likelihood that some factor other than chance (sampling error) accounts for the apparent relationship. Since the null hypothesis states that there is no relationship (the variables are independent), the test merely evaluates the probability that the observed relationship results from chance. As in other tests of statistical significance, it is assumed that the sample observations have been randomly selected.

The computed χ^2 value must equal or exceed the appropriate χ^2 table critical value to justify rejection of the null hypothesis or the assumption of independence at the .05 or the .01 level of significance.

A finding of a statistically significant χ^2 value doesn't necessarily indicate a cause-and-effect relationship, a limitation that was observed when interpreting a coefficient of correlation. A significant χ^2 finding indicates that the variables probably do not exhibit the quality of independence, that they tend to be systematically related, and that the relationship transcends pure chance or sampling error.

There are situations when the theoretical or expected frequencies must be computed from the distribution. Let us assume that 200 residents of a college women's dormitory are blonde, brunette, or redhead. Is the variable, hair color, related to the number of dates the women have in a three-week period? The null hypothesis would indicate that hair color is not related to frequency of dating—that the variables hair color and frequency of dating are independent.

Chi square observations should be organized in crossbreak form. In each category, the expected frequencies (f_e), as contrasted to the observed frequencies (f_o), is the number of cases that would appear if there were no systematic relationship between the variables, a pure chance relationship.

Number of Dates

	Fewer than 10	11–15	More than 15	Total
Blondes	6 (12)	60 (56)	14 (12)	80*
Brunettes	14 (12)	48 (56)	8 (12)	80*
Redheads	10 (6)	32 (28)	8 (6)	40*
	30**	140**	30**	200 grand total

f_e *Σf row   **Σf column

numbers represent the actual observed frequencies f_o
numbers in parentheses represent the expected frequencies f_e

The expected frequency for each of the 9 cells is computed by the formula:

$$f_e = \frac{(\Sigma f \text{ column}) (\Sigma f \text{ row})}{\text{grand total}}$$

Computation of expected frequencies (f_e):

$$\overset{**\quad *}{\frac{(30)(80)}{200}} = (12) \qquad \frac{(140)(80)}{200} = (56) \qquad \frac{(30)(80)}{200} = (12)$$

$$\frac{(30)(80)}{200} = (12) \qquad \frac{(140)(80)}{200} = (56) \qquad \frac{(30)(40)}{200} = (6)$$

$$\frac{(30)(40)}{200} = (6) \qquad \frac{(140)(40)}{200} = (28) \qquad \frac{(30)(40)}{200} = (6)$$

Computation of the χ^2 Value

Formula:
$$\chi^2 = \Sigma\left(\frac{(f_o - f_e)^2}{f_e}\right)$$

$$\frac{(6-12)^2}{12} = 3 \qquad \frac{(60-56)^2}{56} = .28 \qquad \frac{(14-12)^2}{12} = .33$$

$$\frac{(14-12)^2}{12} = .33 \qquad \frac{(48-56)^2}{56} = 1.14 \qquad \frac{(8-12)^2}{12} = 1.33$$

$$\frac{(10-6)^2}{6} = 2.67 \qquad \frac{(32-28)^2}{28} = .57 \qquad \frac{(8-6)^2}{6} = .67$$

$$\chi^2 = 3 + .28 + .33 + .33 + 1.14 + 1.33 + 2.67 + .57 + .67 = 10.32$$

$$\text{degrees of freedom} = (\text{rows} - 1)(\text{columns} - 1)$$

$$= (3-1)(3-1) = (2)(2) = 4$$

χ^2 critical values for 4 degrees of freedom*

.01	.05
13.28	9.49

$\chi^2 = 10.32$

The test indicates that there is a significant relationship between hair color and number of dates at the .05 but not at the .01 level of significance. If we wished to answer the question, "Is there a relationship between blonde hair and number of dates?" we would combine the brunette and redhead categories and use a χ^2 table with 6 rather than 9 cells.

Number of Dates

	Fewer than 10	11–15	More than 15	Total
Blondes	6 (12)	6 (56)	14 (12)	80
Nonblondes	24 (18)	80 (84)	16 (18)	120
	30	140	30	200

$$\frac{(30)(80)}{200} = (12) \qquad \frac{(140)(80)}{200} = (56) \qquad \frac{(30)(80)}{200} = (12)$$

$$\frac{(30)(120)}{200} = (18) \qquad \frac{(140)(120)}{200} = (84) \qquad \frac{(30)(120)}{200} = (18)$$

$$\frac{(6-12)^2}{12} = 3.00 \qquad \frac{(60-56)^2}{56} = .29 \qquad \frac{(14-12)^2}{12} = .33$$

$$\frac{(24-18)^2}{18} = 2.00 \qquad \frac{(80-84)^2}{84} = .19 \qquad \frac{(16-18)^2}{18} = .22$$

* See Appendix D for table of critical values for chi square.

$$\chi^2 = 3.00 + .29 + .33 + 2.00 + .19 + .22 = 6.03 \qquad \text{at } 2\,df:$$

.01	9.21
.05	5.99

The null hypothesis may be rejected at the .05 but not at the .01 level of significance.

In a 2×2 table (4 cells) with 1 degree of freedom there is a simple formula that eliminates the need to calculate the theoretical frequencies for each cell.

Formula:

$$\chi^2 = \frac{N[|AD{-}BC|]^2}{(A + B)(C + D)(A + C)(B + D)}$$

Terms in a 2×2 table

A	B
C	D

Let us use an example employing this formula. A random sample of auto drivers revealed the relationship between experiences of those who had taken a course in driver education and those who had not.

	Reported accident	No accident	
Had drivers' education	44*A*	10*B*	54
No drivers' education	81*C*	35*D*	116
	125	45	170

This is a 2×2 table with one degree of freedom.

$$\chi^2 = 170 \frac{[|(44 \times 35) - (10 \times 81)|]^2}{(54 + 10)(81 + 35)(44 + 81)(10 + 35)} = 170 \frac{[|1540 - 810|]^2}{(54)(116)(125)(45)}$$

$$= \frac{170(730)^2}{35,235,000} = \frac{90,593,000}{35,235,000} = 2.57$$

The χ^2 value does not equal or exceed the critical χ^2 value (3.84) necessary to reject the null hypothesis at the .05 level of significance. There seems to be no significant relationship between completing the course in driver education and the number of individuals who had recorded auto accidents.

Yates' Correction for Continuity   In computing a chi square value for a 2×2 table with one degree of freedom, the formula is modified when any cell has a frequency count of fewer than 10. This formula differs from the previous formula.

$$\chi^2 = \frac{N\left[|AD - BC| - \frac{N}{2}\right]^2}{(A + B)(C + D)(A + C)(B + D)}$$

Example

A pharmaceutical company wished to evaluate the effectiveness of X-40, a recently developed headache relief pill.

Two randomly selected and assigned samples of patients who complained of headaches were given pills. The experimental group was given 6 X-40 pills daily, the control group 6 placebos (or sugar pills) daily, although they thought that they were receiving medication. After a week they repeated their experience.

	X-40 X	Placebo C	
Headaches relieved	30$_A$	40$_B$	70
Headaches continued	4$_C$	10$_D$	14
	34	50	84

A χ^2 test using a 2×2 table at 1 degree of freedom was applied, with Yates correction. Was the effectiveness of the X-40 medication significant at the .05 level?

$$\chi^2 = \frac{84[|(30 \times 10) - (40 \times 4)| - 4|2]^2}{(30 + 40)(4 + 10)(30 + 4)(40 + 10)} = \frac{84[|300 - 160| - 42]^2}{(70)(14)(34)(50)}$$

$$= \frac{84(98)^2}{1,666,000} = \frac{84(9604)}{1,666,000} = \frac{806,736}{1,666,000}$$

$$\chi^2 = \frac{806,736}{1,666,000} = .48$$

The computed χ^2 is far below the χ^2 critical value (3.84) necessary for the rejection of the null hypothesis at the .05 level. The research concludes that the null hypothesis is accepted: There is no significant relationship between the use of X-40 pills at this dosage and headache relief. Any apparent effectiveness was probably the result of sampling error.

The Median Test

This nonparametric test determines the significance of the difference between the medians of two independent groups. It answers the question, "Do medians of these randomly selected samples behave like medians from the same population?" Unlike the *t* test, which determines the significance of the difference between two means, the median test compares medians.

The median test is really an application of the χ^2 test, using a 2×2 table at 1 degree of freedom. The procedure consists of these steps:

1. Compute the median of the combined sample distributions.

2. Count the number of terms at or above the median and below the median for each group.

3. Compute the χ^2 value in a 2×2 table.

A researcher wished to compare the effect of medication upon the number of correct responses on a manipulation test. The experimental group received the medication while the control group received a placebo.

Since one of the cell frequencies was less than 10, Yates' correction is the appropriate formula:

TABLE 8-2 Manipulation Test Scores for Forty Subjects

X (Medication)		f	C (Placebo)		f	
56	24	14	58	16	6	
55	24	↑	56	15	↑	
43	23			52	15		
41	21		40	14		
31	19	Md	38	13	Md	
31	17		28	12		Combined group median $= 20$
27	16		19	10		
26	13		18	10		
26	12	↓	18	9	↓	
25	9	6	17	8	14	

	At or above Md	Below Md
Experimental	14 A	6 B
Control	6 C	14 D

A, B, C, and *D* are all designations of cells.

$$\chi^2 = \frac{N\left[|AD - BC| - \dfrac{N}{2}\right]^2}{(A+B)(C+D)(A+C)(B+D)}$$

$$\chi^2 = \frac{40[|(14 \times 14) - (6 \times 6)| - 20]^2}{(20)(20)(20)(20)}$$

$$\chi^2 = \frac{40[|196 - 36| - 20]^2}{(20)(20)(20)(20)}$$

$$\chi^2 = \frac{40[(160) - 20]^2}{160,000}$$

$$\chi^2 = \frac{40(19,600)}{160,000} = \frac{784,000}{160,000}$$

$$\chi^2 = 4.90$$

Since the χ^2 value of 4.90 exceeds the χ^2 critical value of 3.84 for 1 degree of freedom at the .05 level, the null hypothesis is rejected. There seems to be a significant difference between the scores of the experimental and control groups.

The Mann-Whitney Test

The Mann-Whitney U test is designed to test the significance of the difference between two populations, using random samples drawn from the same population. It is a nonparametric equivalent of the parametric t test. It is more powerful than the median test and lends itself to one- or two-tailed tests of the null hypothesis. It may be considered a useful alternative to the t test when the parametric assumptions cannot be met and when the observations are expressed in at least ordinal scale values.

The basic computation is U_1, and in experiments using small samples the significance of an observed U may be determined by the U critical values of the Mann-Whitney tables.

When the size of either of the groups is more than 20, the sampling distribution of U rapidly approaches the normal distribution, and the null hypothesis may be tested with reference to the z critical values of the normal probability table.

The values of the combined samples, N_1 and N_2, are ranked from the lowest to the highest rank, irrespective of groups, rank 1 to the lowest score, rank 2 to the next lowest, etc. Then the ranks of each sample group are summed individually and represented as ΣR_1 and ΣR_2.

There are two U's calculated by the formulas:

a. $U_1 = N_1 N_2 + \dfrac{N_1(N_1 + 1)}{2} - \Sigma R_1$

b. $U_2 = N_1 N_2 + \dfrac{N_2(N_2 + 1)}{2} - \Sigma R_2$

$N_1 =$ number in one group $\Sigma R_1 =$ sum of ranks in one group
$N_2 =$ number in second group $\Sigma R_2 =$ sum of ranks in second group

Only one U need be calculated, for the other can be easily computed by the formula.

$$U_1 = N_1 N_2 - U_2$$

It is the smaller value of U that is used when consulting the Mann-Whitney U table.

The z value of U can be determined by the formula:

$$z = \frac{U - \dfrac{N_1 N_2}{2}}{\sqrt{\dfrac{(N_1)(N_2)(N_1 + N_2 + 1)}{12}}}$$

It does not matter which U (the larger or the smaller) is used in the computation of z. The sign of the z will depend on which is used, but the numerical value will be identical.

A teacher wishes to evaluate the effect of two methods of teaching

TABLE 8-3 Performance Scores of Students Taught by Method A or by Method B

A	Rank	B	Rank
50	3	49	2
60	8	90	36
89	35	88	33.5
94	38	76	21
82	28	92	37
75	20	81	27
63	10	55	7
52	5	64	11
97	40	84	30
95	39	51	4
83	29	47	1
80	25.5	70	15
77	22	66	12
80	25.5	69	14
88	33.5	87	32
78	23	74	19
85	31	71	16
79	24	61	9
72	17	55	6
68	13	73	18
$N_1 = 20$	$\Sigma\, R_1 = 469.5$	$N_2 = 20$	$\Sigma\, R_2 = 350.5$

$$U_1 = N_1 N_2 + \frac{N_1(N_1 + 1)}{2} - \Sigma\, R_1$$

reading to two groups of 20 randomly assigned students, drawn from the same population.

The null hypothesis proposed is that there is no significant difference between the performance of the students taught by method A and the students taught by method B.

After a period of four months' exposure to the two teaching methods, the scores of the students on a standardized achievement test were recorded. All scores were ranked from lowest to highest and the Mann-Whitney test was used to test the null hypothesis at the .05 level of significance.

$$U_1 = (20)(20) + \frac{20(21)}{2} - 469.50$$

$$= 400 + 210 - 469.50$$

$$= 140.50$$

$$U_2 = N_1 N_2 + \frac{N_2(N_2 + 1)}{2} - \Sigma R_2$$

$$= (20)(20) + \frac{20(21)}{2} - 350.50$$

$$= 400 + 210 - 350.50$$

$$= 259.50$$

Check:

$$U_1 = N_1 N_2 - U_2$$

$$140.50 = 400 - 259.50$$

$$140.50 = 140.50$$

$$z = \frac{U_1 - \dfrac{N_1 N_2}{2}}{\sqrt{\dfrac{N_1 N_2 (N_1 + N_2 + 1)}{12}}}$$

$$z = \frac{140.50 - \dfrac{400}{2}}{\sqrt{\dfrac{(20)(20)(41)}{12}}} = -\frac{59.5}{\sqrt{1366.67}} = -\frac{59.50}{36.97}$$

$$z = -1.61$$

Since the observed z value of -1.61 did not equal or exceed the z critical value of 1.96 for a two-tailed test at the .05 level, the null hypothesis was not rejected. The difference was not significant and the apparent superior performance of the A method group could well have resulted from sampling error.

The Sign Test

The sign test may be used to evaluate the effect of an experimental treatment when certain limiting circumstances prevail:

1. The evaluation of the effect of the experimental variable or treatment cannot be measured, but can only be judged to result in superior or inferior performance.

2. The members of the experimental and control groups consist of more than 10 matched pairs, matched on the basis of IQ, aptitude, members of sets if identical twins, or on some other basis for matching. The subjects may be matched with themselves in a preobservation, postobservation design, serving in one instance as a control group, and in another instance as an experimental group.

Let us assume that 26 pairs of matched individuals were randomly assigned to experimental and control groups. At the end of the experimental cycle each experimental subject was judged by an expert to be superior (+) or inferior (−) in performance to his or her matched subject in the control group.
The results were:

$N = 26$
18 experimental subjects judged superior $+18$
7 experimental subjects judged inferior -7
1 pair indicated no difference   0
Thus $N = 25$

In cases where no difference is discovered, that pair is deleted from further consideration.

The null hypothesis to be tested: The performance of the experimental group did not exceed the performance of the control group at the .05 level of significance. Hypothesis: The number of pluses should equal the number of minuses. Under the null hypothesis using a one-tailed test to evaluate the superiority of performance of the experimental group, the following formula for a test of significance is applied, using the z critical values of the normal probability table:

$$z = \frac{(0 \pm .50) - \dfrac{N}{2}}{\sqrt{\dfrac{N}{4}}}$$

where O = number of signs of researcher's interest. When $O < N/2$, use $(0 + .50)$ in the formula; when $O > N/2$, use $(0 - .50)$ in the formula.

$$*O = 18 \qquad N = 25 \quad \text{(one no-difference observation)}$$

Since $18 > N/2$, use $(O - .50)$ in the formula

$$z = \frac{(O - .50) - \dfrac{N}{2}}{\sqrt{\dfrac{N}{4}}} = \frac{17.50 - 12.50}{\sqrt{\dfrac{25}{4}}} = \frac{5}{2.50} = 2.00$$

Since the z critical ratio for a one-tailed test at the .05 level is 1.64, the null hypothesis is rejected and the superiority of performance of the experiment 1 group is probably established.

The reader is reminded that the sign test is appropriate for determining the difference between dependent, not independent samples. The nonparametric sign test is somewhat insensitive, for it considers only the direction of superiority or inferiority, and does not reflect the magnitude or amount of the difference.

The Wilcoxon Matched-Pairs Signed Ranks Test for $N > 10$ Pairs

The Wilcoxon test is somewhat similar to the sign test, but is more powerful because it tests not only direction but also magnitude of difference between matched groups. If most of the differences favor one group, that group is probably superior. The null hypothesis would assume that the direction and magnitude of difference would be about the same.

The Wilcoxon test, like the sign test, deals with matched samples made up of matched pairs of individuals and is not applicable to independent samples.

The procedure involves a number of rather simple steps.

1. Let d indicate the difference between the pairs under the experimental and control treatment. There would be one d for each pair of scores.

2. Rank the d's without respect to sign, giving rank 1 to the smallest difference, 2 to the next smallest, etc. The number of ranks will equal the number of pairs.

3. Then to each rank affix the sign of the difference.

---

* Superiority (+) signs were the researcher's interest. If, in an experiment, loss of weight (−), for example, were of interest, the researcher would have counted the minus (−) signs.

4. Total the ranks for the + differences and total the ranks for the −
differences. If the sum of the + ranks equaled the sum of the −
ranks, we would conclude that there was no difference between the
effect of the experimental control treatment or variable.

When the scores of a pair are equal, that pair is deleted from the
computation. When two or more differences between ranks are the same,
the ranks are averaged. For example,

	Two equal differences	*Three equal differences*
Differences	20, 21, 21, 26, 27	18, 21, 21, 21, 28
Ranks	1, 2.5, 2.5, 4, 5	1, 3, 3, 3, 5
	$\dfrac{2+3}{2} = 2.5$	$\dfrac{2+3+4}{3} = 3$

The sum of the ranks of the smaller of the like-signed ranks is
designated as T. A z formula is then applied and interpreted by the
critical z values of the normal probability table.

$$z = \frac{T - \dfrac{N(N+1)}{4}}{\sqrt{\dfrac{N(N+1)(2N+1)}{24}}}$$

where $N =$ number of pairs ranked
$T =$ sum of the ranks of the smaller of the like-signed ranks

An example illustrates the computation and application of the Wilcoxon test.

Thirteen pairs of identical twins were separated, with one twin
placed in a heterogeneously grouped class *(H)* and the other in an ability
grouped class *(A)*. After a year they were tested for creativity, and their
performance compared. The null hypothesis that there was no difference
between the performance of the two samples was tested at the .05 level
of significance.

$$z = \frac{9 - \dfrac{(12)(13)}{4}}{\sqrt{\dfrac{12(13)(25)}{24}}} = \frac{9-39}{\sqrt{162.50}} = -\frac{30}{12.75}$$

$$z = -2.35$$

TABLE 8-4   Creativity Scores of Identical Twins Assigned to Heterogeneously Grouped Class *(H)* and to Ability Grouped Class *(A)*

Pair	H	A	d	Rank of d
a	70	80	+10	11
b	62	69	+7	8
c	85	90	+5	6
d	70	68	−2	②
e	54	58	+4	4.5
f	49	58	+9	10
g	80	74	−6	⑦
h		(tie, deleted)		
i	79	80	+1	1
j	90	93	+3	3
k	64	75	+11	12
l	75	79	+4	4.5
m	81	89	+8	9
				$T = 9$

$N = 13 - 1 = 12$ (one no-difference pair)
T = sum of ranks of smaller like sign (−) (d and g)

Since the obtained z value of -2.35 exceeds the z critical value of -1.96 for a two-tailed test at the .05 level, the null hypothesis is rejected. There is probably a difference too great to attribute to sampling error.

SUMMARY

Statistics is an indispensable tool for researchers that enables them to make inferences or generalizations about populations from their observations of the characteristics of samples. Although samples do not duplicate the characteristics of populations, and although samples from the same population will differ from one another, the nature of their variation is reasonably predictable. The central limit theorem describes the nature of sample means and enables the researcher to make estimates about population means (parameters) with known probabilities of error.

The pioneering contributions of Sir Ronald Fisher and Karl Pearson to statistics and scientific method, and William Seely Gosset to small-sampling theory, have made practicable the analysis of many of the types of problems encountered in psychology and education as well as in agricultural and biological research, where they were first applied.

Parametric statistical treatment of data is based upon certain assumptions about the nature of distributions and the types of measures used. Nonparametric statistical treatment makes possible useful inferences without assumptions about the nature of data distributions. Each type makes a significant contribution to the analysis of data relationships.

Statistical decisions are not made with certainty, but are based upon probability estimates. The central limit theorem, sampling error, variance, the null hypothesis, levels of significance, and two-tailed and one-tailed tests have been explained and illustrated. Although this treatment has been brief and necessarily incomplete, the presentation of concepts may help the consumer of research to understand many simple research reports. Students who aspire to significant research activity, or who wish to interpret complex research studies with understanding, will need additional background in statistics and experimental design. They will find it helpful to participate in research seminars and to acquire competence through apprenticeship with scholars who are making contributions to knowledge through their own research activities.

EXERCISES

1. Why is it stronger logic to be able to reject a negative hypothesis than to try to confirm a positive one?
2. A statistical test of significance would have no useful purpose in a purely descriptive study in which sampling was not involved. Do you agree? Why?
3. When a statistical test determines that a finding is significant at the .05 level, it indicates that there is a 5/100 probability that the relationship was merely the result of sampling error. Do you agree? Why?
4. Any hypothesis that can be rejected at the .05 level of significance can surely be rejected at the .01 level. Do you agree? Why?
5. The standard deviation of a sample is likely to be smaller in magnitude than the standard deviation of the population from which it is drawn. Do you agree? Why?
6. The *t* critical value necessary for the rejection of a null hypothesis (at a given level of significance and for a given number of degrees of freedom) is higher for a one-tailed test than it is for a two-tailed test. Do you agree? Why?
7. A manufacturer guaranteed that a particular type of steel cable had a mean tensile strength of 2000 pounds with a standard deviation of 200 pounds. In a shipment, 16 lengths of the cable were submitted to a test for breaking strength. The mean breaking strength was 1900 pounds. Using a one-tailed test at the .05 level of significance, determine whether the shipment met the manufacturer's specifications.
8. Two samples of mathematics students took a standardized engineering aptitude test. Using a two-tailed test at the .05 level of signifi-

cance, determine whether the two groups were random samples from the same population.

Group A	Group B
$N = 25$	$N = 30$
$M = 80$	$M = 88$
$S = 8$	$S = 9$

9. An achievement test in spelling was administered to two randomly selected fifth grade groups of students from two schools. Test the null hypothesis that there was no significant difference in achievement between the two fifth grade populations from which the samples were selected at the .05 level of significance. Use the method of separate variances.

School A	School B
$N = 40$	$N = 45$
$M = 82$	$M = 86$
$S = 12.60$	$S = 14.15$

10. One group of rats was given a vitamin supplement while the other group received a conventional diet. The rats were randomly assigned. Test the hypothesis that the vitamin supplement did not result in increased weight gain for the experimental group. Use a one-tailed test at the .05 level.

X	C
$N = 12$	$N = 16$
$S = 15.50$ g	$S = 12.20$ g
$M = 140$ g	$M = 120$ g

11. A consumer research agency tested two popular makes of automobiles with similar weight and horsepower. Eleven car A's provided a mean miles per gallon of 24.20 with an S of 1.40, while 11 car B's provided a mean miles per gallon of 26.30 with an S of 1.74. Using a two-tailed test at the .05 level, test the null hypothesis that there was no significant difference between the mean gasoline mileage of the two makes of cars.

12. Calculate the number of degrees of freedom when:
   a. Estimating a population standard deviation from a sample standard deviation _____
   b. Computing the statistical significance of a coefficient of correlation _____
   c. Determining the significance of the difference between two means _____

    d. A 2×2 χ^2 table computation is involved   _____

    e. A 3×5 χ^2 table computation is involved   _____

13. In a survey to determine the preference of high school students for a soft drink, the results were:

	Brand A	Brand B	Brand C
Boys	25	30	52
Girls	46	22	28

Was there any relationship between the brand preference and the gender of the consumers? Use a two-tailed test at the .05 level of significance.

14. The number of correct responses on a coordination test was recorded for an experimental group that received a tranquilizer and a control group that received a placebo. Using a median test, test the null hypothesis that the medication had no effect at the .05 level of significance.

X	C
29	30
28	29
28	28
27	26
26	24
26	23
24	17
23	16
23	15
21	14
18	13
16	11
14	8
12	6
10	5

15. Twenty-six members of a local unit of the Weight Watchers Club were weighed two months after the conclusion of the enrollment period. Test the hypothesis that the program was not effective in enabling the former members to sustain their weight loss achieved in the program. Use a sign test at the .01 level of significance.

Initial weight	Two months after
159	148
175	170
170	160

Initial weight	Two months after
200	189
160	163
140	144
125	120
204	200
228	214
270	250
165	164
149	153
122	120
130	144
150	148

Initial weight	Two months after
148	145
129	120
180	169
175	170
168	165
194	190
212	206
235	220
160	165
200	180
245	250

16. A group of 50 college freshmen was randomly assigned to experimental and control groups to determine the effectiveness of a counseling program upon academic averages. Use the Mann-Whitney test to test the null hypothesis that there was no difference between the academic performance of the experimental and control groups at the .05 level of significance.

Experimental	Control
2.10	2.01
3.00	2.69
1.96	3.07
2.04	2.14
3.27	2.82
3.60	2.57
3.80	3.44
2.75	4.00
1.98	3.01
2.00	2.55
2.98	2.77
3.10	3.09
3.69	2.72

Experimental	Control
2.66	3.34
2.56	2.81
2.50	3.05
3.77	2.67
2.40	1.90
3.20	1.70
1.71	1.57
3.04	1.39
2.06	2.09
2.86	3.68
3.02	2.11
1.88	2.83

17. Two groups of junior high school health class students were matched on the basis of intelligence quotients. One group was taught a unit on artificial resuscitation by a traditional lecture discussion method; the other by a prediscussion and film strip presentation. At the conclusion of the unit the groups were tested. Test the null hypothesis that there was no difference in understanding between the groups at the .05 level of significance. Use the Wilcoxon matched-pairs signed ranks test.

	Lecture	Filmstrip
1.	60	70
2.	88	98
3.	78	79
4.	82	80
5.	60	75
6.	54	70
7.	80	87
8.	54	68
9.	50	78
10.	80	89
11.	60	84
12.	90	96
13.	70	88
14.	86	74
15.	60	78
16.	75	65
17.	88	92
18.	60	80
19.	92	70
20.	96	88

18. Compute the t value of the coefficient of correlation:

$$r = +.30$$
$$N = 18$$

Using Student's distribution, is this coefficient statistically significant at the .05 level for a one-tailed test?

BIBLIOGRAPHY

BRADLEY, JAMES V. *Distribution-Free Statistical Tests.* Englewood Cliffs, N.J.: Prentice-Hall, 1968.

CARVER, R. P. "Case Against Statistical Significance Testing." *Harvard Educational Review* 48 (Aug. 1978): 379–389.

DOWNIE, N. M. and R. W. HEATH. *Basic Statistical Methods.* New York: Harper & Row, 1974.

DUBOIS, PHILIP H. *An Introduction to Psychological Statistics.* New York: Harper & Row, 1965.

EDWARDS, ALLEN. *Statistical Methods.* New York: Holt, Rinehart & Winston, 1973.

FERGUSON, G. A. *Statistical Analysis in Psychology and Education.* New York: McGraw Hill Book Co., 1976.

GARRETT, HENRY E. *Statistical Methods in Psychology and Education.* New York: David McKay Co., 1966.

GLASS, GENE V and JULIAN C. STANLEY. *Statistical Methods in Education and Psychology.* Englewood Cliffs, N.J.: Prentice-Hall, 1970.

GUILFORD, J. P. and B. FRUCHTER. *Fundamental Statistics in Psychology and Education.* New York: McGraw Hill Book Co., 1978.

HOPKINS, KENNETH D. and GENE V GLASS. *Basic Statistics for the Behavioral Sciences.* Englewood Cliffs, N.J.: Prentice-Hall, 1978.

HOROWITZ, LEONARD M. *Elements of Statistics for Psychology and Education.* New York: McGraw Hill Book Co., 1974.

McCALL, ROBERT B. *Fundamental Statistics for Psychology.* New York: Harcourt Brace Jovanovich, 1975.

KISH, LESLIE. "Selection of the Sample." Chapter 5 in Leon Festinger and Daniel Kartz, eds., *Research Methods in the Behavioral Sciences.* New York: Holt, Rinehart & Winston, 1953.

MARASCUILO, LEONARD A. and MARYELLEN McSWEENEY. *Non-Parametric and Distribution-Free Methods for the Social Sciences.* Monterey, CA.: Brooks/Cole Publishing Co., 1977.

NUNNALY, JUM C. *Introduction to Statistics for Psychology and Education.* New York: McGraw Hill Book Co., 1975.

POPHAM, W. JAMES. *Educational Statistics: Use and Interpretation.* New York: Harper & Row, 1973.

ROBBINS, HERBERT and JOHN VAN RYZIN. *Introduction to Statistics.* Chicago: Science Research Associates, 1975.

SCHMIDT, MARTY J. *Understanding and Using Statistics: Basic Concepts.* Lexington, MA.: D. C. Heath & Co., 1975.

SIEGEL, SIDNEY. *Nonparametric Statistics for the Behavioral Sciences.* New York: McGraw Hill Book Co., 1956.

SILVERMAN, ELIOT N. and LINDA A. BRODY. *Statistics: A Common Sense Approach.* Boston: Prindle, Webber and Schmidt, 1973.

WEINBERG, GEORGE H. and JOHN A. SCHUMAKER. *Statistics: An Intuitive Approach.* Monterey, CA.: Brooks/Cole Publishing Co., 1973.

WINER, B. J. *Statistical Principles in Experimental Design.* 2nd ed. New York: McGraw Hill Book Co., 1971.

YAMANE, TARO. *Elementary Sampling Theory.* Englewood Cliffs, N.J.: Prentice-Hall, 1967.

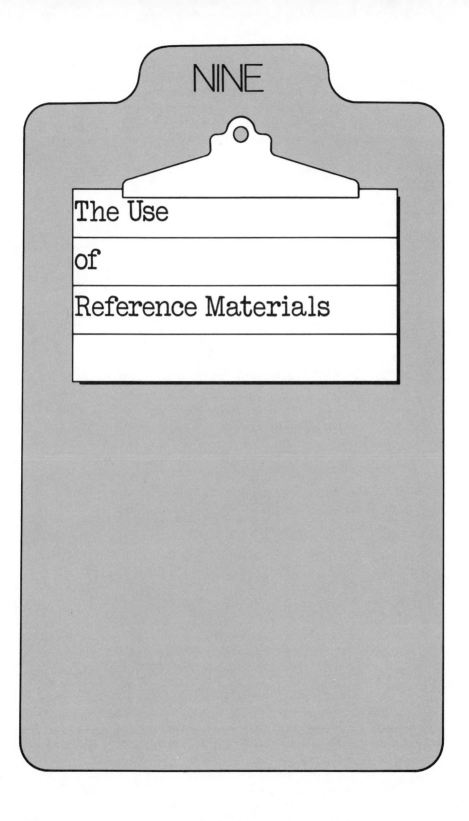

NINE

The Use

of

Reference Materials

Practically all human knowledge can be found in books and libraries. Unlike other animals that must start anew with each generation, human beings build upon the accumulated and recorded knowledge of the past. Their constant adding to the vast store of knowledge makes possible progress in all areas of human endeavor.

Undergraduate students sometimes receive special instruction in the use of the library and its facilities, but too often their library activities are confined to assigned and suggested readings. Graduate students must find their own references. Few graduate students, however, and not all faculty members, have adequate knowledge of the library and its many resources for the effective search for specialized knowledge.

Extensive use of the library and thorough investigation of related literature are essential in preparing graduate term papers and seminar reports, and in planning and carrying out the kind of searching involved in special field problems, theses, and dissertations.

The search for reference material is a time-consuming but fruitful phase of the graduate program. A familiarity with the literature in any problem area helps the student to discover what is already known, what others have attempted to find out, what methods of attack have been promising or disappointing, and what problems remain to be solved. Knowing how to use the library effectively should receive primary emphasis in the graduate program in education. To know what sources to use, what sources are available, and where and how to find them will save many hours of aimless activity.

USING THE LIBRARY

The graduate student should become thoroughly acquainted with the university library, the location of its varied facilities, and the regulations governing the use and circulation of materials. Many university libraries have a printed guide that contains helpful information. A diagram may indicate the location of the stacks, the periodicals room, the reference division, reading rooms, and special collections of books, microfilm or microcard equipment, clippings, manuscripts, or pamphlets. Another useful part of the guide may list the periodicals to which the library subscribes and the names of special indexes, abstracts, and other references available. A third section may deal with the regulations concerning the use of the stacks, the use of reserve books, and the procedures for securing materials held by the library or those that may be procured from another library.

It is beneficial to use the skill and knowledge of librarians, who are anxious to help the student find reference materials. The graduate student should not depend too much on the librarian, however, but should learn to find his or her own references.

Ordinarily, undergraduates fill out call slips for presentation at the circulation desk when they wish to use a book. Faculty members and graduate students are usually issued a card giving them access to the stacks, and thus may carry on the independent searching and browsing not possible when each book must be requested by name.

Most libraries prefer that students not replace books on the shelves after they have been used, for a misplaced book creates confusion both for librarians and for other students seeking it. If students leave the books with which they are finished on the tables, the librarians will return them to their proper position on the shelves.

Sometimes a student learns of a reference that is not available in the local library. Many libraries subscribe to a "union" catalog, which lists references found in other libraries. Most libraries have a union list of serials to indicate the libraries where particular serial publications may be obtained. There are a number of ways in which these materials may be obtained by a library.

1. *By interlibrary loan.* The library may request that the work be sent and then checked out to the user. Note that the library must request this material. It is never sent directly to the user.

2. *By requesting a photostatic copy* of a page or of a number of pages of a desired reference.

3. *By requesting a photostatic print* of selected pages of a microfilm or microfiche.

4. *By an abstracting or translating service.* Some large libraries provide copied or translated portions of needed materials at an established fee.

In connection with any of the above services, the user is expected to bear the costs involved in reproducing, handling, and shipping the materials.

Microfiche

The development of the microfiche has been one of the most significant contributions to library services by providing economy and convenience of storing and distribution of scholarly materials.

A microfiche is a sheet of film that contains micro-images of printed materials. Filmed at a reduction of 1 to 24 or higher, it is possible to reproduce nearly one hundred 8½″ × 11″ pages of copy on one 4″ × 6″ film card. Microfiche readers that magnify the micro-images to original or larger copy size are available at libraries. Some microfiche readers provide up to 40× magnification on screens as large as 15″ × 21″.

There are many document reproduction services that supply microfiche to libraries upon subscription or upon special order.

The Educational Resources Information Center (ERIC) has prepared for the National Institute of Education a directory of nearly 600 libraries that possess extensive collections or receive regular periodic shipments of ERIC microfiche collections. These libraries receive approximately 17,000 microfiche per year. Other document reproduction sources that provide microfiche to libraries or individuals are described later in this chapter.

Super- and Ultra-Microfiche

Recent developments in the field of micro-printing will transform the process of storage, retrieval, and distribution of published materials in libraries of the future. A super-microfiche has been developed that contains up to 1000 pages of printed material on a single 4″ × 6″ transparent card, the equivalent of two or more books. An even more spectacular development is the ultra-microfiche that contains up to 3200 micro-dots on a single card. When projected, each dot contains the equivalent of several pages. Thus, seven to ten volumes could be contained on a single 4″ × 6″ transparent card. Reader printers make hard copy printouts (8½ × 11 inch reproductions) of any page in a few seconds.

THE CARD CATALOG

The card catalog, an alphabetical listing, may be compared to the index of a book. It is the index to the entire library, listing the contents of all publications found in the library, with the exception of serially published periodicals. These compact 3″ × 5″ card forms provide a quick and convenient way to find all of the books, monographs, or pamphlets on the library shelves.

The cabinet drawers of the card catalog are alphabetically labeled, and also numbered sequentially, to facilitate replacing them in the proper place when they have been removed. Printed cards are prepared by the H. W. Wilson Company or by the Library of Congress. College and university libraries usually use these prepared cards. Smaller libraries often prepare their own.

Printed cards contain a great deal of useful information. The card illustrated in Figure 9-1 is a typical Library of Congress card. The "call number" in the upper left corner is written in by the librarian. For the sake of convenience in finding books, the card catalog has two and often three listings for each book. A few libraries have a fourth card for some books.

1. author card

2. subject card

3. title card

4. analytical card

The author card is filed, last name first (Conant, James B.). One can find any or all publications credited to the author. In the case of

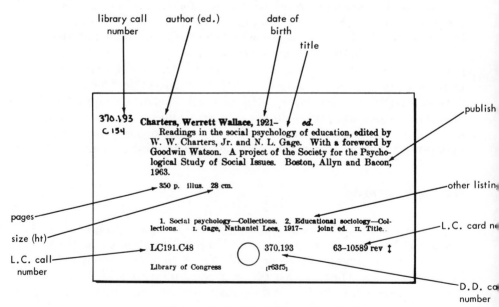

Fig. 9-1. Library of Congress Author Card

joint authorship a card is filed separately for each author. Societies, associations, editors of yearbooks, committees, and government departments are listed as authors when no author is credited with the publication.

The subject card is filed under the appropriate heading. Since headings run from general to specific, *counseling*, a subtopic, would follow *guidance*. When a book is about an author, his or her name is considered a subject. Books about John Dewey are listed under the subject, *Dewey, John.*

The title card is filed under the actual name of the book. Initial articles, *a, an,* or *the,* are disregarded. Thus, *The Elements of Research* is filed under *Elements of Research.*

The analytical card, used by some large libraries, provides a reference to important sections of a book that deal with an important subject or person. For example, De Kruif's *Microbe Hunters* has a section on Ehrlich which can be called to the attention of the reader by the special analytical card. This title, filed separately, indicates that the volume has a section on the person or topic cited.

Ordinarily, the card catalog covers only the books in that specific library. In very large university libraries there may be found the union catalog, which contains duplicates of the card catalog of the Library of Congress, or duplicates of cards found in other important libraries in the United States. Instead of a union catalog, some libraries have a photoprinted, bound-book copy of the Library of Congress catalog, eighteen cards to a page.

LIBRARY CLASSIFICATION

Library systems of book classification are complex but ingenious ways of systematizing the placement and location of books. There is a tremendous amount of detail involved in these systems, but they have been devised in a logical and neat way. Library classification is based upon a methodology that is logical and orderly to the smallest detail. Although it is beyond the scope of this chapter to explain all of the details of book classification, a few principles and procedures are presented that should prove helpful to the library user.

The Dewey Decimal System

The Dewey Decimal system of book classification, designed by Melvil Dewey in 1876, was first used in the Amherst College library where he was acting librarian. The system, or some modification of it, is used

000		General references, periodicals, cyclopedias, biography
100		Philosophy, psychology
200		Religion
300		Social Sciences
	310	Statistics
	320	Political Science
	330	Economics
	340	Law
	350	Administration
	360	Welfare Assns. and Institutions
	370	Education (General)
	370.1	Theory and Philosophy of Education
	370.9	History of Education
	371	Teachers—Methods
	372	Elementary Education
	373	Secondary Education
	374	Adult Education
	375	Curriculum
	376	Education of Women
	377	Religious, Ethical Education
	378	Higher Education
	379	Public Schools (Relation of State to Education)
	379.14	School Law
	379.15	Supervision and Control
	380	Commerce, Communications
	390	Customs
400		Linguistics
500		Pure Science
600		Applied Science
700		Arts and Recreation
800		Literature
900		History

in many college and university libraries and in most public libraries and specialized libraries in the United States and in other parts of the world. The above list indicates the major subject categories.

Library of Congress System

Some of the more extensive libraries, particularly in large universities, use the Library of Congress system of book classification. This system, devised by Dr. Herbert Putnam and authorized by an act of Congress in 1880, is especially useful in large libraries consisting of individual collections housed separately. It provides for twenty main classes instead of the ten of the Dewey Decimal system. Letters of the

A		General Works
B		Philosophy, Religion
C		History
D		World History
EF		American History
G		Geography, Anthropology
H		Social Sciences
I		vacant
J		Political Science
K		Law
L		Education
	LA	History of Education
	LB	Theory of Education
	LC	Special forms and applications
	LD	U. S. Schools
	LE	American Education (Outside U. S.)
	LF	European Education
	LG	Asia, Africa, Oceania
	LH	School Periodicals
	LI	vacant
	LJ	Fraternities, Societies
	LT	Textbooks
M		Music
N		Fine Arts
O		vacant
P		Language, Literature
Q		Science
R		Medicine
S		Agriculture
T		Technology
U		Military Science
V		Naval Science
W		vacant
X		vacant
Y		vacant
Z		Library Science—Bibliography

alphabet are used for the principal headings, but numerals are used for further subgrouping in a fashion somewhat similar to the Dewey Decimal system.

The main classifications in the Library of Congress system have been listed.

Book Placement

All books have a call number or letter that appears in the upper lefthand corner of the author, subject, or title card, and on the spine of the book itself. Books are placed on the library shelves serially by call numbers or letters. Within each classification the books are arranged alphabetically by author's last name. An exception to this rule is that biographies are placed under the subject, rather than the author, of the book.

Most libraries use an additional classification device known as the Cutter-Sanborn system. This system adds author numbers to the basic classification to represent the first letter of the author's name, and additional numbers to distinguish between authors whose names begin with the same initial.

Other systems such as the Bliss, Quinn Brown, Universal Decimal, and Colon systems are described in the specialized literature of book classification in library science.

REFERENCE MATERIALS

There are hundreds of references that may be useful to the graduate student in education. A rather comprehensive list, with a brief description of each source, is presented.

Since the names given to many publications have little common meaning, it is difficult to classify them by title. The contents and information treatment have been used as a basis for classification. Since editorship changes frequently, most editor names have not been included.

References about References

There are a number of publications that identify specific references that cover particular areas of knowledge.

American Reference Books Annual. **Bodhan S. Wynar, ed. Littleton, CO.: Libraries Unlimited, 1970–date.**

Most reference books published or distributed in the United States are reviewed. Reviews, written by more than 200 library specialists, vary in length from 75 to 300 words, and are not cumulated from year to year. This is probably the most complete and up-to-date reference on references available.

A Guide to Reference Books. **Eugene P. Sheehy, compiler. Chicago: American Library Association, 1976.**

This comprehensive work lists, without evaluation, by subject area, by type, and by author or editor, the most important reference books printed in a number of languages. A section is devoted to education. Supplements appear every two or three years.

Wynar, Christine L. *Guide to Reference Books for School Media Centers.* **Littleton, CO.: Libraries Unlimited, 1976. 475 pp.**

This guide includes 2575 entries with evaluative comments on reference books and selection tools for use in elementary schools, junior and senior high schools, and community and junior colleges. It is indexed by author, subject, and title.

Bell, Marion V. and Eleanor Swidan. *Reference Books.* **Baltimore, MD.: Enoch Pratt Library, 1947–date.**

This brief annotated guide describes nearly a thousand reference books.

Reference Books Review Index. **Ann Arbor, MI.: Pierian Press, 1978.**

This annotated listing of references issues supplements quarterly.

Booklist. **Chicago: American Library Association, 1905–date.**

Published biweekly and cumulated every two years, this reference presents an unbiased critical analysis by expert librarians of atlases, encyclopedias, biographical works, dictionaries, and other reference materials in terms of their usefulness and reliability for libraries or homes. Every two years some of the more important reviews are published in a separate publication, titled

Reference and Subscription Books Reviews. **Chicago: American Library Association, 1956–date.**

Published every two years, critical reviews by expert librarians are cumulated from *Booklist.*

Cumulative Book Index. **New York: H. W. Wilson Co., 1898–date.**

This monthly publication, cumulated semiannually and in one- and two-year cumulations, indexes all books published in the English language by author, title, and subject. It is helpful in assuring the student that all pertinent books have been covered in his or her searches.

Books in Print
Subject Guide to Books in Print. **R. R. Bowker Co., 1948–date.**
Vol. I Authors
Vol. II Titles and Publishers

These two-volume comprehensive listings of in-print titles list names of publishers and other publication information.

Union List of Serials in Libraries of the United States and Canada. New York: H. W. Wilson Co., 1965. 5 vols.

This listing of periodicals, foreign and domestic, held by more than 225 libraries does not include government periodicals and other highly specialized materials. *Union List of Serials* is kept up to date by:

New Serial Titles. Washington, D.C.: Library of Congress, 1961–date.

Issued monthly and indexed in the December issue, it lists periodicals, loose-leaf publications, government series, motion pictures, and filmstrips, both domestic and foreign. Also listed are holdings of the Library of Congress and hundreds of participating libraries.

The Standard Periodicals Directory. New York: Oxbridge Publishing Co., 1964–date.

Published every other year, this directory of over 30,000 entries covers every type of periodical, with the exception of local newspapers. Periodicals are defined as publications appearing at least once every two years. Two hundred classifications are arranged by subject. An alphabetical index is provided.

Ulrich's International Periodicals Directory. New York: R. R. Bowker Co., 1966–date. 2 vols.

This classified list of more than 57,000 foreign and domestic periodicals is arranged by subject and title. Publication information is provided.

Irregular Serials and Annuals. An International Directory: Excepting Periodicals Issued More Frequently than Once a Year. R. R. Bowker Co., 1972.

Published biennially, this directory includes more than 20,000 publications.

Sources of Information in the Social Sciences. Chicago: American Library Association, 1973.

Organized by subject area and indexed by author and title, this work contains a comprehensive listing and brief description of reference books, monographs, and scholarly journals.

Leidy, W. Philip. *A Popular Guide to Government Publications.* New York: Columbia University Press, 1976.

This guide lists 119 alphabetically arranged subject headings. Only titles in print at time of publication are included.

Schorr, Alan E. *Government Reference Books: A Biennial Guide to United States Government Publications.* **Littleton, CO.: Libraries Unlimited, 1968/69–date.**

This guide describes more than 1300 publications.

William L. Camp. *Guide to Periodicals in Education.* **Metuchen, N.J.: Scarecrow Press, 1975.**

This reference, which indexes 449 periodicals, is particularly helpful to those who are planning to submit manuscripts for publication. Information is provided about editorial policies, type of readers, and how to submit manuscripts.

Periodicals

Up-to-date treatment of educational problems, contemporary opinions, and the latest reviews and reports of educational research will be found in periodicals or serials. A periodical or serial is defined as a publication issued in successive parts, usually at regular intervals, and, as a rule, intended to be continued indefinitely. Included in this definition are almanacs, yearbooks, directories, handbooks, government documents, publications of societies and associations, newspapers, and magazines.

Periodicals change frequently. In the two-year period from 1977 to 1979, *Standard Periodicals Directory* reported that 21,000 new titles had been added and 9,000 periodicals had ceased publication.

Without comprehensive guides, the search of tens of thousands of periodicals would be a nearly impossible task. Fortunately, a number of indexes and abstracts are available to help scholars in their search for relevant information.

Indexes

A periodical index serves much the same purpose as the index of a book or the card file of a library. Usually listing articles alphabetically under subject, title, and author headings, the sources of periodical articles are indicated. Readers should read the directions for the use of an index before trying to locate references. Most indexes provide complete directions, as well as a list of the periodicals covered, the issue dates included, and a key to all abbreviations used.

Education Index. New York: H. W. Wilson Co., 1929–date. Published monthly (September through June), and cumulated annually.

Since its first publication in 1929, the *Education Index* has served as a comprehensive index of practically all publications in the area of education; it indexes more than 250 educational periodicals, and many yearbooks, bulletins, and monographs published in the United States, Canada, and Great Britain. It includes materials on adult education, business education, curriculum and curriculum materials, educational administration, educational psychology, educational research, exceptional children, guidance, health and physical education, higher education, international education, religious education, secondary education, teacher education, and related subjects.

The cited references listed by subject and title appear in the paperbound monthly edition two or three months after the articles appear in the periodicals. College and university libraries and most public libraries subscribe to the *Index*. The cost of the service is determined by the number of listed periodicals to which the library subscribes, making it less expensive for smaller libraries that do not take as many periodicals.

In using the *Index*, it is often advisable to use past cumulative issues, for references are not carried from one year to the next. It is often helpful to know when a particular problem or topic was of current interest, for *Index* issues from that period will yield better references. For example, in 1968 the author found few citations of articles dealing with cheating or dishonesty in the classroom. However, many references were found in the 1952 and 1965 cumulative issues, for public interest and professional concern had been aroused by the exposures of academic dishonesty at the United States Military Academy and the Air Force Academy in those years.

Canadian Education Index. **Ottawa, Ontario: Canadian Council for Educational Research, 1965–date.**

Issued quarterly, this publication indexes periodicals, books, pamphlets, and reports published in Canada.

Current Contents: Education. **Philadelphia: Institute for Scientific Information and Encyclopedia Britannica Educational Corporation, 1969–date.**

Issued weekly, this publication reproduces the table of contents of more than 500 foreign and domestic educational periodicals. It contains an author index and address directory to facilitate writing for reprints of the articles and to identify the author's organization. Reprints are available directly from the Institute for Scientific Information.

PETERSON, John E.
Life education: a new concept in health education instruction. J Sch Health 45:542-4 N '75
PETERSON, Leo C. and Sawyer, R. C.
How to perpetuate our profession. pors Agric Educ 48:53 S '75
PETERSON, Sterling, and Buttschau, Ray
Innovations in purchasing industrial arts supplies. Ind Educ 64:34-6 D '75
PETROSKY, Anthony R. See Cooper, C. R. jt. auth.
PHARIS, William L.
Principalship; where are we? Natl El Prin 55:4-8 N '75
PHENOMENOLOGY
From phenomenology to subjective method. R. Poole. Univ Q 29:412-40 Aut '75
PHILADELPHIA

E. Washington Rhodes middle school
Philadelphia school study about attitude in inner city students. E. L. Stranix. bibl Education 96:95-100 Fall '75

Public schools
Schools do make a difference. A. A. Summers and B. L. Wolfe. il Todays Educ 64:24-7; Discussion. 27-31 N '75
PHILOSOPHY
See also
Dialectical materialism
Political philosophy
Subjectivity
Values (philosophy and logic)
PHONOLOGY
See also
Bengali language—Phonology
PHONORECORDS
Wider domain of serious contemporary music. R. C. Sheldon. Intellect 104:149 N '75
PHOTOCHEMISTRY

Experiments
Preparation and photochemistry of stilbenes; a synthetic organic chemistry experiment. J. R. Davy and others. bibl il J Chem Educ 52:747-8 N '75
PHOTOGRAMS. See Shadowgrams
PHOTOGRAPHY
See also
Nature photography
Shadowgrams

Printing processes
Darkroom: cropping, burning-in and vignetting. R. W. Cooke. il Sch Arts 75:4-7 D '75
PHOTOGRAPHY, Aerial
Take to the air for a solidly unflighty view of your district; aerial photomaps. il Am Sch Bd J 162:44-5 N '75
PHOTOGRAPHY, Artistic
Photography: an isolated approach. B. R. Carmenati. il Sch Arts 75:12-13 D '75
PHOTOGRAPHY in education
Self-concept and the camera. D. C. Locke. Sch Counsel 23:139 N '75
PHYSICAL defects. See Deformities
PHYSICAL directors

Correspondence, reminiscences, etc.
Boy, a rope, and a truth. E. R. Hill. Todays Educ 64:108 N '75

Duties
Nobody looks at me. B. Bing. J Phys Educ & Rec 46:55-6 F '75

Rating
O.S.U. teacher behavior rating scale. D. Siedentop and C. Hughley. J Phys Educ & Rec 46:45 F '75
PHYSICAL education
See also
Physical education for girls and women

Activities
Ahoy. J. Kautz. J Phys Educ & Rec 46:89 F '75
How we teach it; ed. by M. Hannigan. See issues of Journal of physical education and recreation

Bibliography
Books. See issues of Journal of physical education and recreation

Correlation with other subjects
Interdisciplinary bike tour. il J Phys Educ & Rec 46:40-1 F '75

Curriculum
Education of the whole child: fact or fiction? P. Hunsicker and G. Reiff. NASSP Bull 59:82-5 D '75
Fresh ideas for college physical education; symposium. il J Phys Educ & Rec 46:37-44 F '75

Research
Research; ed. by P. B. Johnson. See issues of Journal of physical education and recreation
Why research? T. P. Martin. J Phys Educ & Rec 46:56+ F '75

Teaching aids and devices
Audiovisual aids. See issues of Journal of physical education and recreation

Teaching methods
Play cards. S. Ravitz. J Phys Educ & Rec 46:30 F '75

Theories and principles
Elementary games and humanism. M. Riley. il J Phys Educ & Rec 46:46-9 F '75

Colleges and universities
Cheyney's phys ed goes co-ed. D. T. Wirth. J Phys Educ & Rec 46:29 Ja '75
Fresh ideas for college physical education; symposium. il J Phys Educ & Rec 46:37-44 F '75
HPER directory of professional preparation institutions. American alliance for health, physical education and recreation. JOHPER 45:37-48 S '74 (cont as) J Phys Educ & Rec 46:26 Ja; 14+ My '75

Elementary schools
Alphabet dance. G. Blanchard. J Phys Educ & Rec 46:65 F '75
Elementary games and humanism. M. Riley. il J Phys Educ & Rec 46:46-9 F '75
Play cards. S. Ravitz. J Phys Educ & Rec 46:30 F '75

High schools
Exercise physiology in secondary schools; a three dimensional approach. E. J. Meyers. J Phys Educ & Rec 46:30-1 Ja '75
PHYSICAL education associations
See also
International federation for university sport
PHYSICAL education departments. See Colleges and universities—Departments of physical education
PHYSICAL education facilities
New Texas-size facilities. A. E. Coleman. J Phys Educ & Rec 46:28 Ja '75
Phys ed facility invites participation; Robert Crown center, Hampshire college, Amherst, Mass. il Am Sch & Univ 48:39 D '75
See also
Playgrounds
PHYSICAL education for girls and women
Self-defense for women. il J Phys Educ & Rec 46:44 F '75
Third HISPA seminar; tr. by M. Spiegel, J. P. Massicotte. J Phys Educ & Rec 46:61-2 F '75
PHYSICAL education for the handicapped
IRUC: what's going on? ed. by J. U. Stein. See issues of Journal of physical education and recreation
Project I CAN' individualized curriculum designed for mentally retarded children and youth. C. Knowles and others. Educ & Train Men Retard 10:155-60 O '75
PHYSICAL education students
Students; ed. by R. Ciszek. See issues of Journal of physical education and recreation
PHYSICAL examinations
See also
School children—Medical inspection
PHYSICAL therapy
Physical activity guidelines for children with developmental hip disorders. R. Adams and M. Puthoff. bibl il J Phys Educ & Rec 46:69,70+ F '75
PHYSICIANS
New oath for physicians. il Intellect 104:147-8 N '75
See also
Pediatricians
PHYSICS

Graduate work
Observations on an obstacle course; U.S. graduate education for the deserving Asian physics student. F. E. Dart and others. Int Educ & Cul Exch 11:29-32 Fall '75

Laboratory work
Developing a laser holographic laboratory for use in secondary school science curriculum. D. J. Record. bibl il Sch Sci & Math 75:691-704 D '75

Teaching
High schools
Developing a laser holographic laboratory for use in secondary school science curriculum. D. J. Record. bibl il Sch Sci & Math 75:691-704 D '75
PHYSIOLOGY
See also
Flexibility (physiology)
Neurophysiology

Fig. 9-2. Page from the Education Index. Used with permission of the H. W. Wilson Company, New York. Education Index copyright © 1976 by The H. W. Wilson Company.

Current Index to Journals in Education. **Phoenix, AZ.: Oryx Press, 1969–date.**

This index is issued monthly and cumulated semiannually and annually, and indexes approximately 20,000 articles each year from more than 700 education and education-related journals, a joint venture with the National Institute of Education. There are five sections:

1. *Source Journal Index* lists the publications from which the articles are selected.

2. *Main Entry Index* is arranged alphabetically and numerically by Clearinghouse Accession Numbers. Initials identify the clearing house that was responsible for preparing the annotated citation.

3. *Subject Index.* Articles are listed alphabetically under as many as five descriptor terms.

4. *Author Index* is listed alphabetically. If there are coauthors, both names are listed.

5. *Journal Contents Index.* Articles are indexed under the alphabetical list of journal names with ERIC number sequences.

Index of Doctoral Dissertations International. **Ann Arbor, MI.: Xerox University Microfilms, 1956–date.**

Published as the issue 13 of *Dissertation Abstracts International* each year, this work consolidates into one list all dissertations accepted by American, Canadian, and some European universities during the academic year, as well as those available in microfilm. It indexes by author and key words selected from dissertation titles.

Comprehensive Dissertation Index **(1861–1972). Ann Arbor, MI.: Xerox University Microfilms, 1974.**

This volume indexes by author name and key word 417,000 doctoral dissertations accepted at 362 accredited institutions from 1861–1972.

Research Studies in Education. **Bloomington, IN.: Phi Delta Kappa, 1953–date.**

This annual publication includes doctoral dissertations in education, both completed and in progress, author and subject indexes, and a research methods bibliography.

Bibliographic Index. **New York: H. W. Wilson Co., 1938–date.**

Fig. 9-3. Page from Current Index to Journals in Education.

Issued semiannually, this guide indexes by subject current bibliographies containing more than 40 citations, including those published in books, pamphlets, and periodicals both in English and in foreign languages. More than 1500 periodicals are examined for bibliographic material.

> *Readers' Guide to Periodic Literature.* **New York: H. W. Wilson Co., 1900–date.**

Issued twice each month, *Readers' Guide* indexes by subject and author articles of a popular and general nature. Prior to 1929, *Readers' Guide* covered many of the educational periodicals. By 1929, the number of educational periodicals had become so great that the *Education Index* was established as a more specialized guide. *Readers' Guide* may be helpful to students in education for finding references to articles in areas outside the field of professional education.

> *Abridged Readers' Guide to Periodic Literature.* **New York: H. W. Wilson Co., 1935–date.**

Fifty-six selected periodicals most likely to be found in smaller libraries are indexed here.

> *New York Times Index.* **New York, 1913–date.**

This index is published biweekly with annual cumulation, and it classifies material in the *New York Times* alphabetically and chronologically under subject, title, person, and organization name. It is also useful in locating materials in other newspapers because it gives a clue to the date of events. Complete issues of the *New York Times* are available in microfilm form in many libraries.

> *Subject Index to the Christian Science Monitor.* **Boston: Christian Science Monitor, 1960–date.**

This publication is issued monthly with annual cumulations.

> *Social Sciences Index.* **New York: H. W. Wilson Co., 1974–date.**

This guide indexes 263 periodicals.

> *Humanities Index.* **New York: H. W. Wilson Co., 1974–date.**

Formerly published as *Social Sciences and Humanities Index* (1965–1973), the *Humanities Index* lists 260 periodicals. These two indexes, each issued quarterly and cumulated annually, index alphabetically by subject and title articles from more than 260 periodicals, including many published outside the United States.

Applied Science and Technology Index. New York: H. W. Wilson Co., 1958–date.

Formerly a part of the *Industrial Arts Index*, this subject index, issued monthly and cumulated annually, covers more than 225 periodicals in chemistry, physics, electricity, engineering, aerospace, metallurgy, machinery, and related subjects.

Business Periodicals Index. New York: H. W. Wilson Co., 1958–date.

Issued monthly and cumulated annually, this subject index covers more than 120 periodicals in the fields of business, accounting, labor and management, marketing, purchasing, office management, public administration, banking, finance, taxation, insurance, and related areas.

Air University Library Index. Maxwell Field, AL.: Air University Library, United States Air Force, 1945–date.

This work indexes quarterly and cumulates every three years more than 76 military periodicals published in the English language.

Music Index: The Key to Current Music Periodical Literature. Detroit: Information Service, 1950–date.

Issued monthly, cumulated annually, more than 300 periodicals are indexed.

Physical Education Index. Cape Girardeau, MO.: Ben Oak Publishing Co., 1978–date.

This quarterly indexes more than 130 domestic and foreign physical education journals by subject, title, and author.

Physical Education/Sports Index. Albany, N.Y.: Marathon Press, 1978–date.

This quarterly covers more than 100 journals. Since *Education Index* and *Current Index to Journals in Education* cover fewer than 10 physical education journals, these indexes provide an important additional source.

Art Index. New York: H. W. Wilson Co., 1929–date.

Published quarterly with cumulation annually and every two years, this publication indexes by author and subject 110 periodicals and museum bulletins, both foreign and domestic. Subjects included are archaeology, architecture, art history, arts and crafts, fine arts, graphic arts, industrial design, interior decoration, photography, planning, and landscape design.

Biological and Agricultural Index. **New York: H. W. Wilson Co., 1916– date.**

Formerly *Agricultural Index,* and issued monthly and cumulated annually, this work indexes by subject and title more than 190 periodicals in such fields of agriculture as chemicals, economics, engineering, animal husbandry, soil science, forestry, nutrition, biology, genetics, ecology, zoology, and veterinary medicine.

Occupational Index. **Jaffrey, NH.: Personnel Services, 1936–date.**

Issued quarterly, this work indexes more than 100 general and technical periodicals by subject, author, and title.

Cumulative Career Index. **Moravia, NY.: Chronicle Guidance Publications, 1971–date.**

This annual publication lists more than 1800 free and inexpensive materials on careers and work opportunities, listed by job titles.

Index to Legal Periodicals. **New York: H. W. Wilson Co., 1908–date.**

Issued monthly and cumulated annually, this index covers nearly 300 legal periodicals, indexed by subject with case notes.

Index Medicus. **Washington, D.C.: National Library of Medicine, 1960.**

Issued monthly, this index includes research reports from most medical journals, and is cumulated annually as:

Cumulated Index Medicus. **Chicago: American Medical Association, 1960– date.**

Abridged Index Medicus. **Washington, D.C.: National Library of Medicine and the A.M.A., Superintendent of Documents, 1970–date.**

Issued monthly, this work cross indexes articles from 118 English language medical journals by subject and author.

Hospital Literature Index. **Chicago: American Hospital Association, 1945–date.**

Issued semiannually with annual and five-year cumulations, this publication covers more than 180 periodicals in the United States and the British Commonwealth dealing with public health, nursing, hospital administration, gerontology, and medicine.

Cumulative Index to Nursing Literature. **Glendale, CA.: Seventh Day Adventist Hospital Assn., 1961–date.**

Issued quarterly with annual cumulation, this work indexes most nursing periodicals.

International Nursing Index. **Philadelphia: American Journal of Nursing, 1966–date.**

This index is issued quarterly with annual cumulation, with citations from more than 200 nursing journals; it lists doctoral dissertations in nursing.

Rehabilitation Literature. **Chicago: The National Society for Crippled Children and Adults, 1940–date.**

Published monthly, this index lists material on the physically handicapped.

Index to Religious Periodical Literature. **Chicago: American Theological Library Association, McCormick Seminary, 1949–date.**

This index to more than 100 religious periodicals is issued every two years.

Catholic Periodical and Literature Index. **Haverford, PA.: Catholic Library Association, 1930–date.**

The quarterly publication indexes more than 135 Catholic periodicals, books, newspapers, and bulletins.

Index to Jewish Periodicals. **Cleveland: Cleveland College of Jewish Studies, 1963–date.**

This index is issued quarterly, and lists by subject and author articles from Jewish periodicals.

Index to Periodicals: Articles by and about Negroes. **Boston: G. K. Hall and Co., 1961–date.**

Issued annually, this work indexes about twenty black interest periodicals not indexed elsewhere.

Public Affairs Information Service Bulletin. **New York: Public Affairs Information Service, 1915–date.**

Published weekly and cumulated quarterly and annually, this publication lists by subject articles in books, pamphlets, government publications, periodicals, and society publications dealing with social, political, and economic affairs throughout the world.

Book Review Index. **Detroit: Gale Research Co., 1965–date.**

This biweekly publication with quarterly cumulations lists book reviews by author from more than 250 periodicals.

Mental Health Book Review Index. **New York: Research Center for Mental Health, 1956–date.**

Published annually and indexed by author, this work lists reviews from more than 200 English language journals.

Microforms in Print
Subject Guide to Microforms in Print. **Washington, D.C.: Microcard Editions Books, 1961–date.**

These annual cumulative guides to microfilms and microfiche do not include theses and dissertations.

Selected United States Government Publications. **Washington, D.C.: Superintendent of Documents, 1928–date.**

Issued biweekly, this small publication, available without cost, lists government books and pamphlets soon after publication.

Index to U.S. Government Periodicals. **Chicago: Infordot International, 1972–date.**

Issued quarterly and cumulated annually, this is a computer-generated guide to selected titles from over 100 major government periodicals.

International Guide to Educational Documentation. **Paris: UNESCO.**

Published every five years, this guide indexes annotated bibliographies covering major publications, bibliographies, and national directories, written in English, French, and Spanish.

United Nations Document Index. New York: United Nations Library, 1950–date.

All U.N. publications are listed by subject and issuing body in this monthly publication.

Abstracts

Another type of reference guide is the abstract, review, or digest. In addition to providing a systemized list of reference sources, it includes a summary of the contents. Usually the summaries are brief, but in some publications they are presented in greater detail.

Dissertation Abstracts International. Ann Arbor, MI.: Xerox University Microfilms, 1955–date.

Issued monthly and indexed annually, *Dissertation Abstracts* is divided into:

A. Humanities and Social Sciences
B. Sciences and Engineering

Dissertations accepted by all universities in the United States and Canada and some in foreign countries are indexed by author and key word. Libraries or individuals may purchase complete xerographic or microfiche copies of any dissertation.

Master's Abstracts. Ann Arbor, MI.: Xerox University Microfilms, 1962–date.

Issued semiannually, this guide abstracts those master's degree theses that are available on microfilm.

Resources in Education. Washington, D.C.: Superintendent of Documents, Government Printing Office, 1966–date.

This monthly abstract journal prepared by the National Institute of Education reports new and completed research projects gathered by the 16 Educational Research Information Centers (ERIC).

Completed Research in Health, Physical Education and Recreation Including International Sources. **Washington, D.C.: American Alliance for Health, Physical Education and Recreation, 1958–date.**

Issued annually, this work indexes by subject and title abstracts of studies conducted throughout the world.

Child Development Abstracts and Bibliography. **Chicago: University of Chicago Press, 1927–date.**

Issued every four months and cumulated every three years, this publication abstracts more than 20 journals.

Review of Child Development Research. **New York: Russell Sage Foundation, 1964–date.**

Research Relating to Children. **Washington, D.C.: Department of Health, Education and Welfare, Children's Bureau, 1948–date.**

Published annually, these abstracts of studies related to the welfare of children are indexed by subject, author, and title.

Research Related to Emotionally Disturbed Children. **Washington, D.C.: Department of Health, Education and Welfare, Children's Bureau, 1968.**

These abstracts are issued irregularly.

Exceptional Child Education Resources. **Arlington, VA.: Council for Exceptional Children, 1969–date.**

Issued quarterly, this publication indexes and abstracts books, periodicals, and government documents.

Mental Retardation Abstracts. **Columbus, OH.: American Association of Mental Deficiency, 1964–date.**

Issued quarterly, this work abstracts more than 200 journals and books, both foreign and domestic.

Deafness, Speech and Hearing Abstracts. **Washington, D.C.: Deafness, Speech and Hearing Publications, 1960–date.**

This quarterly publication abstracts more than 1800 articles each year from over 250 domestic and foreign journals.

Selected RAND Abstracts. **Santa Monica, CA.: RAND Corporation, 1963–date.**

Issued quarterly, these abstracts cover books and reports published by the corporation, many of which deal with education and other social sciences.

College Student Personnel Abstracts. **Claremont, CA.: College Student Personnel Institute, 1965–date.**

Issued quarterly, the abstracts cover more than 275 periodicals. Summaries deal with research practices and developments relating to college students and student services.

Psychological Abstracts. **Washington, D.C.: American Psychological Association, 1927–date.**

Issued bimonthly and indexed annually by subject and author, this publication has excellent signed summaries of psychological research reports. The December issue provides annual cumulative author and subject indexes. Beginning in 1963, each issue is also indexed by both subject and author. Libraries may also provide a cumulative subject index (1927–1960) and a cumulative author index (1927–1963).

Annual Review of Psychology. **Palo Alto, CA.: Annual Reviews, 1950–date.**

Each issue of this annual volume contains critical reviews of the literature in some 15 topical areas of contemporary psychology. Each review is written by a recognized authority on the topic. Although different authors writing in different years may vary considerably in their interpretation and handling of the same topic, all aim for comprehensive coverage of new developments.

Psychological Bulletin. **Washington, D.C.: American Psychological Association, 1904–date.**

Issued bimonthly, the *Bulletin* evaluates reviews of research literature and methodology.

Sociological Abstracts. **San Diego, CA.: Sociological Abstracts, Inc., 1952–date.**

Issued five times a year and cumulated annually, the *Abstracts* cover all areas of sociology, including educational sociology. The work abstracts articles and presents book reviews from several hundred periodicals, both domestic and foreign.

Social Work Research and Abstracts. **New York: National Association of Social Workers, 1965–date.**

Published quarterly, this volume indexes by subject, title, and author. It combines published research with the previously published journal, *Abstracts for Social Workers.*

New Studies: A Guide to Recent Publications in the Social and Behavioral Sciences. **Beverly Hills, CA.: Sage Publications, 1966–date.**

Published as part of the bimonthly journal *American Behavioral Scientist,* this guide abstracts approximately 100 items in each issue from more than 400 journals, reviews, books, and pamphlets, both foreign and domestic.

Crime and Delinquency Abstracts. **Rockville, MD.: National Institute of Mental Health, 1966–1972.**

These abstracts cover published material on delinquency, crime, and penology.

Research Annual on Intergroup Relations. **New York: Anti-Defamation League of B'nai B'rith, 1965–date.**

This annual abstracts major studies in interracial and interfaith relations.

Religious and Theological Abstracts. **Youngstown, OH.: Theological Abstracts, 1957–date.**

The quarterly publication abstracts articles on various phases of religion, including religious education.

Women Studies Abstracts. **Rush, N.Y.: Women Studies Abstracts, 1972–date.**

Issued quarterly, these abstracts cover articles and studies from many journals.

National School Law Reporter. **New London, CT.: Croft Educational Services, 1955–date.**

The biweekly publication abstracts court decisions on school law.

Book Review Digest. **New York: H. W. Wilson Co., 1905–date.**

Issued monthly and cumulated annually, this publication digests reviews of more than 6000 books each year taken from over 70 periodicals.

> *Braille Book Review.* **Washington, D.C.: American Foundation for the Blind and Physically Handicapped, Library of Congress, 1933–date.**

This bimonthly abstracts articles about Braille materials and library services.

Specialized Bibliographies

These specialized bibliographies present extensive lists of periodical articles, monographs, books, and reports.

> *Department of Education.*
> *Price List 31* **Education**
> *Price List 33a* **Occupations**
> *Price List 71* **Children**
> **Washington, D.C.: Department of Education, Superintendent of Documents, Government Printing Office.**

These annual publications list available government publications and are free upon request.

> *National Education Association Publications Catalogue.* **Washington, D.C.: National Education Association, 1930–date.**

Published annually, the *Catalogue* lists all books, pamphlets, periodicals, audio-visual materials, research monographs, and proceedings of the Association.

> **Buros, Oscar K., ed.** *Personality Tests and Reviews.* **Highland Park, N.J.: Gryphon Press, 1972–date. 1679 pp.**

This comprehensive bibliography on the literature of personality scales includes references on constuction, use, and validation of specific tests.

> *Chicorel Index to Reading and Learning Disabilities: An Annotated Guide.* **New York: Chicorel Library Publishing Corp., 1977.**

This work indexes books, yearbooks, monographs, and more than 85 journals, listed by topic and author.

> *Black Higher Education in the United States.* **Westport, CT.: Greenwood Press, 1978.**

This bibliography indexes doctoral dissertations, masters theses, monographs, reports, government documents, and more than 1500 periodicals.

The Gifted Student. **Westport, CT.: Greenwood Press, 1977.**

This annotated bibliography has more than 1300 periodical and book references.

Music Article Guide. **Philadelphia, PA.: Information Services, Inc., 1965–date.**

This quarterly publication presents an annotated guide to feature articles in American music periodicals, directed exclusively to the special needs of school and college music educators. Braille copies and cassette recordings are available from the Music Section of the Division of the Blind and Physically Handicapped, Library of Congress, Washington, D.C.

Music Reference and Research Materials. **New York: Free Press, 1974.**

An annotated bibliography listing nearly 2,000 items including music dictionaries, encyclopedias, bibliographies, catalogues, yearbooks, and directories, indexed by author, editor, and reviewer.

International Bibliography of Research in Marriage and the Family. **Minneapolis: University of Minnesota Press. 2 vols. 1973–74.**

Volume I lists more than 12,000 references to literature from 1900 to 1964. Volume II lists nearly 13,000 items on literature between 1965 and 1972.

Environmental Conservation Education: A Selected Annotated Bibliography. **Danville, IL.: Interstate Printers and Publishers, 1974.**

This volume includes almost 800 books and pamphlets, arranged in six educational levels from primary level through college.

Alcohol Education Materials: An Annotated Bibliography. **New Brunswick, N.J.: Rutgers Center for Alcohol Studies, 1976.**

This decennial work contains information on publications and materials on trade publications, materials from State Boards of Health and Liquor Control, and a list of films on alcoholism and alcohol education.

A Selective Guide to Materials for Mental Health and Family Life Education. **Detroit, Mi. Gale Research Co., 1973–date.**

This annual volume presents a comprehensive list of materials arranged by such subject categories as child growth and development, mental illness, alcoholism and drug abuse, suicide, and divorce. Both print and nonprint materials are described in detail.

Specialized Encyclopedias

Encyclopedia of Education. **New York: Macmillan–Free Press, 1971.**

This ten-volume work presents more than 1,000 articles on most topics of interest in education. Contributions by leaders in all fields of education are signed by the authors.

Encyclopedia of Educational Research. **New York: American Educational Research Association, Macmillan Co. 1939–date.**

Published every ten years, this important reference work cites research on educational problems. Each signed article is written by a specialist and an excellent bibliography is included.

International Encyclopedia of the Social Sciences. **New York: Macmillan Co., 1968. 17 vols.**

Prepared under the direction of ten learned societies, this reference work treats topics in all of the social sciences.

Encyclopedia of Child Care and Guidance. **Garden City, N.Y.: Doubleday & Co., 1968.**

This volume presents a fairly comprehensive treatment of the nature of, and methods of dealing with, problems of childhood.

Encyclopedia of Mental Health. **New York: Franklin Watts, 1970. 6 vols.**

An authoritative and comprehensive reference, this encyclopedia is written by highly qualified contributors who are recognized authorities in the field.

Encyclopedia of Sociology. **Guilford, CT.: Dushkin, 1974.**

A comprehensive treatment of the language, theories, institutions, and leading figures of sociology.

Encyclopedia of Social Work. **New York: National Association of Social Workers, 1965–date. 2 vols.**

Published irregularly in intervals of several years, this work presents extensive articles on all aspects of social work.

Facts on File. **New York: Facts on File, 1940–date.**

A weekly, eight-page, current encyclopedia, *Facts on File* covers world events indexed for quick fact finding, and is cumulated quarterly and annually.

Encyclopedia of the Arts. **New York: Meredith Press, 1966.**

Articles in this reference deal with architecture, painting, theater, cinema, music, drama, and ballet.

Larousse Encyclopedia of Music. **New York: World, 1971. 576 pp.**

An excellent reference work on all areas of music, it is well-written and comprehensive.

Grove's Dictionary of Music and Musicians. **New York: St. Martin's Press, 1970.**

This music encyclopedia includes signed contributions by more than 500 experts on music history, theory, composers, instruments, and artists.

Encyclopedia of Science and Technology. **New York: McGraw-Hill Book Co., 1977, 15 vols.**

More than 7000 articles are written by more than 2000 contributors in all areas of science and engineering. Annual supplements are published.

Encyclopedia of Energy. **New York: McGraw-Hill Book Co., 1976.**

This work consists of more than 300 signed articles on energy prospectives and energy technology. Hundreds of pictures, tables, diagrams, and drawings are included.

Encyclopedia of Philosophy. **New York: Macmillan–Free Press, 1967. 8 vols.**

This outstanding authoritative encyclopedia covering both Western and Eastern thought, ancient, medieval, and modern, is also available in a four-volume edition.

Religions of the World from Primitive Belief to Modern Faiths. **New York: Grosset & Dunlap, 1971.**

This encyclopedic guide to the history and distinctive beliefs of all faiths includes facts and figures on membership and attendance, definitions of religious terms, and an extensive bibliography.

New Catholic Encyclopedia. **New York: McGraw-Hill Book Co., 1967. 15 vols.**

An international reference on the teachings, history, organization, and activities of the Roman Catholic Church, this work also covers all institutions, philosophies, and scientific and cultural movements affecting the church.

Encyclopedia Judaica. **New York: Macmillan Co., 1972. 16 vols.**

More than 25,000 entries, 11 million words, and 8000 illustrations present all phases of Jewish history and culture.

The Negro in America. **Washington, D.C.: Howard University Press, 1970.**

More than 6500 articles and studies about the Negro are provided, indexed by subject and title.

Corpus Juris Secundum. **Vols. 78 and 79. New York: American Law Book Co., 1936–74.**

This work has replaced the older volume, *Corpus Juris,* Vol. 56, long a standard encyclopedia of school law. Annual supplements are available.

American Jurisprudence. **Rochester, N.Y.: Lawyers Co-Operative Publishing Co., 1962–74.**

This series has replaced the older series, *Ruling Case Law.*

Yearbook of School Law. **Topeka, KS.: National Organization on Legal Problems in Education. 1933–date.**

This annual publication reviews the previous year's major cases on school law.

Almanacs, Handbooks, Yearbooks, and Guides

The name of a reference book does not always accurately describe its function, its frequency of publication, or the way in which the subject matter is organized. This general category of references includes those publications that present rather detailed, up-to-date information on a variety of subjects, organized around a given theme. They are the type of reference that one consults to find specific information, often of a statistical nature. Since they are ordinarily not comprehensive enough to be considered encyclopedic and the organization of topics is not alphabetical, they are classified together in this category. Generalized sources are listed first, followed by those with a more specialized emphasis.

World Almanac—Book of Facts. **New York: Newspaper Enterprise Association, 1868–date.**

Published annually, this inexpensive volume is the most comprehensive and most frequently consulted source of miscellaneous information. Statistical data in social, political, religious, geographic, commercial, sports, educational, and economic affairs are presented. One turns to this reference to find such information as the population of cities or countries, the state tax on gasoline in Wisconsin, the enrollment of Lawrence University, the date of the *Andrea Doria* disaster, or the world's record for the mile run. A chronology of important events of the previous year is included and all topics are indexed in detail. The following almanacs are similar to World Almanac:

Information Please Almanac. **New York: Simon & Schuster, 1947–date.**

Reader's Digest Almanac. **Pleasantville, N.Y.: Reader's Digest Association, 1963–date.**

The Official Associated Press Almanac. **New York: Almanac Publishing Co., 1970–date.**

Statistical Abstract of the United States. **Washington, D.C.: Department of Commerce, Superintendent of Documents, Government Printing Office, 1879–date.**

This important volume includes statistical data gathered by all agencies of the federal government, as well as by some private agencies. Of interest to students in education are the data on students, institutions, enrollment, salaries, expenditures, and literacy. All levels from preschool to higher education are covered.

> *The Fact Book: The American Almanac.* New York: Grosset & Dunlap, 1964–date.

This is a privately printed, less expensive paperbound reprint of *Statistical Abstract of the United States.*

> *Book of the States.* Lexington, KY.: Council of State Governments, 1935–date.

Published every even year with supplements in odd years, this work presents authoritative information on all aspects of the governments of the fifty states.

> *Digest of Educational Statistics.* Washington, D.C.: Department of Health, Education and Welfare, Government Printing Office, 1962–date.

Issued annually, this digest provides statistical information in the following volumes:

1. Elementary and secondary

2. Higher education

3. All levels of education

4. Federal programs of education

5. Miscellaneous.

> *Handbook of Research on Teaching.* Chicago: Rand McNally & Co. Vol. I, 1963; Vol. II, 1973.

Comprehensive research on teaching is presented, with in-depth coverage of topics and extensive bibliographies.

> *Education Yearbook.* New York: Macmillan Co., 1972–date.

This annual publication includes statistical data on major educational issues and movements with an extensive bibliography and reference guide.

> *Standard Education Almanac.* Chicago: Marquis Academic Media, 1968–date.

Published annually, this source of statistical information covers practically all aspects of education: elementary, secondary, higher, adult, and vocational; role of the federal government; legislation; finance; enrollments; construction of facilities; international education; and research.

> *Yearbook of Higher Education.* **Chicago: Marquis Academic Media, 1969–date.**

Up-to-date information is provided on all aspects of higher education in the United States, Canada, and Mexico, for more than 3000 junior colleges, colleges, and universities.

> *A Factbook on Higher Education.* **Washington, D.C.: American Council on Education, 1958–date.**

Issued quarterly, the information is statistically presented in tables and figures. One section presents data on all of the universities, colleges, and junior colleges, listed by states. The other section presents data on higher education in general

> *Peterson's Annual Guide to Graduate Study.* **Princeton, N.J.: Peterson's Guides. 5 vols. 1966–date.**

This guide includes descriptions of graduate institutions, programs, administration, enrollment, tuition, financial aid, and other information useful to the prospective graduate student. The same organization also publishes:

> *A Guide to Graduate Study.* **Washington, D.C.: American Council on Education, 1957–date (irregular).**

A useful reference to undergraduates planning graduate study, this book provides information for the selection of a graduate institution.

> *Requirements for Certification of Teachers, Counselors, Librarians and Administrators in Elementary and Secondary Schools and Junior Colleges.* **Chicago: University of Chicago Press, 1935–date.**

Published annually, this guide presents information for the fifty states and territories of the United States.

> *Handbook of Adult Education in the United States.* **Chicago: Adult Education Association of the United States, 1970–date.**

Signed articles deal with various aspects of adult education.

> *Yearbook of Adult and Continuing Education.* **Chicago: Marquis Academic Media, 1975–date.**

Published every other year, this volume presents comprehensive information on all phases of adult education.

Occupational Outlook Handbook. **Washington, D.C.: Bureau of Labor Statistics, Government Printing Office, 1949–date.**

Published every two years, this volume describes job opportunities and requirements in the principal occupational categories. It is useful to guidance counselors, parents, and teachers.

Mental Measurements Yearbook. **Highland Park, N.J.: Gryphon Press, 1938–date.**

This is the most comprehensive summary on psychological measurement and standardized tests and inventories. It contains reviews on all significant books on measurement and excerpts from book reviews appearing in professional journals. More than 800 standardized tests and inventories (achievement, aptitude, interest, and personality) are reviewed by one, two, or three reviewers. Published every few years, this work has been called the "bible of psychological testing." Readers are urged to refer to previous editions, for material is not duplicated from one edition to the next. The 1978 edition was the eighth.

Tests in Print. **Highland Park, N.J.: Gryphon Press, 1974.**

This index to the contents of previous editions of the *Mental Measurements Yearbook* lists practically all standardized tests in print as well as those out of print.

Butler University Bulletin. **Indianapolis, IN.: Butler University, 1854–date.**

A college or university bulletin or catalog yields a great deal of information about an institution, its history, course of study, admission requirements, degrees granted, campus building, tuition, fees, scholarships and grants, and faculty. This is often the best source of information about a particular school, containing more detailed information than is found in any general source. Most institutions maintain a rather complete file of the catalogs of other institutions, either in the library or in the registrar's office.

Yearbook of Special Education. **Chicago: Marquis Academic Media, 1974/75–date.**

Published on every other year, this yearbook includes information on federal and state legislation, programs, teacher training, litigation, and research relating to the physically and mentally handicapped.

Handbook of Denominations in the United States. **Nashville: Abingdon Press, 1975.**

Detailed information is provided about the history and doctrine of more than 250 religious sects and denominations.

Catholic Dictionary. **New York: Macmillan Co., 1961.**

This reference work offers a concise treatment of topics related to Catholic history, philosophy, literature, and doctrine.

Catholic Almanac. **Huntington, IN.: Our Sunday Visitor, 1904–date (present title since 1970).**

This almanac presents a wealth of information on any topic that concerns Catholicism; news, statistics, book clubs, communications offices, and agencies.

American Jewish Yearbook. **Philadelphia: American Jewish Committee, Jewish Publishing Society of America, 1899–date.**

This annual yearbook is a comprehensive statistical reference on all phases of Jewish life throughout the world.

Negro Almanac. **New York: Bellwether Publishing Co., 1978.**

A concise and comprehensive treatment of the Negro in American life, this volume includes biographical materials and information on organization, employment, business enterprise, the arts, sports, military life, and educational activities.

Women's Rights Almanac. **Bethesda, MD.: Elizabeth Cody Stanton Publishing Co., 1974–date.**

This almanac describes the activities of more than 300 women's organizations; statistics, publications, employment of women, women officials, and a chronology of major events.

Sourcebook of Equal-Opportunity Education. **Chicago: Marquis Academic Media, 1974/75–date.**

This sourcebook includes material on federal and state legislation and programs, bilingual education, stereotyping, discrimination, and congressional testimony on the problems of the disadvantaged. The material is arranged by subject and by state, and includes discussion of Blacks, American Indians, Hispanics, Asian-Americans, and women.

References on International Education

This section lists publications that deal with education outside the United States.

> *The World Yearbook of Education.* **New York: Harcourt Brace Jovanovich, 1953–date.**

Issued annually, and prepared under the joint responsibility of the University of London Institute of Education and Teacher's College of Columbia University, each issue is devoted to some aspect of international education.

> *International Yearbook of Education.* **Geneva: International Bureau of Education, UNESCO, 1948–date.**

The *Yearbook* presents in English and French a review of educational developments for the previous year in the United States, Canada, and more than 40 foreign countries.

> *Education Abstracts.* **Paris: UNESCO. New York: Columbia University· Press, 1949–date.**

Issued ten times each year, this annotated guide deals with selected works from a number of international publications dealing with foreign education.

> *Paedagogica Europa: The European Yearbook of Education.* **Amsterdam: Elsevier, 1965–date.**

An annual presentation of papers on education research published in English, French, and German, the publication focuses on a single trend in contemporary educational research.

> *Educational Documentation and Information.* **Geneva: International Bureau of Education, 1971–date.**

This quarterly provides short descriptive articles on national and international institutions, documentation, and research.

United Nations Statistical Yearbook. New York: United Nations, 1949–date.

This annual publication presents statistical data on population, trade, transportation, finance, health, and education.

International Encyclopedia of Higher Education. San Francisco: Jossey Bass, Publishers, 1977.

This ten-volume work presents much new information and is a valuable supplement to existing references.

International Handbook of Universities. Paris: International Association of Universities, 1971. 1216 pp.

This book describes universities and other institutions of higher learning in more than 100 countries outside the United States and the British Commonwealth. It provides information about officials, facilities, history, structure, academic year, admission requirements, fees, scholarships, degree programs, libraries, publications, teaching staff, enrollment, and languages of instruction.

Commonwealth Universities Yearbook. Edinburgh: R. and R. Clark, 1964–date.

Issued annually, this volume gives detailed information on universities in the 23 Commonwealth countries.

World of Learning. London: Europa Publications, 1947–date.

Annual information is provided on universities, colleges, libraries, museums, art galleries, learned societies, and research institutions throughout the world.

Garraty, John A. *New Guide to Study Abroad.* New York: Harper & Row, 1976.

This comprehensive guide for high school, college, and university students includes information on fellowships and awards, academic requirements, and programs available.

Rowland, Howard S. and Beatrice Rowland. *The New York Times Guide to Student Adventure and Study Abroad.* New York: Quadrangle Press, 1976.

This guide describes a wide variety of summer camps, tours, and organized study activities. Programs are listed by countries in such interest areas as sports, exchange programs, language study, and work opportunities.

UNESCO Handbook of International Exchanges. **Paris: UNESCO, 1965–date.**

Information is provided on the purposes, programs, and activities of national and international organizations concerned with educational exchange programs.

Higher Education in Developing Countries. **Cambridge, MA.: Harvard University Center for International Affairs, 1976.**

This is a selected bibliography on students, politics, and higher education.

Specialized Dictionaries

Dictionary of Education. **New York: McGraw-Hill Book Co., 1973.**

This educational dictionary covers 33,000 technical and professional terms. Foreign educational terms used in comparative education writings are included.

Thesaurus of ERIC Descriptors. **Phoenix, AZ.: Oryx Press, 1969–date.**

A definitive vocabulary of education, the *Thesaurus* is a major source of subject headings used for indexing and retrieval of documents and journals in the *Educational Resources Information Center* collection. It is a useful tool for students, teachers, and information specialists.

Comprehensive Dictionary of Psychological and Psychoanalytical Terms. **New York: David McKay Co., 1959.**

More than 13,000 terms are defined in nontechnical language.

Dictionary of Sociology. **Totowa, N.J.: Littlefield, Adams & Co., 1970.**

Most sociological terms are defined in nontechnical language.

Dictionary of the Social Sciences. **New York: Glencoe Press, 1964.**

This work defines approximately 2000 concepts used in the social sciences, and is compiled under the auspices of UNESCO.

Dictionary of Occupational Titles. **Washington, D.C.: Department of Labor, U.S. Government Printing Office, 1977.**

This list of over 40,000 job titles and job descriptions is useful in the study of occupations and industrial processes, and in counseling.

Acronyms, Initialisms, and Abbreviations Dictionary. **Detroit, MI.: Gale Research Co., 1970–date.**

Because of the rapid growth of associations, agencies and bureaus, the use of alphabetical terms has become an important part of communication. Domestic and international terms in such areas as government, business, medicine, science, the computer field, religious organizations, and law enforcement are included in more than 178,000 entries.

Computer Dictionary. **Ormand Beach, FL.: Camelot Publishing Co., 1977.**

More than 21,000 words, phrases, and acronyms arranged in alphabetical order are included. The history of computers, the biographies of computer scientists, and the names of professional organizations are included.

Black's Law Dictionary. **St. Paul, MN.: West Publishing Co., 1951.**

Black's contains definitions of the terms and phrases of American and English jurisprudence.

Ballentine's Law Dictionary with Pronunciations. **Rochester, NY.: Lawyers Cooperative Publishing Co., 1969. 1429 pp.**

This is another highly regarded law dictionary.

Roget's International Thesaurus of Words and Phrases. **New York: T. Y. Crowell, 1977.**

A thesaurus is the opposite of a dictionary. When you have an idea you look for the most appropriate word to convey it. Synonyms and antonyms are listed together. This reference should be used in conjunction with a good dictionary to insure precision of expression. Several inexpensive paper-bound editions are available.

Biographical References

Educational workers often need information about another educator or a prominent person outside the field of education. Some of these occasions relate to the conduct of educational research, while others concern professional contacts.

A partial list of situations in which biographical information would be helpful:

1. To help evaluate writings

2. To recommend a speaker for a professional meeting

3. To prepare a press release about a speaker

4. To introduce a speaker

5. To prepare for an important interview

6. To correspond with a person with greater understanding of his or her background

7. To choose an authority with whom to work professionally (This may involve the choice of a major professor or advisor for advanced study.)

8. To aid in recommending an individual for an honor, such as an award or an honorary degree

There are a number of sources of information about the famous and the not so famous. If a person is really outstanding, a general reference will supply the needed information, but if he or she is less prominent, a more specialized or limited source must be consulted.

Many of these references, particularly the autobiographical type, have been criticized as vanity publications, including in their listings persons of little distinction who are anxious to get their names listed. Hundreds of these autobiographical Who's Whos have been published, covering every city, state, section of the country, foreign country, vocation, profession, ethnic group, religious sect, or denomination. Another criticism concerns the possible lack of accuracy of the information, since persons listed usually send in their own data, which cannot be carefully checked. Another limitation is that some important persons are not listed, for the listings are usually submitted as the results of a questionnaire, and some are not willing to respond.

Without questioning the motive of the publishers, who finance the publication largely by sales of the books to those listed, the reader is urged to evaluate the autobiographical data carefully. Many of these publications are found in libraries and can provide useful biographical data.

The brief sketches include information such as home address, business address, present position and title, former positions, date and place of birth, name of spouse, name of spouse's parents, names of children, schools attended, degrees, honorary positions, honors and awards, membership in professional and social organizations, books published, contributions to periodicals, military experience, travel, and hobbies.

Information about people is usually presented in one of three ways:

1. The Who's Who type. This information is compiled from responses to a questionnaire.

2. The biographical type. This information is taken from published sources which may range from feature articles to carefully documented investigations.

3. The dictionary type. This information usually consists of rather brief biographical data about a number of individuals who have lived in the past and were selected because of their historical importance.

Autobiographical References

Who's Who in America. **Chicago: Marquis Who's Who, Inc., 1899–date.**

Published every two years and listing more than 65,000 names, this general reference is considered one of the most reliable. This company also publishes *Who's Who in the East, Who's Who in the Midwest, Who's Who in the West, Who's Who in the South and Southwest, Who's Who in the World,* and *Who's Who in Government.* The information is autobiographical.

Who's Who of American Women. **Chicago: Marquis Who's Who, Inc., 1958–date.**

This biennial reference is useful because few women have been listed in *Who's Who in America.*

Who Was Who in America. **Chicago: Marquis Who's Who, Inc., 1942–date.**

Published approximately every ten years, this reference lists deceased persons who were prominent.

America's Men of Science. **New York: R. R. Bowker Co., 1906–date.**
Vol. I Physical Sciences

Vol. II Biological Sciences
Vol. III Behavioral Sciences

The information is autobiographical.

Contemporary Authors. **Detroit: Gale Research Co., 1964–date.**

Issued semiannually, this work lists autobiographical sketches of about 4000 authors each year.

Leaders in Education. **New York: Bowker and Jacques Cattell Press, 1932–date.**

This autobiographical publication lists some less-than-prominent as well as prominent educators.

Biographical References

Current Biography. **New York: H. W. Wilson Co., 1940–date.**

Issued monthly and cumulated annually, this reference covers celebrities: kings, prime ministers, presidents, Nobel Prize winners, senators, cabinet members, congressmen, court justices; and sports, radio, film, television, and stage personalities. Biographies are abstracted from feature articles in hundreds of publications. The yearly cumulation is published as *Current Biography Yearbook*.

Directory of American Scholars. **New York: R. R. Bowker Co., 1942–date.**
Vol. I History
Vol. II English, Speech and Drama
Vol. III Foreign Languages
Vol. IV Philosophy, Religion and Law

This directory provides short biographical articles on leaders in various academic fields: teachers, authors, researchers, and administrators.

Biography Index. **New York: H. W. Wilson Co., 1946–date.**

This quarterly index is cumulated annually of biographical material found in more than 2000 periodicals and in the various indexes of the H. W. Wilson Company. Biographies are indexed by name and profession or occupation.

Dictionary of American Biography. **New York: Charles Scribner's Sons.**
11 vols. 1928. Supplements issued in 1944, 1958 and 1973.

This reference, written by recognized authorities in their fields, contains information on more than 15,000 American men and women no longer living, and is prepared under the direction of the American Council of Learned Societies. A one-volume concise edition is available. This is an important source of information about individuals who had some influence upon history, but many of whom are not mentioned in history books.

> *Webster's Biographical Dictionary.* Springfield, MA.: G. & C. Merriam Co., 1969.

This work contains more than 50,000 biographical sketches ranging from a few lines to more than a page in length. It is useful for finding information about persons of any nationality and from any period of history.

Directories

Directories provide information about the purposes and programs of institutions or agencies, and often include information about officers and staff.

> *Education Directory.* Washington, D.C.: U.S. Office of Education, Superintendent of Documents, 1912–date.

This directory is issued annually in five parts dealing with names, educational agencies, officials, institutions, and other relevant data:

1. State Governments
2. Public School Systems
3. Higher Education
4. Educational Associations
5. Federal Government Agencies.

> *NEA Handbook.* Washington, D.C.: National Education Association, 1945–date.

This annual publication contains listings and comprehensive reports of state and national officers of affiliated associations and departments. Information about purposes, membership, and publications is included.

> *Educator's World.* Englewood, CO.: Fisher Publishing Co., 1972—date.

This is an annual guide to more than 1600 education associations, publications, research centers, and foundations.

National Faculty Directory. **Detroit: Gale Research Co., 1964–date.**

Published annually, this work lists alphabetically the names and addresses of more than 300,000 full-time and part-time faculty members and administrative officials of junior colleges, colleges, and universities in the United States.

American Education. **Mt. Prospect, IL.: Educational Directories, 1904–date.**

School officials for practically all schools and school systems in the country, both private and public, are listed by state.

Encyclopedia of Associations. **Detroit: Gale Research Co., 1964–date.**

This directory of more than 14,000 national associations includes business, scientific, educational, health, social welfare, and others of a more general nature. Listing is alphabetical and includes information on membership, address, name of executive secretary, and statement of purpose.

Foundations Directory. **New York: Russell Sage Foundation, 1964–date.**

Foundations are listed alphabetically by state, address, date of incorporation, donors, financial data, purposes, activities, and names of officers. A bimonthly publication, *Foundation News,* supplements the directory.

Directory for Exceptional Children. **Boston: Porter Sargent Publishing Co., 1962–date.**

This directory describes schools, camps, homes, clinics, hospitals, and services for the socially maladjusted, mentally retarded, or physically handicapped. It is indexed by special need and by state location.

Mental Health Directory. **Washington, D.C.: National Institute of Mental Health, Government Printing Office, 1964–date.**

This annual publication lists national, state, and local mental health agencies, both public and private.

A National Catalogue of Financial Aids for Students Entering College. **Dubuque, IA: William C. Brown Co., 1966–date.**

More than 2000 institutional programs are described, with information on sponsors, eligibility, criteria, basis of awards, and application procedures.

Annual Register of Grant Support. **Chicago: Academic Media, 1967–date.**

This list of more than 1000 sources of grants in all areas indicates available funds, purposes, and directions for applying.

Student Aid Annual. **Moravia, New York: Chronicle Guidance Publications, 1955–date.**

Available financial aid consisting of grants, scholarships and loans, for both undergraduates and graduate students, offered by corporations, private associations, labor unions, states and the federal government are described in detail.

The College Blue Book. **New York: C.C.M. Information Corp., 1923–date. 4 vols.**

Published every three years, the four volumes include nine sections which are a most complete source of information on the characteristics of several thousand institutions.

Patterson's American Education. **Mt. Prospect, IL.: Educational Directories, 1904–date.**

Published annually, this guide lists public and private schools, vocational and technical schools, colleges and universities by state and city, with statistical data and names of administrative officials.

Comparative Guide to American Colleges. **New York: Harper & Row, 1964–date.**

Institutions are classified by state, religious orientation, and selectivity. Data for each school include control, admissions, enrollment, facilities, faculty, average SAT scores, and nature of campus life.

American Library Directory. **New York: R. R. Bowker Co., 1923–date.**

This comprehensive biannual guide to private, state, municipal, institutional, and collegiate libraries in the United States and Canada includes information on special collections, number of holdings, staff salaries, budgets, and affiliations.

Instructional aids

The following publications list books, pamphlets, and audio-visual materials that are helpful to classroom teachers. Many are sent free on request; others may be obtained at a nominal cost.

New Educational Materials. **New York: Citation Press, Scholastic Magazines, 1967–date.**

An annual reference and selection guide to recent educational materials, this guide evaluates and reviews instructional aids, and books and articles of reference value, covering all levels, K–12.

Free and Inexpensive Learning Materials. **Nashville, TN.: Division of Surveys and Field Services, George Peabody College for Teachers, 1941–date.**

Published biennially, this list of more than 3000 items is indexed by curriculum-related categories.

Vertical File Index. **New York: H. W. Wilson Co., 1932–date.**

Issued monthly, the catalog indexes pamphlets and current free and inexpensive materials. Since these materials may soon be out of print, they should be ordered as soon as possible.

Programmed Instruction Guide. **Newburyport, MA.: Entelek, 1967–date.**

This semiannual publication lists thousands of programmed instruction units available from more than 300 different sources.

Educators Guide to Free Curriculum Materials, **1944–date.**

Educators Guide to Free Guidance Materials, **1961–date.**

Educators Guide to Free Health, Physical Education and Recreation Materials, **1960–date.**

Educators Guide to Free Science Materials, **1959–date.**

Educators Guide to Free Social Studies Materials, **1960–date.**

Educators Guide to Free Films, **1941–date.**

Educators Guide to Free Filmstrips, **1949–date.**

Educators Guide to Free Tapes, Scripts and Transcriptions, **1955–date.**

Published annually at Randolph, Wisconsin, by Educators Progress Service, these eight references are indexed by subject and title, and include names and addresses of sources listed.

Index to 16 mm. Educational Films. **Los Angeles: National Information Center for Education Media, 1973.**

Index to 35 mm. Educational Films. **Los Angeles: National Information Center for Education Media, 1973.**

The two sources index more than 16,000 educational films by subject, title, length, color, description, producer, distributor, and year of release.

United States Government Films for Public Educational Use. **Washington, D.C.: Government Printing Office, 1964–date.**

Films owned by government agencies and available for free use are listed.

National Center for Audio Tapes Catalogue. **Boulder, CO.: National Center for Audio Tapes, 1965–date.**

Hundreds of audio tapes are listed by subject and title. Duplicate tapes are furnished for a small recording fee.

Research-oriented periodicals

There are many publications in education and in closely related areas that report research activity. Some of these publications are exclusively research-oriented. Others present both research reports and feature-type articles. It is possible that beginning researchers may not be familiar with many of the specialized publications that deal with a problem area selected. Browsing through these periodicals provides an effective introduction to the field. It is also possible that the student may find recent and current reports that have not yet appeared in the appropriate index.

The following list of periodicals may be helpful to those who are planning a research project.

EDUCATION

Administrative Science Quarterly
Adolescence
Adult Education
Adult Jewish Education
Alberta Journal of Educational Research
American Association of University Professors Bulletin

American Behavioral Scientist
American Biology Teacher
American Education
American Educational Research Journal
American Vocational Journal
Arbitration in the Schools
Arithmetic Teacher

Audio-Visual Communications Review
Audio-Visual Language Journal
Black Scholar
Bulletin of the National Association of Secondary Schools Principals
Business Education Forum
Business Education Quarterly
California Journal of Educational Research
Catholic Educational Review
Character Education Journal
Child Care Quarterly
Child Development
Child Study Journal
Child Welfare
Children Today
Childhood Education
Civil Rights Digest
Clearing House
College Board Review
Colorado Journal of Educational Research
Community and Junior College Journal
Comparative Education
Comparative Education Review
Computers and Education
Continuing Education
Convergence
Education and Urban Society
Educational Administration Quarterly
Educational Forum
Educational Leadership
Educational Record
Educational Researcher
Educational Research Quarterly
Educational Technology
Elementary School Journal
Evaluation Quarterly
Harvard Educational Review
High School Journal
History of Education Quarterly
Home Economics Research Journal
Human Development
Independent School Bulletin
Illinois School Research
Indian Historian
Integrated Education
International Journal of Aging and Human Development
International Journal of Educational Science
Jewish Education
Journal for Research in Mathematics Education
Journal for the Study of Religion

Journal of Afro-American Issues
Journal of Alcohol and Drug Education
Journal of American Indian Education
Journal of Business Education
Journal of Communication
Journal of Computer-Based Instruction
Journal of Creative Behavior
Journal of Drug Education
Journal of Educational Data Processing
Journal of Educational Measurement
Journal of Educational Research
Journal of Educational Statistics
Journal of Experimental Education
Journal of Higher Education
Journal of Home Economics
Journal of Industrial Teacher Education
Journal of Law and Education
Journal of Legal Education
Journal of Leisure Research
Journal of Library Research
Journal of Negro Education
Journal of Religion
Journal of Research and Development in Education
Journal of Research in Mathematics Education
Journal of Research in Music Education
Journal of Research in Science Teaching
Journal of Social Studies Research
Journal of Teacher Education
Junior College Journal
Kappa Delta Pi Record
Library Resources and Technical Services
Library Quarterly
Mathematics Teacher
Measurement in Education
Merrill Palmer Quarterly
Microfilm Review
Modern Language Journal
Multivariate Behavioral Research
National Business Education Quarterly
National Catholic Educational Association Bulletin
National Elementary Principal
National Education Association Research Bulletin
National Society for Programmed Instruction Journal
Negro Educational Review
New England Association Quarterly
North Central Association Quarterly
Outlook

Peabody Journal of Education
Phi Delta Kappan
Phylon
Pollution Abstracts
Practical Application of Research
Programmed Instruction
Psychometrika
Public Opinion Quarterly
Religion Teachers Journal
Religious Education
Research in Higher Education
Research in the Teaching of English
Review of Educational Research
Review of Religious Research
School and Society
School Law Journal
School Law Reporter

School Review
School Science and Mathematics
Science
Science Education
Science and Children
Science Teacher
Social Education
Social Science Research
Speech Monographs
Speech Teacher
Teachers College Record
Times Educational Supplement
Theory and Research in Social Education
Theory into Practice
UCLA Educator
Visual Education
Young Children

SOCIOLOGY

American Anthropologist
American Behavioral Scientist
American Journal of Sociology
American Sociological Review
Ethnology
Federal Probation
Human Relations
Journal of American Indian Education
Journal of Applied Behavioral Science
Journal of Correctional Education
Journal of Educational Sociology
Journal of Experimental Social Psychology
Journal of Marriage and the Family
Journal of Research in Crime and Delinquency
Rural Sociology

Social Behavior and Personality
Social Case Work
Social Education
Social Forces
Social Problems
Social Psychology
Social Work
Sociological Methods and Research
Sociological Record
Sociology of Education
Sociology and Social Research
Sociometry
Teaching Sociology
Urban Education
Urban Review

PSYCHOLOGY

American Journal of Orthopsychiatry
American Journal of Psychiatry
American Journal of Psychology
American Psychologist
Applied Psychological Measurement
Behavioral Disorders
British Journal of Psychology
British Journal of Educational Psychology
Catholic Psychological Record

Cognitive Psychology
Contemporary Educational Psychology
Educational and Psychological Measurement
Genetic Psychology Monographs
Journal of Abnormal Psychology
Journal of Abnormal Child Psychology
Journal of Applied Psychology
Journal of Autism and Childhood Schizophrenia

Journal of Clinical Psychology
Journal of Comparative and Physiological Psychology
Journal of Consulting and Clinical Psychology
Journal of Counseling Psychology
Journal of Creative Behavior
Journal of Educational Psychology
Journal of Experimental Child Psychology
Journal of General Psychology
Journal of Genetic Psychology
Journal of Humanistic Psychology
Journal of Mental and Nervous Disease
Journal of Personality
Journal of Personality and Social Psychology
Journal of Personal Assessment
Journal of Psychiatric Research
Journal of Psychology
Journal of Research in Personality
Journal of School Psychology

Journal of Social Psychology
Journal of Verbal Learning and Behavior
Learning and Motivation
Mental Hygiene
Pastoral Psychology
Perceptual and Motor Skills
Personnel Psychology
Psychiatry
Psychoanalytic Quarterly
Psychological Abstracts
Psychological Bulletin
Psychological Monographs
Psychological Record
Psychological Reports
Psychological Review
Psychology in the Schools
Psychology of Women Quarterly
Small Group Behavior
Transactional Analysis Journal

HEALTH AND PHYSICAL EDUCATION

American Journal of Nursing
American Journal of Occupational Therapy
American Journal of Physical Medicine
American Journal of Public Health
Athletic Journal
Health and Education Journal
Health Education
Journal of the American Dietetic Association
Journal of the American Medical Association
Journal of the American Physical Therapy Association
Journal of Clinical Nutrition
Journal of Continuing Education in Nursing
Journal of Drug Education
Journal of Health and Social Behavior
Journal of Health, Physical Education and Recreation

Journal of Medical Education
Journal of Mental Health
Journal of Nursing Education
Journal of Nutrition
Journal of Pediatrics
Journal of Rehabilitation
Journal of School Health
Nursing Mirror
Nursing Outlook
Nursing Times
Nutrition Today
Quarterly Review of Pediatrics
Registered Nurse
Research Quarterly of the American Alliance for Health, Physical Education and Recreation
School Health Review

GUIDANCE AND COUNSELING

American Vocational Journal
British Journal of Guidance and Counseling
California Personnel and Guidance Association Journal
Canadian Counsellor
Counselor Education and Supervision
Elementary School Guidance and Counseling

Focus on Guidance
Guidance Clinic
Measurement and Evaluation in Guidance
Personnel and Guidance Journal
School Counselor
School Guidance Worker
Vocational Guidance Quarterly

SPECIAL EDUCATION

Academic Therapy
American Annals of the Deaf
American Journal of Mental Deficiency
Braille Book Review
Digest of the Mentally Retarded
Education and Training of the Mentally Retarded
Education of the Visually Handicapped
Exceptional Children
Exceptional Child Education Abstracts
Exceptional Parent
Focus on Exceptional Children
Gifted Child Quarterly
Gifted Pupil
Hearing and Speech Action
International Journal for the Education of the Blind

Journal of Learning Disabilities
Journal of Mental Deficiency Research
Journal of Special Education
Journal of Speech and Hearing Disorders
Journal of Speech and Hearing Research
Language, Speech and Hearing Services in Schools
Learning Disorders
Mental Retardation
Mental Retardation Abstracts
New Outlook for the Blind
Sight Saving Review
Special Education
Teacher of the Blind
Teaching Exceptional Children
Training School Bulletin
Volta Review

READING

American Journal of Optometry
Elementary English
English Journal
Initial Teaching Alphabet Bulletin
Journal of the Association for the Study of Perception
Journal of Reading
Journal of Reading Behavior

Journalism Quarterly
Reading Horizons
Reading Improvement
Reading Quarterly
Reading Research Quarterly
Reading Teacher
Reading World

RESOURCES OF THE FEDERAL GOVERNMENT FOR EDUCATIONAL RESEARCH

The federal government has encouraged, promoted, and supported educational activity since the beginning of the nineteenth century. Grants of public land, monetary appropriations, the establishment of special educational institutions, advisory services, dissemination of information, and loans and grants to institutions and individuals have all played an important part in the development of the American educational enterprise.

It has been relatively recently that the federal government has assumed responsibility for the support of educational research. The Eighty-third Congress enacted the Cooperative Research Act of 1954, but allocated no funds. It became operative in 1957, when congress appropriated a little more than one million dollars to improve education through research. The grants of supporting funds to individual colleges and universities, state departments of education, and local school systems provided tangible evidence of congressional awareness of the possible contribution of research to the improvement of education.

Rather than setting up agencies to carry on the needed research, the government entered cooperative agreements, providing funds to those educators who were committed to research and competent to conduct it. By 1960 the appropriations had been increased to 10 million dollars, and by 1966, to more than 100 million.

Although many sources of aid to educational research are scattered throughout various federal agencies, the primary responsibility for the administration of most of the funds lies within the National Institute of Education. Some of the other agencies administering research programs are the National Science Foundation; the Department of the Navy; the Social and Rehabilitation Service; the Office of Manpower, Automation and Training of the Department of Labor; the Office of Economic Opportunity; the Public Health Service; and the Department of Defense. A number of major legislative acts authorized and provided funds for educational research activity.

In 1965 a presidential task force took a critical look at the program of federally supported educational research. The committee approved of much that had been accomplished, but pointed out that there were a number of deficiencies:

1. The individual projects that had been submitted did not provide a coordinated approach to the solution of educational problems.

2. The dissemination of research findings was ineffective.

3. There was an apparent gap between research findings and their implementation. The committee recommended that human resources for research and development should be expanded by establishing training programs for developing research talent, and by utilizing the possible contributions of agencies and institutions previously not eligible for support.

These recommendations were implemented in 1966 by the creation of three new agencies:

1. Research and Development Centers

2. Regional Educational Laboratories

3. Educational Resources Information Centers.

Research and Development Centers

Each center, located at a host university which directs its operations, focuses professional and financial resources on basic research, development when appropriate, and dissemination of research findings and products in a specialized problem area. These centers were established at institutions with the necessary interdisciplinary resources of established staff and experience. In one of the R and D centers, 25 professors, 50 other professionals, and a supporting secretarial staff, representing 13 academic departments of the university, combined their efforts in experimentation, replication of experiments in additional settings, and large-scale field testing. In 1979, there were nine research and development centers.

Center for Educational Policy and Management
University of Oregon, Eugene, Oregon

Center for Educational Research
Stanford University, Palo Alto, California

Center for Social Organization of Schools
Johns Hopkins University, Baltimore, Maryland

Center for the Study of Evaluation
University of California, Los Angeles, California

Learning Research and Development Center
University of Pittsburgh, Pittsburgh, Pennsylvania

National Center for Higher Education Management Systems
Boulder, Colorado

National Center for Research in Vocational Education
Ohio State University, Columbus, Ohio

Research and Development Center for Teacher Education
University of Texas, Austin, Texas

Wisconsin Research and Development Center for Individualized Schooling
University of Wisconsin, Madison, Wisconsin

Regional Educational Laboratories

These laboratories, oriented toward applied research derived primarily from regional problems, emphasize development and dissemination of research findings. Each laboratory, established as a nonprofit corporation not affiliated with a university, serves a particular geographic area, working with school systems, state educational agencies, and other organizations to promote and evaluate changes and innovations in teacher preparation, to disseminate promising educational programs, and to provide consultant services. In 1979, there were eight regional laboratories.

Appalachia Educational Laboratory AEL
Charleston, West Virginia

Central Midwest Regional Educational Laboratory CEMREL
St. Louis, Missouri

Far West Laboratory for Educational Research and Development FWL
San Francisco, California

Mid-Continent Regional Educational Laboratory MCREL
Kansas City, Missouri

North West Regional Educational Laboratory NWREL
Portland, Oregon

Research for Better Schools RBS
Philadelphia, Pennsylvania

South West Educational Development Laboratory SEDL
Austin, Texas

South West Regional Laboratory for Educational Research and Development SWRL
Los Alamitos, California

Educational Resources Information Centers (ERIC)

The third type of agency, and one of the most successful, provided a network of specialized clearinghouses, designed to bring research findings and research-related information to teachers, administrators, researchers, and the public. Located at universities or other host organizations, each center was designated as a specialized information source, selecting, cataloging, indexing, and abstracting research information to be transmitted to the central ERIC agency in Washington. Sixteen ERIC centers currently provide these services:

Adult career and vocational education
Ohio State University
Columbus, Ohio 43216

Early childhood education
University of Illinois
Urbana, Illinois 61801

Educational management	**Reading and communication skills**
University of Oregon Eugene, Oregon 97403	National Council of Teachers of English Urbana, Illinois 61801
Handicapped and gifted children	**Rural education and small schools**
The Council for Exceptional Children Reston, Virginia 22091	New Mexico University Las Cruces, New Mexico 88003
Higher education	**Science, mathematics, and environmental education**
George Washington University Washington, D.C. 20036	Ohio State University Columbus, Ohio 43216
Information resources	**Social studies/social science education**
Syracuse University Syracuse, New York 13210	Social Science Education Consortium Boulder, Colorado 80302
Junior colleges	**Teacher education**
University of California at Los Angeles Los Angeles, California 90024	American Association of Colleges for Teacher Education DuPont Circle, Washington, D.C. 20036
Languages and linguistics	**Tests, measurement, and evaluation**
Center for Applied Linguistics Arlington, Virginia 22209	Educational Testing Service Princeton, New Jersey 08540
Counseling and personnel services	**Urban education**
University of Michigan Ann Arbor, Michigan 48109	Teachers College, Columbia University New York City, New York 10027

The Central Educational Resources Information Agency

The central agency, located at Washington, D.C. provides the following services:

1. Publishes *Resources in Education,* a monthly abstract journal that includes résumés of research documents disseminated by the ERIC clearinghouses.

2. Contracts for the publication of *Current Index to Journals in Education,* providing a complete guide to periodic literature in more than 700

educational and education-related journals. More than 20,000 articles are indexed annually.

3. Contracts for the publication of the *Thesaurus of ERIC Descriptors,* a definitive vocabulary of educational terms, using the subject headings used for indexing and retrieval of documents in the ERIC collection.

4. Contracts for the reproduction and distribution of ERIC documents, available in paper copy or in microfiche form. These reproduced materials are available at a reasonable cost from:

ERIC Document Reproduction Service
P.O. Box 190
Arlington, Virginia 22210

5. Publishes an annual directory of more than 570 organizations that regularly receive monthly shipments of ERIC microfiche. Most of these agencies are university or public libraries, state departments of education, ERIC clearing houses, foundations, or specialized institutes, not only in the United States but in many foreign countries.

The National Institute of Education

The National Institute of Education was established by an act of Congress in 1972 "to support the policy of providing an equal educational opportunity of high quality to every person, regardless of race, color, religion, sex, national origin, or social class." Recognizing the primary role of the states and local governments, the federal government accepted the responsibility for providing leadership in the conduct and support of educational research. The legislation stated four objectives of the Institute:

1. To help to solve or alleviate the problems and achieve the objectives of American education

2. To advance the practice of education as an art, science, and profession

3. To strengthen the scientific and technological foundations of education

4. To build an effective educational research and development system.

Within the National Institute of Education, the *Office of Research Grants* was established to respond to all of these objectives, particularly to strengthen the scientific and technological foundations of education. Handicapped by organizational problems and inadaquate congressional appropriations, it was apparent that the Institute had not realized the expectations of many of its proponents.

In March 1975, a committee of ten prominent educators completed a study of the operations of the Institute. Among their conclusions, several are listed here:[3]

1. The objectives of the agency are too broadly conceived and should be more sharply defined.

2. The relationship between the NIE and the Department of Health, Education and Welfare needs to be improved.

3. Too few individuals are involved in educational research and development activities. Efforts should be made to involve state and local agencies, and the participation of women and members of minority groups.

4. The present existing Regional Laboratories and Research and Development Centers should be reduced in number to not more than six to eight strong agencies.

5. The National Institute of Education should provide a greater sense of direction and more effectively monitor the activities of the laboratories and centers.

The committee endorsed the potential role of the National Institute of Education as an effective agency and, paralleling the National Institutes of Health, trusted that it would eventually provide a much more effective vehicle for the promotion and dissemination of educational research and development than the uncoordinated efforts of the agencies that had previously attempted to attain this objective.

Seeking Research Fund Support

Since policies change from year to year, it would not be practicable to suggest procedures for applying for a research grant from the National Institute of Education. Periodically, the agency selects a focus for research activity and has a general pattern of procedures to be followed:

1. A prospectus must be submitted for preliminary consideration for a grant.

[3] *Research and Development Funding Policies of the National Institute of Education: Review and Recommendations* (Washington, D.C.: Department of Health, Education and Welfare, August 1975).

2. To those submitting proposals, after evaluation of the preliminary prospectus, an invitation to submit a formal research proposal may be extended.

The process is highly competitive, for funds are limited. In 1972, 203 research grants were made from more than 4,000 proposals.

For colleges and universities, public or private agencies, organizations, groups, or individuals that seek grant support, application forms should be obtained from The Office of Research Grants, Proposal Clearinghouse, National Institute of Education, 1832 M Street, Washington, D.C., 20208.

The United States Department of Education In 1979, by an act of the Congress of the United States, the Department of Education was established. Formerly known as the United States Office of Education, a division of the Department of Health, Education and Welfare, the new department head is The Secretary of Education, a member of the President's Cabinet.

SUMMARY

Practically all human knowledge can be found in libraries. Both the professional worker and the graduate student should be familiar with the library's many facilities and services.

The extensive resources of the federal government involved in generating, gathering, and disseminating educational research studies have been described. The *Research and Development Centers,* the *Regional Laboratories,* and the *Educational Resources Information Centers* and their publications are probably the best available sources of information on educational research.

An extensive list of reference materials has been presented, including many more than a student could remember. The course instructor may wish to indicate those that he or she feels are most important. The author trusts that this chapter will provide a convenient and useful source of references when the need arises.

EXERCISES

Reference Exercise

Choose the most likely source for the following information from the list of references that follow:

number

1. A recently completed educational research project   ____
2. List of encyclopedias published in several languages   ____
3. All books on research in a particular library   ____
4. Cost of school building construction in 1975   ____
5. Book reviews on *Jaws*   ____
6. Superintendent of schools at Davenport, Iowa   ____
7. Summary of recent research on spelling   ____
8. A more appropriate word than you have in mind   ____
9. Birth date of the author of a particular book   ____
10. World record for the mile run   ____
11. Chemistry teaching requirements in Iowa   ____
12. Author, publisher, and price of a particular book   ____
13. Teacher liability for a playground accident   ____
14. President of the Illinois Educational Association   ____
15. Biographical sketch of Henry Kissinger   ____
16. Concise history and campus facilities of a college   ____
17. Divorce data for the United States in 1974   ____
18. Faculty rank of a faculty member at Duke University   ____
19. Information on the University of Copenhagen   ____
20. Articles on the Strategic Air Defense   ____
21. Autobiographical sketch of Senator Tower   ____
22. Quotations that deal with trees   ____
23. Computer printout of abstracts on ability grouping   ____
24. Listing of all books published in the English language   ____
25. Articles on homework in professional journals   ____
26. Summary of research on reading   ____
27. A Purdue master's thesis on administrator characteristics   ____
28. Information about a not-too-prominent educator   ____
29. Articles on computer-assisted instruction   ____
30. Definition of the term *core curriculum*   ____
31. Secretary of State under President Woodrow Wilson   ____
32. Up-to-date evaluation of *World Book Encyclopedia*   ____
33. Critical evaluation of the *Kuder Preference Record*   ____
34. A Syracuse University dissertation on merit rating   ____
35. Articles on academic dishonesty   ____
36. Concise information on Roman mythology   ____
37. Proper footnote form   ____
38. Date of the *Andrea Doria* disaster   ____
39. A chronology of events for 1975   ____
40. Enrollment of Temple University   ____
41. History of the word *sheriff*   ____

number

42. List of articles on co-insurance   ———
43. Honorary degrees held by Henry Kissinger   ———
44. Word opposite in meaning to *duplicity*   ———
45. List of articles on steel tempering   ———
46. Illinois tax on gasoline   ———
47. Expert evaluation of a recently published dictionary   ———
48. Information about Simon Vetch, revolutionary war personality   ———
49. Information about the Ford Foundation   ———
50. List of articles on Robert Frost   ———
51. Concise article on computers   ———
52. Article in a publication not available in a local library   ———
53. References on the middle school   ———
54. Price of a U.S. government pamphlet on classroom discipline   ———
55. Information about the Milwaukee City library   ———
56. University of Wisconsin dissertation on labor history   ———
57. Information about the author of a recently published book   ———
58. Articles on home nursing care   ———

List of References

1. Air University Library Index
2. Almanac: World/Information Please
3. American Library Directory
4. American Universities and Colleges
5. Applied Science and Technology Index
6. Bartlett's Familiar Quotations
7. Biography Index
8. Black's Law Dictionary
9. Books in Print
10. Book Review Digest
11. Book Review Index
12. Mental Measurements Yearbook
13. Business Periodicals Index
14. Card Catalogue/Index
15. College Blue Book
16. College/University Catalog/Bulletin
17. Contemporary Authors
18. Corpus Juris Secundum
19. Cumulative Book Index
20. Cumulated Index Medicus
21. Cumulative Index to Nursing Literature
22. Current Biography
23. Current Index to Journals in Education
24. Dictionary of American Biography
25. Dictionary of Education
26. Dictionary of Occupational Titles
27. Digest of Educational Statistics
28. Dissertation Abstracts International
29. Documentation in Education
30. Education Index
31. Encyclopedia of Associations
32. Encyclopedia of Educational Research
33. Encyclopedia Americana/Britannica
34. Foundations Directory
35. Guide to Graduate Study
36. Handbook of Research on Teaching
37. Home Book of Quotations
38. Index to Legal Periodicals

39. International Handbook of Universities
40. Journal of Educational Research
41. Journal of Experimental Education
42. Master's Theses in Education
43. NEA Handbook of Local, State, and National Associations
44. National Tape Recording Catalogue
45. New Serial Titles
46. New York Times Index
47. Oxford English Dictionary
48. Patterson's American Education
49. Price List #31, USOE
50. Personality Tests and Reviews
51. Psychological Abstracts
52. Readers' Guide to Periodic Literature
53. Research Studies in Education
54. Resources in Education
55. Review of Educational Research
56. Roget's Thesaurus
57. School Research Information Service (SRIS)
58. Sociological Abstracts
59. Social Sciences Index
60. Statistical Abstract of the United States
61. Standard Periodicals Directory
62. Subject Guide to Books in Print
63. Twenty Thousand Words
64. Union List of Serials
65. USOE Directory
66. Vertical File Index
67. Webster's Biographical Dictionary
68. Who's Who in America
69. Who Was Who
70. Who's Who in American Education
71. Woelner and Wood: Requirements for Certification
72. World Yearbook of Education

BIBLIOGRAPHY

A Bibliography of Publications About the Educational Resources Information Center. Washington, D.C.: National Institute of Education, 1978.

Funding Opportunities of the National Institute of Education. Washington, D.C.: National Institute of Education, 1979.

Grants for Research on Law and Government in Education. Washington, D.C.: National Institute of Education, 1979.

Guide to Federal Funding in Career Education, Education and Work, and Vocational Education. Washington, D.C.: National Institute of Education, 1978.

How to Use ERIC. Washington, D.C.: National Institute of Education, 1979.

HOWE, HAROLD, "Two Views of the New Department of Education and Its First Secretary: I," *Phi Delta Kappan* 61 (March 1980): 446–447.

National Institute of Education: Summary of the Reorganization Plan. Washington, D.C.: National Institute of Education, 1978.

1979 Guide to Office of Education Programs. Washington, D.C.: National Institute of Education, 1979.

Preliminary Research Plans for Fiscal Year 1979. Washington, D.C.: National Institute of Education, 1978.

Publications and Papers. Washington, D.C.: National Institute of Education, 1979.

Reflections and Recommendations. Fourth Annual Report of the Council on Educational Research. Washington, D.C.: National Institute of Education, 1978.

Research and Development Centers and Regional Educational Laboratories. Washington, D.C.: National Institute of Education, 1979.

Submitting Documents to ERIC. Washington, D.C.: National Institute of Education, 1979.

WYNN, RICHARD, "Two Views of the New Department of Education and Its First Secretary: II," *Phi Delta Kappan* 61 (March 1980): 447–448.

TEN

The

Research Report

Although research reports may differ considerably in scope of treatment, they are expected to follow a similar pattern of style and form that has become conventional in academic circles. These matters of style and form may seem unduly arbitrary to the student. However, they are based upon principles of clarity of organization and presentation, and it is essential that graduate students in education be familiar with them if they are to communicate their ideas effectively.

STYLE MANUALS

Some graduate schools or departments have designated an official manual, or have established their own style manual, to which their theses or dissertations must conform. Students should find out which manual has been adopted officially by their institution or department. Beginning graduate students are disturbed when they discover that these manuals are not always in complete agreement on matters of typography or format. Careful examination, however, will reveal the fact that differences concern minor details. In general, they are in basic agreement on principles of correct presentation.

Regardless of which manual is used as a guide, it should be followed consistently in matters of form and style. The presentation of this chapter is consistent with one of the widely used form and style manuals.

FORMAT OF THE RESEARCH REPORT

The research report, whether it be a thesis, dissertation, or a shorter term paper or report, usually follows a fairly standardized pattern. The following outline presents the usual sequence of topics:

A. Preliminary Section or Front Matter
   1. Title Page
   2. Acknowledgment (if any)
   3. Table of Contents
   4. List of Tables (if any)
   5. List of Figures (if any)
B. Main Body of the Report
   1. Introduction

a. Statement of the problem—specific questions to be answered—hypotheses to be tested
b. Significance of the problem
c. Purposes of the study
d. Assumptions, limitations, and delimitations
e. Definition of important terms
2. Review of Related Literature or Analysis of Previous Research
3. Design of the Study
   a. Procedures used
   b. Sources of data
   c. Methods of gathering data
   d. Description of data-gathering instruments used
4. Presentation and Analysis of Data
   a. Text
   b. Tables
   c. Figures
5. Summary and Conclusions
   a. Restatement of the problem
   b. Description of procedures used
   c. Principal findings and conclusions
   d. Recommendations for further research
C. Reference Section
   1. Bibliography
   2. Appendix

Preliminary Section

The first page of the report is the title page. Although title page forms differ from one institution to another, they usually include: (1) the name of the topic, (2) the name of the author, (3) the relationship of the report to a course or degree requirement, (4) the name of the institution where the report is to be submitted, and (5) the date of presentation.

The title should be concise and should indicate clearly the purposes of the study. One should keep in mind its possible usefulness to the reader who may scan a bibliography in which it may be listed. The title should not claim more for the study than it actually delivers. It should not be stated so broadly that it seems to provide an answer that cannot be generalized, either from the data gathered or from the methodology employed. For example, if a simple descriptive self-concept study were made of a group of children enrolled in a particular inner-city elementary school, the title should not read, "The Self-Concepts of Inner-City Children." A more appropriate title would be "The Self-Concepts of a Group of Philadelphia Inner-City Children."

The title should be typed in capital letters, single-spaced, and centered between the right and left margins of the page. Where more than

THE ATTITUDES OF A GROUP OF FIFTH GRADE TEACHERS
TOWARD THE WEEKDAY RELIGIOUS
EDUCATION PROGRAM

BY
MARY L. PORTER

A Term Report Submitted in Partial Fulfillment
of the Requirements in

Education 548: Introduction to Research

College of Education
BUTLER UNIVERSITY

June 6, 1980

Fig. 10-1. Title page

one line is required, the words in the title are divided into lines so that each successive line is shorter than the one above it and is centered below it in an inverted pyramid style. This format is also used for table titles. Figure 10-1 illustrates a sample page used for a research report, submitted in partial fulfillment of the requirements of a course.

An acknowledgment page is included if the writer has received unusual assistance in the conduct of the study. If used, acknowledgments should be simple and restrained. Flattery and effusive recognition for routine participation by members of the writer's family, faculty advisors, librarians, and clerical helpers are considered unnecessary and in poor taste.

Table of contents. A good table of contents serves an important purpose in providing an outline of the contents of the report. The relationship between principal and minor divisions is indicated by capitalization of chapter numbers and titles, with subheadings in small letters and with capitalized principal letters. Page references for each topic are indicated.

List of tables and figures. If tables and figures are included in this report, a separate page is included for each list. The full titles of figures and tables, worded exactly as they appear in the text, are presented with corresponding numbers and page locations.

All pages in the preliminary section are numbered at the center of the bottom margin with lower-case Roman numerals (i, ii, iii, iv).

The Main Body of the Report[1]

This section may be divided into five divisions. In a thesis or a dissertation these divisions may comprise chapters. In a shorter term paper or report, they may consist of sections appropriately set off by centered headings.

1. The first section serves as an introduction to the area of consideration. A clear statement of the problem with specific questions to be answered or hypothesis to be tested is presented first. A consideration of the significance of the problem and its historical background is also appropriate. Specific purposes of the study are described, and all assumptions, limitations, and delimitations are recognized. All important terms are carefully defined, so that the reader may understand the concepts underlying the development of the investigation.

2. The second section reviews the important literature related to the study. Previous research studies are abstracted, and significant writ-

---

[1] Compare this outline of the main body of the report with the suggested format of the research proposal in Chapter Two.

ings of authorities in the area under study are reviewed. This part of the research report provides a background for the development of the present study and brings the reader up to date. Since good research is based upon everything that is known about a problem, this part of the report gives evidence of the investigator's knowledge of the field. A brief summary, indicating areas of agreement or disagreement in findings, or gaps in existing knowledge, should be included.

3. The third section explains the design of the study in detail. The size of the samples and how they are selected, the variables and the controls employed, the sources and methods of gathering data, the reliability of instruments selected or constructed, and the statistical procedures used in the analysis are carefully described.

4. Section four includes the presentation and analysis of the data. This is the heart of the research report. Through textual discussion and tabular and graphic devices, the data are critically analyzed and reported. Tables and figures are used to clarify significant relationships. Good tables and figures are constructed and titled so that they are self-explanatory. Textual discussion may be used to point out generalizations and significant interpretations, but not to restate the information that they have presented. Good tables and figures are relatively simple, pointing up one or two significant relationships. If complex tables are developed, they should be placed in the appendix.

5. The fifth section consists of a summary. After a brief statement of the problem and a description of the procedures used in the investigation, the findings and conclusions are presented. Findings are statements of factual information based upon the data analysis. Conclusions are answers to the questions raised, or the statements of acceptance or rejection of the hypotheses proposed.

The summary is probably the most difficult section of the report to write. Beginning researchers are sometimes guilty of overgeneralizing on the basis of their limited data. There is a temptation to write persuasively, to mount the soapbox. Previously held convictions, not tested by the analysis, creep into the discussion. The course instructor often has to comment, "Your study to this point has been good. Your summary is disappointing. What you have reported may possibly be true, but there is nothing in your study to justify or support your conclusions."

It is essential that the researcher cultivate the skepticism and the modesty of the scientist. These qualities of scholarly restraint are evidences of the objectivity of scientific analysis and good research reporting.

It may be appropriate in concluding this part of the report to indicate promising side-problems that have been uncovered and to suggest areas or problems for further investigation.

TABLE OF CONTENTS

Fig. 10-2. Table of Contents page

iv

v

Fig. 10-3. List of Tables and List of Figures pages

379

The summary section is the most used part of the research report. Readers who scan research literature to find significant studies examine this section before deciding whether or not further examination of the report is worthwhile.

Reference Materials

The bibliography is preceded by a sheet containing the word BIBLI-OGRAPHY, capitalized and centered on the page. The first page of the bibliography has the center title BIBLIOGRAPHY. References are arranged in alphabetical order, the last name of the author listed first. Each entry is placed flush with the left margin of the page, and subsequent lines are single-spaced and indented five spaces. A double space separates entries. If no author name is given, the name of the publication or the sponsoring organization is listed as the author.

In a short bibliography, books, pamphlets, monographs, and periodical references may be combined in the same list. If the number of references is large, the bibliography may be divided into sections, one for books, one for periodicals, and possibly one for special documents. Ordinarily, a selected bibliography is preferable to an exhaustive list. An annotation, or short statement giving the reader a clear idea of the nature of the reference and the topics that it covers, adds an important quality of usefulness to the bibliography. The annotating statement should be single-spaced, but separated from the bibliographic entry by a double space.

King, Edmund J. <u>Other Schools and Ours</u>. 4th ed. New York: Holt, Rinehart & Winston, 1973. 360 pp.

An interesting and perceptive analysis of school systems in Denmark, France, Great Britain, the United States, the Soviet Union, India, and Japan. The interaction of cultural influences and education is emphasized.

The appendix is preceded by a sheet containing the word APPEN-DIX, capitalized and centered on the page. The first page of the appendix is titled APPENDIX A, and pages are numbered serially, using Arabic numerals. Tables and data—important, but not essential to the understanding of the report—copies of cover letters used, and printed forms of questionnaires, tests, and other data-gathering devices may be placed in the appendix. Each separate entry heading is listed as APPENDIX A, APPENDIX B, etc.

In mounting pictures, standard forms, and other materials on the manuscript sheet, stationers' rubber cement should be used. The materials to be joined should each be coated and allowed to dry before being pressed together. The result will be a permanent bond that will not cause the paper to wrinkle.

STYLE OF WRITING

The research report should be presented in a style that is creative, clear, and concise. Although the phraseology should be dignified and straightforward, it need not be dull or pedantic. Even the most profound ideas can best be explained in simple language and short, coherent sentences.

Slang, hackneyed or flippant phrases, and folksy style should be avoided. Since objectivity is the primary goal, there should be no element of exhortation or persuasion. The research report should describe and explain, rather than try to convince or move to action. In this respect the research report differs from the essay or the feature article.

In the interests of objectivity, the personal pronouns, I, we, you, my, our, and us should not be used. These personal pronouns can be avoided by the use of such expressions as "the investigator" or "the researcher." Instead of saying, "I selected ten students from each class," the passive voice construction would be preferable—"Ten students were selected from each class."

Only the last names of cited authorities are used. Titles such as professor, Dr., Mr., and Dean are omitted. The past tense should be used in describing research procedures that have been completed.

Abbreviations may be used in footnotes, tables, and figures, but they should not be used in the text of the report. A few such exceptions as IQ, PTA, NEA are appropriate, but if there is any doubt, words should be spelled out.

Discussion of quantitative terms. *Few* in number, *less* in quantity are the preferred forms of expression. Numbers beginning a sentence should always be spelled out. Fractions, round numbers, and numbers under 100 should be spelled out, except when they are combined. Use one-half, but 4½ or 4.5. Per cent (meaning per hundred) is spelled out except in tables and figures. Use Arabic numerals with per cent (18 per cent), unless they begin a sentence. Percentage means proportion. In numbers with more than three digits, commas should point off thousands or millions (1,324; 12,304,000).

Ordinarily, standard statistical formulas are not presented in the research report, nor are computations included. If a rather unusual formula is used in the analysis it is appropriate to include it.

Correct Usage

Of course, the ordinary rules of correct usage should prevail. A good dictionary, a spelling guide,[2] a handbook of style,[3,4] and Roget's Thesaurus are helpful references.

The author has noted frequent errors of spelling and agreement between subject and predicate, nonparallel construction, and inconsistent tense sequence. Students who have difficulty in written expression should have a competent friend or relative proofread their copy for correct usage before they type the final manuscript. Inability to write correctly is a serious limitation. Carelessness is an even greater fault.

Effective research report writing is not an easy task. Good reports are not written hurriedly. Even skillful and experienced writers revise many times before they submit a manuscript for publication.

TYPING THE REPORT

Many students type their own term papers or research reports. Anyone with reasonable proficiency and a willingness to learn proper procedures can do an acceptable job. In fact, typing a report is an excellent way to really learn proper form.

Typographical standards for the thesis or dissertation are more exacting. Strikeovers, crossovers, insertions, and erasures are not permitted. Therefore, only typists with great proficiency should attempt to prepare thesis or dissertation copy. Although the expense of professional typing may seem high, the saving of time and excessive effort usually make this arrangement the wiser choice.

It is the writer's responsibility to present manuscript material to the professional typist in proper form. Except for minor typographical matters, the correction of major errors is not the responsibility of the typist. After the material is received from the typist, the student should proofread it carefully before it is turned in.

Typography

1. Good quality of bond, 8½ by 11 inches in size, of 13- to 16-pound weight, should be used for the original and first carbon copy of the thesis or dissertation. A lighter paper may be used for additional copies. For the term paper

---

[2] Twenty Thousand Words (New York: McGraw Hill Book Co., 1951).

[3] William G. Campbell and Stephen V. Ballou. Form and Style for Theses, Reports, Term Papers (Boston: Houghton Mifflin Co., 1974).

[4] Kate Turabian. A Manual for Writers of Term Papers, Theses and Dissertations (Chicago: University of Chicago Press, (1973).

any bond paper is acceptable. Only one side of the sheet is used in typewritten manuscript.

2. Pica type, with ten spaces to the inch, is preferred to elite, which has twelve. The type must be clean, and a medium-inked black ribbon should be used. It is surprising what a new typewriter ribbon and clean type will do to produce effective copy. (Scotch Brand typewriter cleaner or an old toothbrush and some lighter fluid will remove lint and ink particles from the type.) Medium-weight, black carbon paper should be used for the copies. Carbon paper should be replaced often enough to insure clear and even copies. Special symbols not available on the typewriter keyboard should be carefully inserted, using black India ink.

3. To facilitate the proper placement of copy on the page a guide sheet may be constructed, showing the proper margins, the center of the copy portion, and the number of lines from the top and bottom margins. This sheet should be ruled in black ink and placed beneath the first sheet, so that the markings show through. The use of the guide sheet takes much of the guesswork out of copy placement. (See Figure 10-4.) Also helpful is Multicopy carbon paper, which has in the margin a numbered scale representing single-spaced lines.

4. The right margin should be one inch, the top margin 1¼ inches, the bottom margin 1½ inches, and the left margin 1½ inches.

5. Textual material should be double-spaced. Long lists of materials may be single-spaced.

6. Paragraphs should be indented seven spaces for pica type, nine for elite.

7. Words should not be divided at the end of the line, unless completing them would definitely interfere with the margin. A few spaces runover is preferable. In dividing words, consult a dictionary for correct syllabication.

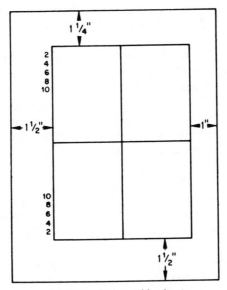

Fig. 10-4. Typing guide sheet

8. Direct quotations not over three typewritten lines in length are included in the text and are enclosed in quotation marks. Quotations of more than three lines are set off from the text in a single-spaced paragraph and indented four spaces from both left and right margins without quotation marks. Original paragraph indentations are retained.
9. The superscript is ordinarily placed at the end of the sentence of quoted material. Where several references are mentioned in one sentence, the superscript is placed after each name reference (Smith,[1] Jones,[2] and Brown[3] reported their findings).

FOOTNOTES

Footnotes serve a number of purposes. They enable writers to substantiate their presentation by citations of other authorities, to give credit to sources of material that they have quoted or paraphrased, and to provide the reader with specific sources that he or she may use to verify the authenticity and accuracy of material used.

Occasionally, in research report writing, the footnote is used to present explanatory statements that, although important, would interfere with the logic and continuity of textual material. In serving these purposes footnotes are very useful devices. They should be used sparingly, however, and never included for the mere purpose of scholarly appearance.

Footnote citations may be inserted in parentheses at the end of the sentence. For example, (18:42) indicates that the citation refers to bibliography listing number 18, page 42. In another procedure all of the citations are placed on one page at the end of the chapter. Each institution or department usually specifies the type of footnote citation permitted or recommended.

Traditionally, footnote citations are placed at the bottom of the page, and are separated from the text by a two-inch horizontal line drawn from the left margin, one double space below the last line of the text. The reference superscript is placed one-half space below the dividing line, the first footnote one line below the dividing line. Each footnote reference is indented the customary number of spaces. If there is a second line in the citation, it is flush with the left margin.

Footnotes are single-spaced, with double spacing between citations. Footnotes are numbered consecutively within a chapter, or consecutively within the entire report if chapter headings are not used.

In consecutive footnote reference the abbreviation Ibid. (Latin, *the same*) may be used. If the page reference is different, the new page citation follows:

[3] Fred N. Kerlinger, Foundations of Behavioral Research (New York: Holt, Rinehart & Winston, 1973), p. 217.

[4] *Ibid.* (indicates same page as previous reference)

[5] *Ibid.*, p. 232. (same work, but a different page)

When references to the same work occur within a page or two, op. cit. (Latin, *the work cited*) may be used, always with the surname of the author and the page reference. Op. cit. is used when another reference intervenes.

[1] Clinton I. Chase, Elementary Statistical Procedures (New York: McGraw-Hill Book Co., 1967), 13.

[2] Philip H. DuBois, An Introduction to Psychological Statistics (New York: Harper & Row, 1965), 24.

[3] Chase, *op. cit.,* 34.

When a second but nonconsecutive reference follows, referring to the same work and same page previously cited, loc. cit. may be used. Again the author's surname must be included.

DuBois, *loc. cit.* (This reference is to page 24.)

Abbreviations

In bibliography or footnote references, abbreviations may be used to conserve space. Students should be familiar with the following standard abbreviations:

art., arts	article, articles
bk., bks.	book, books
c. *(circa)*	about (approximate date)
cf.	compare
chap., chaps.	chapter, chapters
col., cols.	column, columns
div., divs.	division, divisions
ed., eds.	editor, editors
ed., eds.	edition, editions
et al.	and others
e.g.	for example
et seq.	and the following
f., ff.	and the following
fig., figs.	figure, figures
ibid.	same reference
idem.	same person
i.e.	that is
illus.	illustrated
infra.	below
l., ll.	line, lines
loc. cit.	the place cited
mimeo.	mimeographed
ms.	manuscript
n.d.	no date given
n.n.	no name given
n.p.	no place given
no., nos.	number, numbers
op. cit.	previously cited

p., pp.	page, pages
par., pars.	paragraph, paragraphs
<u>passim</u>	here and there (scattered)
pt., pts.	part, parts
rev.	revised
sec., secs.	section, sections
<u>sic.</u>	thus
<u>supra.</u>	above
trans.	translated
<u>vide.</u>	see
vol., vols.	volume, volumes
(. . .)	omissions in quoted matter up to one paragraph in length—(for a full paragraph or more omitted, use a full line of alternating periods and spaces).

(All Latin abbreviations are underlined.)

BIBLIOGRAPHY AND FOOTNOTE FORM

The purpose of the bibliography is quite different from that of the footnote. The bibliography, located at the end of the main body of the report, lists in alphabetical order the references used by the writer in preparing the report. The footnotes, found at the bottom of the page, specifically cite the exact place where quoted or paraphrased materials may be found.

The typographical form of the bibliography listing and the footnote citation also differ. Note the following examples which illustrate the differences for a textbook reference:

Bibliography form:

Vaizey, John. <u>Education in the Modern World</u>. New York: McGraw-Hill Book Co., 1967.

Footnote form:

[1] John Vaizey, <u>Education in the Modern World</u> New York: McGraw-Hill Book Co., 1967.

Additional forms, both bibliography and footnote, most often used in educational writing are illustrated for each type of reference.

Joint Authors

Bibliography form:

Barzun, Jacques and Henry F. Graff. <u>The Modern Researcher</u>. New York: Harcourt, Brace Jovanovich, 1977.

Footnote form:

[1] Jacques Barzun and Henry F. Graff, <u>The Modern Researcher</u> (New York: Harcourt, Brace Jovanovich, 1977), p. 171.

TABLE I
A COMPARISON OF BIBLIOGRAPHY AND FOOTNOTE FORM

	Bibliography	*Footnote*
Indentation	overhanging—first line flush with margin, second line indented five spaces	[1] regular paragraph indentation
Name order	last name first (of first author when more than one author)	first name first
Placement	end of body of report—listed alphabetically by last name of first author	[1] bottom of page with superscript
Punctuation	Author name. Title. Place of publication: Publisher, date of publication.	[1] Author, Title (Place of publication: Publisher, date of publication).
Page reference	414 pp. (total number of pages in book or in article)	p. 23. (specific page location of reference)

More than Three Authors

Bibliography form:
Selltiz, Claire et al. Research Methods in Social Relations. (Rev. in one vol.) New York: Holt, Rinehart & Winston, 1959.
Footnote form:
[1] Claire Selltiz *et al.*, Research Methods in Social Relations (New York: Holt, Rinehart & Winston, 1959), p. 77.

Editor as Author

Bibliography form:
Buros, Oscar K., ed. The Eighth Mental Measurements Yearbook. Highland Park, N.J.: Gryphon Press, 1979.
Footnote form:
[1] Oscar K. Buros, ed., The Eighth Mental Measurements Yearbook (Highland Park, N.J.: Gryphon Press, 1979), p. 179.

Author not Given

Bibliography form:
Author's Guide. Englewood Cliffs, N.J.: Prentice-Hall, 1975.
Footnote form:
[1] Author's Guide (Englewood Cliffs, N.J.: Prentice-Hall, 1975), p. 23.

Publication of an Association, Agency, or Society

If all of the publication is devoted to one topic, treat it as a book. If the article is part of the publication, treat it as a periodical article. Either the name of the article or the name of the sponsoring organization may be listed first.

Bibliography form:

Modern Philosophies of Education. National Society for the Study of Education, Fifty-fourth Yearbook, Part I. Chicago: University of Chicago Press, 1955.

or

National Society for the Study of Education. Modern Philosophies of Education. Fifty-fourth Yearbook, Part I. Chicago: University of Chicago Press, 1955.

Footnote form:

[1] Modern Philosophies of Education, National Society for the Study of Education, Fifty-fourth Yearbook, Part I (Chicago: University of Chicago Press, 1955), p. 220. Quoted by permission of the Society.

This particular organization asks for the inclusion of "Quoted by permission of the Society." Some organizations and publishers request certain forms of acknowledgment when materials are quoted in the thesis, dissertation, or for a manuscript to be published in a book or periodical. For term papers, permission to quote is not necessary.

Part of a Series

Bibliography form:

Terman, Lewis M. and Melita H. Oden. The Gifted Child Grows Up. Vol. 4 of the Genetic Studies of Genius Series, Lewis M. Terman, ed. Stanford: Stanford University Press, 1947.

Footnote form:

[1] Lewis M. Terman and Melita H. Oden, The Gifted Child Grows Up, Vol. 4 of the Genetic Studies of Genius Series, Lewis M. Terman, ed. (Stanford: Stanford University Press, 1947), 7.

A Chapter Written by an Author Other than the Author or Editor of the Book

Bibliography form:

Maccoby, Eleanor E. and Nathan Maccoby, "The Interview: A Tool of Social Science," Chapter 12 in The Handbook of Social Psychology, Vol. 1, Gardner Lindzey, ed. Cambridge, MA.: Addison-Wesley, 1954.

Footnote form:
 [1] Eleanor E. Maccoby and Nathan Maccoby, "The Interview: A Tool of Social Science," Chapter 12 in The Handbook of Social Psychology, Vol. 1, Gardner Lindzey, ed. (Cambridge, MA.: Addison-Wesley, 1954), p. 451.

A Translation

Bibliography form:
Best, John W. Como Investigar en Educacion. Gonzalvo Mainar, trans. Madrid: Morata, 1967.
Footnote form:
 [1] John W. Best, Como Investigar en Educacion, Gonzalvo Mainar, trans. (Madrid: Morata, 1967), 74.

Article in an Encyclopedia

Bibliography form:
Banta, Richard E. "New Harmony." Encyclopædia Britannica (1968) 16: 305.
Footnote form:
 Richard E. Banta, "New Harmony," Encyclopædia Britannica (1968) 16: 305.

Periodical Article

For periodical references, the differences between bibliography and footnote forms are similar to those for book references. Note that the name of the article is enclosed in quotation marks and the name of the publication is underlined. There are a few slight punctuation differences.
Bibliography form:
Walsh, J. Hartt. "Education in 2,000 A.D." Nation's Schools 57 (April 1956), 47–51.
Footnote form:
 [1] J. Hartt Walsh, "Education in 2,000 A.D.," Nation's Schools 57 (April 1956), 47–51.

Quotation from a Primary Source that Cannot Be Located

When using a quotation from a primary source quoted by an author, try to find the original source and quote it directly. If you cannot locate it, quote it, using both primary and secondary references.

Bibliography form:

Kelly, Earl P. "Education for What Is Real." New York: Harper & Row, 1947. As cited by Edward A. Krug, Curriculum Planning. New York: Harper & Row, 1950, 55.

Footnote form:

Earl P. Kelly, "Education for What Is Real" (New York: Harper & Row, 1947). As cited by Edward A. Krug, Curriculum Planning (New York: Harper & Row, 1950), 55.

Newspaper Articles

Ordinarily newspaper items are not listed in the bibliography but they are cited in footnotes.

Footnote form:

[1] Editorial in The Indianapolis News, January 6, 1968.

[1] Associated Press Dispatch, The Milwaukee Journal, December 24, 1968, 1.

The Chicago Daily News, February 3, 1968, 6.

Unpublished Materials

Bibliography form:

Devoe, Donald B. Bibliography on Uses of High Speed Computers in Psychology. Medford, Mass.: Tufts University, Institute for Applied Experimental Psychology, 1957. 5 pp. (Mimeographed.)

Footnote form:

[1] Donald B. Devoe, Bibliography on Uses of High Speed Computers in Psychology (Medford, MA.: Tufts University, Institute for Applied Experimental Psychology, 1957) (mimeographed), 2.

Thesis or Dissertation

Bibliography form:

Best, John W. An Analysis of Certain Selected Factors Underlying the Choice of Teaching as a Profession. Unpublished Doctoral Dissertation, University of Wisconsin, Madison, 1948.

Footnote form:

[1] John W. Best, An Analysis of Certain Selected Factors Underlying the Choice of Teaching as a Profession (Unpublished Doctoral Dissertation, University of Wisconsin, Madison, 1948), 14.

Many dissertations are now reproduced in microfilm form.

Porter, Robert M. Relationship of Participation to Satisfaction in Small

Group Discussions. Doctoral Dissertation. Philadelphia: Temple University, 1955.
Abstract. Dissertation Abstracts 15: 2492–93; No. 12, 1955.

Speeches or statements made, but not published, are listed in the footnotes but not in the bibliography. When quoted in published reports,it is essential that the material be verified by the person who made the statement, and never used without his or her permission.

[1] Statement by Paul Butler, personal interview, January 17, 1980.

[1] Commencement address, Butler University, Indianapolis, Indiana, June 6, 1980.

Quotations from Letters

A letter is legally the property of the writer, not the recipient. When contents are quoted, the written permission of the writer or, if deceased, the permission of his or her heirs, is necessary.

[1] *Letter,* Henry R. Smith to Paul T. Jones, December 7, 1980.

HEADINGS

When the manuscript is divided into chapters, each chapter begins a new page. The word CHAPTER is capitalized, followed by a capitalized Roman numeral, centered and placed four spaces lower than the usual top line of the text. The chapter title is centered and capitalized, a double space below the heading. Textual material follows three spaces below the title.

A major division of a chapter or of a short term paper is introduced with a centered head written in full capitals. Textual materials that follow are placed three spaces below the centered head.

A subdivision of the section of the part of the discussion under the centered head is introduced by a freestanding side head, flush with the left margin. For further subdivision of the discussion, a paragraph side head is used, with the usual paragraph indentation.

CENTER HEAD (FULL CAPITALS)

_____

_____

Side Head (major words captitalized)

_____

_____

Paragraph side head. (only initial letter of first word capitalized)

_____

PAGINATION

Page numbers are assigned to each page of the paper or report. The title page or the initial page of a section (chapter, major subdivision, bibliography, or appendix) does not have a page number typed on it, but a number is allowed for it in the series.

Page numbers are placed in the upper right-hand corner, one inch below the top of the page and aligned with the right margin. Page numbers of the preliminary section of the manuscript use small or lowercase Roman numerals (i, ii, iii), beginning with the title page and ending with the last page preceding the main body of the paper. The page containing Chapter I is page 1, but has no number typed on it. However, the next page is page 2. The bibliography and appendix are numbered serially and consecutively, following the last chapter.

Since correct pagination depends upon the final edited copy, assigning page numbers should be the final step before putting the manuscript into the binder or folder. Preliminary page numbers can be lightly penciled in and changed if additions, deletions, or corrections are made.

TABLES

A table is a systematic method of presenting statistical data in vertical columns and horizontal rows, according to some classification of subject matter. Tables enable the reader to comprehend and interpret masses of data rapidly, and to grasp significant details and relationships at a glance. Tables and figures should be used sparingly; too many will overwhelm the reader.

Good tables are relatively simple, concentrating on a limited number of ideas. Including too much data in a table minimizes the value of tabular presentation. It is often advisable to use several tables rather than to include too many details in a single one. It has been said that the mark of a good table is its effectiveness in conveying ideas and relationships independently of the text of the report.

If a table is large enough to occupy more than a half-page, it should be placed on a page by itself, carefully centered for a balanced effect. If it is short, occupying less than a half-page, it may be placed on the page with texual material, preferably following as closely as possible the textual discussion that relates to it.

Text references should identify tables by number, rather than by such expressions as, "the table above," or "the following table." Tables should rarely be carried over to the second or third page. If the table must be continued, the headings should be repeated at the top of each column of data on each page.

Tables should not exceed the page size of the manuscript. Large tables that must be folded into the copy are always cumbersome, and cannot be easily refolded and replaced. Large tables should be reduced to manuscript page size by photostating or some other process of reproduction. Tables that are too wide for the page may be turned sidewise, with the top facing the left margin, or binding, of the manuscript.

The word TABLE is centered between the page margins and typed in capital letters, followed by the table number in capital Roman numerals. Tables are numbered consecutively throughout the entire report or thesis, including those tables that may be placed in the appendix. The caption or title is placed two spaces below the word TABLE, and arranged in inverted pyramid form. No terminal punctuation is used. The main title should be brief, clearly indicating the nature of the data presented. Occasionally a subtitle is used to supplement a briefer main title, denoting such additional information as sources of data and measuring units employed.

Because they are completely unnecessary, such expressions as "table showing," "distribution of," or "frequency of" should be avoided.

The top of the table is placed three spaces below the last line of the title. Column headings, or box heads, should be clearly labeled, describing the nature and units of measure of the data listed. Such terms as number, per cent, and frequency may be abbreviated by the use of No., %, and f. The percentage symbol (%) should be placed at the top of the column, not with the numbers in the table.

TABLE II
OCCUPATIONS OF FATHERS OF
UNIVERSITY OF WISCONSIN
SENIORS PREPARING TO
TEACH*

Occupations	*Men*		*Women*	
	No.	*%*	*No.*	*%#*
Business proprietor	24	23	32	29
Skilled labor	19	18	10	9
Farming	17	17	19	17
Clerical-sales	16	16	18	16
Profession	15	15	20	18
Unskilled labor	6	6	6	5
No data	5	5	7	6
Total	102	100	112	100

Percentages rounded to equal 100%.
* Adapted from John W. Best, An Analysis of Certain Selected Factors Underlying the Choice of Teaching as a Profession (Unpublished Doctoral Dissertation, University of Wisconsin, Madison, 1948), 47.

If numbers are shortened by the omission of zeros, that fact should be mentioned in the subtitle (in millions of dollars; in thousands of tons). The stub, or label, for the rows should be clear and concise, parallel in grammatical structure, and if possible, no longer than two lines.

Numerical data are usually arranged in descending order of magnitude or frequency, so that comparisons by position can be noted readily. If there are several columns in the table, the first column to the left is arranged in descending order. When data are presented by states, the material is sometimes listed alphabetically by state to facilitate location. Lines of tabular data are single-spaced. Rulings or lines are used only if they facilitate the reading of the table. Few horizontal lines are needed. Vertical lines at left and right margins are omitted.

Decimal points should always be aligned in the column. When no data are available for a particular cell, indicate the lack by a dash, rather than by a zero. Double horizontal lines are placed at the top of the table separating it from the title. A horizontal line is also placed at the bottom to separate the table from the material which follows, three spaces below.

When footnotes are needed to explain items in the table, small Arabic letters or typewriter key symbols are used. Numerical superscripts would be confused with the data contained in the table. Table footnotes are placed just below the table, rather than at the bottom of the page.

FIGURES

A figure is a device that presents statistical data in graphic form. The term figure is applied to a wide variety of graphs, charts, maps, sketches, diagrams, and drawings. When skillfully used, figures present aspects of data in a visualized form that may be clearly and easily understood. Figures should not be intended as substitutes for textual description, but included to emphasize certain significant relationships.

Many of the qualities that were listed as characteristics of good tables are equally appropriate when applied to figures.

1. The title should clearly describe the nature of the data presented.

2. Figures should be simple enough to convey a clear idea, and should be understandable without the aid of textual description.

3. Numerical data upon which the figure is based should be presented in an accompanying table, if they are not included in the figure itself.

4. Data should be presented carefully and accurately, so that oversimplification, misrepresentation, or distortion do not result.

5. Figures should be used sparingly. Too many figures detract from, rather than illuminate, the presentation.

6. Figures that occupy more than a half-page should be placed on a separate page. Those that are smaller and occupy less than a half-page may be placed on the same page as textual material.

7. Figures should follow, not precede, the related textual discussion.

8. Figures are referred to by number, never as "the figure above" or "the figure below."

9. Figures are numbered with Arabic rather than Roman numerals.

10. The title of the figure is placed below rather than above it.

There are several acceptable and frequently used title forms, any of which may be used if followed consistently throughout the report. A block form is illustrated here.

Figure 1. Absences of Students at Washington High During November, 1980.

The line graph

The line graph is useful in showing change in data relationships over a period of time. The horizontal axis usually measures the independent variable, the vertical axis the measured characteristic. Graphic arrangement should proceed from left to right on the horizontal axis; and from bottom to top on the vertical. The zero point should always be represented, and scale intervals should be equal. If a part of the scale is omitted, a set of parallel jagged lines should be used to indicate that part of the scale omitted.

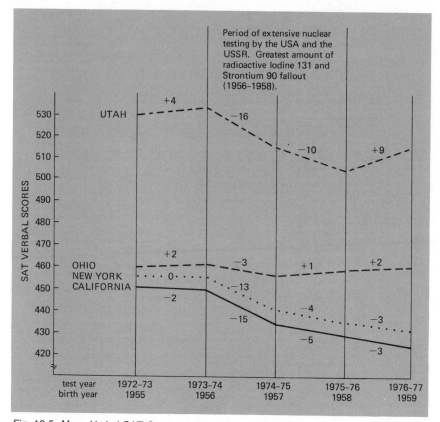

Fig. 10-5. Mean Verbal SAT Scores, 1972–1977, in Four Selected States

Graphic representation by the author, adapted from *Kappan* interview with Ernest Sternglass, "The Nuclear Radiation/SAT Score Decline Connection," *Phi Delta Kappan* 61 (Nov. 1979), 184.

The author devised two figures, a line graph and a bar graph that depict data relationships that were presented textually in two recent periodical articles.

When coordinate graph paper is used, the lines connecting the intersecting points should be made heavy enough to distinguish them from the rulings on the paper. When several lines are drawn, they may be distinguished by using various types of lines—solid, dotted, or alternate dots and dashes. Black India ink is used.

A smoothed curve cannot be obtained by plotting any data directly. Only when infinite data are obtained will the lines connecting the points approach a curved line. The figure formed by the lines connecting the points is known as a frequency polygon.

Fig. 10-6. Decline of Mean Scholastic Aptitude Test Scores from 1963 to 1978. (Throughout the 1970s, verbal scores declined .04 standard deviations each year and mathematical scores declined .025 standard deviations*

* Adapted from Paul Copperman, "The Achievement Decline of the 1970s," *Phi Delta Kappan* 60 (June 1979), 736.

The Bar Graph or Chart

The bar graph may be arranged either horizontally or vertically, and represents data by bars of equal width, drawn to scale length. The numerical data may be lettered within the bar or outside it. A grid may be used to help quantify the graphic representation. A divided bar graph represents the components of a whole unit in one bar.

Horizontal   Vertical   Divided

When comparisons are made, bars or parts of the bars are contrasted by crosshatching. This crosshatching may be done with black India ink. This process is time-consuming, however, and many almost completed drawings have been spoiled by an ink smear in the process.

Fig. 10-7. Commericially Prepared Pressure Sensitive Tapes for Use in Graphs

Pressure sensitive tape with various designs—of stripes, dots, circles, and checks—has largely replaced the inking process, and is available at art supply stores.[5]

In bar graphs, the bars are usually separated by space. If the graph contains a large number of items, the bars may be joined to save space.

Horizontal bar graphs are usually used to compare components at a particular time. Vertical bars are used when making comparisons at different times.

In typed manuscript, horizontal bars are easier to construct. Because of space limitations and typing problems, vertical bars are difficult to label.

The Circle, Pie, or Sector Chart

This type of chart shows the division of a unit into its component parts. It is frequently used to explain how a unit of government distributes its share of the tax dollar, how an individual spends his or her salary, or any other type of simple·percentage distribution.

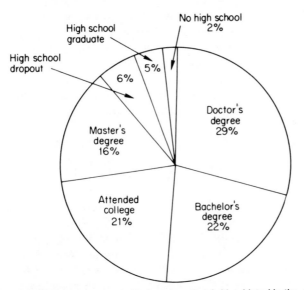

Fig. 10-8. Educational Backgrounds of 129 American Celebrities Listed in the *Current Biography 1966 Yearbook.* *

* Adapted from Adela Deming, "The Educational Attainments of Americans Listed in the Current Biography, 1966 Yearbook," (Unpublished Report, Butler University, Indianapolis, Indiana, 1967), 7.

[5] Available from Chart-Pak, Inc., Leeds, MA. or from Prestape, Inc., New York, NY.

The radius is drawn vertically, and components are arranged in a clockwise direction in descending order of magnitude. The proportion of data is indicated by the number of degrees in each segment of the 360° circle (see Figure 10-8).

This kind of data should be typed or printed within the segment if possible. If there is not sufficient room for this identification, a small arrow should point from the identification term to the segment.

Maps

When geographic location or identification is important, maps may be used. Printed outline maps in 8½ × 11 inch size are available at school-supply stores. Identification may be made by the use of dots, circles, or other symbols, and density or characteristics of areas represented by shading or crosshatching. A key or legend should always be supplied if shadings are used.

Organization Charts

To show staff functions, lines of authority, or flow of work within an organization, an organization chart is a helpful graphic device.

Units may be represented by circles, squares, or oblongs, with names lettered within the units. Distinctions between direct and indirect relationships may be indicated by the use of solid and dotted lines. Ordinarily, authority, supervision, or movement of materials flows from the top to the bottom of the chart, but variations can be indicated by the use of arrows.

EVALUATING A RESEARCH REPORT

Writing a critical analysis of a research report is a valuable experience for the student of educational research. Reports for this purpose may be taken from published collections and such periodicals as the *Educational Researcher*, the *Journal of Educational Research*, or one of the many other publications that publish reports of research in education or in the closely related fields of psychology or sociology.

Another source is the unpublished research reports written by students in previous classes in educational research, or the theses or dissertations found in the university library.

Through a critical analysis, the student may gain some insight into the nature of a research problem, the methods by which it may be attacked, the difficulties inherent in the research process, the ways in which

32 METROPOLITAN AREAS
School Districts of 2,500 or more teachers and 50,000 or more pupils

Boston
Newark
New York
Baltimore County
Philadelphia
Towson
Washington, D. C.
Pittsburgh
Buffalo
Cleveland
Cincinnati
Detroit
Indianapolis
Atlanta
Jacksonville
Duval County
Miami
Dade County
Milwaukee
Chicago
Memphis
St. Louis
New Orleans
Orleans Parish
Minneapolis
Dallas
Houston
Denver
Seattle
Portland
San Francisco
Los Angeles
Long Beach
San Diego

Hawaii

NEA Research Division

Fig. 10-9.

data are analyzed and conclusions drawn, and the style in which the report is presented.

The following questions are suggested as a possible structure for the analysis:

1. The Title
   a. Is it clear and concise?
   b. Does it promise no more than the study can provide?
2. The Problem
   a. Is it clearly stated?
   b. Is it properly delimited?
   c. Is its significance recognized?
   d. Are specific questions raised; hypotheses clearly stated?
   e. Are assumptions, limitations, and delimitations stated?
   f. Are important terms defined?
3. Review of Related Literature
   a. Is it adequately covered?
   b. Are important findings noted?
   c. Is it well organized?
   d. Is an effective summary provided?
4. Procedures Used
   a. Is the research design described in detail?
   b. Is it adequate?
   c. Are the samples described?
   d. Are relevant variables recognized?
   e. Are appropriate controls provided?
   f. Are data-gathering instruments appropriate?
   g. Are validity and reliability established?
   h. Is the statistical treatment appropriate?
5. Data Analysis
   a. Is appropriate use made of tables and figures?
   b. Is the textual discussion clear and concise?
   c. Is the analysis of data relationships logical and perceptive?
   d. Is the statistical analysis accurately interpreted?
6. Summary and Conclusions
   a. Is the problem restated?
   b. Are the procedures described in detail?
   c. Are findings concisely presented?
   d. Is the analysis objective?
   e. Are the findings and conclusions justified by the data presented and analyzed?

SUMMARY

The research report is expected to follow the conventional pattern of style and form used in academic circles. Although style manuals differ in some of the smaller details, students are expected to be consistent in following the pattern of style contained in either the manual required by their institution, or the one that they are permitted to select.

The style of writing should be clear, concise, and completely objective. Of course, the highest standards of correct usage are expected, and careful proofreading is necessary before the final report is submitted.

Tables and figures may help to make the meaning of the data clear. They should be presented in proper mechanical form and should be carefully designed to present an accurate and undistorted picture.

The evaluation of a research project is a valuable exercise for students of educational research. Using a pattern such as the one suggested, the critical analysis of the many aspects of another researcher's report helps students to develop competency in their own research and reporting skills.

BIBLIOGRAPHY

BARZUN, JACQUES and HENRY F. GRAFF. *The Modern Researcher.* New York: Harcourt Brace Jovanovich, 1977.

CAMPBELL, WILLIAM G. and STEPHEN V. BALLOU. *Form and Style: Theses, Reports, Term Papers.* Boston: Houghton Mifflin Co., 1974.

GEPHART, WILLIAM J. *Development of an Instrument for Evaluating Educational Research Reports.* Cooperative Research Project #S-014. Washington, D.C.: U.S. Office of Education, 1964.

HODGES, JOHN C. and MARY E. WHITTEN, eds., *Harbrace College Handbook.* New York: Harcourt, Brace & World, 1963.

KOEFOD, PAUL E. *The Writing Requirements for Graduate Degrees.* Englewood Cliffs, N.J.: Prentice-Hall, 1964.

PERRIN, PORTER G. *Reference Handbook of Grammar and Usage.* New York: William Morrow and Co., 1972.

Publication Manual of the American Psychological Association. Washington, D.C.: The Association, 1974.

STRUNK, WILLIAM and E. B. WHITE. *The Elements of Style.* New York: Macmillan Co., 1962.

TURABIAN, KATE L. *A Manual for Writers of Term Papers, Theses, and Dissertations.* Chicago: University of Chicago Press, 1973.

University of Chicago. *A Manual of Style.* Revised and enlarged. Chicago: University of Chicago Press, 1969.

RESEARCH
METHODS
BIBLIOGRAPHY

ARY, DONALD, LUCY C. JACOBS and ASGHAR RAZAVEIH. *Introduction to Research in Education.* New York: Holt, Rinehart & Winston, 1972.

ASHER, WILLIAM. *Educational Research and Evaluation Methods.* Waltham, MA.: Little, Brown, 1976.

BABBIE, E. R. *Survey Research Methods.* Belmont, CA.: Wadsworth Publishing Co., 1973.

BAKER, ROBERT L. and RICHARD E. SCHUTZ. *Instructional Product Research.* New York: American Book Co., 1972.

BARZUN, JACQUES and HENRY F. GRAFF. *The Modern Researcher.* New York: Harcourt Brace Jovanovich, 1977.

BEST, JOHN W. *Research in Education.* Englewood Cliffs, N.J.: Prentice-Hall, 1977.

BORG, WALTER and MEREDITH D. GALL. *Educational Research: An Introduction.* New York: David McKay, 1971.

BUSWELL, GUY T. *Training for Educational Research.* Berkeley, CA.: Center for the Study of Higher Education, University of California, 1966.

CAMPBELL, DONALD T. and JULIAN C. STANLEY. *Experimental and Quasi-Experimental Designs for Research.* Chicago: Rand McNally & Co., 1966.

COHEN, LOUIS. *Educational Research in Classrooms and Schools: A Manual of Materials and Methods.* London: Harper & Row, 1974.

COOLEY, WILLIAM W. and PAUL R. LOHNES. *Evaluation Research in Education.* New York: Irvington Publishers, 1976.

CRENO, WILLIAM and MARILYN BREWER. *Principles of Research in Social Psychology.* New York: McGraw-Hill Book Co., 1973.

CULBERTSON, JACK A. and STEPHEN P. HENCLEY, eds. *Educational Research: New Perspectives.* Danville, IL.: Interstate Publishers and Printers, 1963.

EDWARDS, ALLEN L. *Experimental Design in Psychological Research.* New York: Holt, Rinehart & Winston, 1972.

ENGLEHART, MAX D. *Methods of Educational Research.* Chicago: Rand McNally & Co., 1972.

FESTINGER, LEON and DANIEL KATZ, eds. *Research Methods in the Behavioral Sciences.* New York: Holt, Rinehart & Winston, 1953.

FOX, DAVID J. *The Research Process in Education.* New York: Holt, Rinehart & Winston, 1969.

GAGE, N. L. *Handbook of Research on Teaching.* Chicago: Rand McNally & Co., 1966.

GALFO, ARMAND J. *Interpreting Educational Research.* Dubuque, IA.: William C. Brown Co., 1975.

GAY, LORRAINE R. *Educational Research: Competencies for Analysis and Application.* Columbus, OH.: Charles E. Merrill Publishing Co., 1976.

GEPHART, WILLIAM J. and ROBERT B. INGLE. *Educational Research: Selected Readings.* Columbus, OH.: Charles E. Merrill Publishing Co., 1969.

GLASER, ROBERT ET AL. *Organization for Research and Development in Education.* Bloomington, IN.: Phi Delta Kappa, 1966.

GOOD, CARTER V. *Essentials of Educational Research.* New York: Appleton-Century-Crofts, 1972.

GOODE, WILLIAM J. and PAUL K. HATT. *Methods in Social Research.* New York: McGraw-Hill Book Co., 1952.

GORDON, IRA J. *Human Development: Readings in Research.* Glenview, IL.: Scott Foresman & Co., 1965.

HARDWICK, CURTIS D. and LEWIS F. PETRINOVICH. *Understanding Research in the Social Sciences.* Philadelphia: W. B. Saunders Co., 1975.

HELMSTADTER, GERALD C. *Research Concepts in Human Behavior.* New York: Appleton-Century-Crofts, 1970.

HOPKINS, CHARLES D. *Educational Research: A Structure for Inquiry.* Columbus, OH.: Charles E. Merrill Publishing Co., 1976.

ISAAC, STEPHEN and WILLIAM B. MICHAEL. *Handbook in Research and Evaluation.* San Diego, CA.: Chandler Publishing Co., 1971.

JOHNSON, M. CLEMENS. *A Review of Research Methods in Education.* Chicago: Rand McNally & Co., 1977.

KAPLAN, ABRAHAM. *The Conduct of Inquiry: Methodology for Behavioral Science.* San Francisco, CA.: Chandler Publishing Co., 1964.

KEPPEL, G. *Design and Analysis: A Researcher's Handbook.* Englewood Cliffs, N.J.: Prentice-Hall, 1973.

KERLINGER, FRED N. *Foundations of Behavioral Research.* New York: Holt, Rinehart & Winston, 1973.

KERLINGER, FRED N. *Scientific Behavioral Research: A Conceptual Primer.* New York: Holt, Rinehart & Winston, 1979.

LEHMANN, IRVIN J. and WILLIAM A. MEHRENS. *Educational Research: Readings in Focus.* New York: Holt, Rinehart & Winston, 1971.

LINDZEY, GARDNER, ed. *Handbook of Social Psychology.* Vol. I. Cambridge, MA.: Addison-Wesley, 1954.

MASON, EMANUEL J. and WILLIAM J. BRAMBLE. *Understanding and Conducting Research.* New York: McGraw-Hill Book Co., 1977.

MOULEY, GEORGE J. *The Science of Educational Research.* New York: Van Nostrand Reinhold Co., 1970.

NEALE, J. M. and R. M. LIEBERT. *Science and Behavior: An Introduction to Methods of Research.* Englewood Cliffs, N.J.: Prentice-Hall, 1973.

Review of Research in Education. Itaska, IL.: F. E. Peacock, Publishers. 1973-date. Volumes 1973, 1974, and 1975 edited by Fred N. Kerlinger. Volumes 1976, 1977, and 1978 edited by Lee S. Schulman.

RUNKLE, PHILLIP and JOSEPH McGRATH. *Research in Human Behavior.* New York: Holt, Rinehart & Winston, 1972.

SAX, GILBERT. *Empirical Foundations of Educational Research.* Englewood Cliffs, N.J.: Prentice-Hall, 1979.

SELLTIZ, CLAIRE, MARIE JAHODA, MORTON DEUTCH, and STUART W. COOK. *Research Methods in Social Relations.* New York: Holt, Rinehart & Winston, 1961.

TRAVERS, ROBERT M. W. *An Introduction to Educational Research.* New York: Macmillan Co., 1978.

TRAVERS, ROBERT M. W. *The Handbook of Research on Teaching.* 2d ed. Chicago: Rand McNally & Co., 1973.

TUCKMAN, BRUCE W. *Conducting Educational Research.* New York: Harcourt Brace Jovanovich, 1978.

TURNEY, B. and G. ROBB. *Research in Education: An Introduction.* New York: McGraw-Hill Book Co., 1973.

VAN DALEN, DEOBOLD B. *Understanding Educational Research.* New York: McGraw-Hill Book Co., 1979.

WANDT, EDWIN. *A Cross Section of Educational Research.* New York: David McKay Co., 1965.

WIERSMA, WILLIAM. *Research Methods in Education.* Itasca, IL.: F. E. Peacock, Publishers, 1975.

APPENDIX A

Statistical Formulas

1. $>$ is greater than
   $<$ is less than

2. Mean M
$$M = \frac{\Sigma X}{N}$$

3. Mode M_0

4. Percentile rank P_r
$$P_r = 100 - \frac{(100R - 50)}{N}$$

5. Variance σ^2
   Standard deviation σ
$$\sigma^2 = \frac{\Sigma x^2}{N} \qquad x = (X - M)$$
$$\sigma = \sqrt{\frac{\Sigma x^2}{N}}$$

   (deviation computation)

$$\sigma^2 = \frac{N\Sigma X^2 - (\Sigma X)^2}{N^2}$$
$$\sigma = \sqrt{\frac{N\Sigma X^2 - (\Sigma X)^2}{N^2}}$$

   (raw score computation)

6. Variance S^2
   Standard deviation S
$$S^2 = \frac{\Sigma x^2}{N-1}$$
$$S = \sqrt{\frac{\Sigma x^2}{N-1}}$$

Glossary of Statistical Symbols

$a > b$ a is greater than b
$b < a$ b is less than a

M arithmetic average
Σ sum of
   X, Y scores
   N number of scores

M_0 mode: score that occurs most frequently in a distribution

P_r percentage of scores that fall below a given value, plus ½ the percentage of space occupied by that score
R rank from the top of a distribution

σ^2 population variance: mean value of the squared deviations from the mean
σ population standard deviation: positive square root of the variance
$x = (X - M)$ deviation from the mean

S^2 variance of a population estimated from a sample
S standard deviation of population estimated from a sample

Statistical Formulas

(deviation computation)

$$S^2 = \frac{N \Sigma X^2 - (\Sigma X)^2}{N(N-1)}$$

$$S = \sqrt{\frac{N \Sigma X^2 - (\Sigma X)^2}{N(N-1)}}$$

(raw score computation)

Variance (S_{DV}^2) or standard deviation (S_{DV}) of a dichotomous variable

$$S_{DV}^2 = \frac{NP(1-P)}{}$$
$$S_{DV} = \sqrt{NP(1-P)}$$

$$S_{DV}^2 = \frac{N}{4}$$

(general formula)

$$S_{DV} = \sqrt{\frac{N}{4}}$$

(when $P = .50$)

7. Standard error of the mean (S_M)

$$S_M = \frac{S}{\sqrt{N}} \qquad \sigma_M = \frac{\sigma}{\sqrt{N}}$$

8. Standard scores z, Z, Z_{cb}

$$z = \frac{X - M}{\sigma} \quad \text{or} \quad \frac{x}{\sigma}$$

$$Z(T) = 50 + 10 \frac{(X - M)}{\sigma}$$

$$\text{or} \quad Z = 50 + 10z$$

$$Z_{cb} = 500 + 100z$$

9. Coefficient of correlation (r)

$$r = \frac{\Sigma (z_X)(z_Y)}{N}$$

$$r = \frac{N \Sigma XY - (\Sigma X)(\Sigma Y)}{\sqrt{N \Sigma X^2 - (\Sigma X)^2} \sqrt{N \Sigma Y^2 - (\Sigma Y)^2}}$$

$$\rho(rho) = 1 - \frac{6 \Sigma D^2}{N(N^2 - 1)}$$

10. Statistical significance of r/ρ

$$t = \frac{r\sqrt{N-2}}{\sqrt{1 - r^2}}$$

$$t = \frac{\rho\sqrt{N-2}}{\sqrt{1 - \rho^2}}$$

Glossary of Statistical Symbols

Dichotomous variable
an outcome is either-or: plus or minus, true or false, heads or tails
N number of events
P probability of an outcome

z sigma score
$Z(T)$ standard score
Z_{cb} College Board standard score

r Pearson product-moment coefficient of correlation

ρ(rho) Spearman difference in ranks coefficient of correlation
D difference between each pair of ranks

Test of the statistical significance of a coefficient of correlation

Statistical Formulas

Glossary of Statistical Symbols

11. Regression line slope

$$r = \frac{\text{rise}}{\text{run}} = \frac{z_Y}{z_X}$$

r the slope expressed in sigma (z) units

$$b = \frac{\text{rise}}{\text{run}} = \frac{Y}{X} \qquad b_Y = r\left(\frac{z_Y}{z_X}\right)$$

b the slope of the line expressed in raw scores

$$b_X = r\left(\frac{z_X}{z_Y}\right)$$

12. Regression equations

$$\tilde{Y} = b_Y(X - M_X) + M_Y$$

$$\tilde{X} = b_X(Y - M_Y) + M_X$$

Predicting a Y from a known X when the coefficient of correlation is known

$\tilde{Y}$ predicted Y

$\tilde{X}$ predicted X

13. Standard error of estimate S_{est}

$$S_{\text{est}} = S\sqrt{1 - r^2}$$

14. Standard error of the difference between two means (independent variances; when variances are not equal)

$$S_{M_1-M_2} = \sqrt{\frac{s_1^2}{N_1} + \frac{S_2^2}{N_2}}$$

(pooled variances; when variances are equal)

$$S_{M_1-M_2} = \sqrt{\frac{(N_1 - 1)S_1^2 + (N_2 - 1)S_2^2}{N_1 + N_2 - 2}\left(\frac{1}{N_1} + \frac{1}{N_2}\right)}$$

15. Significance of the difference between two means

$$t = \frac{\text{difference between means}}{\text{standard error of the difference}}$$

$$t = \frac{M_1 - M_2}{\sqrt{\frac{(N_1 - 1)S_1^2 + (N_2 - 1)S_2^2}{N_1 + N_2 - 2}\left(\frac{1}{N_1} + \frac{1}{N_2}\right)}}$$

(uncorrelated or unmatched groups)

$$t = \frac{M_1 - M_2}{\sqrt{\frac{S_1^2}{N_1} + \frac{S_2^2}{N_2} - 2r\left(\frac{S_1}{\sqrt{N_1}}\right)\left(\frac{S_2}{\sqrt{N_2}}\right)}}$$

(matched or correlated groups)

16. Chi square χ^2

$$\chi^2 = \Sigma\frac{(f_o - f_e)^2}{f_e}$$

f_o observed frequencies

f_e expected frequencies

df degrees of freedom

$$df = (f\text{rows} - 1)(f\text{columns} - 1)$$

$$\chi^2 = \frac{N\left[|AD - BC| - \frac{N}{2}\right]^2}{(A + B)(C + D)(A + C)(B + D)}$$

A	B
C	D

Computation for a 2 × 2 table

Statistical Formulas

17. Median test

$$\chi^2 = + \frac{N\left[|AD - BC| - \frac{N}{2}\right]^2}{(A+B)(C+D)(A+C)(B+D)}$$

18. Mann-Whitney test $(N > 20)$

$$U_1 = (N_1)(N_2) + \frac{N_1(N_1+1)}{2} - \Sigma R_1$$

$$U_2 = (N_1)(N_2) + \frac{N_2(N_2+1)}{2} - \Sigma R_2$$

$$z = \frac{U - \frac{(N_1)(N_2)}{2}}{\sqrt{\frac{(N_1)(N_2)(N_1+N_2+1)}{12}}}$$

19. Sign test (matched pairs)

$$z = \frac{(0 \pm .50) - \frac{N}{2}}{\sqrt{\frac{N}{4}}}$$

20. Wilcoxon matched-pairs signed ranks test

$$z = \frac{T - \frac{N(N+1)}{4}}{\sqrt{\frac{N(N+1)(2N+1)}{24}}}$$

Glossary of Statistical Symbols

Statistical significance of the difference between the medians of two independent groups: at or above common median and below common median

N_1 number in one group
N_2 number in second group
ΣR_1 sum of ranks of one group
ΣR_2 sum of ranks of second group
The significance of U is read from the U critical table. When $N > 20$, the z computation may be used with the normal probability table values.

O number of signs of interest. When $O < N/2$, use $(O + .50)$; when $O > N/2$, use $(O - .50)$

N number of pairs ranked
T sum of the ranks of the smaller of the like-signed numbers

APPENDIX B

Percentage of Area Lying between the Mean and Successive Standard Deviation Units under the Normal Curve

$z\left(\dfrac{x}{\sigma}\right)$	.00	.01	.02	.03	.04	.05	.06	.07	.08	.09
.0	.0000	.0040	.0080	.0120	.0160	.0199	.0239	.0279	.0319	.0359
.1	.0398	.0438	.0478	.0517	.0557	.0596	.0636	.0675	.0714	.0753
.2	.0793	.0832	.0871	.0910	.0948	.0987	.1026	.1064	.1103	.1141
.3	.1179	.1217	.1255	.1293	.1331	.1368	.1406	.1443	.1480	.1517
.4	.1554	.1591	.1628	.1664	.1700	.1736	.1772	.1808	.1844	.1879
.5	.1915	.1950	.1985	.2019	.2054	.2088	.2123	.2157	.2190	.2224
.6	.2257	.2291	.2324	.2357	.2389	.2422	.2454	.2486	.2517	.2549
.7	.2580	.2611	.2642	.2673	.2704	.2734	.2764	.2794	.2823	.2852
.8	.2881	.2910	.2939	.2967	.2995	.3023	.3051	.3078	.3106	.3133
.9	.3159	.3186	.3212	.3238	.3264	.3290	.3315	.3340	.3365	.3389
1.0	.3413	.3438	.3461	.3485	.3508	.3531	.3554	.3577	.3599	.3621
1.1	.3643	.3665	.3686	.3708	.3729	.3749	.3770	.3790	.3810	.3830
1.2	.3849	.3869	.3888	.3907	.3925	.3944	.3962	.3980	.3997	.4015
1.3	.4032	.4049	.4066	.4082	.4099	.4115	.4131	.4147	.4162	.4177
1.4	.4192	.4207	.4222	.4236	.4251	.4265	.4279	.4292	.4306	.4319
1.5	.4332	.4345	.4357	.4370	.4383	.4394	.4406	.4418	.4429	.4441
1.6	.4452	.4463	.4474	.4484	.4495	.4505	.4515	.4525	.4535	.4545
1.7	.4554	.4564	.4573	.4582	.4591	.4599	.4608	.4616	.4625	.4633
1.8	.4641	.4649	.4656	.4664	.4671	.4678	.4686	.4693	.4699	.4706
1.9	.4713	.4719	.4726	.4732	.4738	.4744	.4750	.4756	.4761	.4767
2.0	.4772	.4778	.4783	.4788	.4793	.4798	.4803	.4808	.4812	.4817
2.1	.4821	.4826	.4830	.4834	.4838	.4842	.4846	.4850	.4854	.4857
2.2	.4861	.4864	.4868	.4871	.4875	.4878	.4881	.4884	.4887	.4890
2.3	.4893	.4896	.4898	.4901	.4904	.4906	.4909	.4911	.4913	.4916
2.4	.4918	.4920	.4922	.4925	.4927	.4929	.4931	.4932	.4934	.4936
2.5	.4938	.4940	.4941	.4943	.4945	.4946	.4948	.4949	.4951	.4952
2.6	.4953	.4955	.4956	.4957	.4959	.4960	.4961	.4962	.4963	.4964
2.7	.4965	.4966	.4967	.4968	.4969	.4970	.4971	.4972	.4973	.4974
2.8	.4974	.4975	.4976	.4977	.4977	.4978	.4979	.4979	.4980	.4981
2.9	.4981	.4982	.4982	.4983	.4984	.4984	.4985	.4985	.4986	.4986
3.0	.4987									

Example: Between the mean and $+1.00z$ is 34.13% of the area.
Between the mean and $-.50z$ is 19.15% of the area.

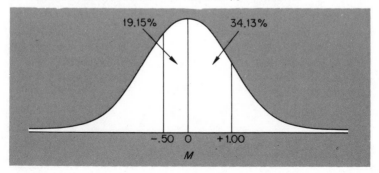

APPENDIX C

Critical Values of Student's Distribution *(t)*

df	*Two-tailed test* level of significance .05	.01	*One-tailed test* level of significance .05	.01
1	12.706	63.557	6.314	31.821
2	4.303	9.925	2.920	6.965
3	3.182	5.841	2.353	4.541
4	2.776	4.604	2.132	3.747
5	2.571	4.032	2.015	3.365
6	2.447	3.707	1.943	3.143
7	2.365	3.499	1.895	2.998
8	2.306	3.355	1.860	2.896
9	2.262	3.250	1.833	2.821
10	2.228	3.169	1.812	2.764
11	2.201	3.106	1.796	2.718
12	2.179	3.055	1.782	2.681
13	2.160	3.012	1.771	2.650
14	2.145	2.977	1.761	2.624
15	2.131	2.947	1.753	2.602
16	2.120	2.921	1.746	2.583
17	2.110	2.898	1.740	2.567
18	2.101	2.878	1.734	2.552
19	2.093	2.861	1.729	2.539
20	2.086	2.845	1.725	2.528
21	2.080	2.831	1.721	2.518
22	2.074	2.819	1.717	2.508
23	2.069	2.807	1.714	2.500
24	2.064	2.797	1.711	2.492
25	2.060	2.787	1.708	2.485
26	2.056	2.779	1.706	2.479
27	2.052	2.771	1.703	2.473
28	2.048	2.763	1.701	2.467
29	2.045	2.756	1.699	2.462
30	2.042	2.750	1.697	2.457
40	2.021	2.704	1.684	2.423
60	2.000	2.660	1.671	2.390
120	1.980	2.617	1.658	2.358
∞	1.960	2.576	1.645	2.326

APPENDIX D

Abridged Table of Critical Values for CHI Square

	Level of significance	
df	*.05*	*.01*
1	3.84	6.64
2	5.99	9.21
3	7.82	11.34
4	9.49	13.28
5	11.07	15.09
6	12.59	16.81
7	14.07	18.48
8	15.51	20.09
9	16.92	21.67
10	18.31	23.21
11	19.68	24.72
12	21.03	26.22
13	22.36	27.69
14	23.68	29.14
15	25.00	30.58
16	26.30	32.00
17	27.59	33.41
18	28.87	34.80
19	30.14	36.19
20	31.41	37.57
21	32.67	38.93
22	33.92	40.29
23	35.17	41.64
24	36.42	42.98
25	37.65	44.31
26	38.88	45.64
27	40.11	46.96
28	41.34	48.28
29	42.56	49.59
30	43.77	50.89

APPENDIX E: RESEARCH COURSE REPORT EVALUATION

RESEARCH REPORT EVALUATION FORM

Name_____Date_____Grade_____

+ adequate   − inadequate

TITLE

clear and concise_____

PROBLEM

clearly stated_____
specific questions raised_____
clear statement of hypothesis_____
testable hypothesis_____
significance recognized_____
properly delimited_____
assumptions stated_____
important terms defined_____

DATA ANALYSIS

perceptive recognition of data relation-
   ships_____
effective use of tables_____
effective use of figures_____
concise report of findings_____
appropriate statistical treatment_____
logical analysis_____

SUMMARY

problem restated_____
questions/hypothesis restated_____
procedures described_____
concisely reported_____
supporting data included_____
conclusions based on data analysis__

REVIEW OF RELATED LITERATURE

adequately covered_____
well-organized_____
important findings noted_____
studies critically examined_____
effectively summarized_____

PROCEDURES

described in detail_____
adequate sample_____
appropriate design_____
variables controlled_____
effective data-gathering instruments or
   procedures_____

FORM AND STYLE

typing_____
spacing_____
margins_____
balance_____
table of contents_____
list of tables_____
list of figures_____
headings_____
pagination_____
citations/quotations_____
footnotes_____
tables_____
figures_____
bibliography_____
appendix_____
spelling_____
punctuation_____
sentence structure_____
proofreading_____
clear and concise style_____

ANSWERS TO STATISTICS EXERCISES

Chapter 7

1. Agree. The median could be lower than the mean if a large proportion of the families had low incomes.
2. Disagree. The median is that point in a distribution above and below which half of the scores fall. It may not be the midpoint between the highest and the lowest scores.
3. $M = 55.33$
   $Md = 58.50$
4. $M = 75$ Range $= 31$
   $Md = 77$
5.   Variance $= 41.33$
   Standard deviation $= 6.42$
6. Disagree. The range does not determine the magnitude of the variance or the standard deviation. These values indicate how all of the scores, not the most extreme, are clustered about the mean.
7. a. no change   d. $+5$
   b. $+5$ e. no change
   c. $+5$ f. no change
8. Percentile rank $= 93$.
9. $M = 72$ standard deviation $= 6$

z	-3	-2	-1	0	$+1$	$+2$	$+3$
heads	54	60	66	72	78	84	90

10.

X	x	z	Z
66	$+5$	$+1.00$	60
58	-3	$-.60$	44
70	$+9$	$+1.80$	68
61	0	0	50
52	-9	-1.80	32

11. a. 11%   f. $-.18z$
    b. 89%   g. $+2.33z$
    c. 87%   h. $-.67_z$ to $+.67_z$
    d. 6%   i. 32%
    e. $+.39z$ j. $0z$
12. a. 119   d. 107
    b. 96   e. 85 to 115
    c. 75%

13.

	Tom	Dick	Harry
algebra z	−1.00	+.33	−.17
history z	+1.25	+.50	−.25

a. Tom   d. Tom
b. Tom   e. Dick
   c. Harry   f. Harry

14. Disagree. The coefficient of correlation is an indication of the magnitude of the relationship, but does not necessarily indicate a cause-and-effect relationship.
15. rho = +.61
16. r = +.65
17. r = +.53
18. r = −1.00

most correct — most incorrect
least correct — least incorrect

19. Agree. $r = \dfrac{\text{rise}}{\text{run}}$ expressed in sigma units

             $b = \dfrac{\text{rise}}{\text{run}}$ expressed in raw scores

The value of r cannot exceed ±1.00
The value of b can exceed ±1.00
20. $S_{\text{est}} = 4.96$
21. a. $\tilde{Y} = 44$
   b. $\tilde{Y} = 36$

Chapter 8

1. Confirming a positive hypothesis provides a weak argument, for the conclusion may be true for other reasons. It does not preclude the validity of alternative or rival hypotheses. Rejecting a negative hypothesis employs stronger logic.
2. Agree. A test of statistical significance provides a basis for accepting or rejecting a sampling error explanation on a probability basis. Only when a sampling process is involved is a test of significance appropriate.
3. Agree. The level of significance determines the probability of a sampling error, rather than a treatment variable explanation. When a researcher finds an observation significant at the .05 level, he or she is admitting that there is a 5/100 chance of a sampling error explanation.
4. Disagree. The .01 alpha level is a much more rigorous criterion than the .05 level. However, any hypothesis that can be rejected at the .01 level can surely be rejected at the .05 level of significance.
5. Agree. The sum of the squared deviations from the mean of a sample is smaller than that calculated from any other point. According to the central limit theorem, the population mean would probably differ from the sample mean. Using the sample mean as a point of reference, the variance and the standard deviation of the population would probably be underestimated. This is partially corrected by considering the loss of one degree of freedom, reducing the size of the denominator in the formula by one, increasing the size of the quotient.

6. Disagree. The *t* critical value for a one-tailed test is lower. The area of rejection is one side of the normal curve and it is not necessary to go out as far to reach it.

t critical values
for rejection

	2*t*	1*t*
.05 level	1.96	1.64
.01 level	2.58	2.33

7. $t = -2.00$ Reject the null hypothesis. The cable did not meet the manufacturer's specifications.
8. $t = 3.49$ Reject the null hypothesis. The means do not behave as sample means from the same population.
9. $t = 1.38$ Do not reject the null hypothesis. There was no significant difference between the achievement of the two groups.
10. $t = 3.77$ Reject the null hypothesis. The weight gain for the experimental group was significant.
11. $t = 3.13$ Reject the null hypothesis. The difference in gasoline mileage was significant.
12. a. $N-1$
    b. $N-2$
    c. $N+N-2$
    d. 1
    e. 8
13. $\chi^2 = 14.06$ Reject the null hypothesis. There seems to be a significant relationship between gender and brand preference.
14. $Md = 21$ $\chi^2 = 1.21$ Do not reject the null hypothesis. The effect of the medication does not seem to be significant.
15. $z = 2.54$ Reject the null hypothesis. The program weight loss seems to have been sustained.
16. $z = .28$ Do not reject the null hypothesis. The effect of the counseling program did not seem to be statistically significant.
17. $z = 2.13$ Reject the null hypothesis. The difference in test scores of the two groups seems to be significant.
18. $t = 1.26$ Do not reject the null hypothesis. The coefficient of correlation was not statistically significant.

Index

AUTHOR INDEX

SUBJECT INDEX